ADOBE® ILLUSTRATOR® 9

Introduction to Digital Illustration

AGAINST THE CLOCK
PERFORMANCE SUPPORT & TRAINING SYSTEMS

PRENTICE HALL
Upper Saddle River, NJ 07458

Library of Congress Cataloging-in-Publication Data

Adobe Illustrator 9: An Introduction to Digital Illustration
        Against The Clock
    p. cm. — (Against The Clock series)
    ISBN 0-13-090827-4
    1. Computer Graphics 2. Adobe Illustrator (computer file)
    I. Against The Clock (Firm) II. Series
    T385.A35775 2001
    006.6'869—dc21

                                    00-056678

Executive Editor: Elizabeth Sugg
Developmental Editor: Judy Casillo
Supervising Manager: Mary Carnis
Production Editor: Denise Brown
Director of Manufacturing and Production: Bruce Johnson
Manufacturing Buyer: Ed O'Dougherty
Editorial Assistant: Lara Dugan
Formatting/Page Make-up: Against the Clock, Inc.
Prepress: Photoengraving, Inc.
Printer/Binder: Press of Ohio
Cover Design: Joe Sengotta
Icon Design: James Braun
Creative Director: Marianne Frasco

Prentice Hall International (UK) Limited, London
Prentice Hall of Australia Pty. Limited, Sydney
Prentice Hall Canada Inc., Toronto
Prentice Hall Hispanoamericana, S.A., Mexico
Prentice Hall of India Private Limited, New Delhi
Prentice Hall of Japan, Inc., Tokyo
Pearson Education Asia Pte. Ltd., Singapore
Editora Prentice Hall do Brasil, Ltda., Rio de Janeiro

10 9 8 7 6 5 4 3 2 1

ISBN 0-13-090827-4

Contents

PURPOSE

The Against The Clock series has been developed specifically for those involved in the field of graphic arts.

Welcome to the world of electronic design and prepress. Many of our readers are already involved in the industry — in advertising and design companies, in prepress and imaging firms, and in the world of commercial printing and reproduction. Others are just now preparing themselves for a career somewhere in the profession.

This series of courses will provide you with the skills necessary to work in this fast-paced, exciting, and rapidly expanding business. Many people feel that they can simply purchase a computer, the appropriate software, a laser printer, and a ream of paper, and begin designing and producing high-quality printed materials. While this might suffice for a barbecue announcement or a flyer for a yard sale, the real world of four-color printing and professional communications requires a far more serious commitment.

THE SERIES

The applications presented in the Against The Clock series stand out as the programs of choice in professional graphic arts environments.

We've used a modular design for the Against The Clock series, allowing you to mix and match the drawing, imaging, and page-layout applications that exactly suit your specific needs.

Titles available in the Against The Clock series include:

Macintosh: Basic Operations
Windows: Basic Operations
Adobe Illustrator: Introduction and Advanced Digital Illustration
Macromedia FreeHand: Introduction and Advanced Digital Illustration
Adobe InDesign: Introduction and Advanced Electronic Mechanicals
Adobe PageMaker: Introduction and Advanced Electronic Mechanicals
QuarkXPress: Introduction and Advanced Electronic Mechanicals
Microsoft Publisher: Creating Electronic Mechanicals
Microsoft PowerPoint: Presentation Graphics with Impact
Microsoft FrontPage: Designing for the Web
MetaCreations Painter: A Digital Approach to Natural Art Media
Adobe Photoshop: Introduction and Advanced Digital Images
Adobe Premiere: Digital Video Editing
Macromedia Director: Creating Powerful Multimedia
File Preparation: The Responsible Electronic Page
Preflight: An Introduction to File Analysis and Repair
TrapWise and PressWise: Digital Trapping and Imposition

ICONS AND VISUALS

We've designed our courses to be "cross-platform." While many sites use Macintosh computers, there is an increasing number of graphic arts service providers using Intel-based systems running Windows (or WindowsNT). The books in this series are applicable to either of these systems.

All of the applications that we cover in the Against The Clock series are similar in operation and appearance whether you're working on a Macintosh or a Windows system. When a particular function does differ from machine to machine, we present both.

There are a number of standard icons that you will see in the sidebars. Each has a standard meaning. Pay close attention to the sidebar notes as you will find valuable comments that will help you throughout this course and in your everyday use of your computer. The standard icons are:

The **Pencil** icon indicates a comment from an experienced operator or instructor. Whenever you see the pencil icon, you'll find corresponding sidebar text that augments or builds upon the subject being discussed at the time.

The **Bomb**, or **Pitfalls** icon indicates a potential problem or difficulty. For instance, a certain technique might lead to pages that prove difficult to output. In other cases, there might be something that a program cannot easily accomplish, so we might present a workaround.

The **Pointing Finger** icon indicates a hands-on activity — whether a short exercise or a complete project. Note that sometimes this icon will direct you to the back of the book to complete a project.

The **Key** icon is used to point out that there is a keyboard equivalent to a menu or dialog-box option. Key commands are often faster than using the mouse to select a menu option. Experienced operators often mix the use of keyboard equivalents and menu/dialog box selections to arrive at their optimum speed.

If you are a Windows user, be sure to refer to the corresponding text or images whenever you see this **Windows** icon. Although there isn't a great deal of difference between using these applications on a Macintosh and using them on a Windows-based PC, there are certain instances where there's enough of a difference for us to comment.

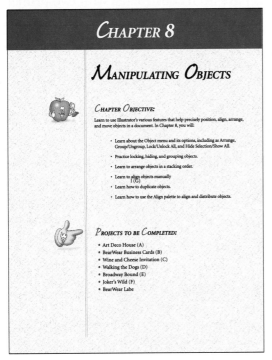

Chapter openers *provide the reader with specific objectives.*

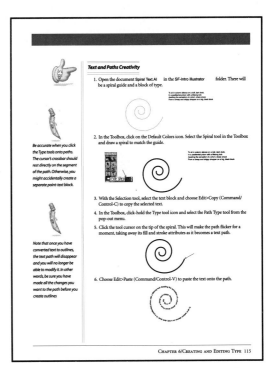

Sidebars and hands-on activities *supplement concepts presented in the material.*

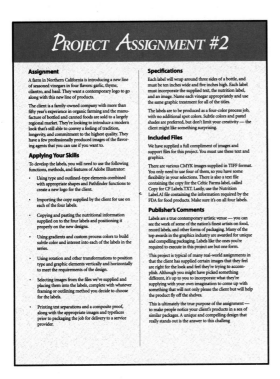

Project assignments *allow you to use your imagination and new skills to satisfy a typical client's needs.*

Step-by-step projects *result in finished artwork — with an emphasis on proper file construction methods.*

Against The Clock course materials have been constructed with two primary building blocks: exercises and projects. Projects always result in a finished piece of work — digital imagery typically built from the ground up, utilizing photographic-quality images, vector artwork from illustration programs, and type elements from the library supplied on your student CD-ROM.

This course, *Adobe Illustrator: Introduction to Digital Illustration*, uses several step-by-step projects on which you will work during your learning sessions. (There are also open-ended project assignments immediately preceding the two reviews.) You will find images of the step-by-step projects that you will complete by the end of the course displayed on the inside front and back covers of the book. Here's a brief overview of each:

PROJECT A: ART DECO HOUSE

Effective use of paths isn't limited to creating the proper shape. Stroke weight, color, stacking order, and the way paths are joined at corners are all taken into consideration by professional artists. To achieve the look of this drawing, strokes of various weights, joined to create correct corners and intersections, are all incorporated. This design uses perspective to create the feel of a three-dimensional object. Another consideration is the limited use of tones — there are only white, black, and 30% gray shades.

PROJECT B: BEARWEAR BUSINESS CARDS

Some of the most popular and commonly-used layouts and designs rely on standard formatting of type and logo elements. In this project, grids and non-printing guides are used both to frame the individual business card and to allow the elements to be accurately duplicated for "four-up" printing. Type selection, alignment, and positioning are required to create the basic layout as well as the central logo element. Trim marks, necessary for the printer to use when cutting the individual cards, are also created and positioned.

PROJECT C: WINE AND CHEESE INVITATION

This project makes use of Illustrator's ability to "mold" type and paste it into almost any shape. This invitation is composed from several discrete elements. The shape of the glass is provided as a template, and the Pen tool is used to trace the object. Corner and smooth points are created and edited to accomplish this task. The same methods are used to create the shape representing the bouquet rising from the glass. The text element is then pasted into the object and adjusted until the fit is perfect.

PROJECT D: WALKING THE DOGS

Walking the Dog is another example of simple shapes being used to develop complex and effective illustrations. The project requires the use of a common set of techniques, including stacking and coloring. Additionally, the Paintbrush tool is used to give a more freehand feeling to the piece. Since a template is used to establish the shape and the position of the drawing's components, there are several layers — one for the template, the others for the illustration. A popular coloring technique is used for the creation of colored shapes that don't quite fit the boundaries of individual objects (the dogs, the girl's legs, and the background shape). A custom brush technique is also employed to create the hatch-mark pattern of the girl's hose. Lastly, the illustration is prepared and output as spot color separations.

PROJECT E: BROADWAY BOUND

The appearance of folded cloth presents a unique challenge to the designer and illustrator. Subtle shading and highlights must be balanced with the basic design. The Broadway Bound project incorporates the use of gradients to achieve this effect. Special attention is paid to how the gradient direction in each object interacts with contiguous paths. Notice how colors and shades seamlessly join in and beneath each fold, within the woman's shoe, and throughout the background. Only the man's wing-tips are solid black and white. Details such as the reflection on the dancer's shoe are stacked custom shapes. Additionally, the border around the dancers acts as a window on a much larger scene — another popular and effective design technique.

PROJECT F: JOKER'S WILD

The Joker playing card is an excellent example of a design that takes advantage of Illustrator's stacking order and arranging techniques. The stars make use of the Star tool dialog to create specific shapes and are colored using the Color menu. This complex (and fun) drawing makes extensive use of templates, layers, creative drawing techniques, operations, and filters.

PROJECT G: BEARWEAR LABEL

Packaging is an important aspect of the graphic arts industry, and the BearWear Label project represents a simple example of this specialized application. The project starts with the use of guides to ensure accuracy — a critical issue in packaging, where cutting dies are used in the manufacturing process. All designs must fit these dies. The final cuts, which remove the corners of a basic rectangle, result in a custom shape. This shape is reduced and converted to guides to ensure compliance with the shape of the die. Simple gradients fill the top and bottom panels, and a placed TIFF file of the bear comprises the center. The BearWear logo created in an earlier project is used to identify the clothing company, and the design incorporates type on a circular path positioned over the photographic elements.

FOR THE STUDENT

On the CD-ROM you will find a complete set of Against The Clock (ATC) fonts, as well as a collection of data files used to construct the various exercises and projects.

The ATC fonts are solely for use while you are working with the Against The Clock materials. These fonts will be used throughout both the exercises and projects.

A variety of student files have been included. These files are necessary to complete both the exercises and projects.

FOR THE INSTRUCTOR

The Instructor Kit consists of an Instructor's Manual and an Instructor's CD-ROM. It includes various testing and presentation materials in addition to the files that come standard with the student books.

- **Overhead Presentation Materials** are provided and follow along with the course. These presentations are prepared using Microsoft PowerPoint and are provided in both "native" PowerPoint format as well as Acrobat Portable Document Format (PDF).

- **Extra Projects** are provided along with the data files required for completion. These projects may be used to extend the course, or may be used to test the student.

- **Finished artwork (in PDF format)** for all projects that the students complete is supplied on the CD-ROM.

- **Test Questions and Answers** are included on the instructor CD-ROM. These questions may be modified, reorganized, and administered throughout the delivery of the course.

- Halfway through the course is a **Review** of material covered to that point, with a **Final Review** at the end.

ACKNOWLEDGMENTS

I would like to give special thanks to the writers, illustrators, editors, and others who have worked long and hard to complete the Against The Clock series. Foremost among them are Gary Poyssick, Pamela Griffin, Jean-Claude Tremblay, and Don Poyssick, whom I thank for their long nights, early mornings, and their seemingly endless patience.

Thanks to the dedicated teaching professionals whose comments and expertise contributed to the success of these products, including Rainer Fleschner of Moraine Park Technical College, and Joanne Floydd of Mt. San Antonio College.

A special thanks to Bill Morse and Scott MacNeil for their wonderful artwork contributions.

Thanks to Toni Toomey, copy editor and final link in the chain of production, for her tremendous help in making sure we all said what we meant to say.

A big thanks to Judy Casillo, developmental editor, and Denise Brown, production editor, for their guidance, patience, and attention to detail.

Ellenn Behoriam, July 2000

AGAINST THE CLOCK

Against The Clock (ATC) was founded in 1990 as a part of Lanman Systems Group, one of the nation's leading systems integration and training firms. The company specialized in developing custom training materials for such clients as *L.L. Bean, The New England Journal of Medicine, Smithsonian,* the *National Education Association, Air & Space Magazine, Publishers Clearing House,* The *National Wildlife Society, Home Shopping Network,* and many others. The integration firm was among the most highly respected in the graphic arts industry.

To a great degree, the success of Lanman Systems Group can be attributed to the thousands of pages of course materials developed at the company's demanding client sites. Throughout the rapid growth of Lanman Systems Group, Founder and General Manager Ellenn Behoriam developed the expertise necessary to manage technical experts, content providers, writers, editors, illustrators, designers, layout artists, proofreaders, and the rest of the chain of professionals required to develop structured and highly effective training materials.

Following the sale of the Lanman Companies to World Color, one of the nation's largest commercial printers, Ellenn embarked on a project to develop a new library of hands-on training materials engineered specifically for the professional graphic artist. A large part of this effort is finding and working with talented professional artists, writers, and educators from around the country.

The result is the ATC training library.

ABOUT THE AUTHORS

Every one of the Against The Clock course books was developed by a group of people working as part of a design and production team. In all cases, however, there was a primary author who assumed the bulk of the responsibility for developing the exercises, writing the copy, and organizing the illustrations and other visuals.

In the case of *Adobe Illustrator: An Introduction to Digital Illustration,* that author was Dean Bagley. Dean is an experienced marketing and advertising expert. One of Dean's most effective skills is the development of hands-on activities, which, as you'll see, is the foundation of the ATC series.

Dean is a professional cartoonist, well-known for his imaginative and entertaining "Baggy Gator" series of comic characters. Dean lives in Winter Haven, Florida.

GETTING STARTED

Platform

The Against The Clock series is designed to apply to both Macintosh and Windows systems. Adobe Illustrator runs under Macintosh, Windows 98, Windows 2000, and Windows NT. There are separate student files for Macintosh and Windows students.

Naming Conventions

In the old days of MS-DOS systems, file names on the PC were limited to something referred to as "8.3," which meant that you were limited in the number of characters you could use to an eight-character name (the "8") and a three-character suffix (the "3"). Text files, for example, might be called *myfile.txt*, while a document file from a word processor might be called *myfile.doc* (for document). On today's Windows systems, these limitations have been, for the most part, overcome. Although you can use longer file names, suffixes still exist. The Macintosh does not rely on the file extension at all. You see the characters as part of the file name.

When your Windows system is first configured, the Views are normally set to a default that hides these extensions. This means that you might have a dozen different files named *myfile*, all of which may have been generated by different applications and consist of completely different types of files.

You can change this view by double-clicking on *My Computer* (the icon on your desktop). This will open the file. Select View>Folder Options. From Folder Options, select the View tab. Within the Files and Folders folder is a checkbox: Hide File Extensions for Known File Types. When this is unchecked, you can see the file extensions. It's easier to know what you're looking at if they're visible. While this is a personal choice, we strongly recommend viewing the file extensions. All the files used in this course have been named using the three- or four-character suffix.

Key Commands

There are two keys generally used as *modifier* keys — they do nothing when pressed, unless they are pressed in conjunction with another key. Their purpose is to alter the normal functions of the other key with which they are pressed.

The Command (Macintosh) or Control (Windows) key is generally used when taking control of the computer. When combined with the "S" key, it functions to save your work. When combined with "O," it opens a file; with a "P," it prints the file. In addition to these functions, which work with most Macintosh and Windows programs, the Control key may be combined with other keys to take control of specific functions in Adobe Illustrator.

Another special function key is the Option (Macintosh) and Alt (for alternate) (Windows) key. It, too, is a modifier key, and you must hold it down along with whatever other key (or keys) is required for a specific function. The Option and Alt keys are often used in conjunction with other keys to access typographic characters having an ASCII number higher than 128. Under Windows, they are used in conjunction with the numeric keypad. For example, Alt-0149 will produce a bullet character. Alt-F4 will close the program. The Option key is combined with alphanumeric keys, instead of the numeric keypad. Option-8, for example, will produce a bullet.

The keys on the top row of the keypad, F1–F12, also accomplish specific tasks in conjunction with the computer. F1 will bring up the Help menu. F6 and Shift-F6 will move elements to the front or the back of a "stack" of text and graphic objects.

The Macintosh and Windows access context-sensitive menus in similar but different ways. On the Macintosh, holding down the Control (not the Command) key while clicking the mouse button will bring up context-sensitive menus. Under Windows, this is accomplished by clicking the right mouse button (right-clicking). We generically call accessing the context menu "context-clicking."

The CD-ROM and Initial Setup Considerations

Before you begin using your Against The Clock course book, you must set up your system to have access to the various files and tools to complete your lessons.

Student Files

This course comes complete with a collection of student files. These files are an integral part of the learning experience — they're used throughout the course to help you construct increasingly complex elements. Having these building blocks available to you for practice and study sessions will ensure that you will be able to experience the exercises and complete the project assignments smoothly, spending a minimum of time looking for the various required components.

In the Student Files folders, we've created sets of data. Locate the **SF-Intro Illustrator** folder and drag the icon onto your hard disk drive. If you have limited disk space, you may want to copy only the files for one or two lessons at a time.

We strongly recommend that you work from your hard disk. However, in some cases you might not have enough room on your system for all the files we've supplied. If this is the case, you can work directly from the CD-ROM.

Creating a Project Folder

Throughout the exercises and projects you'll be required to save your work. Since the CD-ROM is "read-only," you cannot write information to it. Create a "work in progress" folder on your hard disk and use it to store your work. Create it by context-clicking, while at your desktop, then selecting New Folder (Macintosh) or New> Folder (Windows). This will create the folder at the highest level of your system, where it will always be easy to find. Name this folder "Work in Progress".

Fonts

You must install the ATC font library to ensure that your lessons and exercises will work as described in the course book. These fonts are provided on the student CD-ROM.

Instructions for installing fonts are provided in the documentation that came with your computer. In general, drag them into your System>Fonts folder on the Macintosh, or, under Windows, from your Start>Settings>Control Panel>Fonts, select File>Install New Font. Navigate to the Fonts folder on the CD, select the fonts, and click OK.

System Requirements

On the Macintosh, you will need a Power PC 604 processor or above, running the 8.5 operating system or later; 64 MB of RAM; a monitor with a resolution of at least 800 × 600 or greater; Adobe PostScript Level 2 or higher printer; and a CD-ROM drive. You will need 105 MB of free hard drive space for installation.

On a Windows operating system, you'll need a Pentium II or faster processor; Windows 98/NT 4.0, or Windows 2000 or higher; 64 MB RAM; a monitor with a resolution of at least 800 × 600 pixels; Adobe PostScript Level 2 or higher printer; and a CD-ROM drive. You will need 105 MB of free hard drive space for installation.

Prerequisites

This book assumes that you have a basic understanding of how to use your system.

You should know how to use your mouse to point and click, and how to drag items around the screen. You should know how to resize a window, and how to arrange windows on your desktop to maximize your available space. You should know how to access pull-down menus, and how checkboxes and radio buttons work. Lastly, you should know how to create, open, and save files.

If you're familiar with these fundamental skills, then you know all that's necessary to utilize the Against The Clock courseware library.

Notes:

INTRODUCTION

This course has been designed to familiarize you with the fundamentals of Adobe Illustrator. Illustrator is an industry standard in the graphic arts, and is used by thousands of artists around the world. Illustrator produces *vector* artwork; that is, artwork comprised of mathematical descriptions of shapes, curves, fills, and patterns.

It would be restrictive to think of Illustrator purely as a drawing program. In fact, Illustrator can handle a number of critical tasks and produce an almost unlimited array of special effects — including several that might be considered the domain of a painting or image-editing program such as Adobe's popular Photoshop program.

As you learn to use Illustrator, you will soon realize that the basic functionality of the program has to do with its control over *paths.* Paths are PostScript objects built of *anchor points* (locations where you click the mouse) and *segments* (lines that connect the anchor points). In their simplest form, these connecting segments are straight lines; in their most common use, however, they're *curves.* The ability to control the shape of curved segments (also called *Bézier Curves*) is one of the hallmarks of Illustrator and perhaps the most powerful tool available to today's digital artist and designer.

Paths have attributes, including color and weight. Using paths, the artist is able to construct lines (called *open paths*) and shapes (called *closed paths*). Paths can also have *fill* attributes, which provide total control of the appearance of objects drawn in the program. Additional functions allow for stacking of objects, and the ability to develop segregated collections of objects on a kind of virtual "overlay" called *layers.* Elements on single layers can be locked or hidden, as can entire layers and all the components they contain. Objects can also be merged, rotated, scaled, and distorted in unlimited ways.

Control over color in Illustrator is equally powerful; the program allows colors to be defined based on the industry standard four-color ink set known as CMYK (cyan, magenta, yellow, and black). Additionally, you can define so-called "spot colors," and access a range of industry standard color models such as the Pantone™ swatch library. These options ensure that your work will comply with the workflows of the commercial printing and imaging industry. Tools for saving files in formats compatible with the World Wide Web are also part of the program, as are processes for outputting your artwork to a vast array of PostScript devices. You can choose to send your work to color printers, digital proofing systems, imagesetters, platesetters, and digital presses — all without changing the original format. Illustrator objects can also be imported into all major page layout and photo-editing programs.

Illustrator's functionality doesn't end here, either. With the ability to import high-resolution images from scanners, clip art, or image editing software such as Adobe Photoshop, the designer isn't limited to using the program solely to draw components for other uses. Many top designers — particularly those working in display advertising and packaging environments — never leave the application. They choose to import their images, develop patterns, and complete their designs within the scope of Adobe Illustrator.

During this introductory course, you will be exposed to many of the powerful features offered by Adobe Illustrator. As your experience and knowledge of the program evolves, you will probably agree that the program is among the most powerful tools available to the designer today. We hope you like the course and find it effective.

CHAPTER 1

THE ILLUSTRATOR ENVIRONMENT

CHAPTER OBJECTIVE:

To understand Illustrator's powerful working environment; to learn how to customize Illustrator's tools and palettes for an individualized working environment; to become familiar with how Illustrator works. In Chapter 1, you will:

- Learn how to create, open, and save documents, and the different saving file formats available.

- Learn how to use Document Setup to control the Page Tiling, Orientation, and Artboard.

- Learn about Page/Print Setup.

- Learn the basic elements of the Toolbox, menus, palettes, and the working page.

- Know how to access the Toolbox tools and its various pop-out tools.

- Develop a better understanding of how to use palettes, and how to manage them to mximize your working environment.

- Become familiar with Illustrator's General Preference options and how to alter them to suit your coming needs in this course.

In Illustrator, there is rarely only "one way" to perform most techniques. Ten Illustrator artists could look at a design, and each one could have their own way of approaching the end result. Illustrator is just that versatile.

Just for fun, when you hold Option/Alt and click on the Status menu you get further information that probably has nothing to do with the job at hand, such as the moon phase, mouse clicks, shopping days til Christmas, and even Ted's home phone number (if you like Illustrator, he'd like to know.)

The Illustrator Environment

Whether they are mechanics, chefs, or graphic artists, true professionals must know the tools of their trades. To work efficiently and produce quality products, they must know which tool is best for the job and how to use it. The Adobe Illustrator program is a highly complex collection of tools for the digital artist.

Illustrator can be intimidating at first glance. However, as you learn your way around the various elements of this software environment, you will discover that it provides you with everything you need to work efficiently and productively.

The Environment

Later we will show you how to customize a document window to suit your needs. The basic elements available will include menus, palettes, the working page, and the treasure trove of tools in the Toolbox.

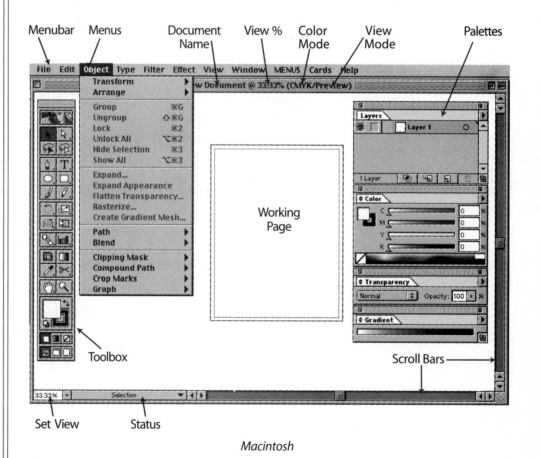

Macintosh

Several documents can be open at the same time. They can be accessed at the bottom of the Window menu, where they will be listed by name. Another way to navigate through the open documents is to manually resize the document windows so that some parts of the windows are visible behind the active window. By clicking on the visible portion of a document, it comes to the front as the working document.

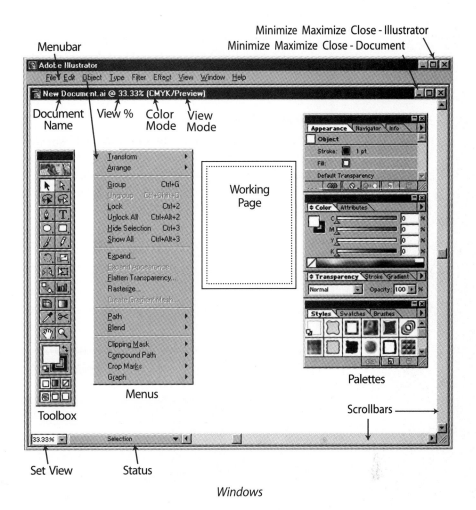

Windows

Both the Windows and Macintosh document windows contain the same elements.

- **Menubar.** Shows the menus that offer many (but not all) of Illustrator's features, functions, and operations.

- **Title bar.** Shows the document name, followed by the percentage of the document you are currently viewing, the Color mode (CYMK or RGB), and the Viewing mode (Preview or Artwork).

- **Palettes.** Give you instant access and control over most document elements, such as color, line weight, font style, and numerous others.

- **Toolbox.** Contains tools necessary for creating and modifying objects in the document.

- **Working Page.** Area where your illustrations will be created.

- **Set View.** Percentage at the bottom of the document window allows you to either enter the view size directly, or use its menu to select the size percentage.

- **Status pop-up menu.** Can display pertinent information from the current tool selected, date and time, free memory, and the number of "Undos" available.

Creating and Opening Documents

There's nothing unique or surprising about creating and opening documents in Illustrator. Like most popular Macintosh and Windows software, File>New, File>Open, and Command/Control-N or Command/Control-O will get you started; from there, you have some choices to make.

Creating New Documents

When you create a new document with File>New, you get the New Document dialog box. Now you can name the file, choose either CMYK or RGB color, and customize the Artboard Size. Color mode depends on what you are creating the image for — commercial press or the Web (more about this later). The Artboard Size should be left to the default standard letter-size (612 × 792 points).

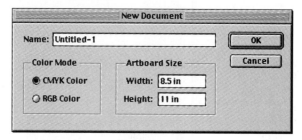

Macintosh

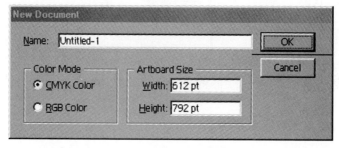

Windows

If the file is for commercial press, you should choose CMYK as the Color Mode. If the image is going to be a graphic on the Internet, you should choose RGB, which is the color standard for the Web.

Opening Documents

In addition to being able to open documents created with earlier versions of Illustrator, the program also supports most major graphic formats.

The File>Open Feature

A saved Illustrator document can be opened using File>Open. For Macintosh users, there are two important buttons to consider in Show and Show Preview.

Show

The Show option of the Open dialog box defaults to All Readable Documents, which are documents types that Illustrator is familiar with and can open. The All Documents option will show every file in a folder or directory. The Show menu also lists file types that, when selected, will narrow the listing down to this type of file only.

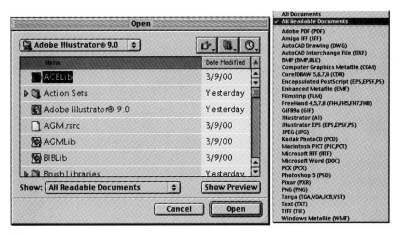

Show Preview

When clicked, this option shows a small thumbnail preview of the selected document.

On the Macintosh, the Show Preview option of the Open dialog box only shows previews of EPS files that have been saved with Include Document Thumbnails.

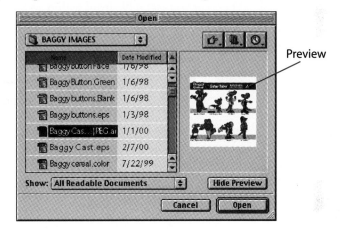

Macintosh

In Windows, the Open dialog box defaults to Files of Type>All Formats. If the selected file has a thumbnail preview, it will appear in the square at the bottom.

Windows

Open Recent Files

The File menu has an option that keeps track of the last ten Illustrator files that have been opened or saved. This is called Open Recent Files. This is useful for accessing documents that might have been accidentally saved in the wrong folder, and/or briefly lost.

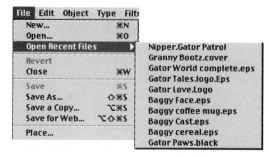

Saving Your Work

Whenever you save a file from within an application, it is normally saved in what is known as "native" format. Saved Illustrator files contain all the information that was used to create the images in the file. There are three things you can do with an Illustrator file: Save, Save As, and Save a Copy. The exact file format you choose depends on how you eventually intend to use the image.

This Save option can save a previously saved Illustrator document only. If the new document was not named in the New Document dialog box, it will retain the "Untitled" name. In this case, Save will be grayed in the File menu. Pressing Command/Control-S defaults to the Save As dialog box, so the format and name of the file can be set. Once a document is saved, choosing File>Save (Command/Control-S) will update the file to your disk without displaying any dialog boxes.

The Save As option offers formats that are compatible with many other applications and even other hardware platforms. Use Save As when you want to save an existing file with another name, another file format, or to a different location.

Once either Save or Save As is chosen, the Save dialog box appears. It has a Name field where you can name the file, and a Format menu from which to choose the format of the saved document. There are three to choose from: Adobe PDF (PDF), Adobe Illustrator Document, and Illustrator EPS (EPS).

If you make unwanted changes to your artwork, the Revert option, found in the File menu, will close the file and open the last version you saved. The keyboard shortcut for Revert is F12.

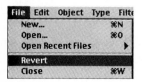

Macintosh users, if you mistakenly press Save, all changes made are saved to the current file. Perhaps you don't want this. If this happens, all is not lost. Edit>Undo will undo this Save, as long as you don't close the document.

(This feature is not available for Windows users.)

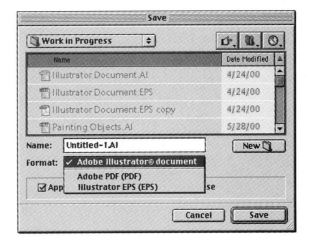

*To close several open
documents quickly, hold the
Option/Alt key when closing
the first document. All
others will close as long as
they don't need any
changes saved.*

*When Save As is used on a
previously saved document
to change its name, the
newly named document
becomes the working file,
and the former is closed,
without saving its changes.*

When you choose Adobe Illustrator format in the Save dialog box, the following dialog box
will appear. If you intend to print your artwork from within Illustrator, this native format is
sufficient. It will keep the file size small while retaining all Illustrator features. This format,
however, cannot be placed or imported as a graphic into most layout programs. When the
Adobe Illustrator Document option is selected in the Format/Files of Type menu, the
following dialog box will appear when Save is pressed. The default settings are best; clicking
OK will save the file.

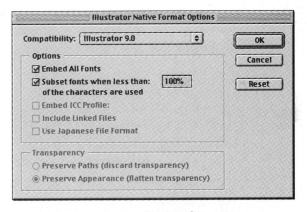

Macintosh

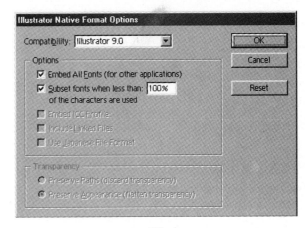

Windows

Adobe PDF (PDF)

Adobe PDF allows you to save your document as a PDF file (Portable Document Format). It's been steadily gaining in popularity since its introduction five or more years ago.

Actually, there are several system level components to this option, as well as the built-in capacity to save or open PDF files directly from Illustrator. Several of these components are included with your Macintosh or Windows system, and others are available commercially from Adobe. Included with your system are:

- **Acrobat PDFWriter**. This is a print driver that lets you print your documents to PDF. You don't need to print to PDFWriter from Illustrator, because you can save into the format directly. You can, however, print a PDF file from any other application, and then use Illustrator to open the file — a useful function if you ever want to use output from one application as a component in an Illustrator drawing. PDF files can be viewed (but not modified) using the second system component:

- **Acrobat Reader**. Acrobat Reader is a free product manufactured by Adobe and distributed both by them directly as well as by many third party companies who distribute it with PDF files so that the viewer can open them on their computer.

The amazing thing about a PDF file is that once the file has been saved into this format, it can be viewed and printed — with every detail, including fonts, images, pages, and more — on any computer that has Acrobat Reader installed. Whether or not someone has Illustrator, they can view and print your documents as if they did.

The not-for-free parts of Acrobat are tools that allow you to add buttons, animation, interactivity, contents listing, export the files to other applications, and modify them in other ways. The name of the product is Adobe Acrobat and is available from a wide variety of sources. It comes with a product called Acrobat Distiller, which is an industrial-strength program designed to process multiple documents into Acrobat format in a single batch. There are two PDF dialog boxes you can access when saving in PDF file. The General settings is the first.

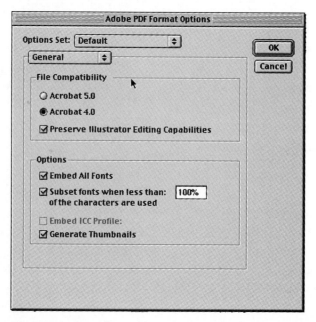

The second dialog box available to you when you save a PDF file from within Illustrator is the Compression options. These control the downsampling of image files and can produce a screen-ready version of your Illustrator file that can be viewed by anyone with Acrobat Reader.

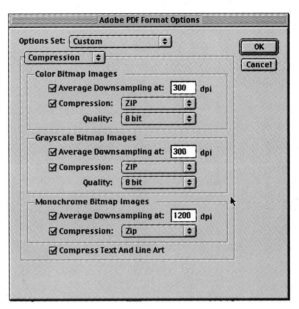

The Acrobat Reader program provides a "player" that can be used to fan through pages, attach notes, and print any PDF document to your own printer. It's becoming a very popular method of moving "rich" documents (ones that contain their original formatting, fonts, images, and layout) across the Internet.

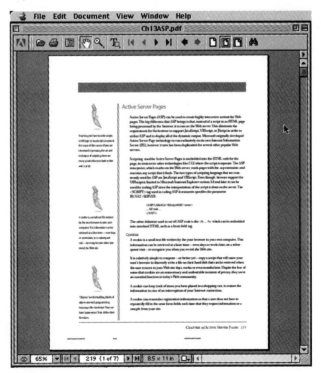

Acrobat Reader, which is available free of charge, can be used to view, annotate, and print files which have been output to Portable Document Format (PDF).

Documents created in older versions of Illustrator can be opened by 9.0, but if any new 9.0 features are applied to the file, it must be saved as 9.0 version format to retain these changes.

The Compatibility option in all of the save dialog boxes allows you to save the file in previous versions of Illustrator, which is useful when giving the file to someone who has an older version. If they don't have Illustrator 9.0, they cannot open an 9.0 file. A warning stating that the file format is unreadable will appear.

> ✓ **Version 9.0**
> **Version 8.0**
> **Version 7.0**
> **Version 6.0**
> **Version 5.0/5.5**
> **Version 4.0**
> **Version 3.0/3.2**

Acrobat Resources

The best place to find out more about PDF is from the Adobe web site, at http://www.adobe.com. Another great site that we make use of is called planetpdf.com. You sign up as a member (free) and gain access to thousands of PDF users from around the nation and around the world, discussing every possible aspect of PDF use, particularly in the graphic arts environment.

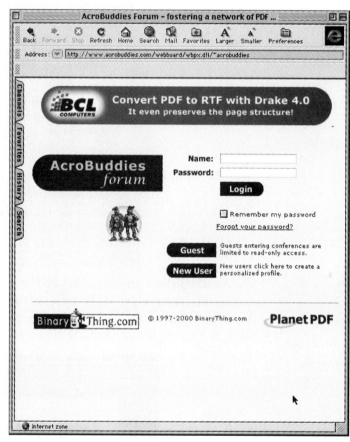

The PlanetPDF web site is a great resource for information about using Acrobat in the real world, and provides information about add-on products that can enhance the program's functionality.

It's a good idea to experiment with PDF, and to explore the possibilities that it presents for making documents platform independent — meaning that a document you create can be viewed and output exactly as you intended it to look — on Macs, Windows or Unix computers. Although this book isn't the place for a fully detailed discussion of all the possibilities, PDF is increasingly becoming a standard file format in both the graphics arts world as well as the general business community.

Illustrator EPS (EPS)

EPS (Encapsulated PostScript) is a universal file format meaning that a wide variety of programs support importing and exporting images in EPS format for printing to Postscript printers. If an image is going to be placed in another application, the file should be saved in the EPS format. When Illustrator EPS is selected in the Save As dialog box, an EPS Format Options dialog box appears after Save is pressed. The default settings can be changed as you learn more about file formats and EPS in particular.

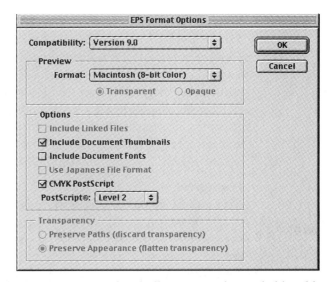

Since you are just getting acquainted with Illustrator, we've probably told you all you need to know about saving documents — at least for now. It won't be long, however, before you will need to make additional decisions when you save files. Be aware of the following Save options, then when you need them, you can refer to the details that follow.

Preview

When you save an EPS file you can select a Preview option, which determines how the document will be viewed on the monitor when it is placed in another document. With None, the EPS image, when placed, will be a big gray rectangular object with no preview. The two TIFF previews (Black & White, 8-bit Color) are primarily made for PC (IBM and compatibles) monitors. The Macintosh previews are for the Apple Macintosh. Black & White gives a coarse 1-bit preview of the image. The 8-bit Color selection is in vivid color, and is best for seeing what will place and print.

Macintosh

The Windows Preview Format does not offer a Macintosh selection, therefore choose either of the two TIFF options. TIFF formats are usually cross-platform and will show up on the Macintosh.

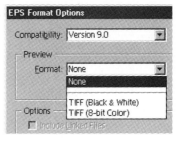

Windows

Don't be mislead by the word TIFF in the Preview>Format selection. You are not actually saving the file as a TIFF. On a Macintosh, the raster format of the Preview is PICT. Windows formats do not support PICT, so they show the Preview on screen using the TIFF format.

Options

The Options section in the dialog box gives you some additional saving features to select. The Include Linked Files will save placed images into the document. To save a thumbnail that can be seen in the File>Open dialog box, select Include Document Thumbnails. The Include Document Fonts saves the fonts used in the file inside the document. Use Japanese File Format to the file in a Japanese computer language. CMYK PostScript allows the document, if it contains RGB images, to be printed in applications that do not support RGB. PostScript gives the choices of three levels of PostScript output when the document is printed — Level 1, Level 2, and Level 3.

Transparency

The Transparency option allows you to retain or remove any transparency features that may have been used on the paths in the document. Your choices include Preserve Paths (discard transparency), which removes any transparency from the paths it was applied to, and Preserve Appearance (flatten transparency), which keeps the applied appearance of the object's preview.

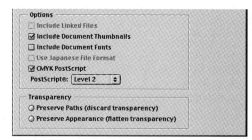

The Save a Copy option in the File menu saves a duplicate of the open document. Selecting Save a Copy gives you the Save As dialog box where you can accept the name, format, and location of the document or change any these attributes of the document. Illustrator adds the word "copy" to the name of the document in the dialog box. You can highlight the name and retitle to any name you desire.

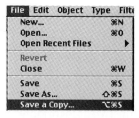

Save for Web

The Save for Web option in the File menu saves the document images and objects as a raster image (either JPG, GIF, or PNG) that can be used as an Internet graphic. Save for Web offers many variables for format, depth, color and resolution, and should only be used by those who are used to creating graphics for the Web.

Get in the habit of using standard naming conventions and standard extensions such as Filename.AI or Filename.EPS so your files can be transported back and forth between Macintosh and Windows. This is important because the extension is the only way Windows can identify which software application was used to create the document.

Windows users will notice that even if they add a capital letter extension to a file name when saving, Windows will automatically change it to lower case.

Creating, Saving, and Opening a Document

1. In the File menu, select New to create a new untitled document.

2. The New Document dialog box will appear. Leave the file named "Untitled-1." We will suppose that the document is to be printed as four-color process (CMYK) on a commercial printing press. Click the CMYK Color button. Leave the Artboard Size set as it is, then click OK.

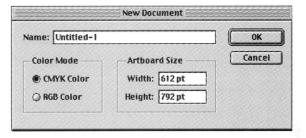

The size of the Artboard can be set when creating a New document. If, however, it needs changing afterwards, the Document Setup>Artboard section must be used.

3. Go to the File menu. For Macintosh users, the Save option will be grayed out. The only saving options you will use are Save As, or Save a Copy. Choose Save As.

4. Go to your **Work in Progress** folder. Leave the Format/Files of Type set for Adobe Illustrator Document. Change the name of the document to "Illustrator Document.AI". Click Save.

Windows users can toggle between Landscape and Portrait orientation in Document Setup>Artboard by placing the cursor in the Height field and pressing the Tab key.

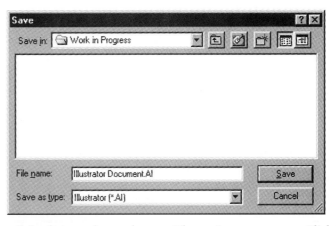

5. In the next dialog box, make no changes. The settings are correct. Click OK.

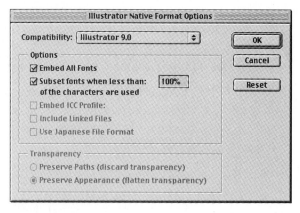

6. In the document, look at the heading across the top of the window. The new name will be present, and the file is now a saved document.

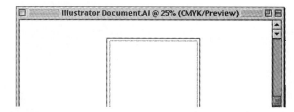

7. Press Command/Control-W to close the document.

8. Use the File menu to select Open. In its dialog box, navigate to your **Work in Progress** folder and open the **Illustrator Document.AI** file.

9. From the File menu, select Save As. In the dialog box, click on the Format/Files of Type menu and select Adobe Illustrator EPS (EPS). Rename the file "Illustrator Document.EPS". Click Save.

10. In the EPS dialog box that appears, leave the Compatibility set for Version 9.0. Macintosh users, set the Preview Format to Macintosh (8-bit Color). Windows users, set the Format to TIFF (8-bit Color). Make no other changes. Click OK. The saved file is now an Encapsulated PostScript (EPS) image. Notice that the active document is the new EPS document. To make changes that will be saved to a separate file without changing the current document, Save a Copy must be used.

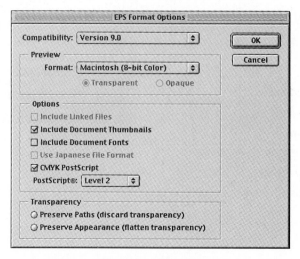

11. From the File menu, select Save a Copy. The familiar Save As dialog box will appear. Notice that the word "copy" has been added to the file name.

12. In the Format menu, select the Adobe PDF option and click Save.

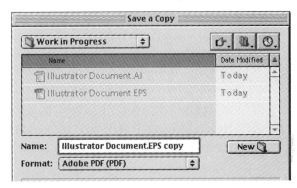

13. In the Adobe PDF Format Options dialog box, make no changes. Click OK.

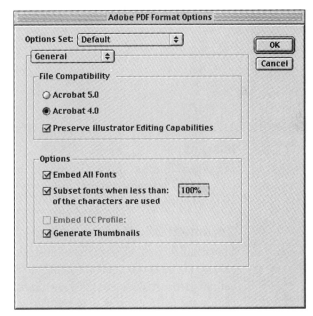

14. You will notice that the copy you just saved does not become the current working file. The copy is saved externally and must be opened to perform any work on it.

15. You have experienced how to create, open, and save Illustrator documents.

16. Close the file without saving.

Page Tiling and the Artboard

As you get started using Illustrator, your main concern will be learning how to use the tools and features that allow you to create images. However, every artist needs a work space and a piece of paper to draw on. Illustrator calls these the Artboard (work space) and Page Tiling (piece of paper).

New Documents

By default, a new Illustrator document contains only one Page Tile. Also by default, a new Illustrator document starts you out with a standard 8.5 in. × 11 in. page. Your working page (Page Tiling) is on the Artboard, which corresponds to the drawing table you would use if you were working with traditional media, such as pen and ink. The space you see on your monitor around the Artboard is like the floor around your drawing table (and just like your floor, the junk you toss on this space stays there until you clean it up).

By default, the Artboard and the Page Tiling are the same size. Therefore, when you create a new document in Illustrator, the lines defining the Page Tiling and the Artboard appear to be only one line with the Page Tiling on top.

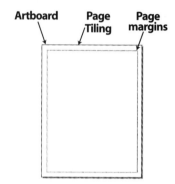

Margins

The dotted line that appears inside the Page Tiling is the margin. When you create a new document, Illustrator automatically sets the margin to correspond to the printable area of your default printer.

Document Orientation and Size

The default orientation in a new Illustrator document is Portrait. You can change the orientation to Landscape of the Artboard and Page Tiling using the File>Document Setup>Artboard dialog box. If you change the orientation of the Artboard, you must also change the orientation of the Page Tiling. However, the Size, Width, Height, and Orientation options in File>Document Setup>Artboard only pertain to the Artboard. To change the orientation of Page Tiling you must use the Page Setup/Print Setup button on the lower right of the Artboard dialog box.

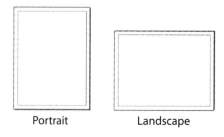

Portrait   Landscape

Changing Artboard and Page Tiling Orientation

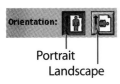

Portrait
Landscape

1. Create a new document set for CMYK Color Mode, leave it untitled and the Artboard Size at the default setting.

2. From the File menu, select Document Setup>Artboard.

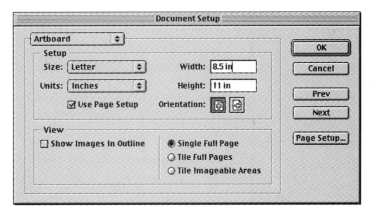

3. The Portrait orientation icon is selected by default. Click on the Landscape icon. Click OK. Look at your document page. Do you notice something odd? The Artboard changed to Landscape, but the Page Tiling is still set at Portrait. Select Edit>Undo.

4. Go back to File>Document Setup>Artboard. Select Use Page/Print Setup. Click on the Page/Print Setup button at the right of the dialog box. In the dialog box that appears, select the Landscape icon. Click OK. In Document Setup click OK. This changes the orientation so both the page tiling and artboard are the same.

5. When changing the orientation of the page, make sure you have Use Page Setup selected in Document Setup>Artboard, and use the Page/Print setup dialog box to choose a different Orientation.

6. Close the document without saving.

The Toolbox

Illustrator's center piece is the Toolbox. This powerful floating palette provides you with a range of tools for creating and modifying almost any image you desire. Every time you launch Illustrator, the Toolbox will appear on your monitor. But you get much more than you first see. If you click-hold on the small arrow that you see in some of the tool icons, a pop-out menu appears with even more tools to choose from.

At the end of each pop-out menu is a small "end piece" that allows you to tear-off the menu and place it on the screen so it is easier to access. While the pop-out menu is showing, touch the end piece with your mouse, release the button, and the pop-out will separate from the Toolbox. You can then move the menu around your screen to customize your work space.

To close the tear-off menu, click on the Close box in the toolbar at the top of the menu.

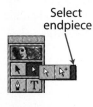

Select endpiece

Close button

Tear off menu

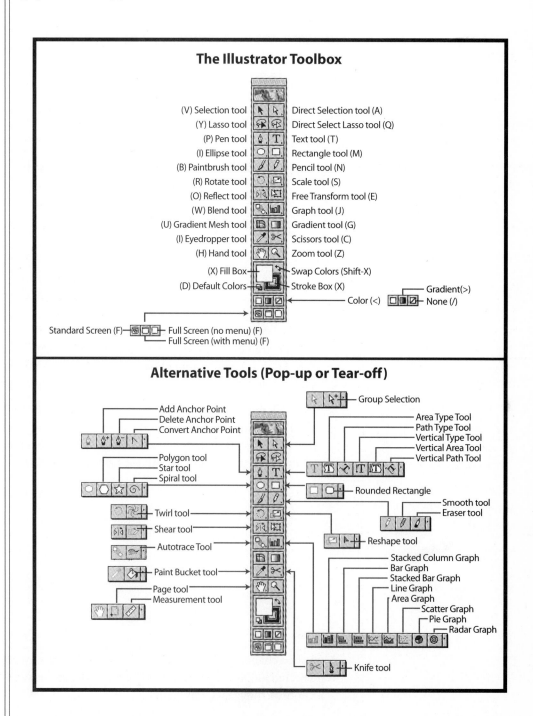

The Illustrator Toolbox

(V) Selection tool — Direct Selection tool (A)
(Y) Lasso tool — Direct Select Lasso tool (Q)
(P) Pen tool — Text tool (T)
(I) Ellipse tool — Rectangle tool (M)
(B) Paintbrush tool — Pencil tool (N)
(R) Rotate tool — Scale tool (S)
(O) Reflect tool — Free Transform tool (E)
(W) Blend tool — Graph tool (J)
(U) Gradient Mesh tool — Gradient tool (G)
(I) Eyedropper tool — Scissors tool (C)
(H) Hand tool — Zoom tool (Z)
(X) Fill Box — Swap Colors (Shift-X)
(D) Default Colors — Stroke Box (X)
Gradient(>)
Color (<) — None (/)
Standard Screen (F) — Full Screen (no menu) (F)
Full Screen (with menu) (F)

Alternative Tools (Pop-up or Tear-off)

Group Selection
Add Anchor Point
Delete Anchor Point
Convert Anchor Point
Area Type Tool
Path Type Tool
Vertical Type Tool
Vertical Area Tool
Vertical Path Tool
Polygon tool
Star tool
Spiral tool
Rounded Rectangle
Smooth tool
Eraser tool
Twirl tool
Shear tool
Reshape tool
Autotrace Tool
Stacked Column Graph
Bar Graph
Stacked Bar Graph
Line Graph
Area Graph
Paint Bucket tool
Scatter Graph
Pie Graph
Page tool
Radar Graph
Measurement tool
Knife tool

The Toolbox Explained

Although at this early stage in your studies you won't understand each of these brief explanations, as you begin to learn the tools and their functions, they will become clear.

Using the correct tool for the job at hand is an important knowledge set that you'll only develop over time. On the other hand, there are usually several ways to accomplish any task in Illustrator, and most experienced users develop preferences for which tool they use to achieve the effect they're looking for.

Selection tool selects entire paths, groups of objects, and blocks of text.

Direct Selection tool selects individual paths and objects.

Group Selection tool selects objects within a group.

Lasso Selection tool selects anchor points in a freeform fashion.

Direct Lasso Selection tool selects individual anchor points in a freeform fashion.

Pen tool draws paths with anchor points and path segments.

Add Anchor Point tool puts new anchor points on paths.

Delete Anchor Point tool removes anchor points from paths.

Convert Direction Point tool interchanges smooth and corner points.

Type tool enters text that can be edited.

Area Type tool enters text inside closed paths.

Path Type tool enters text on paths.

Vertical Type tool enters text vertically.

Vertical Area Type tool enters vertical text inside closed paths.

Vertical Path Type tool enters vertical text on paths.

Ellipse tool draws ovals and circles.

Polygon tool draws multi-sided figures.

Star tool draws multi-pointed figures.

Spiral tool draws a curled path.

Rectangle tool draws four-sided figures, including squares.

Rounded Rectangle tool draws four-sided figures with rounded corners.

Paintbrush tool draws paths resembling brush strokes.

Pencil tool draws freehand lines.

Smooth tool modifies freehand lines.

Eraser tool deletes path segments and anchor points.

Rotate tool revolves objects.

Twirl tool twists objects.

Scale tool changes the size of objects.

Reshape tool adds anchor points.

Reflect tool mirrors objects.

Shear tool skews objects.

Free Transform tool rotates, scales, and reflects objects.

Blend tool blends colors and repeats objects along a path.

Graph tools create the type of graph shown on the each tool button.

Eyedropper tool samples paint attributes from objects.

Paint Bucket tool creates colors objects with the currently selected stroke and fill.

Scissors tool cuts paths.

Knife tool cuts a path and closes it.

Hand tool moves document view around the monitor.

Page tool moves the Page Tiling position on the Artboard.

Measure tool works as a movable ruler in the document window.

Fill box, **Swap Fill/Stroke** tool, **Stroke** box, **Default Colors** tool, **Color Palette** button, **Gradient** button, and **None** button modify the colors in objects.

Standard Screen, **Full Screen with Menu Bar**, and **Full Screen No Menu Bar** buttons modify how the document window is viewed.

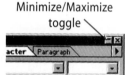

Palettes

In addition to the Toolbox, menus, and dialog boxes, Illustrator makes extensive use of self-contained dialog boxes called palettes. Many Illustrator functions — particularly those that set the attributes of objects and type — are available in the palettes. Here are some samples.

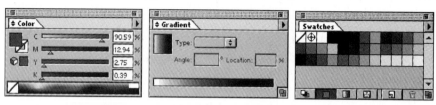

The Palettes use familiar icons and features seen in menus and dialog boxes throughout Illustrator. A basic palette is displayed below.

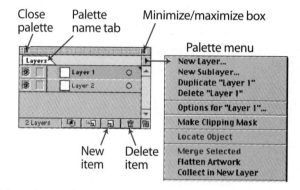

Tab. The name of the palette is located in its tab. To the far right of the tab is an arrow that, when pressed, shows the palette menu. Each palette has its own menu with options that pertain to its features.

New Item icon. The New Item icon creates new palette items within the palette. For example, in the Layers palette, the New Item icon creates a new layer. In the Swatch palette, it creates a new color swatch.

Delete Item icon. The Delete Item icon deletes any item that is selected within the palette.

Minimize/Maximize box. When the whole palette is showing, the Minimize/Maximize toggle box rolls the palette up like a window shade. This minimizes the room the palette occupies on the screen while keeping it available for easy access. When you click Minimize/Maximize box again, the palette comes into full view.

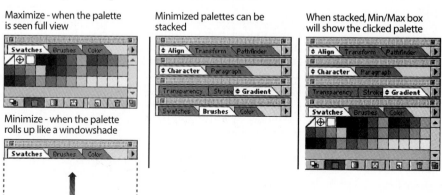

In the name tab of some palettes, you will see an icon of triangular arrows depicting up and down movements.

Minimize/Maximize icon

You can click on this icon to toggle between minimizing the palette up to the title bar and maximizing the entire palette, including its options. Not all palettes have these icons. **Palettes with icons:** *Color, Transparency, Attributes, Stroke, Info, Gradient, Align, Pathfinder, Character, and Paragraph.* **Palettes with no icons:** *Layers, Links, Actions, Brushes, Appearance, Navigator, Transform, Swatches, and Styles.*

Docking palettes is another way to reduce the clutter on your monitor.

Combining Palettes

Palettes can be combined by dragging their name tabs to another palette. This activity is known as "grouping" palettes.

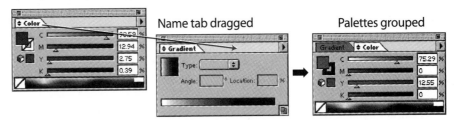

Name tab dragged   Palettes grouped

This speeds up efficiency by allowing related palettes to be combined. Each palette can be activated by clicking on the name tab. The tab that is white will be the active palette.

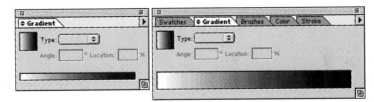

Another combination method is called "docking." The name tab of one palette is dragged to touch the bottom of another palette. When the Selection arrow touches the bottom of the receiving palette, a small bar on the bottom of its palette becomes dark, meaning that contact has been made, and the docking was successful. When palettes are docked, only one title bar appears above the top palette. This is the bar to drag on when the docked palettes need to be moved.

Name tab is dragged

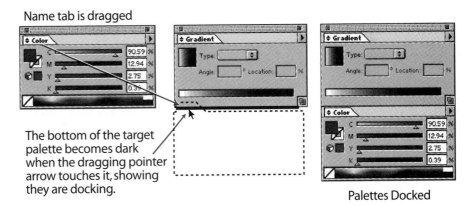

The bottom of the target palette becomes dark when the dragging pointer arrow touches it, showing they are docking.

Palettes Docked

Palettes can also be dragged from a group or docking, and become a single palette.

Palettes can be put away by pressing the Tab key. To put all palettes away, but keep the Toolbox open, hold the Shift key while pressing the Tab key.

Menus

Illustrator's menus offer features for modifying, editing, or arranging artwork. Many menus have sub-menus marked with a triangle that, when highlighted, will show further choices and options.

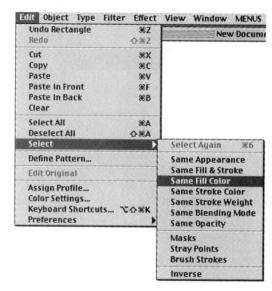

Contextual Menus

One of the most useful pop-up menus is the Contextual menu, accessed by Control-click/Right-click anywhere on the screen. This menu pops up wherever the Selection tool arrow is located and pressed. The menu changes depending on the selected object, thus the name "Contextual."

Some examples of contextual menus include selecting a path and Control-clicking/Right-clicking, which shows you the pop-up menu with options for modifying paths. When text is selected, type options are shown. If no object is selected, Zoom, Rulers, Show Grid, and Guides commands are available that affect the document itself. Raster images can be transformed, arranged, and selected from the Contextual menu.

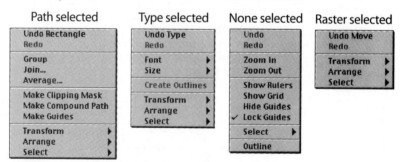

Preferences

Preferences are just that — customized settings to fit the way one prefers to work. Examples of Preferences in Illustrator include whether objects are measured (and rulers displayed) in inches, picas, or millimeters. There are many other examples that we will discuss later. Found at the bottom of the Edit menu, Preferences offers further options that allow you to adjust Illustrator's operations. When Preferences are accessed, several choices appear, but the General Preferences options are most important for now.

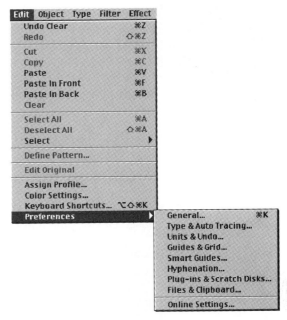

General Preferences

The Preferences>General dialog box offers some choices about Keyboard Increments, Tool Behavior, and some other options affecting tool tips, warnings, stroke weights, cursors, and others.

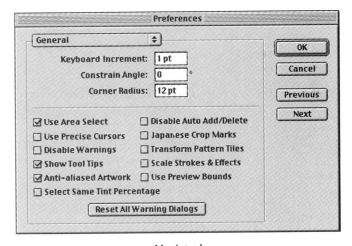

Macintosh

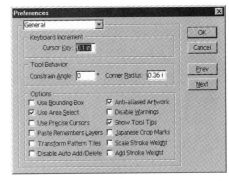

Windows

- **Use Bounding Box (Windows).** Other than the Show/Hide Bounding Box option found in the View menu, for Windows users the Bounding Box can also be toggled on and off from this Preference selection. We suggest that you keep this option unchecked and use the View menu to access the Bounding Box.

- **Use Area Select.** Makes it possible to click on a painted object in Preview mode and select it. This does not work in Outline mode. Keep this checked.

- **Use Precise Cursors.** Changes the shape of a tool cursor to a cross-hair for more precision when using certain functions. It is not needed when learning the tools, so keep this option unchecked.

- **Paste Remembers Layers (Windows).** This option pertaining to Layers (covered in Chapter Nine) and is not necessary for now. Keep it unchecked.

- **Disable warnings.** As bothersome as warnings can be, they can prove helpful — especially for new users. This option should not be selected.

- **Show Tool Tips.** Turns on balloon tips that explain the functions of tools in the Toolbox and on floating palettes. This option should be selected.

- **Anti-Alias Artwork.** This option affects how the artwork looks when seen in the document. Anti-Alias smooths and improves the visual appearance. Select this option.

- **Select Same Tint Percentage.** This option controls some of the selecting methods in the Edit>Select menu. It is necessary to access tints of colors used, so check this option.

- **Disable Auto Add/Delete.** Keep this anchor point related option unchecked until anchor points and segments are discussed in greater detail.

- **Japanese Crop Marks.** Sets crop marks for Japanese measurement standards. This option can be unchecked for this book.

- **Transform Pattern Tiles.** This should only be checked when using patterns. Patterns are not part of this course, so this option should be unselected.

- **Scale Strokes & Effects.** Automatically adjusts line weights in proportion to the selected scaling factor. This option should be checked.

- **Scale Strokes & Effects (Macintosh).** Automatically adjusts line weights in proportion to the selected scaling factor. This option should be checked. The Windows equivalent, **Scale Stroke Weight**, does the same thing with Strokes.

- **Use Preview Bounds (Macintosh).** Affects the increments in the Transform and Info palettes. If this option is not selected, the measurements reflect the size of the object based on the path. If selected, the measurements are based upon the outer boundaries of the Preview. Keep this option unchecked. The equivalent to this is the **Add Stroke Weight** found in the Windows dialog box, which does the same thing.

More Preferences, Later

As the course progresses, we will see the other Preferences that can be altered. During this course, it is not a good idea to make adjustments until the actual features and functions are introduced, explained, and there is a good understanding of why the changes need to be made.

Chapter Summary

You have observed the working environment of Illustrator and used many of its features. You have created, saved, and renamed files. You have changed the orientation of the Artboard. You have learned how menus and palettes offer you options for altering your tools and functions, as well as how Preferences affect the way certain tools and features work.

Notes:

CHAPTER 2

GRIDS AND GUIDES

CHAPTER OBJECTIVE:

To understand the similarity between art created traditionally and art created with the digital tools available in Illustrator. To learn how the tools in Illustrator can be used to create and modify art. To learn about Grids, Guides, and Rulers, and how they relate specifically to measuring and placing artwork. In Chapter 2, you will:

- Learn how Illustrator's document background can become a digital blue-line matrix with the Grid.

- Learn how to control the Grid to customize its color, style of appearance, alter each gridline with Gridline Every, and change the number of subdivisions.

- Learn more about Rulers, the Zero Point, and how to manage ruler measurement units.

- Understand how Guides are used to keep measurements and alignments consistent in designs and layouts. Become competent at converting paths to guides, and guides to paths.

- Learn how to customize the color and style of guides.

Grids and Guides

Before digital tools became part of the industry, commercial art had to be created by hand, and no artist was without their "non-repro blue" pen to map out their dimensions, borders, margins, and guidelines. Today, with all of our digital tools and the ability to create and modify art on the fly, guides are still a prerequisite to maintaining exact measurements and dimensions of artwork. Since so many drawings require the measuring of objects and placing them in proper position — relative to other objects as well as relative to the page — it's very important to learn how to use the various measurement tools available in the Illustrator environment.

The three features in Illustrator that relate specifically to the measuring and placement aspect of the document are Grids, Guides, and Rulers.

Grids

Artists working in traditional media often use pads of non-photographic (non-repro) blue-line grid sheets. In the same way that these blue-line grids are used for measurements, dimensions and creating exact artwork, Illustrator can turn the background of any document into a blue-line grid. The artboard and page tiling can still be seen without distractions, and the grid does not print.

The grid and guides are easy to customize in the Edit>Preferences>Guides & Grid dialog box.

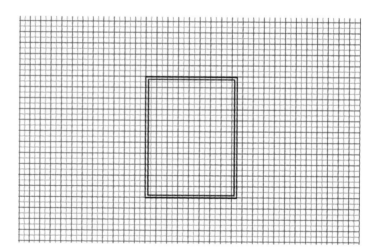

If the color of the grid is distracting or if it conflicts with similarly colored objects, its color can be changed with Edit>Preferences>Guides & Grid.

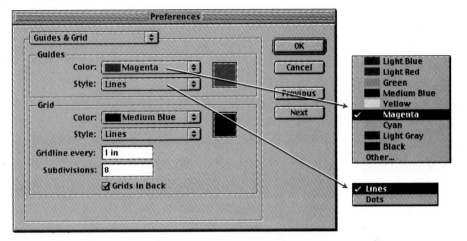

If the grid is not shown, and you still find objects snapping to invisible points as they are moved, and Snap to Point is turned off, check to see if Snap to Grid is selected. Regardless of whether the grid is visible or not, Snap to Grid remains active and will attract the artwork as it is moved.

- **Color.** Choose a different color for the guides or grid lines. Double-clicking the swatch square brings up the Color Picker to alter colors.

- **Style.** The style of guides or a grid can be either solid lines or dots.

- **Gridline Every.** The distance between the thicker lines (gridlines) can be set for your own needs. One inch is the default standard.

- **Subdivisions.** The subdivisions are the small squares between the gridlines. The number of subdivisions can be customized.

Using the Grid

1. From the **SF-Intro Illustrator** folder, open the document **Grid and Guides.AI**. Select Fit in Window from the View menu to adjust the view to see the page clearly.

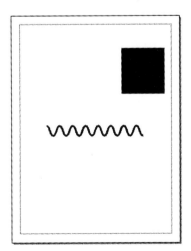

The thicker gridlines are set up to be 1" apart. This makes page dimensions easier to see, and the aligning of objects more precise.

2. In the View menu, select Show Grid. With the Selection tool, click on the black square to drag it around. Drag the square so that its upper left corner is aligned with the thicker gridlines in the upper left area of the page.

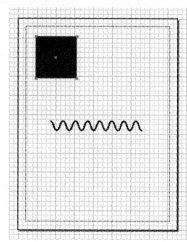

3. Are you being exact? To be certain that the square is accurately touching the thicker grid lines, it is best to have Snap to Grid turned on. In the View menu, select Snap to Grid. Reselect the square and move it around the page slowly, to see how it now snaps to the gridlines.

4. Move the square up to the upper left area and, when it snaps, release the mouse. Select the squiggle-lined object and do the same moving around the page. Turn Snap to Grid off, and again move this object. Move the object to the center of the page.

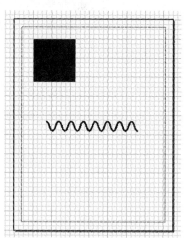

5. Use View>Hide Grid to hide the feature. Turn Snap to Grid back on and move the objects around. Notice how, despite the grid not being active, it still attracts the objects as they move. Be aware of this in case you feel objects snapping to unseen parts of the document.

6. Close the document without saving.

The rulers can also be shown/hidden by using the Contextual menu.

You can change the units to the next available increment type by pressing Command/Control-Shift-U. Each time you press, it goes to the next type of increment.

All new documents default with the Zero Point set for the bottom left corner. If you prefer the zeros to originate from the upper left corner, drag the Zero Point from its origin to the desired spot.

Rulers

As simple as the document rulers seem, they have properties and abilities that are indispensable when creating guides or measuring objects and distances. There are two rulers: Horizontal (spanning across the top of the document), and Vertical (appearing on the left side of the document). They are accessed with either View>Show Rulers, or by pressing the keyboard shortcut Command/Control-R, both of which toggle the ruler on and off.

Zero Point

The Zero Point is where the zeros of both rulers meet. This point can be relocated by dragging from the Zero Point origin where the two rulers meet in the upper left corner of the document. It defaults to the lower left corner of the page.

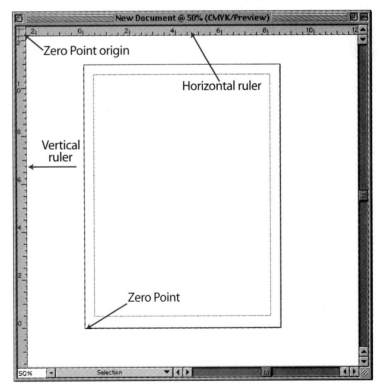

Paths can be converted to a guide by pressing Command/Control-5, or by using the Contextual menu.

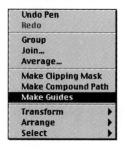

You can make objects snap to guides by selecting Snap to Point in the View menu. You will know the object has snapped and made contact with the grid when the Selection tool cursor appears hollow.

Guides made while on different layers will be controlled by the specific layer that they were made on. If the layer is hidden, its guides are hidden, too.

Ruler Measurement Units

Units of measurement can be changed in either File>Document Setup or Edit>Preferences>Units & Undo. They are independent of each other. If one is changed to different units, the other remains the same until it is changed. Get into the habit of using only one of these for setting the Units.

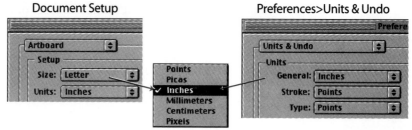

Guides

Guides are useful and may be used to maintain heights and widths, keep objects aligned on a level plane, or position objects relative to others in the design. They are useful (and sometimes essential) in keeping measurements and alignments consistent in designs and layouts. Guides can appear as either solid or dotted lines. This appearance can be changed with Edit>Preferences>Guides & Grid.

There are two methods to creating guides.

- **Rulers.** With the Selection tool, simply click-hold in the ruler area and drag the mouse onto the page to pull a guide into the drawing area.

- **From Path.** Selecting a path (or paths) and choosing View>Guides>Make Guides converts the path to a guide. You can also use the Contextual menu.

Managing Guides

The Guides section of the View menu offers several options for managing guides.

- **Hide Guides.** This feature removes the guides from view. They are, however, still there.

- **Lock Guides.** This option locks the guides, making them inaccessible and eliminates the possibility that a guide could be accidentally moved, modified, or deleted.

- **Make Guides.** This option allows you to convert a path into a guide.

- **Release Guides.** This option works only when guides are unlocked. Use this feature to convert guides to paths. It doesn't matter if the guides were previously paths — this function also works with ruler guides.

- **Clear Guides.** This feature deletes all existing guides. Be careful!

Using Guides

Your imagination is the only limit to ways to use guides. Ruler guides can show the center of a page. They can divide the page into specific areas, such as showing the page center, a matrix for repeating labels, or columns that could be used for text.

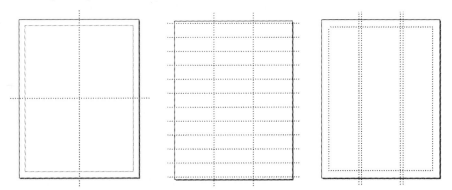

Guides created from paths can be of any shape or size and aren't restricted to just horizontal or vertical guides, as are regular ruler guides.

In this example, the far left oval was drawn, then duplicated to the right. The four ovals were selected and turned into guides with Make Guides. This presented a good template of guides so the Pen tool could be used to trace the black line on top.

Custom guides made from paths and true ruler guides have no differences, other than shape. A guide is a guide is a guide. They both serve one purpose — to assist your accuracy in creating the design.

A good example of both custom and ruler paths used for a functional means is shown in this business card matrix of guides. It started with a simple rectangle. To actually create this series of guides, go on to the next exercise.

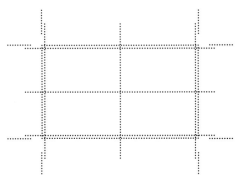

Experimenting with Guides

1. From the File menu, select New to create a document in CMYK Color mode, leave the artboard size as is, save the file as "Business Card Guides.AI" to your **Work in Progress** folder. Go to Edit>Preferences>Guides & Grid. Change the guides to Dots, and the color to Black.

2. Use View>Show Rulers to see the rulers, if they are not currently active. Set the Units for Inches. If the units are set for Points (Illustrator's default setting), then press Command/Control-Shift-U, which moves the check mark to Inches.

3. Click on the Rectangle tool in the Toolbox.

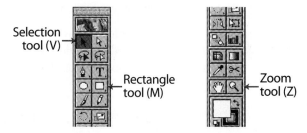

4. Hold the Option/Alt key and click the tool cursor on the top center of the page. In the Rectangle tool dialog box enter 3.5 in. in the Width box, and 2 in. in the Height box.

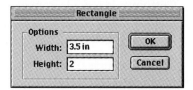

5. Select the Zoom tool in the Toolbox. Drag a marquee around the upper left corner of the rectangle. This will enlarge the view of the area for more detailed work. In the upper-left corner of the document, where the two rulers meet is the Zero Point origin box. Click-hold this box and drag toward the upper-left corner of the rectangle so that you move the Zero Point to this location.

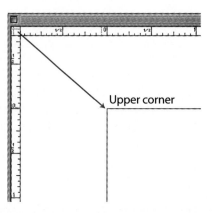

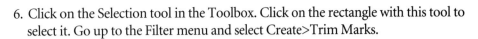

6. Click on the Selection tool in the Toolbox. Click on the rectangle with this tool to select it. Go up to the Filter menu and select Create>Trim Marks.

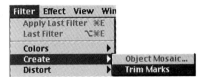

7. The trim marks will appear outside the business card. Trim Marks are used by the commercial printer to know where to cut the business card after printing. Click on the Trim Marks to select them, then hold the Shift key and click the rectangle. In the View menu, go to Guides>Make Guides, turning these objects into guides. Use View>Fit in Window to see the entire image.

8. To mark the center of the business card, you will drag guides from the rulers. The card is 3.5 in. wide. Half of this is 1.75 in. From the vertical ruler on the left of the document, drag a guide over to the middle of the card and look up at the horizontal ruler at the top of the screen. Set the guide on the 1.75 in. mark of this ruler.

9. From the horizontal ruler, drag down another guide so that it matches the 1 in. (half of the 2 in. height) mark of the vertical ruler at the left. You have used guides to give a better idea of the center of the card.

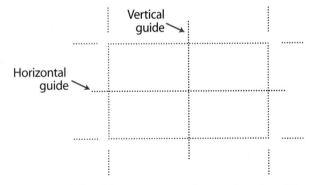

10. Type on a business card should never get too close to the edges. The closest you should allow type to come to the edge is $1/8$ in. Use the Zoom tool to enlarge the view of the card to see details better. Use your vertical and horizontal rulers to drag guides that are $1/8$ in. inside the border of the rectangle guide.

Double-clicking the Hand tool icon in the Toolbox will execute the Fit in Window selection. The full page will fit into the viewing window.

If you miss your mark on the rulers when creating guides, don't bother going to the trouble of unlocking the guides to relocate. Just use Edit>Undo to undo the errant guide.

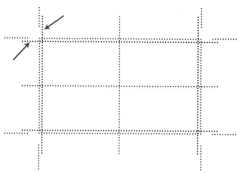

11. The business card guide matrix is finished, except for the trim marks, which are still guides. They would have to print in order for the printer (or graphic arts service provider that is outputting and printing your cards) to see them. You will need to select these guides and release them. Select View> Guides>Lock Guides which toggles the guides to be unlocked. You cannot select guides when they are locked. Click on the Trim Marks guides to select them. Go to View>Guides>Release Guides and they will become paths again. Relock the guides in the View>Guides menu.

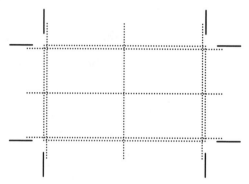

12. Use the View menu to Hide Guides to see your items that will print (trim marks). Go back to the View menu and click on Show Guides to see your guide matrix.

13. Save your changes and close the document.

Chapter Summary

You have learned about the three features used for organizing and measuring the page: Grid, Guides, and Rulers. You have manipulated objects on the grid, created and deleted guides, and relocated the Zero Point. You have also used some of these functions in the practical application of creating a business card guide matrix.

Unlocked guides can be selected and moved around like path objects. It is easy to accidentally select and move them, so be careful.

CHAPTER 3

VIEWING MODES

CHAPTER OBJECTIVE:

To develop an understanding of the importance of document views in designing your artwork. To learn the difference between Outline and Preview modes, and to learn which view is best to use when working with paths. In Chapter 3, you will:

- Observe the difference between the two primary viewing modes: Outline and Preview.

- Use the Outline, Preview, and Pixel Preview views.

- Learn about New Views — how they work, how to create them, and how to use them.

- Understand the power of Illustrator's New Window option, and how to use its multiple windows to see different document views at one time.

- Become familiar with the Navigator palette and use it to move around within a document.

- Work with the various views, use their viewing functions, and know when it is best to apply them.

Viewing Modes

Viewing your work is very important when developing artwork, particularly complex or detailed illustrations. Sometimes it's necessary to look very closely at small detail in the artwork. At other times, the whole page must be viewed from a distance to check the position of elements in the entire drawing. There are also situations in which you will only want to see certain objects in color, leaving the other objects viewed as outlines.

There are several viewing modes that Illustrator provides to give the artist more control when working on or proofing designs in a document. Your work will become more efficient when you understand and use the Preview and Outline modes, know how use the Navigator palette to zoom in and out of an illustration, and know how to create and save customized views of your work with New View and New Window.

Outline and Preview Viewing Modes

At the top of the View menu are the two most important viewing modes that Illustrator uses to display objects — Outline and Preview. The two modes are toggled back and forth when selected in the menu, or by pressing the keyboard shortcut Command/Control-Y.

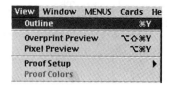

Outline

The Outline mode shows elements in their raw, "wire-frame" outlines. It removes all painting effects from view, and allows the paths to be seen without color or line thicknesses, displaying only the anchor points, connected by the segments, that define the shapes.

The advantage of Outline mode is that the anchor points, segments, and curve control handles are more easily accessed for adjusting and fine-tuning. In Preview mode (showing colors) the painted effects sometimes get in the way, keeping certain parts of a design from being selected easily. The circle below is displayed in Outline mode:

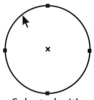
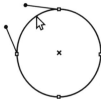

| Unselected circle | Selected with Selection tool | Selected with Direct Selection tool |

When an object is deselected (in Outline mode), its segments and center-point are visible, but not its anchor points. Anchor points are only visible when the object is selected.

When circles or objects containing curves are selected with the Direct Selection tool, the segment that the user clicks on shows its curve control handles.

Objects can be painted in Outline mode, but the colors, gradients, or patterns will not be visible. Preview mode must be toggled on to see these attributes.

To select a whole object with the Direct Selection tool, you must press Option/Alt while clicking on a segment or anchor point in the object.

Outline view is the fastest mode to work in. If there are gradients, styles, and colors in the design it could take quite some time to redraw the screen.

Preview

Preview shows the illustration in color, with gradients, patterns, or other effects, displaying how it will look when printed.

Any object can be painted and modified while in Preview mode. The objects can still be selected, and anchor points and curve handles clicked on, though it is sometimes not as easy to isolate or select these details in Preview mode.

Below is the same circle, as seen in Preview mode.

Unselected circle   Selected with Selection tool   Selected with Direct Selection tool

When deselected, the painted path of the object appears, but the center and anchor points are not visible. If selected with the Selection tool, the anchor points and center point become visible. The center point of a previewed object looks like a small square.

When curving objects have their segments clicked with the Direct Selection tool, the anchor points touching the segment show their curve handles.

Drawing lines in Preview mode has some disadvantages. If the Toolbox is set for objects to have a fill, the line segments may look confusing as you draw the object. In this example, the curvy line drawing (A) is meant to be just that — a line, however the toolbox Fill box was set for a black fill, so as the line was being drawn, it looked like drawing (B).

Drawing in Preview Mode

A.   B.

Sometimes it is necessary to draw objects in Outline mode to see the paths more clearly as you are developing them. This eliminates confusing your eye with interference from a painted object.

Views to Maximize Efficiency

Your personal working style will dictate whether to draw in Preview or Outline mode. There are times, however, when objects either overlap, obscure other elements, or cause problems that a change in viewing mode can remedy. Here are some guidelines for selecting which mode (Preview or Outline) to work in as you create and view objects.

Preview mode is best when you are merely drawing circles, ovals, and squares, or when you are arranging objects to fit a particular design.

Preview mode is sometimes not good for drawing paths with the Pen tool because it may show unexpected fills that obscure the true shape.

Outline mode is best when drawing with the Pen tool, to see the shape exactly as it is drawn. Preview can then be toggled to see the object painted.

Outline mode is best for editing intricate or complex drawings with many overlapping elements.

Coloring and finalizing a drawing will almost always be easier in the Preview mode.

Pixel Preview

Illustrator allows you convert its vector paths into raster (bitmapped) images made up of pixels, suitable for photographic programs, such as Photoshop, or the Internet. You can access Illustrator's Pixel preview to see how the design would look when you export or save it as a raster image.

Overprint Preview

Printing multicolored designs falls into the category of separations, and, as most artists working with commercial presses know, the subject of overprint and trapping comes into play. Trapping is based on applying overprint to certain portions of the design where two or more colors touch. Overprinting is overlapping the colors so there are no flaws between the colors when the job is printed. Overprint View shows the colors as they overlap, the overprinting color being darker where the two colors intersect.

New Views

Using New Views, you can only access one document view at a time. To see multiple views together, use the Window>New Window feature. (Read on to find out more about this feature.)

If you find yourself constantly zooming in and out of the same general region of a document, the New Views feature will help you work more efficiently. New Views allows you to customize and save views at any magnification and regions of the document that you specify. Then instead of using the Hand tool to move around the document and the Zoom tool to achieve the magnification you want, you can simply select the desired view from the New Views you've saved. At the bottom of the View menu are two options, New View and Edit Views.

To create and save a customized view of a document, first use the Hand and Zoom tools to create the desired magnification region you want to work on. Click on View>New View, then, in the dialog box that appears, name the view and click OK to save it.

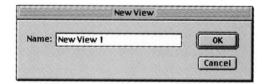

Once new views are saved, their names appear at the very bottom of the View menu, where they can be selected.

Edit Views

The name "Edit Views" at the bottom of the View menu is rather misleading. The only changes you can make are to rename or delete a new view from the list.

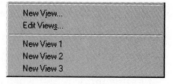

To actually change a view, you have to delete it in Edit Views and recreate it in New Views.

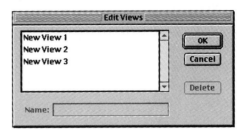

In the example below, the designer wanted to display the document at 50% to see the full page and stars. The view was created and named "Full Page." Next, a second custom view was created and saved with a close-up of the smallest star. One of the stars, the smallest one, needed further modifications.

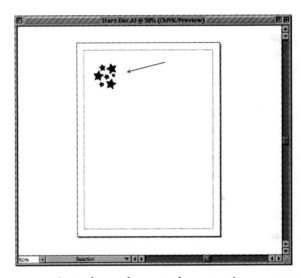

Since a closeup of the star was going to be used, a second custom view was created by zooming in on the star and naming the new view "Star Close-up." Now the designer could toggle back and forth between the two views by selecting either one from the New View menu instead of repeatedly using the Zoom tool and repositioning the page with the Hand tool.

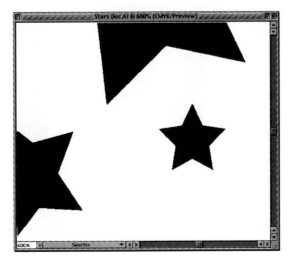

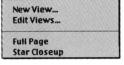

Whenever you have to move scroll bars, or you use the Hand tool too often, it's time to consider saving several New Views. We know mapmakers who use Illustrator and often have dozens of New Views in a single document.

New Windows

A powerful but often ignored feature in Illustrator is the New Window option in the Window menu. This creates another window view that displays the working document. The number of windows that will fit on the screen is limited only by the amount of space you have on your monitor.

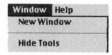

Each new window can have attributes applied to them to see the document in a different setting. Changes made while you are working in any of these new windows will affect the working document.

For example, let's suppose you are working on a job with gradients, patterns and other complex fills that make it hard to select and adjust anchor points while in Preview mode, but you need to see how changing anchor points affects the finished look of the document. The answer is to show the same document in both Preview and Outline mode at the same time. New View shows only one view of the document at a time, so it wouldn't help with the problem of needing to see more than one view at a time.

Creating New Windows

To create a new window from the toolbar, choose Window>New Window. A second window appears next to the original document view, and both windows are automatically given a number.

In the example below, the original window on the left was set to display in Preview mode, and the window on the right was customized to display in Outline mode. Any changes made to the document in one window will affect the objects in the other window. These changes appear simultaneously in both windows.

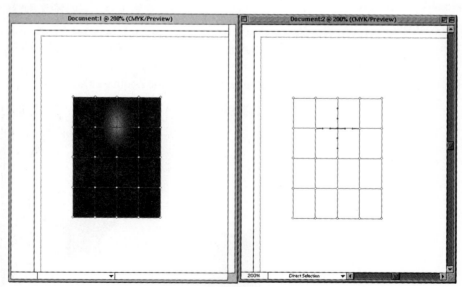

If a New View was saved while the document was in Preview mode, and the document was in Outline mode at the time that the custom view was accessed, the document automatically changes to Preview mode, including the viewing mode of the layer.

In the example that follows, two more new windows were created, and Illustrator automatically numbered them Documents 3 and 4. The designer turned on the rulers in Document 3. Notice that the rulers do not appear in the other windows. This is because Show Rulers is a feature of the document *window*, not the document itself. Document 4 was set for Preview mode, and the Window>Show Grid was selected.

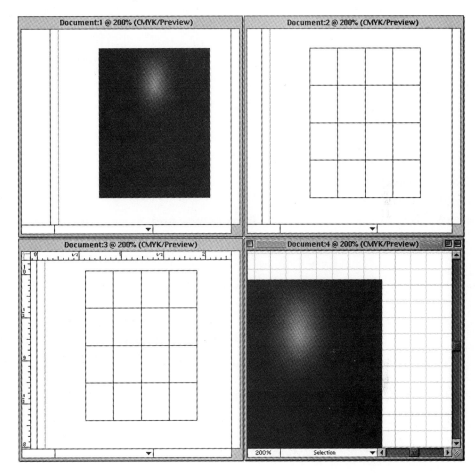

With New Window, some page features such as Show/Hide Rulers affect the window, but not the document itself. Rulers set in one new window will not show rulers in all other windows. At the same time, features such as guides affect the document. Changes to the drawings do "roll over" to each document view.

Windows are numbered sequentially, in the order that you create them. If one of the windows is closed, Illustrator automatically renumbers the windows that remain. For example, if Document 3 in the above example were closed, Document 4 would be become Document 3.

Navigator Palette

The Navigator palette is one more feature found in the Window menu that allows you to move around in the document to select different views. The Navigator palette displays objects on the working page as well as any that are on the artboard around it. The Proxy Preview Area (outlined by the marquee) corresponds to the current viewing area of your working page. As you move the Proxy Preview Area in Navigator, the view of your document also changes. This method avoids tedious scrolling and the use of the Hand tool.

Navigator Features

Illustrator provides you with numerous ways to accomplish the same task. In this chapter, we have already seen more than one way to zoom in and out of a document. The Navigator palette offers yet another way to do this.

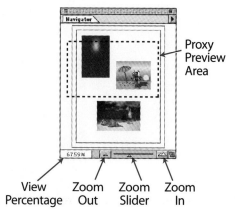

The larger the viewing percentage of the document, the smaller the Proxy Preview Area box becomes.

- **Proxy Preview Area.** As you move this box around the Navigator palette, the actual document view changes. The screen portion within the Proxy Preview area will be the part that displays in the document window.

- **View Percentage.** This box can be highlighted and percentages typed directly in. Return/Enter must be pressed to apply the new percentage.

- **Zoom Out.** This option reduces the view in the document.

- **Zoom Slider.** The View Percentage changes as the slider is moved.

- **Zoom In.** You can enlarge the view in the document using this option.

Working with the Various Views

1. In the **SF-Intro Illustrator** folder, open the **Viewing Methods.AI** document. The document will be set for Preview mode when you first open it.

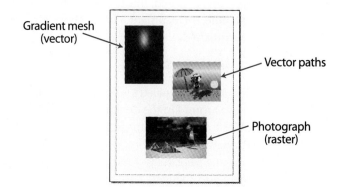

2. From the View menu, select the Outline option at the top of the menu. This will toggle the view to Outline mode. The images will be seen in their raw wire-frame path outlines. Select the objects individually and move them around. Notice how fast you can work in Outline mode without the painting and repainting of Preview mode.

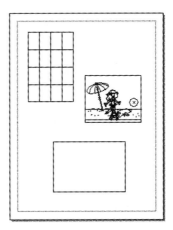

3. Go back to the View menu and highlight Preview to toggle back to Preview mode.

4. With the Selection tool, click only on Snipper Gator on the beach image to select her and her shadow. Drag her down to be on the sailboard photo underneath. Vector paths can be positioned on raster images to give interesting effects.

5. Just to see how Pixel Preview affects the objects on the page, use the View menu to select Pixel Preview. Keep in mind that the purpose of this view is to show you how vector paths will look once rasterized, and in pixel format. The two top images are vector, but the bottom image is a raster object already. Keep in mind that Pixel Preview is limited to 72 dpi resolution. It is primarily for you to see how vector paths will look when saved for the Web. Use the Zoom tool to zoom in close to the objects and see how their previews look in this view.

6. Once you have observed how the images look in this viewing mode, go back to the View menu and select Pixel Preview again to toggle it off.

7. Use the Zoom tool to draw a marquee around Snipper. This will isolate and zoom her up to fill the screen.

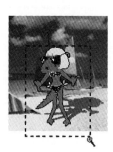 

8. At the bottom of the View menu, select New View. In the dialog box, name the view "Snipper closeup". Click OK.

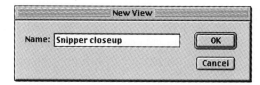

9. In the View Percentage menu at the bottom left of the document, select 25%.

10. Choose View>New View and name the view "25% View". Click OK.

11. With the Zoom tool, drag a marquee selection around the sun in the vector outlines beach scene. Select the Hand tool and drag it on the sun, moving the view to the right.

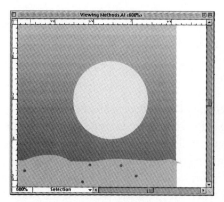 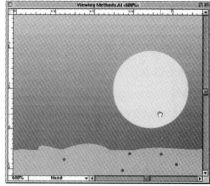

12. Select New View from the View menu and name this view "Sun Closeup".

13. At the bottom left of the document window use the View Percentage menu to select 50% view percentage. The view will adjust to fill the entire page.

14. You now have three New Views to select from. Try using them. In the View menu, select one of the views and see how the view changes to that exact position. Continue to choose other New Views from this menu, and observe how the screen display is affected as you do.

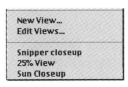

15. Return to 50% view, if your screen is not in this mode.

16. In the Window menu, select New Window. Another window of this same document will appear. Adjust the windows so that they can both be seen in their entirety at the same time on your screen. Click on Window 2 and, in the View menu, select Outline to send it to Outline mode.

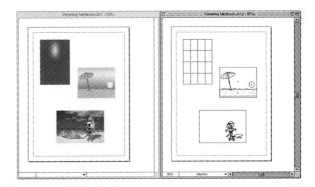

17. Click on Snipper with the Selection tool and move her back up to her original beach scene with the umbrella. Notice how this movement simultaneously occurs in Window 1.

18. Go to the Window menu and select New Window. Window 3 will appear. Return to Window>New Window again. Window 4 will appear. Adjust all four windows so that they all appear on the screen.

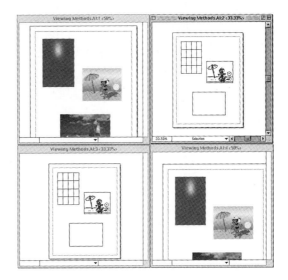

19. Click on Window 1 and use the View menu to select the 25% View custom view.

20. Click on Window 2 and select the Sun Closeup custom view. Notice that the view also changed to Preview mode, which was the mode the document was in when the view was saved.

21. Click on Window 3. Go to the View menu and select the Snipper Closeup custom view. This view will also change to Preview mode. Where is Snipper? She was moved earlier. The only thing a custom view is concerned with is the location of the area saved in the view. This is the same view position and percentage, but without Snipper.

22. Click on Window 4. In the View menu select Fit in Window. The page will reduce to fit into the window.

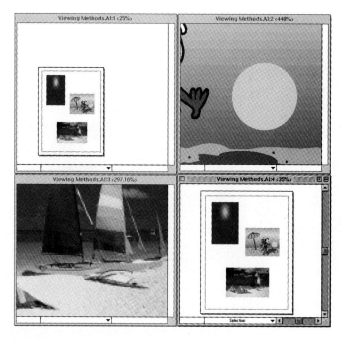

23. Getting rid of the extra windows is simple. Just click on the Close box of each window. Close Windows 4, 3, and 2 by first clicking on each window to make it active, and then clicking their Close boxes.

24. The original window should be the only one showing.

25. In the Window menu, select Show Navigator. Its palette will appear on the page.

26. Click on the View Percentage box of the Navigator palette and highlight the number. Type in "300" and press Return/Enter to apply the percentage. The document view will enlarge to 300%. You will see the Proxy Preview Area box in the Navigator.

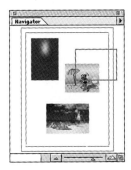

27. Drag on the Proxy Preview Area box and center it on the small gradient. Notice how this object appears in the center of the document window.

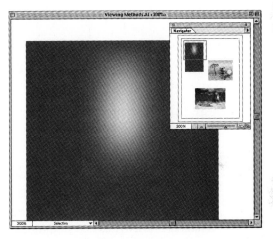

28. Move the Proxy Preview Area box to center the beach scene. Click the palette's Zoom Out icon twice to reduce the view. Notice how the Proxy Preview Area box gets bigger as the document view percentage is reduced.

29. Move the Proxy Preview Area box to center the bottom sailboard beach image. Drag the palette Zoom slider to the right and observe how it rarely moves in even increments. The palette's View Percentage box shows the zoom percentage as the slider is moved. Raise the percentage to approximately 197% and stop. Now click on the palette Zoom icon. It will round off the view to 200%.

30. You have observed and used the many features Illustrator offers for viewing objects and pages in your drawings.

31. Close the document without saving.

Chapter Summary

You have observed how viewing objects and images in the document gives you almost unlimited flexibility in customizing how you view a work page. You have seen and used Outline, Preview, Pixel Preview modes. You have also seen how New Views help in viewing your work, and how creating New Windows can show multiple windows of a single document. You have used the Navigator to change and manipulate the views of the document.

CHAPTER 4

CREATING
PRIMITIVE SHAPES

CHAPTER OBJECTIVE:

To learn how to create primitive shapes such as squares, rectangles, circles, and ellipses. To become familiar with the tools and features that Illustrator provides for creating simple shapes. In Chapter 4, you will:

- Learn about the Ellipse tool, and the many shapes you can create with it.

- Understand how to control the origin point and how it affects the location of an ellipse as it is drawn.

- Learn about the Rectangle and Rounded Rectangle tools and how to customize rounded corners.

- Learn how to use other drawing tools such as the Twirl, Spiral, Star, and Polygon tools.

Creating Primitive Shapes

Whether very simple or complex, drawn by hand, or developed with digital tools, almost all drawings make use of primitive shapes like squares, rectangles, circles, and ellipses. This section will introduce you to the tools Illustrator provides for creating these simple elements. We'll discuss ways to create these shapes both visually and mathematically. Each method is useful depending on the requirements of your design project. Later on, as you learn more about paths and shapes, you will understand that circles and squares, drawn with the tools discussed in this chapter, are actually collections of paths and anchor points.

Ellipse Tool

You can create circles, ovals, and any remotely convex shapes manually with the Ellipses tool. Select the Ellipses tool and click-drag the cursor to create any size or shape figure.

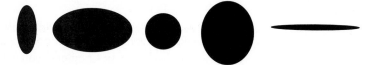

Using the Dialog Box

You can create any ellipse mathematically by setting the exact desired dimensions in the Ellipse dialog box. To access the dialog box, select the Ellipse tool and click once on the work page. In the dialog box that appears, enter the dimensions and click OK. The ellipse that appears will be centered where you first clicked the cursor.

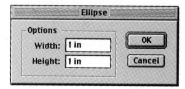

Circles

To create a circle, click and drag the Ellipse tool while holding down the Shift key (this constrains the shape to be proportional).

The Ellipse dialog box remembers the dimensions of the last ellipse drawn. If you draw an ellipse manually, and want to see its actual dimensions, select the Ellipse dialog box.

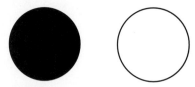

The Starting Point of an Ellipse

You can click anywhere on your working page to draw an ellipse. This location determines the starting point of the ellipse. Then you have two choices for determining where the center of the object will be.

Note that in the figures that follow, the Shift key was held down to constrain the ellipse to a circle, but the steps we describe apply to any ellipse. When you click-drag the cursor from the starting point, the upper-left outside edge of the ellipse will remain at the starting point, as shown in figure (B). If you hold down Option/Alt while click-dragging the cursor, the ellipse will be centered at the starting point, as shown in figure (C).

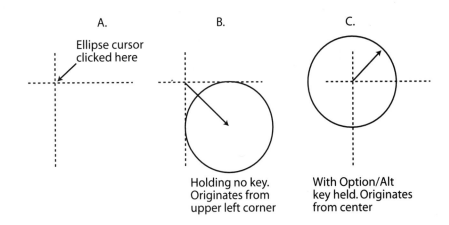

A. Ellipse cursor clicked here

B. Holding no key. Originates from upper left corner

C. With Option/Alt key held. Originates from center

The keyboard shortcut for selecting the Default Colors box in the Toolbox is to press the "D" key.

Whenever you're working on a hands-on activity, try to visualize what it is you're learning, as opposed to simply following the steps. There's always a reason we've used an exercise.

Experimenting with the Ellipse tool

1. Use File>New to create a new document of CMYK Color mode, leaving it untitled and the Artboard Size set as is. Click on the Default Colors icon in the Toolbox.

Default Colors

2. Select the Ellipse tool in the Toolbox. Pressing the mouse button, drag the tool cursor on the page to experiment with drawing an ellipse by moving the mouse around to see how the ellipse changes shape. Release the mouse when you have drawn an ellipse you like. Release the mouse to end the drawing process.

3. With the Ellipse tool selected, and while the Pressing the Option/Alt key, create several different sizes and shapes. Observe how this operation creates the ellipse from its center.

4. While drawing and holding the Option/Alt key, add the Shift key. Observe how this draws a perfect circle originating from the center.

5. Release the Option/Alt key, but still press the Shift key. Observe how the circle is drawn, but does not originate from its center.

6. Select and Delete the ellipses drawn on the page. Leave the document open for the next exercise.

Creating Customized Ellipses

1. Continue working in the open document. Choose View>Outline.

2. With the Ellipse tool still selected, draw a simple oval ellipse. Notice how it originates from where you first clicked the tool cursor on the page.

3. The ellipse has a visible center point. Press the Option/Alt key as you click-hold the crosshair cursor on this center point to draw another ellipse, originating from the center. Try to adjust the ellipse as you drag to make it a little larger, but keep the same shape and contours of the first ellipse. When satisfied with the fit, release the mouse.

4. Again press the Option/Alt key, adding the Shift key. Click-hold the crosshair cursor on the center again, and draw a circle from the center, making it larger than the other two ovals. This is not an artistic masterpiece, but an example of how it is sometimes easier to control the placement of an ellipse or circle when its origin point is controlled as well.

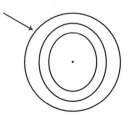

5. To the right of this ellipse group, draw one more ellipse, smaller than the first oval. With the Selection tool, select and move this ellipse over to the others and match its center point with the others. This is to show you how randomly drawing an ellipse and moving it into position adds additional work and leaves some room for error.

6. Close the file without saving.

When drawing objects with the various tools shown in this chapter, you can actually move the object around the page as you draw by holding the Spacebar. Try it!

The Option/Alt keys, as well as Shift, have the same effect on the Rectangle tool as they do on the Ellipse tool. A key that is added to another key command to change its function is called a modifier key.

The Ellipse and Rectangle tools draw complete closed paths with center points. The center point looks like an "X" in Outline mode and a small square in Preview mode. In the menu Window>Show Attributes, the Show Center Point attribute will turn the display of the center point on and off. When the center point is turned off, you can't see it, but the center point is still there. Later, you will see that center points are critical when developing certain types of objects.

Rectangle Tool

We use the Rectangle tool to draw rectangles and squares. These figures can be drawn manually with the mouse or mathematically with the Rectangle tool dialog box.

Drawing with the Mouse

To draw manually, click anywhere on the page with the Rectangle tool and drag. Use the Shift key while dragging to constrain the rectangle to a square.

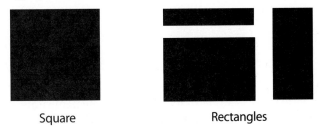

Square   Rectangles

Using the Dialog Box

To create a rectangle mathematically with exact dimensions, use the Rectangle tool dialog box. Click anywhere on the page with the Rectangle cursor, and enter the desired dimensions in the dialog box that appears. Click OK and the figure will appear at the spot on the page where you first clicked the cursor.

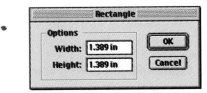

The Starting Point of a Rectangle

Note that in the figures below, the Shift key was held down to constrain the rectangle to a square, but the steps we describe apply to any ellipse. When you drag the cursor from the starting point (A), the upper-left outside edge of the rectangle will remain at the starting point as shown in figure (B). If you hold down Option/Alt while click-dragging the cursor, the rectangle will be centered at the starting point, as shown in figure (C).

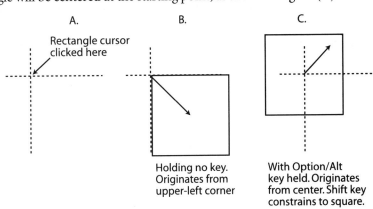

A.
Rectangle cursor clicked here

B.
Holding no key. Originates from upper-left corner

C.
With Option/Alt key held. Originates from center. Shift key constrains to square.

Rounding Square Edges

Any object with squared corners can have rounded corners, which are created manually or mathematically. The roundness of the corner is determined by size of the corner radius, and the overall appearance of the figure is determined by the size of the corner radius in relation to the size of the figure. For example, if you apply a rounded edge with a small radius to a large rectangle , you will get a very different effect from a rounded edge with a large radius applied to a small rectangle.

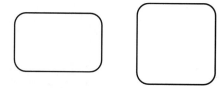

Corner radius is based, as the name implies, on the radius of a circle. If you divide a circle in quarters, you actually have four round corners. The curvature of the corners is determined by the radius of the circle when whole.

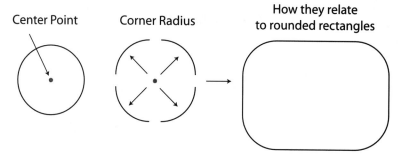

Center Point   Corner Radius   How they relate to rounded rectangles

Changing the Corner Radius

There are several ways to create and modify a corner radius both mathematically and manually. Use the method that best suits your working style and your project.

Manually

Select the Rounded Rectangle tool and draw the object by click-dragging the cursor on the page. The corner radius of this tool is set in the Preferences>General dialog box.

Preferences>General

When using the Rounded Rectangle tool, the corner radius can be set before drawing in the Edit>Preferences>General window. There is a Corner Radius option where the radius used by the Rounded Rectangle tool can be entered.

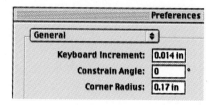

Dialog box

Select the Rounded Rectangle tool and single-click its cursor on the page. Then set the Width, Height, and Corner Radius and click OK.

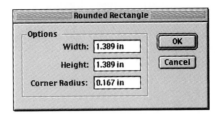

Filters

Square-cornered objects can be drawn with the regular Rectangle tool and then changed into a rounded-corner object. From the Filter menu, use the first Stylize option to access Round Corners and enter the desired radius in the dialog box. Click OK to apply the change to the object.

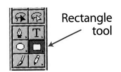

Experimenting with the Rectangle Tool

1. Create a new document set for CMYK Color mode, leave it untitled and the artboard set for default.

2. Click on the Rectangle tool in the Toolbox.

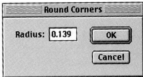

Rectangle tool

3. Drag the tool cursor on the page to experiment with drawing a rectangle by moving the mouse around to see how the rectangle changes shape as you drag. Release the mouse when you have drawn a rectangle you like.

4. Draw several different sizes and shapes with the Rectangle tool, pressing the Option/Alt key as you draw. Observe how this starts the rectangle from its center point.

5. While drawing and holding the Option/Alt key, add the Shift key. Observe how this constrains the shape to a square (still originating from the center).

6. Release the Option/Alt key, still holding the Shift key. It is still a square, but it doesn't originate from its center point. Delete all the rectangles and squares on the page.

7. Leave the document open for the next exercise.

If you want objects to have a solid white fill with a black stroke, select the object, then click on the Default Colors box in the Toolbox, or press the "D" key.

Default Colors

Creating Rounded-Corner Objects

1. In the open document, select File>Document Setup and make certain that Units is set for inches. Select the Rounded Rectangle tool in the Toolbox.

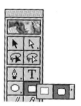

2. Experiment with drawing rectangles with rounded corners.

3. Single-click the tool cursor on the top-center of the page. In the dialog box set the Width and Height to 2 in. and the Corner Radius to 0.25 in. Click OK. The rounded rectangle will appear. Note the roundness of the corners.

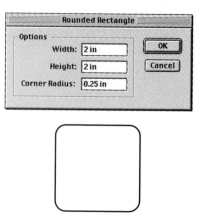

4. Choose Edit>Preferences>General. Type "0.10" into the Corner Radius box. Click OK. Select the Rounded Rectangle tool and draw a rectangle. It will have the corner radius you specified. Observe the difference in this corner radius, compared to the square drawn in step 3.

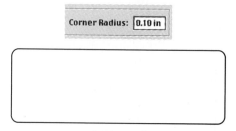

5. Change back to the regular Rectangle tool with squared edges. Draw a rectangle. Click on the object with the Selection tool to select it.

6. Choose Filter>Stylize>Round Corners. In the dialog box that appears, leave the number at 0.139. Click OK. Observe that the rectangle you drew with squared off corners now has rounded corners.

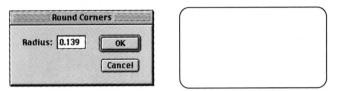

7. Close the file without saving it.

Other Drawing Tools

Besides circles and squares, Illustrator provides tools to draw other shapes, such as stars, polygons, swirls, and spirals. In the Toolbox you will find the tools that either apply different effects to objects, or create shapes of their own. Some of these tools have dialog boxes, accessed by clicking the tool's crosshair on the page.

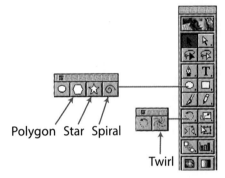

Polygon Star Spiral

Twirl

Twirl Tool

You can use the Twirl tool to create an unlimited variety of effects. As with other tools, you can change objects manually or mathematically.

Manual twirling   Dialog Box

In the examples of dialog box twirling notice that the changes were applied to open paths. Try twirling some closed paths to see what you get.

Dialog Box Twirling

The examples below were created by selecting the objects, then using the Twirl dialog box to apply the exact increments. Positive numbers rotate the twirl in a clockwise direction. Negative numbers twirl or rotate the object counter-clockwise. The anchor points, and how many there are in an object, determine how much curvature is created by the twirling.

Text can also be twirled, but must first be turned into path outlines.

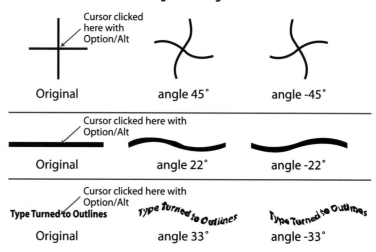

Twirling with dialog box

Cursor clicked here with Option/Alt

Original   angle 45˚   angle -45˚

Cursor clicked here with Option/Alt

Original   angle 22˚   angle -22˚

Cursor clicked here with Option/Alt

Type Turned to Outlines   Type Turned to Outlines   Type Turned to Outlines

Original   angle 33˚   angle -33˚

Manual Twirling

When manually applying the Twirl tool, the idea is to click the cursor on the selected object and drag away from it. This requires experimentation to determine where to click and how far to drag to achieve the desired effect.

- When an object is selected and you click-drag the Twirl tool cursor, the center of the twirl (origin point) defaults to the exact center of the object, regardless of where you click-drag the tool.

- To set the origin point to a different location, single-click the cursor on this new point, then click-drag to twirl the selected object.

To twirl objects more smoothly, single-click the tool cursor a moderate distance from the selected object, then click-drag the cursor from this point.

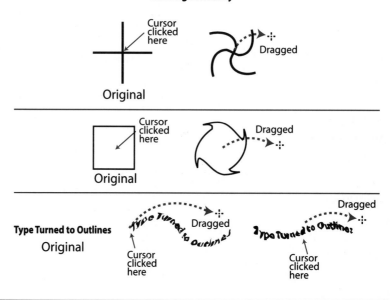

Twirling Manually

Cursor clicked here

Original   Dragged

Cursor clicked here

Original   Dragged

Type Turned to Outlines

Original

Type Turned to Outlines   Dragged   Type Turned to Outlines   Dragged

Cursor clicked here   Cursor clicked here

Some objects are meant to be a stroke (line) without a fill. The spiral looks odd when a fill is applied, unless this is your intent.

A.

B.

Pressing the Command/ Control key as you drag the Spiral tool forces the spirals to a concentric circular shape. Be careful! This requires some experimentation, because the effects can become quite explosive.

Spiral Tool

Like most tools, the Spiral tool is used by clicking and dragging. It creates new objects, and doesn't affect existing elements of the drawing. The direction of the drag determines where the opening of the spiral occurs. Dragging upward, as shown in sample A, points the opening toward the top. Dragging downward (sample B) points the opening toward the bottom. While dragging the crosshair, simultaneously press the Up Arrow of the keyboard to add anchor points to the center. Pressing the Down Arrow will delete anchor points from the center (samples C, D, and E).

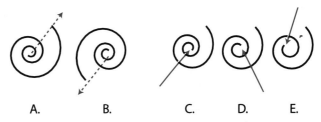

A.   B.   C.   D.   E.

Clicking on the page with the Spiral tool shows a dialog box that allows you to modify the tool's attributes.

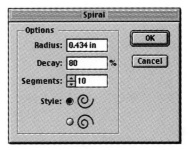

Star Tool

The Star tool draws various forms of stars when its cursor is dragged on the page. There are several keyboard options available which change its attributes while dragging.

If dragged without pressing any key, the star will have slightly bloated stems, as shown in sample A. Hold the Option/Alt key while dragging and the stems will straighten out (B).

A.   B.

When dragging the star, the Up Arrow key will add points. The Down Arrow key will subtract points. You can construct a star with as few as three points.

Like the Spiral tool, the Star tool has a dialog box, which is accessed by single-clicking the Star cursor on the page.

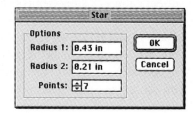

Polygon Tool

The Polygon tool draws a multi-sided closed object. Holding the Shift key while dragging constrains the drawing of the object to a polygon with equal sides. The Up Arrow key adds sides; the Down Arrow key deletes sides while the object is being drawn manually.

The Polygon tool also provides a dialog box (accessed by single-clicking the cursor on the page) that allows changes to such attributes as the radius of the object and how many sides the polygon has. When OK is clicked, the object appears on the page.

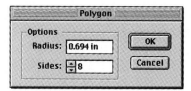

Experimenting with Geometric Tools

1. Create a new document set for CMYK Color mode, leave it untitled and the artboard set for default. Click the Default Colors icon in the Toolbox.

2. With the Rectangle tool, draw a 2-in. square, leaving it selected.

3. With the Twirl tool, click on the upper-right corner of the square, and drag in a circular motion toward the lower-right corner. Observe the results. Delete the twirled object after you've experimented with the tool.

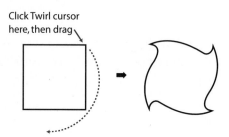

Click Twirl cursor here, then drag

With the Star and Spiral tools, you can use the arrow keys to increase the number of sides as you're drawing the object.

4. With the Rectangle tool, draw a very thin rectangle. With the Twirl tool, click on the right end of the rectangle, then drag toward the upper-left direction. Observe how the object twirls as you drag. Delete the object when you're done experimenting.

Click Twirl cursor here, then drag to the left

5. Select the Spiral tool. Drag the cursor downward while holding the Shift key. Continue to hold the mouse button down as you draw the spiral. Release the Shift key and press the Up Arrow key three times. Observe how extra points are added to the center of the object. Press the Down Arrow key three times to subtract points from the interior of the spiral. Delete the object.

6. With the Spiral tool still selected, click the crosshair on the page to display the dialog box. Set the Radius to 2 in., Decay to 80, Segments to 20, and set Style to the top option. Click OK. Notice how the settings affect the shape of the object. Delete the object.

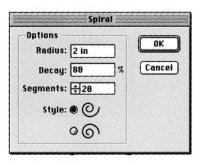

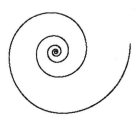

7. Select the Star tool. Drag the tool on the page to create a star. While dragging, press the Option/Alt key. Add the Shift key at the same time, and observe how it constrains the position of the star. Do not release the mouse button.

Drawn with no keys held

Drawn with Option/Alt key held

Drawn with Option/Alt and Shift key held

8. With your left hand, press the Up Arrow key twice to see how star points are added with each pressing. Press the Option/Alt key to see how the star's radius attributes are changed. Press the Down Arrow key several times to see how the points are subtracted. Delete the star.

9. With the Star tool still selected, click the crosshair on the page to display the Star dialog box. Set the Radius 1 to 2 in., Radius 2 to 1 in., and Points to 7. Click OK. Delete the star when you're done.

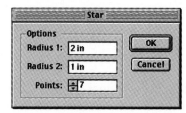

10. Select the Polygon tool. Drag the tool on the page to create a polygon. While holding down the mouse button, try pressing the Up Arrow or Down Arrow keys. This increases or decreases the number of sides of the Polygon. Release the mouse button. Observe the polygon and then delete it.

11. Click the Polygon tool's cursor on the page to display its dialog box. Enter the following settings and click OK. Note that the Radius attribute determines the length of the polygon's sides — unlike the radius of a circle.

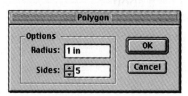

12. Close the file without saving.

Chapter Summary

You have learned how to create and use primitive objects. Creating rectangles, squares, ellipses, and custom shaped objects, you have learned how the objects can be drawn either through manual or dialog box means. You have learned how the Origin Point of the drawn object determines many aspects of its creation and location. You have seen how to customize these objects with modifier keys.

CHAPTER 5

CREATING PATHS

CHAPTER OBJECTIVE:

To understand vector paths — the fundamental component of any Illustrator shape. To understand the anchor points and segments of a vector path. To learn how to create and control paths. To learn the effective use of the Pen tool. In Chapter 5, you will:

- Learn how to create paths with the Pen tool.
- Understand anchor points and segments.
- Learn about open and closed paths.
- Learn about the Pen tool symbols, and what they tell you about the functions of the tool.
- Understand how to draw paths with the Pen tool using modifier keys.
- Learn about drawing curves and how to control their many different shapes.
- Learn how to create and use two types of anchor points — Smooth point and Corner point.
- Learn how to modify paths, and develop an understanding of the path editing tools.

PROJECTS TO BE COMPLETED:

- Art Deco House (A)
- BearWear Business Cards (B)
- Wine and Cheese Invitation (C)
- Walking the Dogs (D)
- Broadway Bound (E)
- Joker's Wild (F)
- BearWear Label (G)

Anchor points are created any time you use the Pen, Pencil, and Paintbrush tools. Segments are the lines that connect the anchor points. When you use the Rectangle or Ellipse tools, the shapes you create are a combination of segments and anchor points.

We should mention that you actually can increase the size of a bitmap image using specialized software, which retains most of the original detail when you size up the image. The end result isn't perfect, though; vector artwork retains its exact specifications and quality.

Creating Paths

Illustrator is known as a vector illustration program. There are two ways to create and save electronic images, vector and bitmap. Vector refers to artwork that is created and saved as a collection of mathematical statements. Raster images are normally created from scanners or digital cameras, and comprise a series of pixels arranged on a grid. Vector images remain sharp and clear as they are enlarged, whereas raster images are fixed at their original resolution and become grainy as they are enlarged. The two fundamental components of any vector object created in Illustrator are the anchor points and segments that make up the shape's outlines or paths.

Anchor Points and Segments

Anchor points and segments are the building blocks of vector artwork. All vector paths, regardless of the tool that created them, are made up of anchor points and segments. The smallest path possible is made up of two anchor points connected by a segment.

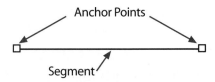

Regardless of the complexity of the design, it all comes down to anchor points and segments. Each individual series of anchor points and segments is known as a *path*.

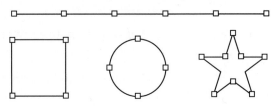

A path can be a series of anchor points connected by segments

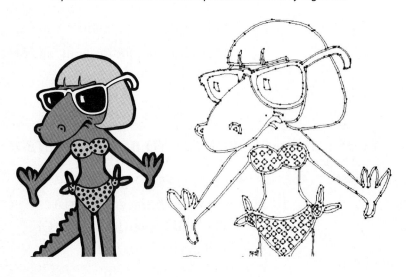

Every time you click the Pen tool, an anchor point is created. As you continue to click, the anchor points are connected with lines called segments.

It is easier and faster to draw paths in Outline mode. This way you won't see the painted segments showing their fills or strokes.

Pen Tool

The Pen is the most important of all the Illustrator tools because it allows the widest range of creation and control over custom paths. Anchor points are created any time you click the Pen tool, with segments connecting them as you click. There are other Illustrator tools that create shapes, but the Pen tool is the most critical drawing tool for creating shapes from scratch.

A beginning point is made by clicking once to start the process. The mouse is moved in any direction, then clicked again to create a second anchor point. A segment appears connecting the two points. Until the Pen tool is deselected, continual clicking creates one uninterrupted path, sometimes called an "outline."

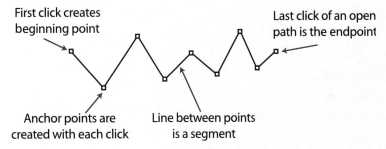

Once you start clicking a path with the Pen tool, you can finish either by clicking on the beginning point, resulting in a closed path, or by deselecting the path (choose the Selection tool and click on the page away from the path), which leaves an open path.

Open and Closed Paths

The versatility of vector paths allows you to start, finish, interrupt, or modify a path at any time. Despite all these attributes, there are only two kinds of paths: open paths and closed paths.

An open path is made when the endpoints of the path do not meet. There is an open gap between the two.

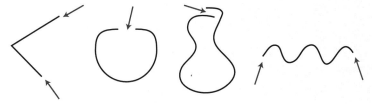

Some open paths are meant to be open. If you are drawing lines or graphic rules, they might look like this, which is the desired effect. All the paths below are open, which was meant to create the design.

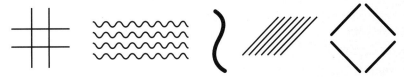

There will be times that, when drawing a path, interruptions will occur in which the path must be deselected in order to come back to it later. In most situations, open paths should not be filled with color. The two endpoints of the open path will be connected by the filling color when in Preview mode.

If any other anchor points of the path intersect this connecting fill, the fill obscures them. Here's an example:

A filled open path seen
in Outline mode. Note endpoints.

The same path seen
in Preview mode. Endpoints
fill in across the open void.

When the continuity of the path has no beginning or end, this is called a closed path. Closed paths are made by finally, after all the necessary clicks are made to create the shape, clicking the Pen tool on the first anchor created. The endpoints meet and enclose the shape.

Pen Tool Symbols

The small symbol at the lower right side of the tool's icon is meant to help the artist develop illustrations. When the tool is first selected, the symbol looks like an "X." This changes as the tool moves over anchor points.

A.   B.   C.   D.   E.

A.   The symbol is an "X" when the Pen tool is starting a new path.

B.   It becomes a circle when it touches the endpoint of an open path.

C.   The slash "/" appears when the Pen tool moves over the beginning or endpoint of an unselected open path. Clicking on the beginning or endpoint at this time will let you continue the open path.

D.   The angled "V" appears when the Pen tool touches the beginning or endpoint of a selected open path that is in progress of being drawn.

E.   When drawing one path, if the Pen tool passes over the beginning or endpoint of another unrelated path, this symbol appears, letting you know that clicking on that point will connect the two lines.

The more you use the Pen tool to click on anchor points, the more you will come to appreciate the symbols that tell you if the tool is positioned where you want it. This is particularly true if you want to continue working on an existing open path, or if you want to connect two open paths that already exist.

Holding the Shift key constrains the path to 45°/90° increments.

Pressing the Spacebar when you click an anchor point with the Pen tool allows you to relocate the point if needed.

Clicking once then deselecting leaves individual anchor points scattered around the page. They're called "stray points," and they can cause problems when you're importing your drawings into other programs or when you go to print your work. The Object>Path>Cleanup feature finds and eliminates these troublesome, usually invisible, points.

Drawing Paths with the Pen Tool

1. Create a new document set for CMYK Color mode, leave it untitled and the artboard set for default.

2. Select the Pen tool from the Toolbox. In the View menu, set the display to Outline mode.

Pen tool

3. With the Pen tool, click on the page in a zigzag pattern. You will see the anchor points appear as you click. After clicking about nine times, stop — but do not deselect the path. Position the tool over the last anchor point. You will notice the angled "V" symbol indicating the path is in progress.

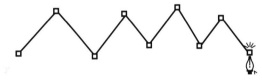

4. Position the tool over the first anchor point, but do not click. The symbol will become a circle, indicating that if this point is clicked, the path will be closed.

5. Press the Command/Control key. This temporarily changes the Pen to the Selection tool arrow. Click this on the page to deselect the path. Let go of the Command/Control key. You will see the Pen tool again.

6. Touch the Pen tool to the last point you created. The symbol will show the slash (/), indicating that if you click the point, the flow of the path will continue.

7. Click the Pen tool on the last anchor point to continue. Click several times under the path to add a few more anchor points, heading to the left. When near the beginning point, click on it. You have now created a Closed path.

First and last click here

8. You have used some of the basic Pen tool drawing techniques. Select the object with the Selection tool. Click on the Default Colors box in the Toolbox. Go to View>Preview mode to show the drawn object in Painted mode. Observe how the anchor points are harder to see in Preview mode.

9. Delete this path and keep the document open.

Constraining a Path

1. Continue in the open document in Preview mode. From the vertical ruler on the left of the screen, drag a guide anywhere on the page. In the View menu, make sure that Snap to Point is selected. (If a menu item has a check mark, you know it's selected.) Click the Fill box in the Toolbox. Now click the None box so the object will have no distracting colors.

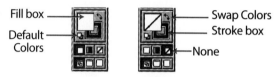

2. Select the Pen tool. Click once on the guide to create the beginning point (step A). Press the Shift key and move the Pen tool to the right and click again to create a second anchor point (step B). Observe how pressing the Shift key constrains the line to a straight horizontal line. Move the tool down and position the cursor below the second anchor point. Press the Shift key and click again to make a third anchor point (step C). No matter how far off from a 90° angle you click the Pen tool, the new line jumps to exactly 90° to the first one.

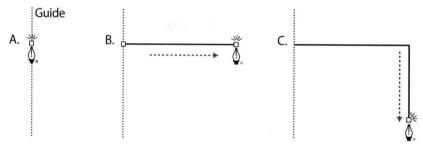

The Snap to Point option (in the View menu) allows Pen tool points to snap to guides you may have.

4. Move the tool to the left of the last click, so the tool is under the original anchor point. Pressing the Shift key, click again. Be certain to click on the guide so the point will snap to the guide, keeping the new point aligned exactly under the beginning point.

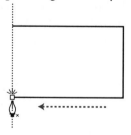

5. Click on the Selection tool in the Toolbox and click on the page to deselect this path. There are times, while drawing a path, you might be interrupted. It is quite simple to pick up where you left off. Select the Direct Selection tool and click it on one of the path's segments to see its anchor points.

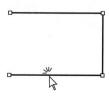

The Pen tool can be quickly accessed by pressing the "P" key.

6. Select the Pen tool. Click the pen tip once on the last point you created. This lets you resume drawing the same path.

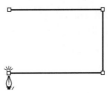

7. Move the tool up to the first anchor point and click on it to close the shape.

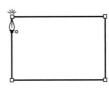

8. You have manually created a rectangular closed path.

9. Delete the path and keep the file open for the next exercise.

Creating Multiple Simple Paths

1. In the open document, remain in Preview mode.

2. Select the Pen tool. The task is to draw many independent segments that crisscross each other. Click the tool once to set the beginning point. Move down and right about an inch, hold the Shift key to constrain to a 45° angle, then click again.

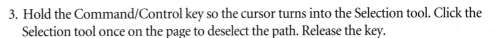

3. Hold the Command/Control key so the cursor turns into the Selection tool. Click the Selection tool once on the page to deselect the path. Release the key.

4. The tool will revert back to the Pen tool. Continue to make many segments this way (click beginning point, click endpoint, deselect). Draw the segments so they cross over one another. Continue to click-click-deselect until you have created an interesting collage of segments that crisscross each other.

5. With the Selection tool, select some of these paths individually and move them around. Select some anchor points with the Direct Selection tool, and move the points around to see how flexible they are.

6. Delete all the paths and keep the document open for the next exercise.

Drawing Curves

We've already discussed how to create straight line segments using the Pen tool (click a point, move the mouse, and click a second point). Drawing curves takes a little more practice with the Pen tool because you have to use it to drag on anchor points to create a curve "control handle." Knowing when to drag on a point is the secret to drawing the curve you want.

Control Handle

As the illustrations below show, the position of a control handle affects the general shape of a curved path. The distance of the control handle from the anchor point controls the depth of a curve.

Curving segments are also known as Bézier curves, named after the Frenchman who created the adjustable curves of vector graphics.

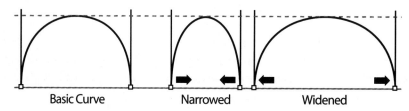

Basic Curve   Narrowed   Widened

Remember, dragging anchor points is the way you develop curves. The more you pull, the bigger the curve.

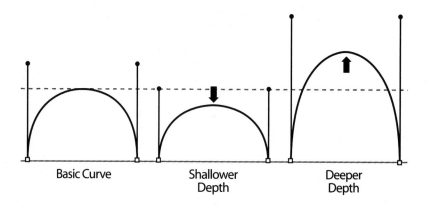

Basic Curve   Shallower Depth   Deeper Depth

Expect to work with curves for a while before you feel completely comfortable with them.

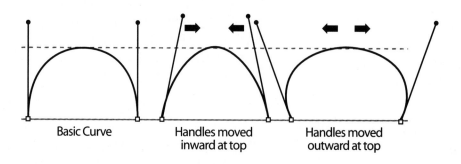

Basic Curve   Handles moved inward at top   Handles moved outward at top

Smooth Point

The smooth point is aptly named since curving segments passing through it are smooth, continuous lines. The smooth point is identified by the two control handles that protrude from it in opposite directions. Use the smooth point to create free-flowing, elegant curves.

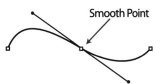

Creating a Smooth Point

1. Continue in the open document. With the Pen tool, click-hold the mouse on the page and drag a curve handle upward at roughly a 45° angle to create the first point (step A). Move the mouse to the right and click-hold-drag upward to create the smooth point (step B).

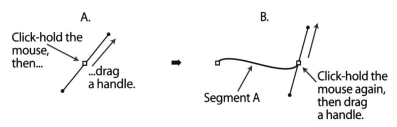

2. Single-click again to the right to create an endpoint, completing the smooth point sequence (segment A before — smooth point — segment B after).

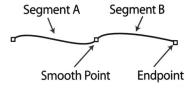

3. Click on the smooth point with the Direct Selection tool. You will see its control handles. Click-hold on the top handle's round endpiece and drag upward at a slight angle (step A). Now click-hold on the endpiece of the bottom handle and drag downward toward the left (step B). Observe how as you move the control handles, both segments are affected.

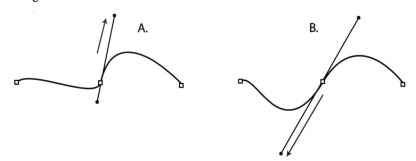

4. Delete this path. Keep the document open.

Corner Point

A corner point has handles that move independently of each other in different directions. There are three places to have a corner point: between two straight segments, at the end of a straight segment, and between consecutive curves linked together.

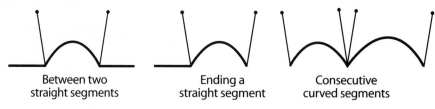

| Between two straight segments | Ending a straight segment | Consecutive curved segments |

The corner points that bridge a segment can go in different directions giving you the ability to create custom shapes that you could not accomplish with smooth points

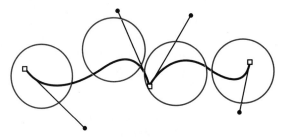

Each handle controls the area of the segment extending from its anchor point.

If you need to change a corner point to a smooth point, use the Convert Direction Point tool (in the Pen tool pop-out menu) to convert the point. If you click-drag the tool on the point, new smooth point control handles will appear.

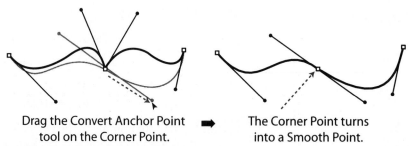

Drag the Convert Anchor Point tool on the Corner Point. ➡ The Corner Point turns into a Smooth Point.

Creating Corner Points

1. Continue in the open document. With the Pen tool, click-hold the mouse on the page and drag up and right to create the first curving point.

Click-drag

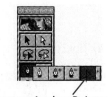

After curves have been set on an anchor, such as a smooth or corner point, the only tool that can modify or transform the anchor point is the Convert Anchor Point tool.

Convert Anchor Point tool

When dragging to create curves, you'll normally drag toward the area where you intend to create the next anchor point. This helps avoid creating really drastic curves that have hard-to-control handles.

Recognizing smooth and corner points boils down to this: Corner point segments are independent of any other segment. Smooth point handles control the segments on either side of the point.

2. Move the mouse to the right, and click-drag upward, creating a smooth point. Release the mouse button, but don't deselect.

3. Hold the Option/Alt key and click-drag on this same endpoint, pulling the second control handle to the right. Do not deselect.

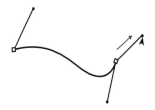

4. Move the mouse to the right, then drag upward creating an ending curve point.

5. Click on the first segment with the Direct Selection tool. You will see its control handles.

6. Click-hold the right control handle (on center anchor point) and rotate it upward. Observe how only the left segment curve changes.

7. Using the right and left control handles of the first segment, adjust the curve to look like this.

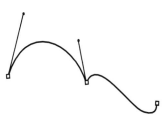

8. With the Direct Selection tool, click on the second segment to see the control handles. Adjust the curve to look like this.

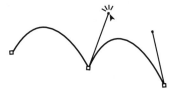

9. You have created and adjusted corner points and have observed how maneuverable they are for modifying segments. Keep the document open.

More Corner Point Techniques

The previous exercise showed how to create corner anchor points with two handles that adjust the segments before and after the point. There are, however, other circumstances in which you will want to create a simple corner point without using the Option/Alt key with all the clicking and dragging.

If you have a straight line segment (A) that is going to extend into a curve, the simplest method is to deselect the path after the straight line is made. With the Pen tool click-drag the line's endpoint, pulling out a corner point curve handle (B). Finally, move the mouse to the right and single-click to end the corner point segment (C). Click on the corner point or its segment with the Direct Selection tool to show the control handle that adjusts the curve (D).

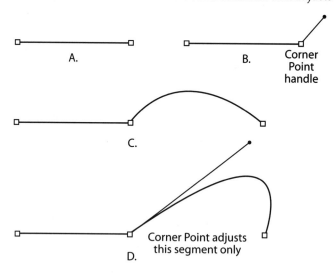

Combining Straight Lines with Curves

1. Continue in the open document. With the Pen tool, single-click to establish a beginning point. Move the mouse to the right and up, then single-click again.

2. Click-drag the Pen tool on the second anchor point, and pull out a control handle. Release the mouse button. Move the mouse to the right and down, then single-click to establish a third anchor point. With the Direct Selection tool, click on the second anchor point to see the control handle. Use it to adjust the curve to look like the example below.

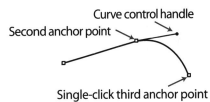

3. Select the Pen tool. Click on the third anchor point and move the mouse to the left and down. Single-click to create the fourth point.

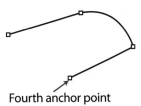

4. Click-drag the Pen tool on the fourth point, and pull out a corner point control handle.

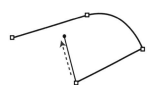

5. Release the mouse button. Single-click the Pen tool on the first point you created. This will make the object a closed path.

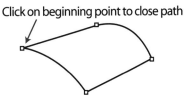

6. Use the Direct Selection tool to click on the fourth point to see its control handle. Use it to adjust the curve to look like the example below.

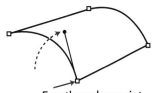

7. You have now created a complete object, composed of both straight and curved segments.

8. Close the file without saving.

To see curve handles more clearly for making adjustments, go to Outline mode.

Budgeting anchor points is not done just for aesthetic reasons. The size of an Illustrator document increases with the number of points in the document.

Strategies for Making Curves

Making a smooth or corner point is not a random, click-anywhere process. The idea is to click the anchor points at the most strategic places along the path so as to draw the path with the fewest anchor points possible. A half a circle created with the Ellipse tool is shown in figure A. We have shown where Illustrator places its anchor points. Figure B shows that you will not meet with much success if you try to make this shape with only two anchor points. A series of continual curves has the anchor points placed in the best locations so the smooth points can achieve the desired flow (C).

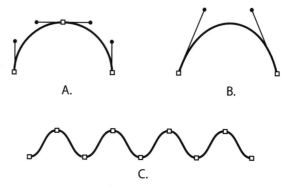

Here is a curving object (A). Let's suppose that it was given to you as a template, and your task was to use the Pen tool to trace the shape. Where would you click the anchor points along this path? In figure B we have shown you a suggested series of anchor points. Do you agree with the placement?

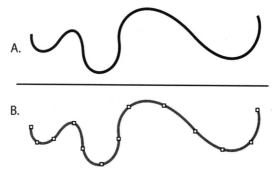

If you *don't* agree, then you are beginning to grasp the logic behind anchor point placement for curves. Below is the path showing the only anchor points you would need to create it.

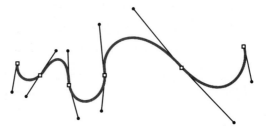

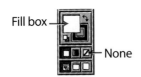

Fill box ——

—— None

When tracing templates with the Pen tool in Preview mode, it is best to set the stroke color at black and the fill at None. A white fill will cover up and obscure the template so that you can't see what to trace. The black stroke will give you a better idea of the path as it is drawn.

Pen Tool Practice

Before going on, we are going to give you time to practice what you have learned about the Pen tool and its abilities to create straight lines and curves. Open the **Pen Practice.AI** file in the **SF-Intro Illustrator** folder.

Click the Default Colors box in the Toolbox. To set the Fill to None, click the Fill box, then click the None box. Using the Pen tool, try to accurately trace these template images. Remember to use the least number of anchor points necessary to achieve the shape.

Tracing a Template

1. Open the **Banana Trace.AI** file in the **SF-Intro Illustrator** folder. The template image is a simple banana, composed of both curves and some straight lines.

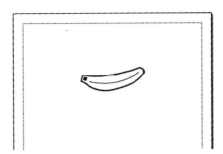

2. In the Toolbox, click the Default Colors icon to set the stroke color to Black, and the fill to White. Click on the Fill box and select None.

Fill box ——

Default —— Colors

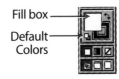

—— Swap Colors

—— Stroke box

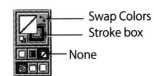

—— None

The Selection tool selects an entire path and its anchor points. With the Direct Selection tool, hold the Option/Alt key to accomplish the same task.

3. Select the Pen tool to begin tracing the outlines. Click-drag a starting curve point on the banana's end piece. Your next click will be the upper-right corner of the banana, so drag the curve in that direction.

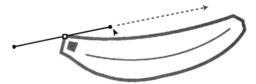

4. Click the Pen tool on the upper-right corner of the banana.

5. Click two more times for the next two corners to create the curved end of the banana. Now click-drag the Pen tool on the last anchor point clicked. A curve handle will pull out of the point.

6. The curve will not extend to the other end of the banana and still fit the template. It needs a midpoint. Click an anchor point midway, along the template. Click-drag on this anchor point to pull out a curve handle.

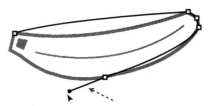

7. Moving to the left, click the Pen tool to create the first corner on the left side of the banana. Now click on the next corner. The last and final click should be on the first anchor point you created. This will complete a closed path defining the banana's shape. This is why paths are also called "outlines."

Final click here

8. Fine-tuning is necessary to accurately fit the curves to the template. There are only three curves that need adjustment. The anchor points must be selected with the Direct Selection tool, which shows the corner handles. Click on the first anchor you made. Drag on its corner handle and fit the curve to the template.

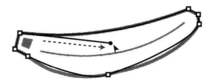

9. When finished, click the Direct Selection tool on the anchor point from which the second curve was dragged. Drag its control handle to fit the curve of the template.

10. Click on the next curving anchor point at the bottom of the banana. You will see its control handle. Drag the control handle to fit the curve. Deselect the path.

11. The black "shadow" that suggests the stem of the banana requires just four clicks of the Pen tool to make the four corners, with a fifth click on the first point to make it a closed path. Click the stem with the Selection tool to select it. Click the Swap Colors icon in the Toolbox. This flip-flops the paint attributes of the stem to a black fill, no stroke. Deselect the "stem" path.

12. To reset the Fill to None and the Stroke to black, click on the outline path of the banana. Notice how the Fill/Stroke boxes in the Toolbox change. Now, anything drawn will have these attributes. We will move on to draw the single segment.

13. Select the Pen tool and click-drag it on the left end of the side piece, dragging a curve handle. Click the second point on the right end of the piece. Use the Direct Selection tool to adjust the curve to fit the template.

14. Now you can paint the object. With the Selection tool, click on the banana outline path. In the Window menu, select Show Stroke to see the Stroke palette. Set the Weight to 2 pt. Press Enter/Return to apply. Keep the path selected.

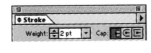

When clicking the Fill or Stroke boxes in the Toolbox, if the box you want is already active, clicking it will bring up the Color Picker, which might not be what you expected. Simply click Cancel to put it away.

15. Use Show Color in the Window menu to access the Color palette. Click on the Fill box in the palette to apply a color to the fill. Drag the Y (Yellow) slider to 100%. Set all of the other colors to 0%. The banana is now drawn and painted. Click Return/Enter if the banana does not readily accept the color change.

Fill box

Yellow

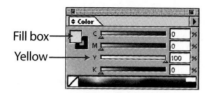
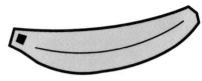

16. You have succeeded in drawing a series of curves and straight lines, adjusting them to fit, then painting them. Congratulations.

17. Close the file without saving.

Modifying Paths

Drawings don't just happen; they're developed through a progression of tool operations until the final product is achieved. Professional artists constantly tweak and fine-tune drawings until they're satisfied with the results.

All drawings — even small, simple illustrations — usually require the ability to modify paths. This section will discuss how to edit and change segments and anchor points so that the objects and shapes are exactly correct.

Anchor Points and Segments

When we spoke of how to create circles and squares with the Ellipse and Rectangle tools, we mentioned that all these shapes (as well as the stars, polygons, and spirals) were actually "automatic" versions of shapes that can be drawn from scratch.

All shapes comprise anchor points and segments and can therefore be modified on a point-by-point basis. Knowing how to select specific anchor points and segments is critical to working with paths. Anchor points and segments are the building blocks of objects. The ability to create, edit, and modify points and segments is a core Illustrator skill. Here are the basics:

The Selection tool automatically selects all anchor points in an object or group of objects. The Direct Selection tool selects individual anchor points and segments.

- When a path is clicked with the Selection tool, the whole path is selected and all of the anchor points are solid (selected).

- When a segment of the same path is clicked with the Direct Selection tool, all anchor points appear, but are hollow (unselected). Only the selected segment can be moved, or deleted.

- When a single anchor point is clicked with the Direct Selection tool, it becomes solid, indicating it is selected. Only the selected point can be moved or modified. The other anchor points are unselected. If, for instance, you needed to move three anchor points on an object possessing many points, you would hold Shift and click on the three individual points to select them. You could then move these points without affecting the other points.

In the real world, you'll find yourself using the Direct Selection tool (the hollow arrow) more often than the black Selection tool.

Drag-duplicating objects with Option/Alt is used quite a bit, in as much as Illustrator does not have a "duplicate" menu feature, which is available in other programs.

After you have deleted a single segment, the remaining portion of the object will become selected. You will erase the entire object if you press Delete again.

Selecting Single Anchor Points

Selecting a single anchor point is often necessary when modifying an object. Selecting one anchor point can be done in two ways:

- Drag the Direct Selection tool to create a small marquee around the anchor point (A).

- Click directly on the single point with the Direct Selection tool, isolating it (B).

Regardless of the selection method, the single selected point can be moved (as shown in figure B), or deleted.

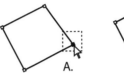
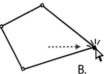

Moving Segments

Only the Direct Selection tool can select a segment (A). When selected (and the mouse button held), the segment and its connected anchor points can be moved (B).

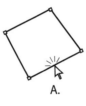
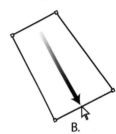

Deleting Single Segments

Single-click on a segment with the Direct Selection tool to select it (A). Press the Delete key to remove the segment (B).

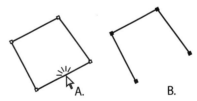

Duplicating Paths and Objects

The easiest way to duplicate a path is to click on it with the Selection tool, and hold down the Option/Alt key as you drag the object. Adding the Shift key after the move has begun will constrain the movement to 90°.

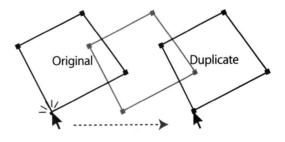

Path Editing Tools

Occasionally, the need arises to make more drastic changes to a path than simply moving a point or segment around. The Scissors, Add Anchor Point, Delete Anchor Point, and Convert Anchor Point tools can perform these alterations to a path without disturbing other points or control handles.

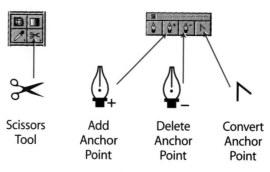

| Scissors Tool | Add Anchor Point | Delete Anchor Point | Convert Anchor Point |

At the place where the Scissors tool cuts the path, it will look like there is only one anchor point.

Don't be misled. There are actually two anchor points present, one positioned on top of the other.

Deselect, then, using the Direct Selection tool, you can move them apart to see the points.

- **Scissors tool.** This tool cuts a path by clicking it on either an anchor point or a segment. Be aware that the cut is not readily apparent. If the anchor points are nudged or you move one of the segments, the split will show.

- **Add Anchor Point tool.** Use this tool to add an anchor point anywhere on a segment. It will not place an anchor point on top of another point. The new anchor point can be used to reshape the path.

- **Delete Anchor Point tool.** This tool removes an anchor point from a path when the point is clicked on. Other points on the path remain undisturbed, but the removal of the point may cause the path to change shape.

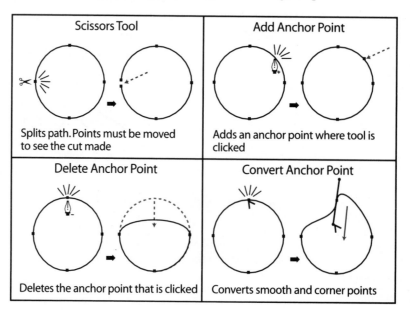

Scissors Tool	Add Anchor Point
Splits path. Points must be moved to see the cut made	Adds an anchor point where tool is clicked
Delete Anchor Point	**Convert Anchor Point**
Deletes the anchor point that is clicked	Converts smooth and corner points

Connecting Anchor Points

Often, separate anchor points need to be connected to other points to complete a path. The Group command, which is used to bind whole paths and other objects together, does not connect paths between unconnected anchor points.

Here are two techniques that can be used to bridge the gap between anchor points:

- Use the Direct Selection tool to select two anchor points (either beginning or endpoints) by either drawing a selection marquee around them or Shift-clicking directly, then using Object>Join to connect them.

- Click the Pen tool on two separate anchor points (either beginning or endpoints).

Editing and Modifying Paths

1. Create a new document set for CMYK Color mode, naming it "Border Design.AI". Leave the artboard set for the default letter size. In the View menu, set the view for Outline mode. This way you will see the paths better to modify them. In the Edit>Preferences>Guides & Grid window, set the Guides Color for Light Blue and the Style for Dots.

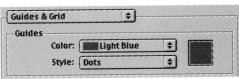

The keyboard shortcut for Join is Command/Control-J.

2. Select the Rectangle tool and, holding the Option/Alt key, click its cursor on the top center of the page. Its dialog box will appear. Set the Width at 5 in. and the Height at 1 in. Click OK.

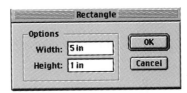

3. The rectangle will appear where you clicked the tool cursor. You will see it has a center point. If the rulers are not showing, select Window>Show Rulers.

4. Drag a horizontal guide from the horizontal ruler at the top of the document window, releasing the guide directly on top of the rectangle's center point. Drag a vertical guide to the rectangle's center. Select the rectangle and press Command/Control-5 to turn it into a guide.

5. Click the Default Colors box in the Toolbox. Change the Fill box to None. Now, select the Ellipse tool, hold the Option/Alt key, and click the cursor anywhere on the guides. The Ellipse dialog box will appear. Set the Width and Height for 1 in. Click OK. The circle will appear. Select it with the Selection tool, and move it so that it fits the left side of the rectangle guide.

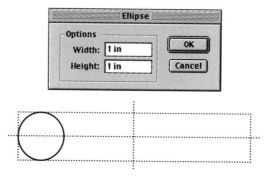

6. When in place, let go of the mouse. Reselect the circle and, holding the Option/Alt key, drag the circle over to fit in the right side of the rectangle. Be sure to press the Shift key after the drag has begun, to constrain the move to 45° or 90°.

7. With the Direct Selection tool, hold down the Shift key while clicking on the inside middle anchor points of the circles to select them. Press Delete.

8. You now have two half-circles to work with. Deselect the paths.

9. Use the Direct Selection tool to draw a marquee that includes the two top anchor points of the half-circles. This will select the points. Press Command/Control-J to Join the two points.

10. Select the Pen tool. We will use another way to connect points on the bottom of the figure. Click first on the bottom anchor point of the left half-circle. Now, click on the bottom anchor point of the right half-circle. This creates a new segment and closes the path.

11. You have created a custom shape using modified circles.

12. Select the Ellipse tool. Hold the Option/Alt key and click the crosshair cursor on the center where the two guides meet. The Ellipse dialog box will appear. Set the Width and Height for 2 in. and then click OK. A circle will appear.

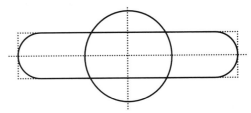

13. Select the Scissors tool in the Toolbox. Click the cursor on the two side anchor points of the circle to cut the path. Deselect the paths.

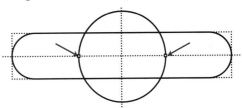

14. With the Selection tool, click on the top half of the cut circle. Move it up holding the Shift key to constrain movement to a vertical direction. Move the top half of the circle so its bottom anchor points touch the first object you created. Select the bottom half of the cut circle and drag it down (while holding the Shift key) so its top points touch the first object. Drag vertical guides over to mark the places where the anchor points touch.

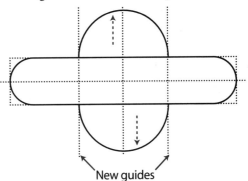

New guides

15. Select the two half-circle paths. Press Command/Control-3 to hide them. Use the Scissors tool to cut the modified object where the guides touch it. Shift-click the middle paths with the Selection tool and press Delete.

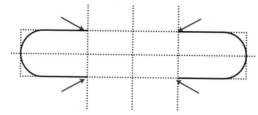

16. Use Object>Show All to bring the half-circles back to view. With the Direct Selection tool, draw a marquee around the points where the half-circles meet the modified object points. Press Command/Control-J to Join the points. If a dialog box appears asking whether you want smooth or corner points, simply click OK. It doesn't matter in this instance.

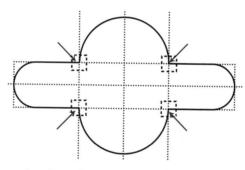

17. Select the Scissors tool and cut the modified object on its two farthest left/right points.

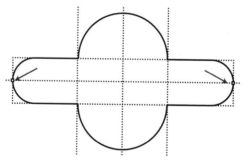

18. Select the bottom half with the Selection tool and press the Down Arrow key 15 times to move it down about 1/4 in.

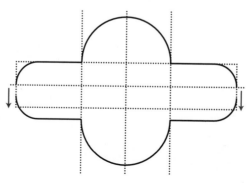

19. Use the Pen tool to click on the two anchor points on one side to connect them. Connect the anchor points on the other side.

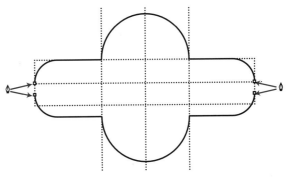

20. You have used methods for editing paths to create an attractive object that could be used for a logo. Did you accurately join all the specified points?

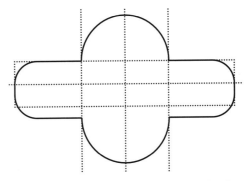

21. We will paint the object. Use View>Guides to clear the guides. Use the View menu to go to Preview mode. Select the object with the Selection tool. Click the Default Colors box in the Toolbox.

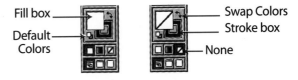

In the Window menu, select Show Stroke. In the Stroke palette, set the Weight for 10 pt. and apply with Return/Enter.

22. Press Command/Control-C to Copy the path. Press Command/Control-F to Paste in Front the duplicate on top of the original. Click the Swap Colors icon in the Toolbox to make the Stroke white. In the Stroke palette, set the Weight for 2 pt. Click on the Fill box in the Toolbox and click the None box underneath so the duplicate will have no fill, but will have a 2 pt. white rule.

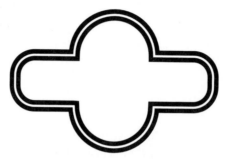

23. You have created a graphic piece starting from scratch and modifying paths with the methods shown.

24. Save As the file to your **Work in Progress** folder for your own use if ever you need a decorative border. Believe us, there is nothing like a handy clip-art collection that you can immediately draw from in an emergency.

Avoiding Mishaps

Releasing guides back to paths is a convenient way to have paths the exact shape and size you need them. However, there are mishaps that might occur, and when your EPS file, consisting of only a few paths becomes an astronomical file size, gigantic in physical size when placed in other programs, you will scream, "What happened?"

The answer is simple. A path (you will learn later) is composed of a single segment with anchor points at either end.

If, for instance, you release a vertical or horizontal ruler guide back to a path, then quickly click on it with the Direct Selection tool and click Delete, you are only succeeding in deleting the segment, not the anchor points.

This leaves them in the document, and since they are way off in the far, reaches of the document, this makes the file an incredible size.

The rules for avoiding or fixing this mishap are:

- When selecting a guide-turned-to-path to delete it, always use the Selection tool (black pointer tool).

- If you have already accidentally deleted only the segment, not the anchor points, go to the Object menu and make sure that Unlock All is not black and accessible. If it is, then some objects are locked, and these could be the anchor points. If so, use Unlock All to unlock objects. Select only the objects you wish to keep in your design. Lock (Object>Lock) the necessary pieces. Then select All to select any unnecessary anchor points or segments, and press Delete. You can select Object>Unlock to unlock the necessary paths.

- Go to the Object menu selection Path>Cleanup. In the dialog box select the Stray Points option, which looks for single anchor points and deletes them when you click OK.

Chapter Summary

You have experienced the relationship of paths and vector graphics, as well as the importance of the Pen tool for creating both open and closed paths. You have learned how to draw straight lines, curves, and trace templates. You have learned the differences between smooth and corner points in curves and have observed the most strategic points to click the Pen tool to create these curves. You have also learned how to edit and modify paths and how to use this to create designs.

Complete Project A: Art Deco House

Notes:

CHAPTER 6

CREATING AND EDITING TYPE

CHAPTER OBJECTIVE:

Develop skill in using type in a design. To learn how to create and manipulate typographic elements. In Chapter 6, you will:

- Understand how to place type on the page.
- Learn the difference between Point text and Area text.
- Learn the various ways to select text.
- Study typographic basics, including fonts, font weight, font style,leading, tracking, kerning, scaling, and baseline shift.
- Understand paragraph settings and type alignment.
- Learn to recognize overset text blocks and how to access the hidden text.
- Learn about converting text to path outlines.
- Learn to create different effects with text in the form of path outlines.
- Learn how to fit type to a template.

PROJECTS TO BE COMPLETED:

- Art Deco House (A)
- **BearWear Business Cards (B)**
- Wine and Cheese Invitation (C)
- Walking the Dogs (D)
- Broadway Bound (E)
- Joker's Wild (F)
- BearWear Label (G)

You can select type either by highlighting the text with the Type tool cursor, or by clicking on the text block with the Selection tool. This second method selects all the type, while the Type tool cursor can be used to select portions of the type.

Creating and Editing Type

It goes without saying that the digital artist must know how to develop shapes, control paint attributes, and accurately position objects within a drawing. Many experienced artists might also argue that the ability to manipulate type elements is equally important in creating designs that use type. Knowing how to create and edit type allows the designer to select the most appropriate typeface for a project, then style and position the type to enhance the overall design of the project.

Illustrator's type controls allow you set attributes such as line spacing, character spacing, text alignment and even the shape of individual characters. In this chapter we will explore ways to create or modify type elements.

Getting Type on the Page

Illustrator provides two basic ways to apply a block of text to a document — using the Type tool from the Toolbox to create point text and area text, or using one of the specialized type tools available in the Type tool pop-out menu. These specialized tools allow you to create lines of text along open paths or areas of text inside pre-drawn closed paths.

Creating Point Text with the Type Tool

Point-text blocks are created by selecting the Type tool from the Toolbox, clicking its I-beam cursor on any position in the document, and entering the desired text. The text begins at the point where you clicked the cursor. A point-text block has no right margin, so it will not "wrap" to the next line. In other words, one line of type will go on endlessly until you either stop typing or press Return/Enter to start a new line. Use this kind of text block for small quantities of type, such as headlines, short sentences, and phrases that don't require the text to wrap to the next line.

<u>This is a point-text block</u>

Creating Area Text with the Type Tool

An area-text block is set into a text container, which has margins automatically set to the size of the container. Use an area-text block whenever you want quantities of text to appear in structured columns positioned on specific regions of the page.

To create area text, click on the Type tool to activate the I-beam cursor. Move the cursor to any position on the page, then drag the cursor diagonally to create a text container the desired size. The I-beam cursor will automatically appear in the upper left corner of the box, and you can begin typing. As you type, the text will wrap to the next line when it reaches the right side of the box.

Don't be alarmed when you deselect the text container and it seems to disappear. It will reappear again anytime you click on the text with the Type tool or with one of the selection tools.

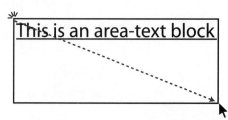

This is an area-text block

When area-text blocks have too much text for the type container, a small square with a plus (+) sign appears to the right to show that there is more text than shows in the box.

Sirens screamed and emergency lights flashed as firemen arrived on the scene and began unwinding yards of fire hose, donning their gas masks and chopping down a tall fence to get to the blaze. The neighbors who had called them peered over their wooden fences, gaping and pointing at what was

Single words can be instantly selected with the Type tool cursor by double-clicking it on the word. Triple-clicking will select an entire paragraph. You can also select a contiguous range of text by clicking at the start of the desired range, then holding the Shift key, and clicking at the end of the range.

Be certain to select View>Hide Bounding Box when working with text containers. Bounding boxes obscure the text containers and make them more difficult to work with.

If you double-click on a text block with the Selection tool, the cursor turns into the Type tool cursor, placed in the text and ready to go.

Selecting Text

Before you can modify any element in a block of text, you must select the text to be changed. You can use the Selection tool or the Type tool, depending on how much text you want to edit. To select text with the Type tool, click and drag the I-beam cursor over the desired text. The selected text will appear highlighted. To select all of a point- or area-text block, click anywhere on the text with the Selection tool. Text selected this way will appear underlined.

Another very popular species, this warm-growing orchid is found in the old-world tropics: places like Vietnam, Thailand, New Guinea, and Australia. It is often grown in slatted wooden baskets, which closely mimic its natural habit of growing in the "crotches" of

Another very popular species, this warm-growing orchid is found in the old-world tropics: places like Vietnam, Thailand, New Guinea, and Australia. It is often grown in slatted wooden baskets, which closely mimic its natural habit of growing in the "crotches" of

Type tool highlighting   Selection tool clicking

The Type Area Select option in the Edit>Preferences>Type & Auto Tracing dialog box offers the ability to select a text block with the Selection tool by clicking within the text block. If this option isn't turned on, it's necessary to click directly on the text's baseline to select the text block.

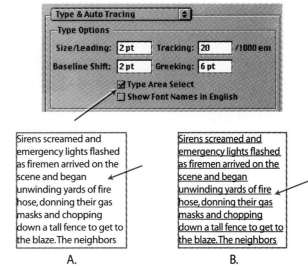

When Type Area Select is checked, the text block can be selected by clicking the Selection tool anywhere within the block (A). If Type Area Select is unselected, the Selection tool must be clicked directly on one of the baselines of the text (B).

Fonts are attractive but don't get carried away with putting too many typefaces on a document. This is the sign of the amateur. Be conservative in your use of type. In general, limit yourself to three different fonts in a project. To add variety, apply different sizes and styles to the fonts you've chosen to use.

Old-time typographers used an arcane measurement system that had a fraction more than 72 points to an inch. All graphics programs today round the amount down to 72 points to an inch.

"Sans" in the term sans serif is French for "without" and rhymes with "dawn."

Resizing a Text Container

In some cases, the area-text box you created may be too small once you have entered all of the text. To make the text fit, resize the Bounding box by selecting and moving one of the handles (small squares) on the bounding box. If the bounding box is not active, use View>Show Bounding Box (Command/Control-Shift-B).

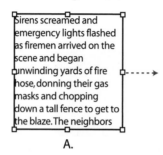

A.   B.

Typographic Basics

Volumes have been written on the art of typography. Indeed, fine typesetting is an art form. If we dedicated this entire course to type, we could only begin to cover the fine points. To teach you how to use type in Illustrator, we will try to cover most of the basics. The Character palette provides control over most of Illustrator's type attributes. The Show Options arrow has been selected in the palette menu below.

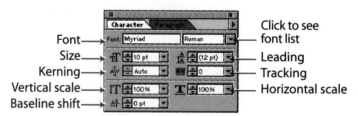

Fonts

In digital art, we use the term "font" to refer to the entire collection of characters in any given typeface. To access a list of fonts available in Illustrator, click on the arrow menu button to the right of the Font field in the Character palette. Here is a sampling of various fonts available in Illustrator.

Avant Garde   Cheltenham   **Cooper Black**

Helvetica   Souvenir   **STENCIL**   Tekton   Times

Typefaces fit into one of four categories: Serif refers to the small extensions from the characters' stems. Sans serif means "without serifs." Decorative is a hybrid style of features that can't be classified as "serif" or "sans serif." "PI" fonts are pictographs, or picture fonts like Dingbats, Carta (used for maps) or musical notes.

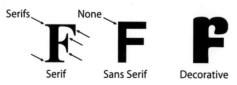

Serif
Sans Serif
Decorative

Double-clicking the Leading icon in the Character palette will change the leading number to match the size of the type.

Hold Command/Control and click on the icons in the Character palette to reset the values to the Illustrator default settings.

The keyboard commands make changes in leading and baseline shift in increments of point sizes. Illustrator defaults to 2-pt. increments with each key pressed. If any setting has to be fine-tuned by 1 pt., this can be changed in the Character palette.

Font Styles

Most font families contain a basic style called Roman or Normal, depending on the font's design. Some fonts also have a bold style, and many have an italic and bold italic style. Other fonts may include styles such as oblique, book, heavy, light, or ultra, which are variations on the bold and italic styles.

Size

The size of a character is measured vertically in "points." There are 72 points in one inch. The vertical measurement of a font extends from the bottom of the descender to the top of the ascender.

Leading

Leading is the distance between the baseline of a line of type from the baseline of the line above it. It may also be measured form ascender to ascender, expressed in points or hundredths of an inch.

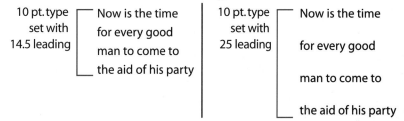

| 10 pt. type set with 14.5 leading | Now is the time for every good man to come to the aid of his party | 10 pt. type set with 25 leading | Now is the time for every good man to come to the aid of his party |

The keyboard shortcut for adjusting leading is Option/Alt-Down Arrow key (to increase increments) and Option/Alt-Up Arrow key (to decrease increments). The leading increases/decreases by 2 pts. each time you press the keys. If the Command/Control key is added, the increments change to 10 pts. each time you press the keys, which means if the leading is at 12 pt., the leading will change to 22 pt.

Tracking

Tracking is the spacing between characters. There are several descriptive words often used to describe tracking, such as loose, normal, or tight. In Illustrator, the tracking is measured in numeric increments that refer to thousandths of an "em." The zero setting is considered normal; increments in the negative numbers are tight (less space between the letters); and increments in numbers above zero means the tracking is loose (more space between the letters). The increments are adjusted in the Character palette. Any type or text blocks selected can be modified in this palette.

The Tracking menu

	-100
	-75
	-50
	-25
	-10
	-5
✓	0
	5
	10
	25
	50
	75
	100
	200

Examples:

This tracking is set for 0.

This tracking is set for -25.

This tracking is set for -50.

This tracking is set for 15.

This tracking is set for 25.

This tracking is set for 50.

The keyboard shortcut for adjusting tracking of selected text is Option/Alt-Left Arrow key (to decrease spacing) or Option/Alt-Right Arrow key (to increase spacing).

Kerning

Kerning refers to the spacing between two contiguous characters. Most high-quality fonts have certain common "kerning pairs" built into the font. Most typefaces, especially the larger type in ad headlines, need some kerning to look their best.

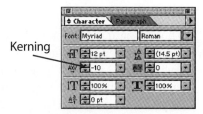

| Letter's left/right dimensions butt up to each other | This looks bad and makes reading difficult | Kerning makes the letters fit better |

You may kern a pair of characters by placing the type cursor between the two characters and pressing Option/Alt-Left Arrow key (to decrease increments) or Option/Alt-Right Arrow key (to increase increments). Each time you press an arrow key, the space between the pair of characters increases/decreases by 20/1000 em, which is the default Tracking setting in the Edit>Preferences>Type & Auto Tracing dialog box. Adding the Command/Control key to the short increases/decreases increments by 10 times the default setting.

You can also adjust the spacing between two characters from the Kerning field on the Character palette. To do this, place a type cursor between two characters, then use the arrow buttons in the Kerning field to modify the kerning.

Setting increments preferences. The keyboard shortcuts for Size, Leading, Tracking/Kerning, and Baseline Shift can be modified in Preferences>Type & Auto Tracing.

Scaling Type

You can condense or expand the height and/or the width of characters using scaling fields in the Character palette or the Scaling tool in the Toolbox. To change the scaling of one or more characters using the Vertical Scaling and Horizontal Scaling fields in the Character palette, select the desired text, then use the arrow buttons in the scaling fields to make your changes.

As your eye becomes attuned to tracking and kerning, you will begin to notice examples of text that is too loose or too tight, and headline text where kerning has not been well applied.

To kern the spacing on a more than a few characters of text, use Tracking.

You may wonder why we stress the Character palette instead of the Type menu, as you get more fluent in using type in Illustrator, you will appreciate having all the typographic settings in one movable palette. If you have a large monitor you will get tired of constantly making the journey up to the top of the screen to access the Type menu, especially to make setting changes. The time spent taking all those trips adds up.

If you want to reset the Vertical and Horizontal scaling fields in the Character palette back to 100%, press Command/Control-Shift-X.

Drop caps can be easily made in Illustrator using Baseline Shift. To create a drop cap, highlight a single character, increase its size and style, then use Baseline Shift to align it with the rest of the text.

Drop caps

If we show a palette full of options, and all you see when you access the palette is a limited top half. Use the palette menu to Show Options and you will see all the features available.

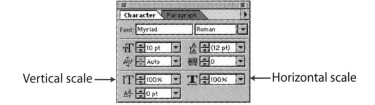

Vertical scale →   ← Horizontal scale

The scaling increments are applied in percentages of the characters' initial setting.

This text is set to 50% Horizontal Scale

This text is set to 150% Horizontal Scale

This text is set to 75% Vertical Scale

This text is set to 200% Vertical Scale

Baseline Shift

The imaginary line that characters sit on is called the baseline. Illustrator's Baseline Shift feature allows you to move a baseline up or down. This feature is extremely valuable when creating logos where you want letters to rise above or go below the adjoining characters.

To alter the baseline of characters by 2-pt. increments, select the desired text and press Option/Alt-Shift-Up Arrow or Option/Alt-Shift-Down Arrow. If you add the Command/Control key to this shortcut, the increments will increase/decrease times 5.

Baseline 0 pt. ⟶ A Stitch in Time......

Baseline -4 pt. ⟶ A Stitch in Time-----

Baseline 4 pt. ⟶ A Stitch in Time

Paragraph

In the Paragraph dialog box, further type formatting adjustments can be made. From alignment and indentations, to word and letter spacing, customizing these settings can make the type look exactly as desired. The Paragraph palette menu has a Show Options selection that will show all the features available.

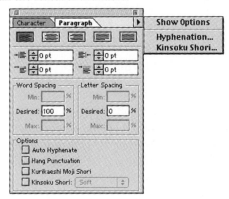

Some of the Paragraph controls are for more advanced typographic typefitting. We will only address the Alignment feature of the dialog box for now.

You can go from field to field in a palette by pressing the Tab key. Using the Tab key when text is selected will insert a tab indent. Be careful.

Alignment

There are nicknames that the typographers use for how the margins of blocks of text are aligned. Align Left is called either "flush left" or "ragged right" by typographers, because the left margin is even, or flush, and the right margin is ragged, or uneven. Align Right is known as "flush right" or "ragged left." Align Center centers all type in the middle of the text block, with ragged left and right margins.

Justify Full Lines creates evenly aligned (called "justified") right and left margins. Justify Full Lines does not justify lines that are not "full", such as last lines in a paragraph. Justify All Lines justifies every line in the text, including lines that are not full. Study some magazines, books, and advertising materials to see how alignment varies from media to media. Some publications prefer justified type, others like the casual look of Align Left. When you are deciding how to align text, focus first on readability then on visual appeal.

To align blocks of text, select the text and click on the desired alignment button in the Paragraph palette.

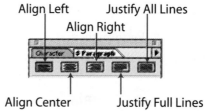

Creating Type

1. Create a new document set for CMYK Color Mode, leave it untitled and the Artboard set for default. Select View>Preview mode. Be sure that the Bounding box (View menu) is not active. Select the Type tool and click the cursor on the page to create a point-text block.

2. Type your name for the first line, press Return/Enter; your address on the second line, (Return/Enter); your city, state, and zip code on the third line.

   User's Name <return>
   12234 Silicon Valley Rd. <return>
   Anywhere, USA 33615

3. With the Type tool cursor, highlight all this text. Press Command/Control-T to access the Character palette. Use the Palette menu to Show Options.

4. Click on the arrow to the right of the Font field and scroll up the pop-up menu to select ATC Cabana, Normal. Apply a 14-pt. character Size, and 24-pt. Leading. Set Tracking at -20, Kerning at Auto, Horizontal Scale at 125%, and Vertical Scale at 110%, and set the Baseline Shift at zero.

Take note of the tracking in publications with justified margins. When you decide on justified margins for large blocks of text, you are asking for headaches tracking loose and tight text.

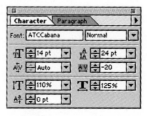

Once you have set the font features, every time you activate the Type tool, the same features will be applied to any new text you enter, until they change again.

To save time scrolling through the list of font names, highlight the Font field and enter the name of the typeface you want.

Watch out!

If you draw a large area-text block, for example 5 × 5-inches, but only type three words, the file, when saved in Illustrator EPS format, will be as big as the text block, regardless of the wasted white space.

5. Double-click the Type cursor on your first name to select it. Keep this selected. Hold the Shift key and go to your last name. Single-click the cursor on the middle of your last name. You will see all letters, up to that point, become selected. Continue pressing the Shift key and double-click the cursor on your last name. This will select your whole name. Change the font style to Bold. Change the tracking of your name to 200.

6. Highlight the first letter of your first name. Change the Size to 20 pt. Hold the Shift key and the Option/Alt key, and press the Down Arrow key two times to change the Baseline shift. Highlight the first letter of your last name, and repeat these changes to this letter.

7. Click the text cursor between the first and second letters of your first name and press Option/Alt-Left Arrow three times.

U ser's N ame
12234 Silicon Valley Rd.

Anywhere, USA 33615

8. Perform the same kerning on the first and second letters of your last name. You are gaining experience in entering and formatting type in Illustrator. Close the document without saving.

Overset Text Blocks

Be careful when creating area-text blocks. Depending on how small the block is drawn, more words can be typed than will show in the block. If this happens, a small box with a "+" in it will appear. This is the overset text indicator, which signifies that more type is available. To see more type, the text container must be enlarged.

```
Sirens screamed and
emergency lights
flashed as firemen
arrived on the
scene and began
unwinding yards of
fire hose, donning
their gas masks and
chopping down a
tall fence to get
to the blaze. The
neighbors who had
called them peered
over their wooden ⊞
```

In this example, an area-text block was drawn with the Type tool. A name and address was typed, but the size of the container was made too small. The city, state, and zip code line is not accessible. The overset text icon appears in the bottom right of the block (A). The View>Show Bounding Box option was selected, then the bottom handle of the Bounding box was dragged down to enlarge the area (B). The unseen type is now visible and can be highlighted if needed.

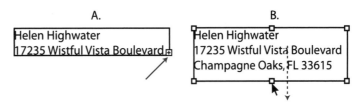

Formatting Text

1. Open the document **Format Text.AI** from the **SF-Intro Illustrator** folder.

2. With the Selection tool, click on the text container. Press Command/Control-T to access the Character palette.

3. Set the font to ATC MaiTai, Normal, the Size to 14 pt., and the Leading at 21 pts. Set the Tracking at 0, the Horizontal Scale at 100%, the Vertical Scale at 100% and the Baseline Shift at 0 pt. Press Return/Enter to apply.

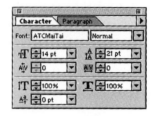

4. Enlarging the size and leading has moved the text down past the text container's boundaries. The Overset Text icon now shows, indicating that there's more text.

5. The bottom part of the container must be moved down to enlarge the text block. Select View>Show Bounding Box to apply this feature to the text container. Click on the bottom handle of the Bounding box and pull down. The text container will extend and display the overset text.

6. With the Type tool, highlight the words "Latin Nonsense by Oedipus Wrecks." Style the type ATC MaiTai, Bold. Set the Size at 18 pt. and Leading at 24-pt.

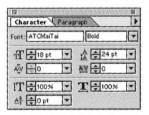

7. With the Type tool, highlight all the text in the block. In the Paragraph palette, click on Justify Full Lines, then select Justify All Lines. Observe how the spacing between the words is affected. Click on Align Left, then on Align Right. Observe the difference. Finally, click on Align Center.

8. You will notice that the word "magna" is on a line by itself. Highlight just the body text with the Type tool and, holding the Option/Alt key, press the Left Arrow key one time. This will tighten the Tracking to -20 and the spacing will bring "magna" up to the previous line.

9. Highlight only the title "Latin Nonsense." Change the font size to 24 pt. Select the text block with the Selection tool, and move it to the center of the page.

10. You have experimented with some of Illustrator's features for formatting type.

11. Close the file without saving.

Text Effects

Working with text as a designer goes far beyond merely typesetting. The use of type in logos, artistic headlines, and decoration challenges the designer's imagination. Illustrator offers many features and functions that can affect type in ways impossible with standard typesetting methods.

Fit Headline

Letter spacing sometimes becomes a designer's tool. If there is a set width for a background and just a few words is not enough to fill it, Illustrator's Fit Headline option in the Type menu will spread the letters out evenly across the width.

In the example below, the one word "HEADLINE" was not enough to fill the rectangle. The text was highlighted with the Type cursor, and Fit Headline applied. The feature spaced the tracking of the letters from end to end. Further fine-tuning of the spacing can be done in the Tracking option of the Character palette.

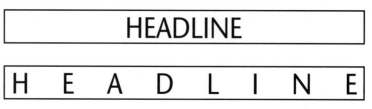

Working with Type Outlines

As you have seen, when you apply formatting changes, such as scaling, the change is applied uniformly to the selected characters. To be truly creative with text, you must first convert the characters to paths with anchor points and segments by selecting the text block with the Selection tool and choosing Type>Create Outlines.

You need these paths so you can stretch, distort, and curve individual elements of each character. This is because most of Illustrator's special operations and filters will only work on path outlines. The text characters below had to be converted to outline paths before the special effects could be applied.

The Fit Headline option will only work on Area text blocks, and the text must be highlighted with the Type tool cursor.

Outlined type is no longer text in its true sense. Once converted, unless Undo is used, the outlines cannot return to being text, and type attributes from the Character palette no longer have any effect. Type turned to outlines will look somewhat thicker and heavier on screen than when it was pure text. This is the screen preview of vector outlines, and is shown in a rough raster format. Don't worry though; the output of vector artwork to a PostScript printer produces a 100% clean image.

Creating outlined type can also be used to prepare Illustrator files that need to be opened and printed from a remote computer without the need for the exact fonts used. It can be useful, for example, in creating ads that will be incorporated in a page layout package as an EPS file.

Creating a Design with Type Outlines

1. Create a new document set for CMYK Color Mode; leave it untitled and the Artboard set for default. Press Command/Control-R to activate the Rulers. You will be working in Outline mode, so set this in the View menu.

2. Select the Type tool in the Toolbox. Click the cursor on the page and type these words on separate lines in one text block:

   LOGO

   TYPE

3. Press Command/Control-T to access the Type Character palette.

4. Highlight the text and style it ATC Cozumel, Normal, and set the Size 72 pt. Set Leading at 65, Tracking at 0, and Horizontal Scale at 100%. Press Return/Enter to apply. Use the Paragraph palette to set alignment for Align Left. Select the text block with the Selection tool. From the Type menu select Create Outlines (Command/Control-Shift-O). Select Object>Ungroup (Command/Control-Shift-G) to ungroup the letters so you can work with them individually.

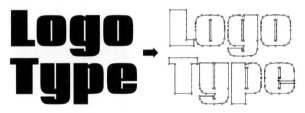

5. From the ruler at the top of the document, drag a horizontal guide down to the bottom of the descender in the "g" in "Logo." Drag another guide to the bottom of the "p" in "Type."

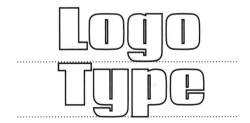

6. Zoom in on the "L, " and use the Direct Selection tool to marquee and select the lower anchor points. Holding the Shift key (to constrain the move), drag the points so that the bottom segment touches the guide.

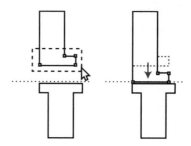

7. With the Selection tool, select the "ogo" letters and move them closer to the "L." Hold the Shift key to constrain the move to 90°.

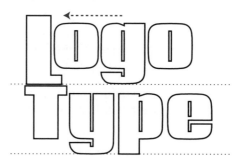

8. With the Direct Selection tool, marquee the bottom anchor points of the "T." Drag them down, holding the Shift key, so the bottom segment touches the guide.

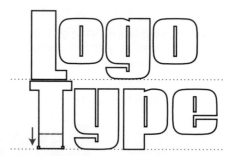

9. With the Direct Selection tool, select the top anchor points of the "T." Drag the points upward, holding the Shift key, so that the top of the "T" matches the lower leg of the "L."

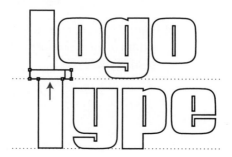

When modifying type by keyboard and visual means, it is easier to see the letters when the text block is selected with the Selection tool. If the type is highlighted by the Type tool, the black selection marker detracts from seeing the type clearly.

10. Select the "ype" outlines with the Selection tool, and drag them closer to the "T." Hold the Shift key to constrain the move.

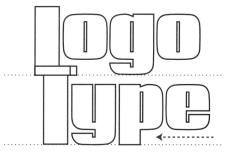

11. With the Direct Selection tool, highlight the bottom anchor points of the last "o" in "Logo." Drag so that the bottom of the "o" touches the guide. Hold the Shift key.

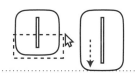

12. Marquee the left-side anchor points of the "g" descender. Drag them, holding the Shift key, to the left so that it almost touches the Upper leg of the "T."

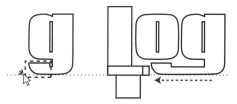

13. With the Direct Selection tool, marquee the top points of the "ype" letters. Drag them up until they are just under the letters "ogo."

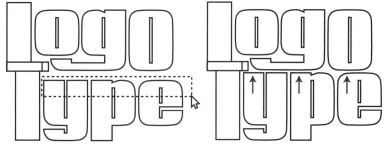

14. You have edited and modified the type in a way that would be impossible to do if the letters were to remain in text format. Preview your finished logo.

15. Close the file without saving.

Creating Text on a Curved Path

1. Create a new document set for CMYK Color Mode; leave it untitled and the Artboard set for default. Set the document for Preview mode. In the Toolbox, click the Default Colors icon. With the Pen tool, draw a curving path no more than 2 in. long. Click-hold on the Type tool in the Toolbox to access the pop-out menu, and select the Path Type tool.

Default Colors

Path Type tool

2. Lay the crossbar of the text cursor on top of the path and click once. Don't be alarmed when the path you drew loses its paint attributes. It has become a text path. Set the font ATC Seagull at 12 pt. Type the words "Typing text on a path."

3. With the Selection tool, click on the path. You will see the I-beam text cursor in front of the word "Typing." Drag the I-beam to the left with the Selection tool.

4. Increase the font size to 22 pt. You will see the type extend to the right, disappearing at the end of the path. The text overflow square will appear (A). Click the text path with the Direct Selection tool to see the anchor point better at the end of the path. Select the Pen tool, click on this endpoint and drag a curve handle. Click further to the right and the rest of the text will appear (B). Click on the endpoint with the Direct Selection tool and pull it down to the right. Adjust the path to flow as shown (C).

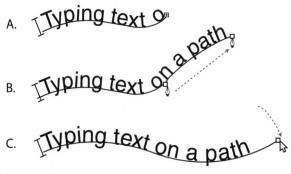

5. You have observed how text can be set on a path. You have modified both the text and path. Close the document without saving.

Be accurate when you click the Type tools onto paths. The cursor's crossbar should rest directly on the segment of the path. Otherwise, you might accidentally create a separate point-text block.

Note that once you have converted text to outlines, the text path will disappear and you will no longer be able to modify it. In other words, be sure you have made all the changes you want to the path before you create outlines.

Text and Paths Creativity

1. Open the document **Spiral Text.AI** in the **SF-Intro Illustrator** folder. There will be a spiral guide and a block of type.

2. In the Toolbox, click on the Default Colors icon. Select the Spiral tool in the Toolbox and draw a spiral to match the guide.

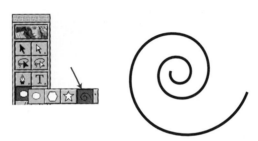

3. With the Selection tool, select the text block and choose Edit>Copy (Command/Control-C) to copy the selected text.

4. In the Toolbox, click-hold the Type tool icon and select the Path Type tool from the pop-out menu.

5. Click the tool cursor on the tip of the spiral. This will make the path flicker for a moment, taking away its fill and stroke attributes as it becomes a text path.

6. Choose Edit>Paste (Command/Control-V) to paste the text onto the path.

Vector paths can be turned into a text path by clicking any of the Type tools on the object.

7. The other way to combine text and paths is to place text inside a closed path with the Area Type tool.

8. Deselect the spiral text object. In the Toolbox, click on the Default Colors icon. Select the Polygon tool in the Toolbox. Click its cursor on the page. In the dialog box, set the Radius to 1.25 in., the Sides to 8. Click OK. The polygon will appear.

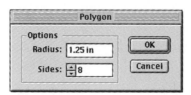

9. Edit>Copy the polygon, then choose Edit>Paste in Back to make a copy. Use Object>Hide Selection to hide this duplicate. The text is still copied into the Clip-board, available to be pasted. Select the Area Type tool in the Type tool pop-out menu.

10. Click the Type tool I-beam's crossbar anywhere on the path of the polygon. It will flicker as it changes to a text container, losing its black outline. Press Command/Control-V to paste the text into the polygon. Select the text block with the Selection tool.

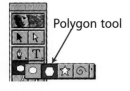

Polygon tool

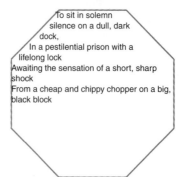

11. Press Command/Control-Shift-">" once. The size of the type will increase by 2 pts. from 8.5 pt. to 10.5 pt. To increase the leading, hold the Option/Alt-Shift key, and press the Down Arrow key twice. Open the Paragraph palette and click the Align Center button, or press Command/Control-Shift-C to align center the text.

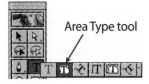

Area Type tool

12. The polygon will have lost its paint attributes when changed into a text container. To have a border for text, a copy of the path is needed before turning it into a text container. This is what you did with the original polygon.

13. Choose Object>Show All to bring the hidden painted polygon back into view.

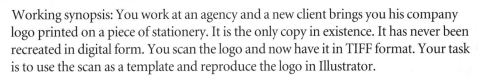

To sit in solemn
silence on a dull, dark
dock,
In a pestilential prison with a
lifelong lock
Awaiting the sensation of a short,
sharp shock
From a cheap and chippy
chopper on a big,
black block

14. The text will now have a polygon border. You have experimented with some of the creative aspects of combining text and paths.

15. Close the file without saving.

Fitting Type to a Template

Working synopsis: You work at an agency and a new client brings you his company logo printed on a piece of stationery. It is the only copy in existence. It has never been recreated in digital form. You scan the logo and now have it in TIFF format. Your task is to use the scan as a template and reproduce the logo in Illustrator.

1. Create a new document set for CMYK Color Mode; leave it untitled and the Artboard set for default. Choose View>Show Rulers to see the rulers.

2. Use File>Place and select the **Wow Logo.TIF** document in the **SF-Intro Illustrator** folder to place the file. In the Place dialog box, click the Template button so that the image will become a template in the document. Click Place and the template will appear on the page.

3. Marquee the Zoom tool around the template to bring it up to a larger view. When matching other artist's work, you will have to experiment with some features to try and match their settings. In most cases, it won't be exact, but to come very close is acceptable for this exercise.

4. Press Command/Control-T to access the Character palette. When no type is selected, the setting you make in the Type palette will determine the settings of the next text created. You recognize this typeface as ATC Plantation. The template type looks about 60 pt., so start to work from this setting. Set both the Tracking and Baseline Shift to zero. Set the Vertical and Horizontal scaling at 100%. Be sure that Alignment is set for Align Left in the Paragraph palette.

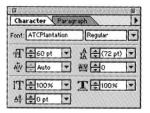

5. Select the Type tool and click its crossbar (located at the bottom of the I-beam cursor) at the base of the template's left "W." Note that when you increase any type size, it will enlarge upward from the baseline. The crossbar of the Type cursor designates where the baseline will be located.

Crossbar

If the Type Character palette shows only these options,

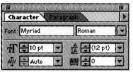

use its palette menu to select Show Options

and all options of the palette will be available

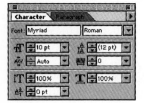

6. Type the word "WOW" and select the text block with the Selection tool to move the block so that the "O" is centered over the "O" in the template.

7. Because you used the Selection tool in step 6, the entire text block is active. Any changes will affect all letters. Hold the Command/Control-Shift keys, then continue pressing the greater-than (>) key that enlarges the type 2 points each time you press the key. Try to get your W's to match the ones in the template as closely as possible.

8. Highlight the "O" with the Type tool cursor. Enlarge it by pressing the shortcut keys as done above. The enlarging also raises the letter above the baseline. Hold the Option/Alt-Shift keys, and press the Up or Down Arrow keys to adjust the Baseline Shift. Continue fine-tuning the point size and baseline shift to fit the "O" as closely as possible to the template.

9. The letters will now almost fit those in the template, but there seems to be some horizontal scale needed. Select the text block with the Selection tool. Then, in the Character palette, set the Horizontal Scale to 125%. Too much? Set it to 110%.

10. The tracking needs to be tighter to bring the letters closer together. Hold the Option/ Alt key and press the Left Arrow key to close up the gaps between the letters. Some adjusting may be needed between two letters. If so, click the Type cursor between the two letters, and hold the same key, pressing the Left or Right Arrow keys to kern the spacing. The letters should just about fit right on the template. Deselect the text block.

11. The next stage will be to paint the letters. It is a two-color logo, blue and red, and the client will need stationery, ads, and specialty products printed with the two colors. This means that they will have to be spot colors.

12. In the Window menu, select Show Swatches to see the Swatches palette. Return to the Window menu and highlight Swatch Libraries to select the Pantone Coated library. This library of colors will appear as a palette separate from the Swatches palette. View both the palettes by Name View.

13. In the Pantone palette, scroll down to the Pantone 185 2x CVC color. Click on the name. You will see this color appear in the Swatches palette. In the Swatches palette, double-click on the Pantone 185 2x CVC name. The Swatch Options dialog box will appear. The Color Type field in the dialog box is set at "Spot Color." Make no changes. Click OK.

14. In the Pantone palette, scroll down to the Pantone 273 CVC color. Click on the name so that it will appear in the Swatches palette. You now have two spot colors to paint with. They are easier to access in the Swatches palette, rather than scrolling and scrolling through the Pantone library.

15. With the Type tool, highlight the three letters. Click the Pantone 273 CVC color swatch in the Swatches palette. Highlight the "O" and click the Pantone 185 2x CVC color swatch.

16. Select the text block with the Selection tool and choose Object>Hide Selection to hide it as we continue. With the Rectangle tool draw a rectangle to match the top rectangle in the template. Click on it with the Selection tool and drag downward, holding the Shift key to constrain. Match the rectangle to that of the bottom rectangle in the template. When in position, press the Option/Alt key, and release the mouse button to duplicate.

17. You are about to set text on the rectangles. Select both rectangles and Object>Lock them so that clicking the Type tool on the rectangle doesn't turn it into a text block.

18. In the Type Character palette, set the font to ATC Seagull, Regular. Set the font size to 12 pt., the Leading to Auto, and the Tracking to zero. Set the Vertical and Horizontal scales at 100%, and Baseline Shift at zero. In the a Paragraph palette, set the Alignment to Align Left.

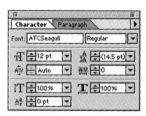

19. Select the Type tool and draw a text container that fits just inside the top rectangle. Hold the Command/Control key to turn the cursor into the Selection tool. Click this on the white of the page to deselect the text block. Release the key, and the cursor becomes the Type tool cursor again. Draw another text container on the bottom rectangle.

20. The alignment is set for Center. This means that to click back in the top area-text block, you must click the cursor in the center of the text block to make it active. Do this now. Type the words "CHILDREN'S TOYS". Deselect the top text block. Click the Type tool cursor into the center of the bottom text block and type "WITH A DIFFER-ENCE". Deselect the text block.

21. Unlock the rectangles by choosing Object>Unlock All. Select both rectangles and press Command/Control-3 to hide them to see the template rectangles.

22. The type in the template is evenly spaced from the left to right sides of the rectangle. Click the Type tool cursor into the top text block, and choose Edit>Select All. Go to the Type menu and select Fit Headline.

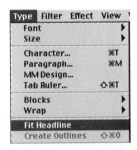

23. The selected text will automatically set the tracking to space the letters evenly in the text block. Highlight the letters in the bottom text block and apply Fit Headline to the text.

24. While pressing the Option/Alt key, along with the right and left Arrow keys, fine-tune the logo by highlighting the letters in question and manually tracking them. Further refinement can be done in the Character palette by typing in smaller or larger numbers in the Tracking field, then pressing Enter/Return to apply.

25. Choose Object>Show All to see the hidden objects. With the Selection tool, select both text blocks. Access the Eyedropper tool. A shortcut to setting a white Fill to objects is to click on the white of the page or Artboard. Do this now, and the selected type will become white.

Fit Headline will only work if the text is selected with the text cursor in an area-text block.

26. You have now recreated this logo, based on the template supplied by your fictional client.

CHILDREN'S TOYS

WOW

WITH A DIFFERENCE

27. Choose Edit>Select All to select everything, including all text blocks in the operation. From the Type menu select Create Outlines. The last and most important step to take is to turn all the text into outlines or paths. This is a necessary precaution to take when working with new printers or ad agencies where the issue of fonts may arise. If these fonts were left as text, the receiver would have to possess this particular font. When text is turned to outlines, the characters become vector paths and all font issues are eliminated.

28. Save As the file in Illustrator EPS format to your **Work in Progress** folder. Name it "Wow Logo.AI".

29. Close the document.

Chapter Summary

You have learned the typographic controls of the Illustrator program. From point size, leading, kerning, tracking, and vertical and horizontal scaling, you have created and formatted type that can be used in practical applications, such as business cards, brochures, flyers, and advertisements. You have learned to create both point- and area-text blocks, manipulate them, and look for overset type and correct it. You have also turned type into outlines that were modified for designing purposes and experienced how to match type to a supplied template.

Complete Project B: BearWear Business Cards

CHAPTER 7

PAINTING OBJECTS

CHAPTER OBJECTIVE:

To explore Illustrator's painting tools and techniques. Learn how to add color to paths. In Chapter 7, you will:

- Learn about fill and stroke and how to apply them to a path.
- Understand the difference in painting open paths and closed paths.
- Learn the many techniques for applying fills and strokes to path objects.
- Learn the features of the Swatches palette and its palette menu.
- Understand the Color palette, how to use it to create colors, and how to use its palette menu to change color mixes.
- Learn the difference between process (CYMK) colors and spot colors and how to use them.
- Learn how to import colors from color libraries.

PROJECTS TO BE COMPLETED:

- Art Deco House (A)
- BearWear Business Cards (B)
- Wine and Cheese Invitation (C)
- Walking the Dogs (D)
- Broadway Bound (E)
- Joker's Wild (F)
- BearWear Label (G)

Painting Objects

A wide variety of painting tools is available in Illustrator. In this section we're going to see how these painting tools can be used to add color to objects and shapes. Color dramatically expands the artist's ability to communicate visually, and effective use of color is a critical skill.

Fill and Stroke

Imagine sitting in front of a blank piece of paper with a box of colored markers. You select a blue marker and draw an oval. If you did the same thing in Illustrator, the blue line you drew would be the *stroke*. The width of the marker's point determines the thickness (weight) of the stroke. Pick up a yellow marker and color in the oval inside the lines. The yellow is the *fill* of the object.

The Fill
(filling the inside)

The Stroke
(outline or path)

Objects created in Illustrator — whether generated with the Pen, Pencil, Ellipse, Rectangle, or other tools — have stroke and fill attributes. Even if these attributes are set to none, and the object is essentially invisible, the fill and stroke exist. There are three ways to color an object. They are:

- **Stroke only.** The object has a colored outline (stroke) but has no fill color. The weight of a stroke is measured in points. A 6-pt. black stroke was applied to the examples here.

- **Fill and stroke.** Both the fill and stroke of an object color attributes. The sample below is filled with 30% black and has a 6-pt. black stroke.

- **Fill only.** Objects can be painted with a fill and no stroke (the stroke is set to None). The fill can be a solid color, a tint of a solid color, a gradient, or a pattern as shown in the three samples here. Type is a good example — they normally have a black fill and a stroke of none.

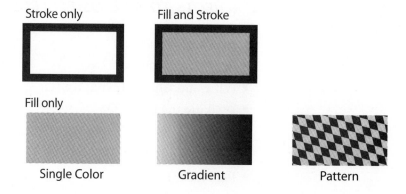

Stroke only   Fill and Stroke

Fill only

Single Color   Gradient   Pattern

Picas and points are the standard measurement system used throughout the graphics industry. Illustrator's default stroke weight is set in points. You can change the units of measure from points to picas in Edit>Preferences >Units & Undo. We recommend that you to stay with points at first. You can always change back and forth for job-specific requirements later.

Although you can apply a pattern to a stroke, there is a good chance that you will have problems printing the artwork. If you're thinking of using a pattern on a stroke, we suggest you experiment with some simple shapes and determine if the project will output correctly — before you decide to incorporate the process in an important drawing.

Open and Closed Paths

A path whose starting and ending points connect is a closed path. A path whose end points do not touch is an open path. You could think of a path (open or closed) as a fenced yard with or without the gate closed.

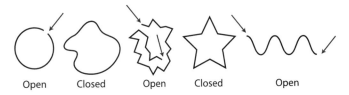

Open   Closed   Open   Closed   Open

Strokes

The stroke's *weight* is its thickness of a path. As the weight of the stroke increases, the preview of the path gets thicker. A stroke can be painted with any color, including "None" (or transparent) as well as with a pattern.

Strokes can be solid lines or dashed. For creating custom dashed lines, you can set the length of dashes and the size of the gaps between them. You can even alternate the size of the dashes and spaces. There is a variety of end caps you can choose for the dashes. You can also assign different appearances to how segments are joined.

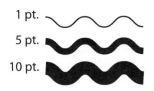
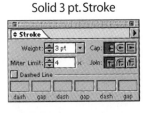
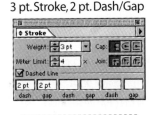

Getting Creative with Dashes and Gaps

The ability to create custom dashed lines — combined with a little imagination and creativity — offers almost unlimited design options.

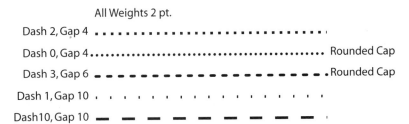

If you select a palette and only see the upper half, you can select Show Options from the palette menu to show the complete palette features.

Strokes thinner than about 1/4 point will not print properly on high-resolution output devices. Remember that when you reduce an object you might reduce its strokes below this minimum setting.

If you were to create several objects with no stroke or fill and print the page, you would find that it takes longer to output than an empty page. That's because the printer images everything on the page — even if you can't see it!

Stroke Palette

To set a stroke's attributes, open the Stroke palette by choosing Window>Show Stroke. In this palette you can set the attributes of any selected path, and press Enter/Return to apply the attributes. Here's a look at the options offered within the palette:

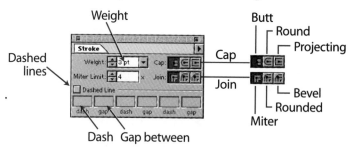

- **Weight.** This is the thickness of the stroke.

- **Dashed lines.** Check the box to create a dashed stroke.

- **Dash and Gap.** When Dashed Line is clicked, the value entered in the Dash box determines the length of the dash (in points). The value entered in the Gap box determines the length of the gap. If you only use the first two boxes, the dashes and gaps will remain constant for the length of the stroke.

- **Cap and Join.** Caps are the ends of open paths (Illustrator treats dashes as open paths). Join is the corner where two segments meet at a corner point.

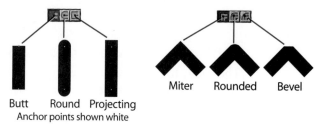

Butt   Round   Projecting
Anchor points shown white

Miter   Rounded   Bevel

Fill

Applying a color attribute to a path's interior is known as a fill, because you're "filling" the object. You can fill an object with a solid color, a gradient, or a pattern.

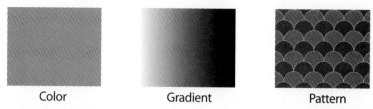

Color   Gradient   Pattern

A fill can be applied to both open and closed paths. Take care when applying a fill to an open path. If the path's stroke is set at None, or if it is the same color as the fill, it is easy to mistake the object for a closed path.

You can apply a gradient or color fill from the Toolbox by clicking on the Gradient button or the Color button below the Fill/Stroke boxes. The settings in the button you choose will be applied to the selected object.

Don't be fooled by objects with empty-looking white interiors. Are they filled with White or None? The quickest way to tell is to click the object and look at the Fill box on the bottom of the Toolbox.

Here are some samples of filling open and closed paths.

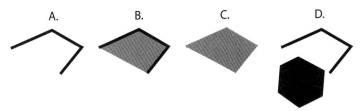

A. This path looks like a open path, with no fill. In fact, it is an open path with a white fill, which cannot be distinguished from the white background of the working page.

B. The same path is now filled with 30% black, making it apparent that it is an open path.

C. This is the same open path with the stroke set to match the 30% black fill. The difference between the fill and the stroke can't be seen.

D. All of the sides of the polygon should be equal, but they don't appear to be. This is because the open-path object from sample A has been positioned on top of the polygon, and its white fill is obscuring the polygon. To show the entire polygon without moving either object, change the fill of the open path to None.

Applying Fills and Strokes from the Toolbox

You can apply both fill and stroke attributes to a selected object directly from the Toolbox. If you set the attributes before you activate a drawing tool, they will be applied to the next object as you draw.

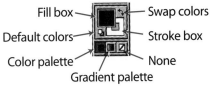

- **Fill and Stroke boxes.** One box will always be in front of the other, indicating which one is active. The active box determines whether changes to a selected object will affect its fill or stroke.

- **Swap colors.** Switches the paint attributes between the fill and stroke boxes. If you have a red fill and a blue stroke, clicking this button will set the fill to blue and the stroke to red.

- **Default colors.** Restores the default attributes, which are a solid white fill and a black stroke.

- **Color palette.** Clicking this icon brings up the Color palette for adjusting or creating colors. If an object painted with a gradient is selected, clicking this icon will remove the gradient and paint the object with the current color in the palette.

- **Gradient palette.** Brings up the Gradient palette to adjust or create gradients.

- **None.** A white fill is opaque. An object with the fill set to None is transparent. A stroke can also be set to None.

Swatches Palette

The Swatches palette is used for painting an object's fill and stroke with colors, gradients, or patterns. The default palette provides a limited range of colors, gradients, and patterns, but you can create any number of new attributes and store them in the Swatches palette. A swatch can be dragged onto any (unselected) object or clicked to apply the color to a selected object.

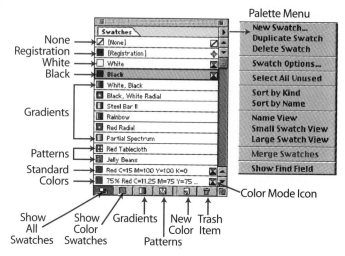

- **None.** No value (transparent).

- **Registration.** A color that appears on all printing plates for aligning separations.

- **White.** Paints object white.

- **Black.** Paints object 100% black.

- **Show All Swatches.** Shows all colors, gradients, and patterns available in the palette.

- **Show Color Swatches.** Shows all color swatches, including RGB, CMYK, HSB, and Spot color.

- **Gradients.** Shows all gradients in the Swatches palette.

- **Patterns.** Shows all patterns in the Swatches palette.

- **Palette Menu.** Provides options for managing the features in the Swatches palette.

- **Show Find Field.** Brings up a dialog box for finding a color by name. If you know the name of the color you want, you can find it by activating the Show Find field from the palette menu. This adds a search field to the palette, where you can enter the name of the color. In this example, pressing the "Y" key selected the first color beginning with that letter, in this case "Yellow." In the Find field, you can type the name or number of the color you want, and the selection will jump to those colors.

Double-clicking the Fill or Stroke boxes in the Toolbox is a quick way to access the Color Picker so you can create new colors or modify existing ones.

If you select Large Swatch View from the palette menu in the Swatch palette, pointing to a swatch causes the color name to appear in a stool tip. If you want to see the color names in Small Swatch View, select Show Tool Tips in Edit>Preferences>General.

Pressing the "D" key returns the stroke and fill to their default status — a white fill with a black stroke.

Painting Objects

It's often necessary to apply colors to existing objects. To avoid coloring the wrong Fill or Stroke attribute, it is important that the correct attribute box is active (on top of the other). In this example, the Fill box is active. It is in front of the Stroke box. Any colors now assigned will be applied to the fill of the selected object.

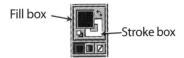

Fill box

Stroke box

When you're coloring objects, remember to double-check which attribute is active — the Fill or the Stroke — whether you're working in the Toolbox, the Color palette, or the Appearance palette.

Painting Selected and Unselected Objects

There are many methods available for painting objects. They fall into two categories: methods that require the object be selected, and methods that work on objects that aren't currently selected.

Painting Selected Objects

An object that you wish to paint can be selected with any of the selection tools. Text can be selected either by highlighting it with the Type tool or by clicking on its text block with a selection tool.

Clicking a Swatch

You can apply a color to the stoke or fill of a selected object by activating the Fill or Stroke box on the Toolbar then clicking on the desired color swatch in the Swatches palette. In the example below, the Fill box is active, so the color clicked in the palette fills the polygon.

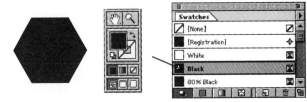

Dragging a Swatch

You can also apply a color to the stroke or fill of a selected object by dragging a swatch from the Swatches palette to the Fill or Stroke box in the Toolbox. The color here was dragged to the Stroke box, which in turn painted the stroke of the selected polygon.

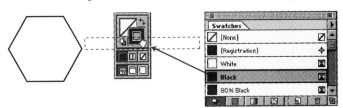

You can toggle between the Fill and Stroke boxes by pressing the "X" key. Adding the Shift key swaps colors between the two, which is the same as clicking the Swap Colors icon.

The ability to apply color attributes to objects that aren't selected saves time when you're changing a number of objects. You just drag and drop. Alternatively, you can Shift-Click a series of objects and apply your changes at one time.

The Paint Bucket is a pop-out tool accessed by clicking on the Eyedropper tool. You can also access the Paint Bucket tool, when the Eyedropper tool is active, by pressing the Option/Alt key.

Color Palette

The Fill and Stroke boxes on the Color palette also show the currently active colors. As you change the color attributes in the Fill or Stroke box, the selected object automatically takes on the new colors.

 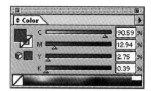

Eyedropper Tool

The Eyedropper tool is another quick way to grab color attributes from one object and apply them to another. To paint a selected object, click the Eyedropper tool on an object with the desired fill and stroke attributes. The selected object will assume those attributes. In the example below, the star was selected and circle clicked with the Eyedropper tool; the star automatically took on the same fill and stroke attributes.

Painting Unselected Objects

To paint an object that is not selected, you must touch it with a swatch or with the painting tool. You can use any one of three methods.

Drag a Color from the Swatches Palette

Simply dragging a swatch onto an object will apply that color. When you do, either its stroke or fill (depending on the active icon) will take on the color. In this example, the Fill box was active and a swatch dragged onto the unselected star.

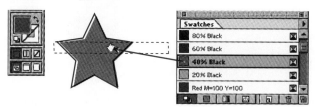

Dragging from the Color Palette

You can drag the swatch from the Color palette onto an unselected object. In this example, the Fill box was active, and the color was dragged from the Color palette to touch the star.

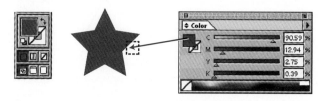

Painting an object with the Paint Bucket tool does not select the object. Also, keep in mind that painting with this tool by default changes both the fill and the stroke of the object.

Dragging from the Toolbox

Dragging the Fill or Stroke box from the Toolbox will apply the color to an unselected object. In this example, the black Stroke box was dragged onto the star, applying black to the stroke.

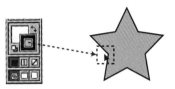

The Paint Bucket

The Paint Bucket applies both the active fill and stroke attributes. To paint an unselected object, select the Paint Bucket and click on the desired object. In this example, the circle was painted with a gray fill and a black stroke in one click.

Applying colors to objects

1. Open **Painting Objects.AI** from the **SF-Intro Illustrator** folder.

2. Make certain the View menu is set for Preview mode.

3. With the Selection tool, click on the zigzag path at the top of the page.

4. Choose Window>Show Swatches to access the Swatches palette. Click the Show Color Swatches icon at the bottom of this palette. In the Palette menu, select Name View. You will notice that the None, Registration, White, and Black color attributes are at the top of the list.

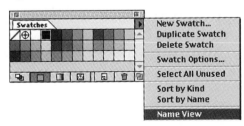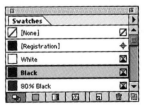

5. In the Toolbox, click on the Default Colors icon. The default attributes are a white fill with a black stroke.

Default Colors

6. The zigzag is an open path, so it is best to have it filled with None. Click on the Fill box, then click the None box.

7. The stroke of the zigzag path is black and you need to paint it a different color. Click on the Stroke box in the Toolbox to bring Stroke attributes to the front.

8. Click on any color in the Swatches palette. Observe how the path changes to this color. Click a few other colors and watch the stroke change. Choose any relatively dark color that you like.

9. Choose Window>Show Stroke. The top portion of the palette will be visible. Select Show Options to display all of the available features. The thickness of the stroke is determined by the value entered in the Weight field.

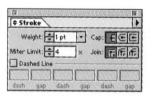

10. Highlight the Weight field and type "3". Click the Dashed Line checkbox and press Return/Enter. This will apply the 3-pt. stroke and the default 12-pt. dash to the path. Zoom in and look at the effect.

11. Set the Dash box to 2 pts. and the Gap box to 4 pts. Press Return/Enter.

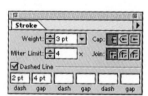

12. Zoom in and look at the stroke:

13. On the page click on the left rectangle with the Selection tool. Activate the Fill box in the Toolbox. Select a color of your choice from the Swatches palette and drag it over the Fill box. Observe how the rectangle's fill assumes this new color.

The part of the Paint Bucket tool that actually paints an object is the tip of the "spilling paint."

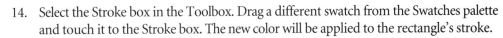

14. Select the Stroke box in the Toolbox. Drag a different swatch from the Swatches palette and touch it to the Stroke box. The new color will be applied to the rectangle's stroke.

15. With the Selection tool, click on the oval directly underneath the rectangle we just worked with. Select the Eyedropper tool click the star. Observe how the oval takes on the star's paint attributes.

16. With the Selection tool, click anywhere on the page to deselect all objects.

17. Click on the Fill box in the Toolbox. Drag a swatch from the Swatches palette onto the unselected star (use any color you like). Drag another color from the Swatches palette onto the oval, and another onto the rectangle. Observe how their fills became painted with these colors.

18. Click on the Stroke box in the Toolbox to make it active. Click on any color in the Swatches palette to assign it to the Stroke box.

19. Drag the Stroke box to touch the rectangle. Drag it again to touch the oval, and once more for the star.

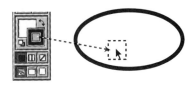

20. Click on the square above the star. Notice how its paint attributes are now shown in the Fill and Stroke boxes in the Toolbox.

21. Click on the Eyedropper tool in the Toolbox to select it. Hold down the Option/Alt key to toggle from the Eyedropper to the Paint Bucket tool. Click the Paint Bucket icon on the rectangle, the oval, and the star to paint them with the new attributes. Notice that both the fill and the stroke color attributes are taken on by all three clicked objects.

A tint is a percentage of a color less than 100%. For example, 100% black is solid black; 50% black is a medium gray; 10% black hardly noticeable as a light gray.

22. Holding the Shift key, use the Selection tool to select all four of the objects.

23. Click on the Swap Colors icon in the Toolbox. Notice how the fill and stroke attributes of the selected objects change.

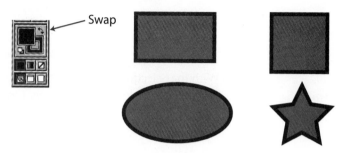

24. Select the Eyedropper tool and use it to click the zigzag object. The four selected objects will take on its dashed lines and no fill.

25. Close the file without saving.

Color Modes

Illustrator comes with a broad choice of colors from the swatch libraries. There may be times, however, when one of your projects require a color not available in these supplied collections. To have full control over color and tints, it's necessary to learn to use the Color palette. It is here that new colors are created, existing colors modified, colors applied to objects, or saved in the Swatches palette.

Tints of a process (CYMK) color can be created in either the Color palette or in the Swatch Options dialog box. To create a tint of a process color, press the Shift key while moving a color slider. The Shift key will make all of the sliders move together.

Illustrator provides five color modes to choose from in the Color palette menu: Grayscale, RGB, HSB, CMYK, and Web Safe RGB. Commercial color printing is a complex science where as much can go wrong as can go right. For this reason we recommend that you use only the Grayscale and CMYK modes for commercial printing. If the design is going to be used on the Web and not commercially printed, then use Web Safe RGB colors.

Using the Proper Color Mode

Whether a piece of art is created digitally or using traditional media, there are two types of color that may be used when the art is printed: Process (CYMK) color and Spot color. In this digital age, is benefits an artist to have at least a rudimentary understanding of what happens when a job is printed.

Although today's requirements often include preparing files for use on the Internet, the rules there are much simpler to understand, because the display that you're working on is essentially the same as someone else's display. When it comes to putting ink on paper, the number and complexity of the variables increases geometrically.

There are four primary color modes that you will be dealing with:

- **RGB**. Stands for Red, Green, and Blue and is the mode in which your color monitor operates. When you're preparing images for the Internet, this is the mode to work in. One of the most important considerations when coloring objects for the Web is that you use a palette that's "safe" when viewed on Windows, Macintosh, WebTV, Unix, or Linux computers. A web-safe palette of RGB colors is included as a color library. Use it whenever you're creating images that will be eventually used on the Internet or an interactive CD.

- **Grayscale/Black and White**. Think regular laser printers, high-speed copiers, and black and white newspapers. When you're working with just one ink — black or any other — you can achieve shades of gray. The proper mode to work in when you're going to use only one color of ink is Grayscale. There is a Grayscale library to use when you need to produce this type of image.

- **Spot color**. Spot colors are created by mixing inks together in a bucket at the printer — literally. Printers have a collection of colored inks, with names like Rubine Red, Reflex Blue, Violet, and Green. Companies like Pantone and TruMatch print books showing what various combinations of these solid inks will look like when printed on certain types of paper (one for coated, or shiny stock and one for uncoated, or dull stock). Spot colors are used for two primary purposes: adding a second color to a regular black print job (two-color printing), or adding a 5th color, such as that required for a corporate logo, to a four-color job. If you want to use a spot color, you must either pick it from a Pantone or TruMatch book, or from the supplied Pantone Coated and Uncoated libraries supplied on your Illustrator CD. You can't create custom spot colors because the printer won't know which inks to mix together to reproduce what you create on your monitor.

- **Four-color process, or CMYK printing**. Color printing is actually an illusion. When you look at *Sports Illustrated, New Yorker, Smithsonian Magazine,* or your local color newspaper, you might think there is a complete range of colors in the images, but there isn't. There are four colored inks — Cyan (C), Magenta (M), Yellow (Y), and Black (K). Using these four transparent (Process) inks, printers are able to simulate over 18,000 different colors — flesh tones, blue skies, green grasses, yellow bananas, or rich red velvet. But look closely and there are only four inks.

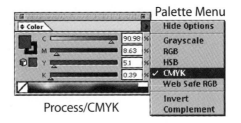

Process/CMYK

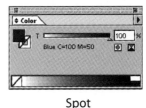

Spot

*Illustrator will allow you to create custom colors — but **don't** do it. Because spot colors are created by mixing together solid inks at the printer, you can't simply add some Cyan, or some "Forest Green" together to a yellow spot color and expect the printer to reproduce it. If you need a custom color, build it from Cyan, Magenta, Yellow, and Black inks — that way the printer will be able to create the color on press almost exactly as it appears on your computer.*

If you do make the mistake of generating a custom spot color, make sure that you tell the printer to convert it to process colors before they print the job — this will avoid extra printing plates from being generated at output time.

Color Palette

Process colors are shown with sliders representing the four CMYK (cyan, magenta, yellow, black) colors. You can use these sliders to build custom process colors or adjust existing ones. Depending on what mode you're creating in, the sliders display either RGB (for Web images), or Grayscale, Spot, or CMYK for printing. Here is what the Color palette and its features look like.

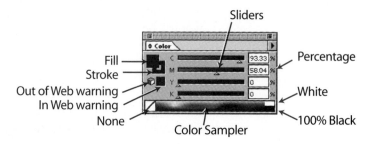

- **Sliders and Percentage.** The color sliders are moved to adjust the percentages of CMYK to achieve the desired color, or you can type a percentage into the box next to the sliders. If an object is selected while adjusting the sliders, the changes are immediately reflected in the object.

- **Fill, Stroke.** These are the same Fill and Stroke boxes of the Toolbox. In fact, colors can be applied to the fill and stroke of objects directly from this palette, which eliminates moving the mouse to the Toolbox. Keeping the Color palette close by the working area will save you a considerable amount of time.

- **None, White, Black.** These are the three most basic paint attributes used, and can be applied to selected objects by clicking on them in this palette.

- **Color Sampler.** This spectrum can be used to select a wide range of colors. When the cursor is clicked in any color region, the sliders show the percentages of the selected color mode. Selected objects will automatically take on the new color.

- **Out of Web Color Warning.** This icon lets you know that the chosen color does not meet the standards for colors used on the Web. Clicking on the icon will select the nearest Web-safe color.

- **In Web Color Warning.** This alert tells you when you are in the Web safe gamut, or range, for cross-platform color displayed on the Web.

- **Last Color Used.** This swatch appears when a Gradient is applied to a fill, and displays the last color you used. Clicking this swatch will reinstate the color.

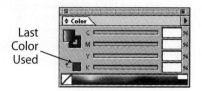

Spot Colors

The Color palette displays a Spot Color bar when a Spot color is the selected from the Swatches palette. Notice that the CMYK sliders are no longer present. All that can be modified in this palette is the tint, or percentage, of the single color. You can select a tint either by moving the slider, or typing in the desired percentage in the field to the right of the slider. Changing the tint is the only option you have for customizing the appearance of a spot color, but you can use as many tints as you like. Using shades or tints of one color adds interest and variety to a one- or two-color illustration.

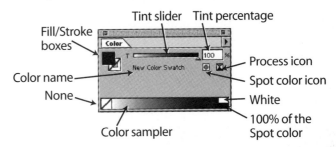

- **Fill/Stroke.** These act the same as the Fill and Stroke boxes in the Toolbox.

- **Color name.** The name of the Spot color is shown here.

- **None, White, Black.** These are the three most basic paint attributes used, and can be applied to selected objects by clicking on them.

- **Color Sampler.** This is a 0-100% range of the selected color. Clicking in this tonal range changes both the slider and the percentage number.

- **Tint slider, percentage.** If a known percentage is required, it can be achieved by using the slider or typing the percentage number into the box.

- **Process, Spot icons.** These icons identify the type of color.

Color Palette Menu

The Color palette menu offers several color models. Do not bother using the Color palette's menu to select RGB if the document is set for CMYK (and vice versa). Even though the alternate color model can be selected, it will not take effect.

- **Grayscale.** These are the standard 256 levels of gray between black and white.

- **RGB.** Red, Green, and Blue are common to computer monitors and televisions.

- **HSB.** This is Hue, Saturation, Brightness, based on the perception of color.

- **CMYK.** Cyan, Magenta, Yellow, and Black are the colors that make up Process color printing.

A perfect example of using a spot color in a four-color job is for a corporate logo. If you look at companies like Canon, IBM, Compaq, or any large firm, they're logo is normally a solid colored ink — not a process color "build." This calls for the use of a fifth ink, a spot color ink created specifically for that logo. It's added as a fifth plate in a four-color job.

Another reason that many companies require spot colors for their logos is because sometimes these ink colors cannot be perfectly duplicated using four-color process. They're either too dark or too light. That's because four-color process has a very limited "gamut" or range of available colors.

Make certain you confirm with your print house or service provider what spot color libraries you can use. It is pointless to use TruMatch colors, for example if they use only Pantone inks.

- **Web Safe RGB.** These are the 216 varied colors that are standard with the Web.

- **Invert.** Creates an inverse, or color "negative" of the color in the active Fill or Stroke box.

- **Complement.** Creates the color complement (as it would be found on a color wheel) of the color in the active Fill or Stroke box.

Using the Swatches Palette

Illustrator provides the Swatches palette primarily for storing and managing colors. This is the main palette for applying colors to objects. There are several sections holding Process/Spot colors, Gradients, and Patterns. These sections may be view individually, or from the Show All Swatches section. The Swatches palette is the only place to store colors, gradients and patterns that have been imported or custom-made. When you create new color swatches, they reside in the Swatches palette.

Creating New Color Swatches

A new color that can be created in the Color palette can also be created in the New Swatches options to be saved in the Swatches palette, there are two ways to create it: using either the Color palette or the New Swatch dialog box accessed in the Swatches palette menu.

Color Palette

You can use the sliders in the Color palette to create a color. When you have the desired color, you can then drag it to the Swatches palette, where it can be saved and accessed in the future. By default a new process (CMYK) color swatch will appear, named New Color Swatch until you assign a specific name to it. To do this, double click on the new swatch and enter the name in the dialog box that appears.

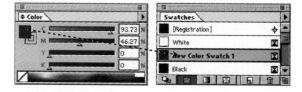

Swatches Palette

The Swatches palette provides two ways to create a new color swatch: by clicking the New Swatch icon (A) at the bottom of the palette, or by using the palette menu's New Swatch option (B). Creating a new color with either of these two methods locates the New Color Swatch at the bottom of the color list, and you may have to scroll down the list to see it.

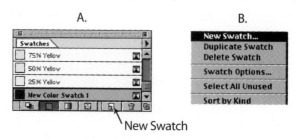

New Swatch

When the New Swatch method is used to create a custom color, the color sliders in the Swatch Options dialog box reflect whatever color is currently selected in the Swatches palette.

Dragging a new color from the Color palette puts the color in the Swatches palette positioned where you dragged it. Using either the New Swatch icon or palette menu option creates the new color at the very bottom of the color list (when viewed by Name View). Access the palette menu's Sort by Name feature to put the colors in alphabetical order.

Swatch Options

Regardless of how a new process (CYMK) color swatch is created, it may need modifications, such as renaming it, setting it as a Global color, or making adjustments to its hue using the CMYK color sliders. All of these modifications can be done in the Swatch Options dialog box, which appears when you double-click the new swatch in the Swatches palette. As the sliders are moved, the Preview button in the dialog box can be selected to see the color change on a selected object in a document and in the Preview window.

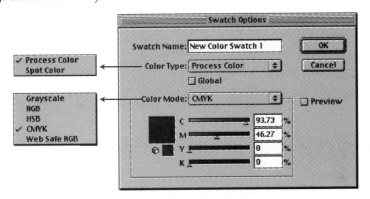

- **Name.** Color names are "case sensitive," meaning that upper and lower case versions of the same characters have different values. The names "Spot Remover" and "spot remover" are two different colors. Be careful.

- **Color Type.** Offers the choice of the color being a Process Color or Spot Color. Be careful, if you assign process color status to a spot color it will no longer be a spot color. By the same token, even though Illustrator allows you to call a process color a spot color, it will remain process.

- **Global.** When a color is global, any changes made to the original color will affect all tints and objects painted with this color. Spot colors are automatically global.

- **Color Mode.** Allows the choice of the various color modes available.

- **Preview.** When this box is selected, the adjusted color appears in the Swatches palette, the Color palette, and in any selected objects in the document.

- **Swatch.** Shows the color as the sliders are moved when Preview is clicked.

The Color Icons

In one document, there can be only one color mode; Grayscale, two-color, three color, CMYK, or RGB. When the Swatches palette is set for Name View these modes are displayed with icons to the right of the color name.

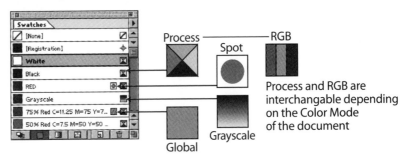

The only real use for a custom spot color is when you're creating a plate for varnish or a die-cut shape. In this case there isn't a concern that the color can't be recreated using mixes of solid inks — there isn't any color in a varnish or a die — only shape. Remember that the shape must be a solid color for either use.

Assigning a color to Global status affects the color's behavior within a document, but in no way does it affect how the color will be printed.

- **Process (CMYK) or RGB.** Depending on the color mode of the document, this will be either the Process icon or the RGB icon.

- **Spot Color.** The Spot color icon is represented by the circular "spot" on the square.

- **Grayscale.** This color model provides black and tints of black. Grayscale is frequently used for creating black-and-white documents, or for converting color documents to black and white.

- **Global.** This icon indicates whether a color has been assigned Global status.

Spot Colors and Tints

Although Illustrator will allow you to create new Spot colors, we strongly recommend that when you need to use a spot color ink, you either select it from the Pantone or TruMatch books or from the Pantone library that comes with Illustrator. As we've already stated, creating a custom spot ink will only result in frustration, because the printer will have no idea how to create the color you envisioned. The color can be converted to process color during output, but there's an excellent chance that the colors will change when this occurs.

When Window>Swatches Libraries is accessed, and a library imported, its palette will appear with all of the available colors. The square icon with a circle inside it (when viewed by Name View) indicates that it is a spot color. When you single-click on a spot color in one of the imported libraries, this color will automatically be added to the Swatches palette for that document, and the Color palette will automatically show the spot color slider.

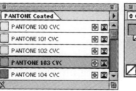 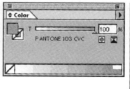 

Imported Libary   Color Palette   Swatches Palette

When you move the slider in the Color palette, different tints of the color will appear in the palette's active Fill or Stroke box. You can save this tint for future use in your document by dragging and dropping it in the Swatches palette. The new swatch will automatically be named with its preset Pantone identification number plus the percentage tint of the color.

Creating and Applying Custom Colors

1. From the **Work in Progress** folder, open the **Painting Objects.AI** document.

2. Use the Window menu to access the Color and the Swatches palettes. Position them near each other. In the Color palette, view the CMYK sliders (accessed from the palette menu). View the Swatches palette by Name View.

3. In the Color palette, click the Fill box to make it active. Use the sliders to set it to 100% Cyan. Drag the Fill swatch to the Swatches palette.

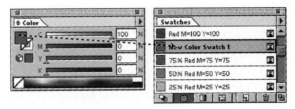

4. Double-click the New Color Swatch in the Swatches palette.

5. In the Swatches Options dialog box, name the color "Ocean Blue." Set it to be a Global Process color. Make no other changes. Click OK.

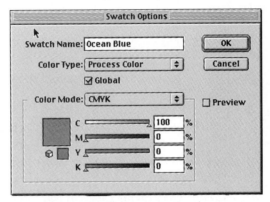

6. The new colors will change in the Swatches palette. The two icons to the right of the name indicate that it is a global color built from Process (CMYK) inks.

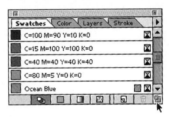

7. Create the rest of the custom colors listed below using the three methods for creating colors (Color palette, New Swatch icon in the Swatch palette, and palette menu option). Make certain when you use the Color palette that you set the colors for CMYK from the palette menu. When you are through creating the colors, use the palette menu to sort by name.

Beach Sand C: 0, M: 25, Y: 50, K: 0

Sunshine C: 0, M: 0, Y: 100, K: 0

Palm Fronds C: 100, M: 0, Y: 100, K: 0

Palm Trunk C: 50, M: 85, Y: 100, K: 0

When selecting a range of tints of a spot color, we recommend that you limit yourself to a five-step range of tints: 20%, 40%, 60%, 80% and 100%. This range covers most of what eye can perceive and makes it less complicated to apply the tints to painted objects.

8. Choose View>Preview. In the Toolbox activate the Fill box. From the Swatches palette, drag the Ocean Blue swatch over to touch the ocean background path, filling it with this color. Select the ocean background path and change its stroke to None. Deselect this path. Click the Fill box to make it active again.

9. The waves will need to contrast with the ocean, so the ocean color needs to be tinted. Click on the ocean path. In the Color palette the Ocean Blue custom color will appear. Move the eyedropper tool about midway in the tint area until the ocean is lighter.

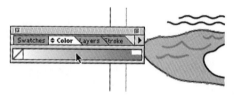

10. Click on the Deserted Isle Beach to select it. Activate the Fill box. In the Swatches palette, click on the Beach Sand color.

Deserted Isle Beach

11. Deselect the beach. In the Swatches palette, click on the Palm Frond color so the Fill box is set with this color. Select the Eyedropper tool and hold the Option/Alt key to change it to the Paint Bucket. Click the Paint Bucket on the frond of the palm tree to turn it green. Change the stroke of the frond to None.

Imported swatch libraries are locked so that the original file cannot be accidentally modified.

✓ **Default_CMYK**
Default_RGB
Diccolor
Earthtones_1
FOCOLTONE
Harmonies_1
HKS E
HKS K
HKS N
HKS Z
PANTONE Coated
PANTONE Process
PANTONE Uncoated
Pastels
System (Macintosh)
System (Windows)
Toyo
Trumatch
VisiBone2
Web
Other Library...

12. Click the Fill box in the Toolbox to make it active again. Click on the palm trunk with the Selection tool. From the Swatches palette, drag the Palm Trunk swatch over to touch the Fill box. Change the stroke of the frond to None.

13. Deselect the trunk. With the Selection tool, pressing the Shift key, select all the trunk bands. With the Eyedropper tool, click on the palm frond to paint the trunk bands with this same paint attribute.

14. Deselect the trunk bands. In the Toolbox, set the Fill box for None, and click the Stroke box to make it active. Show the Stroke palette from the Window menu and set the weight to 3 pt. with rounded caps.

15. In the Swatches palette, click on the Ocean Blue color. Change the Eyedropper tool in the Toolbox to the Paint Bucket tool, then click it on the waves that are above the background ocean.

16. Click the Swap Color icon in the Toolbox to switch the stroke color over to the Fill box. Use the Paint Bucket tool to click on the waves that are within the background ocean.

17. Click the Fill box in the Toolbox to make it active. From the Swatches palette, drag the Sunshine color to touch the sun, to fill it with this color. Select the sun object and change its stroke to None.

18. Use the Selection tool (while pressing the Shift key) to select the five sun rays above the sun. With the Eyedropper tool, click on the sun to paint the rays yellow. Deselect all of the objects.

19. You have succeeded in creating custom colors and have used several painting techniques to color the various components of the illustration.

20. Save your changes to the document and close.

Importing from Swatch Libraries and Custom Colors

Illustrator provides collections of thousands of predefined colors supplied by leading companies in the graphics industry. These swatch collections are listed by product name in Window>Swatch Libraries. In addition to the pre-made color libraries, you can create your own customized gradients, colors, and patterns, which can be imported from other documents using Windows>Swatch Libraries>Other Library.

Swatch Libraries

When selected from Windows>Swatch Libraries, a library of color swatches will appear as a palette on your desktop. Any color you select can be imported into a document's Swatch palette by dragging it to the palette. Clicking on a spot color will import it to the Swatches palette for that document, though other colors and paint attributes must be dragged to the palette. To keep your screen from becoming too cluttered, you can drag the name tabs of active libraries into one palette to group them together, but keep the document's Swatches palette by itself.

Any libraries opened for one document will remain active in all other documents opened or created until you quit Illustrator. The next time you launch Illustrator, you will have to open these libraries again.

Customized Colors

Perhaps you have a saved Illustrator document with some paint attributes — gradients, colors, or patterns — you want to use in your current document. As paint attributes are created or selected for a document, they can be stored in that document's Swatches palette. Illustrator allows you to import customized paint attributes from one document to another using Window>Swatch Libraries>Other Library. This eliminates the tedious process of having to rebuild custom colors, gradients, or patterns that you intend to use from one document to the next.

When Other Library is selected from the Swatch Libraries menu, a dialog box appears with the file names of previously saved Illustrator documents. Opening a file that contains the desired customized paint attributes brings up a the Swatch palette from the saved document. This palette can be identified on your work page by its tab, which has the same name as the document from which it was selected.

Importing from Color Libraries

The CMYK makeup of an imported color can be viewed in the Color palette, changing the palette's color mode to CMYK.

1. Create a new document set for CMYK Color Mode, leave it untitled and the Artboard set for default. Choose Window>Show Swatches to show the Swatches palette in the document.

2. Go to the Window menu and choose Swatch Libraries>Pantone Coated.

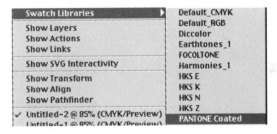

3. The colors will appear in their own named palette, viewed by small swatches. In its palette menu, view the colors by Name View. The list of names will appear. Scroll through the colors to see all that are available.

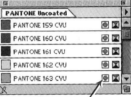

Triangle with spot indicates a Spot Color

Circle in square indicates a Spot Color

4. Click any one of the colors in the Pantone Uncoated palette. Click again on another color in this palette. In the Swatches palette, scroll down to the bottom of the list and you see that these colors are now present. You have imported these colors into the Swatches palette of the active document only. When you quit Illustrator, then launch it again, these imported colors will not be in the Swatches palette. They will only be in the previously saved document you imported the colors into. Also, when you open this imported colors document, the Pantone palette will not be present. It will have to be accessed again if you want to import additional colors.

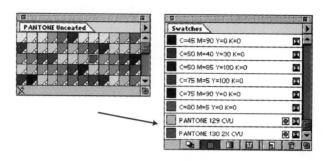

5. Create a new CMYK document from the File menu. When the new document opens, notice that the two palettes opened from the Swatch Libraries remain active. These libraries will be available until they are either put away, or Illustrator is quit.

6. Go to the Window menu and select Swatch Libraries>Other Library. Use its dialog box to go to the **Work in Progress** folder. Click on **Painting Objects.AI** and press Open.

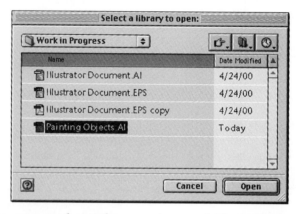

If you want Styles to be available in all new documents, create or paste the styled object to the appropriate Startup file found in the Plug-ins folder.

7. There will be a pause as the attributes are imported. The **Painting Objects.AI** Swatches palette will then appear. Use the palette's menu to view by Name View. The pencil icon with the slash through it in the lower left denotes that all the colors, gradients, patterns are locked, and cannot be modified for saving into this palette.

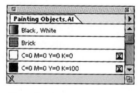

8. Scroll down to a color created in the last exercise and drag it to the Swatches palette. This paint attribute has now been imported to the new document's Swatches palette.

9. You have observed and used ways to import paint attributes from various swatch libraries into an Illustrator document. Close the document without saving.

Styles, Effects, and Appearances

The Styles feature in Illustrator allows you to create and save customized fills and strokes. There are three parts to this feature.

- **Styles palette.** Special effects (or *styles*) applied to fills and strokes are created here and stored for later use.

- **Effect menu.** Provides a vast number of alterations you can apply to fills and strokes to create new styles. (Note that the Filter and Effect menus have many of the same options for creating visual effects. Illustrator's filters serve a different purpose from the effects, and the two features are *not* interchangeable. We will discuss the Filter menu in a later chapter.)

- **Appearance palette.** Records and stores a detailed list of the steps you took to create a special effect for fills and strokes. Once an effect has been applied to a fill or stroke, it can be fine-tuned from dialog boxes accessed in the Appearance palette.

The subject of the styles, effects, and appearance features is so complex that we can only scratch the surface in this course. We will discuss and illustrate the collaboration of these three features.

Styles Palette and Style Libraries

The Styles palette, accessed from Window>Show Styles, is used to create and store special effects. Illustrator provides a number of default styles in the palette in addition to the collections of graphic effects in Window>Style Libraries.

Styles palette

Every style you want to create, access, alter, or apply begins and ends in the Styles palette.

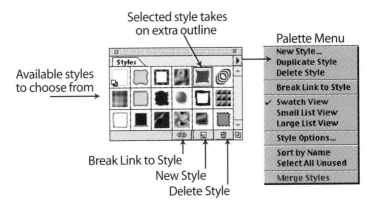

- **Available Styles.** Each style is represented by a swatch (in Swatch View) so you can see the special effect it will create when applied to an object. There are two other views in the palette menu, but Swatch View shows the image best.

- **Selected Style.** A double border around a swatch indicates that this is the currently active style.

- **Break Link to Style.** This option will break the connection between an object in a document and a style so that if the style is edited, the object will remain the way it looked when it was first painted.

The spot colors available in the Pantone Coated and the Pantone Uncoated swatch libraries are very similar, however, they are not interchangeable. Which type of ink to use is a technical issue that should be settled with your client and the printer before you begin the project.

- **New Style.** This button will turn the attributes of a selected object into a style and add it to the Styles palette.

- **Delete Style.** A selected style can be deleted by clicking this button, though a warning will appear asking if you really want to delete. Dragging the style swatch directly to the Trash icon will delete it without the warning.

- **Palette Menu.** This menu offers several options for creating, duplicating, deleting, viewing, sorting, and merging styles.

Styles Libraries

The style libraries accessed from Window>Style Libraries is a good starting place to find additional ready-made styles or to get ideas for creating your own. Notice that each library is offered in two color modes, CMYK and RGB. You can alter any of the styles in these libraries using features from the Effect menu and the Appearance palette, but you can only store your changes using the New Style feature from the Styles palette menu.

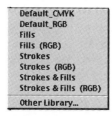 

Styles Unlimited

You can apply a style to any path, open or closed, simply by clicking the desired swatch in the Styles palette while the path is selected. Here are some samples of the default styles in the palette that appear to be limited to closed paths. From the simple beginnings of a plain object, there are few, if any, limits on the images you can create using Illustrator's Styles feature. Keep in mind that styles can be applied to open as well as closed paths.

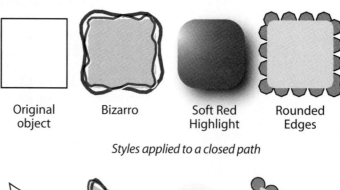

| Original object | Bizarro | Soft Red Highlight | Rounded Edges |

Styles applied to a closed path

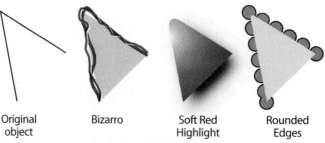

| Original object | Bizarro | Soft Red Highlight | Rounded Edges |

Styles applied to an open path

Regardless of how many styles you create while Illustrator is running, they will not be in other documents the next time Illustrator is launched. The only way to have any colors, gradients, patterns or styles present in all open Illustrator documents is to create them in the Adobe Illustrator Startup (your choice, CMYK or RGB) file found in the Plug-ins folder where the Illustrator application is located.

Creating a Style

A new style is created by first selecting an open or closed path in a document. The path is then painted with fill and stroke attributes and any desired effects. To convert the object's attributes to a new style, the object is either dragged into the Styles palette or, with the object selected, the New Style button is clicked at the bottom of the palette. Now the new style can be applied to any object.

In this example, a square was drawn (A). It was painted with a gold fill, then Effect> Distort>Zig Zag was applied (B). Effect>Path>Offset Path was applied to the selected object along with Effect>Stylize>Drop Shadow (C). The object was then dragged into the Styles palette (D). This style can now be applied to any object in this document, by selecting the object and clicking on the style swatch in the palette.

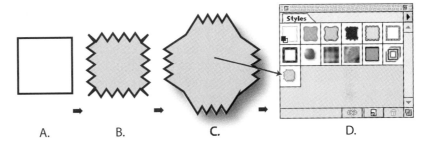

A.   B.   C.   D.

Creating Basic Styles

A style does not have to be as elaborate as the ones we've discussed so far. Any frequently used fill attributes (color, gradient, pattern) and stroke attributes (color, stroke weight, and dashes) can be added to the Styles palette. Keep in mind that new styles created in one document are not automatically available in other documents, but they can be imported from other documents in the same way customized swatches are imported.

Editing Styles

There are two locations where you can edit an existing style: in the document, by making changes to an object, or by making changes directly in the Appearance palette. There are different ways to save and apply an edited style depending on what you are trying to accomplish.

Creating a New Style from an Existing Style

Once a style has been applied to a number of objects in a document, it may be desirable to change the appearance of one or two of the objects, but not all of them. You can edit the object any way you desire and leave it at that, or drag the changes to the Styles palette as a new style, then select other objects and apply the new style. Now you have objects painted in two different styles.

Replacing an Existing Style with a New Style

Suppose there are a number of objects with the same style that are scattered throughout a document and they need to be altered in the same way. Making these alterations by selecting each object and applying an edited style is not practical. In this case you can make desired changes to one of the objects in the document, then select Replace from the palette menu in the Appearance palette. You will see the old style swatch in the Styles menu is replaced with the new style swatch. At the same time, all of the objects painted in the original style will automatically take on the attributes of the replacement style.

Keep the Styles palette set for Swatch View, which shows you a small preview of each style.

It is not obvious at first, but the Styles palette has a few different default styles depending on whether the document is set for CMYK or RGB.

Creating a New Style and Keeping the Old Style

Now let's suppose you want to apply a replacement style to all of the objects in a document, but you don't want to lose the original style. In this case, you can select the original style swatch, then go to the Styles palette menu and select Duplicate Style. A duplicate swatch will appear, but this is not the one you want to edit. Make sure the original swatch is selected, then you can edit whatever elements you desire. Going to the Appearance palette menu and selecting Replace will apply the edited style.

Tips on Styles

We have barely scratched the surface of creating and using styles. Here are some suggestions to keep in mind as you explore this feature of Illustrator.

- Styles can be as simple or elaborate as suits your needs.

- Whenever a style is applied to an object, the fill and stroke attributes will be activated in the Toolbox. When the style is no longer selected, these fill and stroke attributes (but *not* the effects) will be applied to any new objects created until the attributes are changed in the Toolbox or another style is selected.

- A single style can take on different appearances, depending on the shape of the path it is applied to.

- Keep in mind that to apply changes to every object with the same style applied, the original style must be replaced in the Appearances palette menu.

- Break Link to Style will break the global connection between an object and its assigned style. If the style is then edited and replaced, the object will remain the way it looked when the original style was applied.

- Only one object at a time may be dragged to the Styles palette and turned into a style. If you try to drag more than one object at a time to the palette, all of them will be rejected.

Effect Menu

The Effect menu only applies modifications to the *appearance* of a path, not the path itself. When you see the menu, you will note that it offers two sets of options. The first set of options contain effects that can be applied only to vector paths, and the second set can be applied only to raster images.

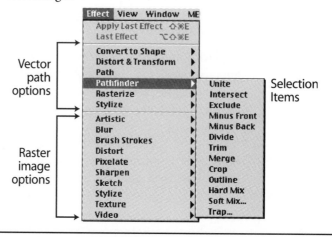

Effects for Vector Paths

Here are samples of some of these effects as they appear on vector paths. Keep in mind that the original path is still present and unaltered. These visual effects are applied only to the object's appearance.

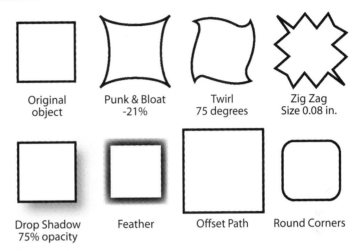

Original object   Punk & Bloat -21%   Twirl 75 degrees   Zig Zag Size 0.08 in.

Drop Shadow 75% opacity   Feather   Offset Path   Round Corners

Effects for Raster Images

There are various way to have a raster image in an Illustrator document, but the two primary methods are either by placing (importing) the image from an external source, or by selecting vector paths and rasterizing them (from the Object menu). Here are samples of how some of the raster effects work on raster images.

Original Raster Object   Paint Daubs   Plastic Wrap   Spatter

Glass   Graphic Pen   Glowing Edges   Patchwork

Appearance Palette

The Appearance palette is a powerful feature in Illustrator that allows you to view and fine-tune the appearance of any object or style. When you select an object or style, it automatically becomes active in the Appearance palette, where you see the paint attributes of the fill and stroke, along with a list of the effects that were applied to create its appearance.

Within the Appearance palette you can modify any effect in the list. Double-clicking on an effect brings up its dialog box that allows you to customize the attributes you want for that effect. Double-clicking on either the Fill or the Stroke item in the Appearance palette will activate only the Color palette. The other palettes, such as Swatches or Stroke, that affect the fill and stroke cannot be accessed this way.

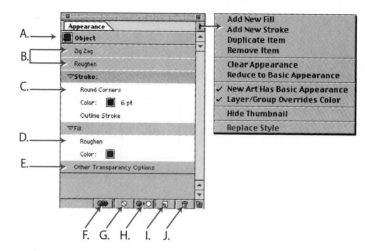

A. **Appearance swatch.** The swatch is too small to provide more than a clue about the item's appearance, but if you've selected a style, its name will appear here.

B. **List of applied effects.** This list names the effects you applied to the whole object and the order in which you applied them. Double-clicking on an effect brings up a dialog box where the effect can be fine-tuned.

C. **Stroke section.** This section shows the color swatch of the painted stroke, the stroke's weight, and lists the effects that have been applied to the stroke.

D. **Fill section.** This section shows a swatch of the painted fill, and lists the effects that have been applied to it.

E. **Transparency option.** Shows the transparency settings of the appearance.

F. **Appearance option.** This button toggles between the two options that determine how new objects will appear when drawn. These are the options:

New Art has **Basic Appearance.** (Button is selected) When this icon is selected, any new objects drawn will have only the standard fill and stroke paint attributes applied and will not have the previous used effect applied.

New Art Maintains Appearance. (Button unselected) New objects will have the fill and stroke (plus additional strokes, if any) attributes of the last painting or style used.

G. **Clear Appearance.** Removes all paint attributes and applied effects from the selected object. They will both be reduced to None.

H. **Reduce to Basic Appearance.** Removes the effects from the object, but keeps the paint attributes. Also removes all extra fills and strokes, leaving one of each.

I. **Duplicate Selected Item.** This option duplicates an item selected in the palette. For example, a stroke color and weight might need to be duplicated and other stroke attributes applied to it.

J. **Delete Selected Item.** Items may be dragged to this icon and deleted without a warning appearing on the screen.

Tips on the Appearance Palette

Using the Appearance palette will be second nature before long. Below are some pointers to keep in mind as you become accustomed to this feature.

- Only objects that have been applied from the Effect menu will show these effects in the Appearance palette.

- Filters and other operations outside the Effect menu will not show up in the Appearance palette.

- The Appearance palette reflects all the attributes of selected single objects only. If more than one object is selected, for example, objects in a group, the Appearance palette merely states "Object: Mixed Appearances."

- If an effect is dragged from one item to another in the palette, with the Option/ Alt key pressed, the effect will be duplicated and be immediately applied to the receiving item.

- If an object does not have an effect or style applied to it, only the object's fill and stroke attributes will be listed in the Appearance palette.

- When you click on the Fill or the Stroke item in the Appearance palette, the corresponding boxes in the Toolbox and the Color palette are activated.

- The Stroke and Fill items in the Appearance palette are movable. For instance, a Stroke item residing at the bottom of the Appearance palette can be dragged up and relocated at the top of the Appearance list, the corresponding attribute in the selected object's appearance will be moved to be in front of other attributes.

Working with Styles and Effects

1. Create a new Untitled document, setting the Color Mode to RGB, and leaving the Artboard set for default. Make sure you are in Preview mode.

2. From the Window menu, select Show Styles to see the Styles palette.

3. Using the Rectangle tool, draw a 2-in. square in the top center of the page.

4. Click the Selection tool in the Toolbox, leaving the square selected.

5. One at a time, click on the various Styles in the palette and observe how the square's appearance changes with each click.

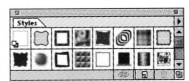

Top row: Default, Blizzard, Black Red Dashes, Fantasmic, Purple Puddle, Patriotic Ribbon, Rainbow Plaid, Rounded Edges, Scribbly. Bottom row: Soft Red Highlight, Rustic Pen, Textured Rainbow, Sketchy, Cast Shadow, Rough Steel, Froth, Endorific, Bristly.

6. Leave the square painted with one of the styles. This is because an effect changes the appearance of the path but not the path itself. Go to Outline view and observe how the square path has not been altered. Return to Preview mode.

7. From the Window menu, select Show Appearance. This will bring up the Appearance palette. Observe how the makeup of the selected style is shown in this palette. Click on several other styles in the Styles palette and note how their components are listed in the Appearance palette.

8. In the Appearance palette, click the Clear Appearance button in the palette menu. Click on Windows>Show Swatches. Select Name View then Sort by Name from the palette menu.

9. Fill the square with Bright Blue, and set the stroke with a 3-pt. weight and apply the Blue color. Go to the Effect menu and select Distort & Transform>Punk & Bloat. In the dialog box, set the Punk at 45, then click OK to apply.

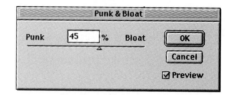

10. The square will take on the Punk & Bloat appearance as set. Look at the Appearance palette and note how Punk & Bloat has appeared in the list.

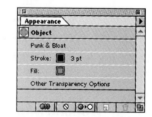

11. Go to the Effect menu and select Distort & Transform>Twirl. In the Twirl dialog box, set the Angle for 80, and click OK. The appearance of the bloated object will now twirl.

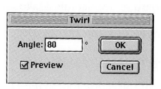

12. Observe how the Twirl effect has been listed in the Appearance palette. Keep in mind that when these effects appear above the Stroke and Fill sections, this means that they have been applied to both the fill and the stroke. If an effect is applied to only the stroke or fill, it will appear in the corresponding section.

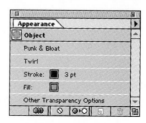

13. Up until now, nothing has been selected in the Appearance palette. If neither the Stroke nor Fill section is selected, they will both be altered when effects are applied. Clicking on either one will isolate the application of the effect. Click on the Stroke section in the Appearance palette. Choose the Effect>Stylize>Feather option. In the next dialog box make no changes, just click OK. The feathering will be applied. Look at the Appearance palette and note that the Feather effect appears only in the Stroke section.

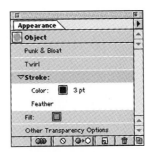

14. We will now apply an effect to the fill. Click on the Fill section in the Appearance palette. In the Effect menu, choose Texture>Patchwork. Make no changes in the dialog box, and click OK. The patchwork grid will be applied to the fill of the selected object. Observe how the name Patchwork appears only in the Fill section of the Appearance palette.

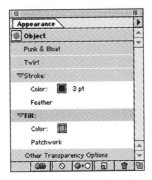 

15. The effect names in the Appearance palette are not just for informing you what has been applied. If you double-click on any one of these names, the appropriate dialog box will appear, allowing you to make modifications.

16. Double-click on the Twirl item in the Appearance palette. In the dialog box, change the Angle to 0 (zero) and click OK. Observe how the object appears now with zero Twirl applied. Undo this change so the 80 degree Twirl is back.

17. With this object selected, click on the New Style button in the Styles palette. This object will appear in the palette as a new style. Deselect the object.

New Style appears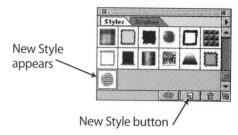

New Style button

18. In the Toolbox, click on the Default Colors icon. With the appropriate tools, draw a rectangle, a circle, and a star. Click on the new style you created in the Styles palette to paint the objects with this style.

19. Observe how the shapes of the objects determine how the style looks.

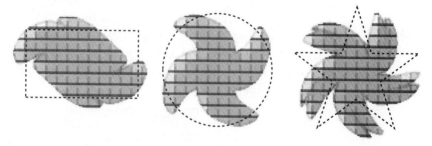

20. You have experimented with creating and applying styles, used the Effect menu to observe how its options affect paths, and experienced the many practical uses of the Appearance palette.

21. Close the file without saving.

Chapter Summary

You have learned the many features that are used to alter a path's appearance. You have learned the difference between the stroke and fill of a path, how to apply colors, gradients, patterns, and use the Swatches palette. You have learned to use the many methods available to paint objects, and created, modified and applied colors from different palettes. You have had an introduction to the Styles palette, the Effect menu, and use of the Appearance palette.

Complete Project C: Wine and Cheese Invitation

CHAPTER 8

MANIPULATING OBJECTS

CHAPTER OBJECTIVE:

Learn to use Illustrator's various features that help precisely position, align, arrange, and move objects in a document. In Chapter 8, you will:

- Learn about the Object menu and its options, including as Arrange, Group/Ungroup, Lock/Unlock All, and Hide Selection/Show All.
- Practice locking, hiding, and grouping objects.
- Learn to arrange objects in a stacking order.
- Learn to align objects manually
- Learn how to duplicate objects.
- Learn how to use the Align palette to align and distribute objects.

PROJECTS TO BE COMPLETED:

- Art Deco House (A)
- BearWear Business Cards (B)
- Wine and Cheese Invitation (C)
- Walking the Dogs (D)
- Broadway Bound (E)
- Joker's Wild (F)
- BearWear Label (G)

Some Illustrator menu options that include the words Hide/Show in the View and Window menus can be toggled back and forth. For example, you can activate Show Rulers with Command/Control-R, then Hide Rulers with the same keystroke.

Other functions have related pairs of keystrokes that allow you to quickly toggle back and forth between functions. Here is a useful set of keystroke shortcuts from the Object menu:

Lock/Unlock All

Lock: Command/Control-2
Unlock: Command/Control-Option/ Alt-2

Hide Selection/Show All

Hide Selection: Command/ Control-3
Show All: Command/ Control-Option/ Alt -3

Group/Ungroup

Group: Command/Control-G
Ungroup: Command/ Control-Shift-G

Manipulating Objects

Even the most simple designs can get confusing, especially when parts of objects are obscuring each other so they can't be selected or modified. Illustrator offers several features that help you work around such problems and dramatically speed up production time. In this chapter we discuss and demonstrate various features and functions to use when objects need to be repositioned, aligned, arranged, or moved into the correct position to meet the requirements of your design.

Object Menu

The Object menu provides the most flexibility for managing objects. While the Layers palette (which we get into later in the course) performs some of the same hiding and locking functions, the Object menu works primarily on elements within a layer, allowing the artist to arrange them in front of or in back of other objects in the same layer.

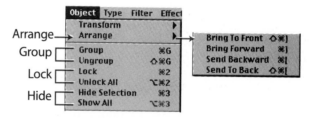

Arrange

The four options in the Object>Arrange menu are restricted to manipulating the objects within a single layer. In the logo exercise in Chapter 6, you saw how "stacking" objects in front or in back of each other makes it easier to modify them. Use these options when you need to change the "stacking" order of objects.

Bring to Front and Send to Back are the extreme positions for objects. However, you can also use Bring Forward and Send Backward to move an object up and down one position in the stack.

Group/Ungroup

Objects within a document can be selected and grouped into one unit. Groups of objects can be grouped with other groups. Using Ungroup will only undo the last grouping performed. Ungroup will have to be selected several times to get multiple groups of objects back to their original, independent status.

Lock/Unlock All

Locked objects cannot be selected, moved, or modified. This is a very handy way of getting objects in complex designs to stop interfering with attempts to click and select other objects. Unlock All does just that — unlocks all locked objects. You cannot lock or unlock individual objects with this feature. We will show you later how you can use the Layers palette to lock or unlock single objects.

Hide Selection/Show All

Hiding selected objects removes them from view without deleting them. If the document is closed with hidden objects, they will return to view when the document is next opened. Show All brings hidden objects back to view. It cannot pick or choose. Show All does just that — shows all hidden objects. If you need to view specific hidden objects, they all have to be brought back into view with the Show All command, then unwanted objects must be hidden again.

Although you can hide several objects in sequence, one after another, to show any single object from a hidden group is impossible. The Show All option releases all hidden objects at once.

Locking, Hiding, and Grouping Objects

1. Create a new document set for CMYK Color Mode; leave it untitled, and the Artboard set for default. Save the document in Illustrator format to your Work in Progress folder as "Locking Objects.AI". With the Rectangle tool, draw a rectangle on the page. Use the Option/Alt key to drag two duplicates to the right.

    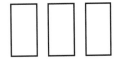

2. Click on the middle rectangle to select it, and go to Object>Lock.

    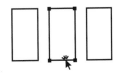

3. Marquee the three rectangles with the Selection tool. Notice that the locked path did not get selected.

    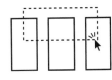

4. Go to Object>Unlock All. The locked rectangle, when unlocked, becomes the selected object. It will now be accessible. Leave it selected.

5. Go to Object>Hide Selection. The selected rectangle disappears.

Groups of objects can be combined with other groups. They can be ungrouped, but only in the same order that they were originally grouped. To ungroup objects back to their individual status, the Ungroup command must be applied as many times as the Group command was originally applied. Whatever objects were grouped first will be the last to be ungrouped.

Grouping has some drawbacks. If objects from different front/back locations are grouped, they will all be brought to the front of the stacking order. If objects on different layers are selected and grouped, they will all be relocated to the topmost of the layers from which the groups were selected.

6. Click on the remaining two objects and hide them the same way. Use File>Save to save the document. Close the document. With File>Open, open this same document from the **Work in Progress** folder. Notice that the hidden rectangles have all come back to view. Select the three rectangles and delete them.

7. Use the Rectangle and Ellipse tools to create several objects, as shown here.

8. Marquee-select the large circle and square. Press Command/Control-G to Group them. Deselect the group. Click on the large circle with the Selection tool. Notice that both objects become selected.

9. Select the five smaller circles and group them, using the Object>Group.

10. Select the four long rectangles and press Command/Control-G to Group them. Keep this group selected.

11. Hold the Shift key and click on the group of five circles. Press Command/Control-G to Group them. Keep this group selected.

12. Hold the Shift key and click on the first group of circles and squares. Press Command/Control-G to group them.

13. You have now grouped individual objects, and then combined them into larger groups. This is called "nesting." Deselect the groups and activate the Direct Selection tool. Click on any object in a group and notice that only that object is selected. Hold down the Shift key and click on one or two additional objects. Notice that the Direct Selection tool activates only those objects that you clicked on. This is how you can modify individual objects in a group without ungrouping them first. Deselect the selected objects.

14. Activate the Selection tool and click on any object to select the entire group. Go to the Object menu and select Ungroup. This will return the groups to the state they were in just prior to the last Group command. Deselect all objects. The five-circle group and the four-rectangle group will still be grouped together. Click on one of the five circles. You will observe that all the circles, including the rectangles, became selected.

15. Go to Object>Ungroup again. The two nested groups will be ungrouped.

Object	Type	Filter	Effect
Transform			▶
Arrange			▶
Group			⌘G
Ungroup			⇧⌘G
Lock			⌘2

Notice that the following features have closely related keyboard shortcuts.

Bring to Front
Command/Control-Shift-]

Send to Back
Command/Control-Shift-[

Bring Forward
Command/Control-]

Send Backward
Command/Control-[

Moving objects around with the Front/Back command is different than using layers. You often need to stack objects on top of each other within their own layer.

16. We won't go on ungrouping, but it was important to show you how the grouping can be executed any number of times. Nesting, however, can affect output if there are too many groups nested together. Use nesting sparingly.

17. Notice that it is not always easy to spot objects that are grouped. If any objects are accidentally left selected during a grouping, they will be grouped too. If this happens, you must ungroup the objects and group them again as desired.

18. Close the document without saving.

Arranging with Front/Back

All newly created documents, by default, contain only one layer. For the sake of this discussion, let us assume that everything is happening on that one default layer. Within a layer objects are "stacked" in the order they were created or pasted into the document. That is to say, each new object is on top of the stack. Once an object has been added to the document, its "stacking order" can be changed using the options in the Object>Arrange menu.

This example shows the objects stacked in the order they were added to the document. The square was drawn first, then the circle and star were drawn. The polygon was pasted into the document, and finally, the spiral was drawn. Notice the front-to-back position.

If a filled object is on top of (in front of) another object, it can ruin the effect you are trying to achieve. The Arrange feature in the Object menu offers four options for stacking objects in a document.

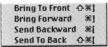

In this example, to start off with, the word "COFFEE" was created with white type. A black object with rounded corners was drawn to be the background for the type. As you can see, the black object hides the type. A diamond shaped object was drawn last, putting it in front of all other objects (A). This is a simple example, but it's often difficult to draw objects and manage their stacking order at the same time, nor is it necessary to try.

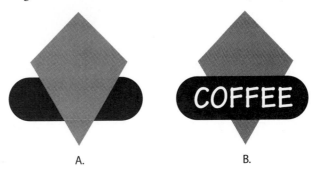

A.   B.

The black object was created just after the type, meaning it was one step in front of the type. The object was selected, then Arrange>Send Backward chosen from the Object menu. The diamond shape was selected, but if Send Backward were applied, it would only go behind the type and remain in front of the black object. Instead, Arrange>Send to Back was chosen, sending the diamond behind both objects (B). This is an example of how the elements of a design can be created individually then Illustrator's Arrange feature applied to complete the design.

Arranging Objects' Stacking Order

1. Open the document **Arranging Objects.AI** from the **SF-Intro Illustrator** folder. You will see four objects on the page. They are not touching or overlapping each other, so their stacking order is unknown. With the Selection tool, move all the objects into one place, centered on top of each other.

2. The first thing you'll notice is that the circle is in front of the other objects.

3. Click on the circle and select Object>Arrange>Send to Back. The circle goes all the way to the back and appears behind the other objects, but you still cannot see the spiral.

4. Select the star and chose Object>Arrange>Send Backward. The Send Backward command only sends the star back one level, which exposes the spiral while keeping the square and circle in position.

5. We need to add a background to this design. With no objects selected, click on the Eyedropper tool in the Toolbox. With the tool, click on the square in the design to set the fill for the next object you draw. Select the Rectangle tool and draw a rectangle that encloses the other objects. Like all new objects, it defaults to the front position, covering the objects in back of it.

6. Select the rectangle and press Command/Control-Shift-[to send it to the back. Now the other objects are visible.

7. To experiment with grouping, select the rectangle and the square and choose Object>Group (Command/Control-G). The square is the frontmost object in this grouping, so the stacking order of the group defaults to the square, which, as you can see, obscures the circle. Select Edit>Undo (Command/Control-Z) to undo the action.

8. You have observed how an object's stacking order can be rearranged with the Object>Arrange menu.

9. Close the document without saving.

Precision Alignment Techniques

In an earlier chapter, we discussed how to use Illustrator's rulers — how to set them and how to move them onto the page as guides. Let's build on this knowledge and focus on some methods for accurately positioning items on the page.

There are times when two or more identical objects need to be positioned exactly on top of each other. What is seen on the screen, however, is very seldom an exact alignment. How can you be certain that the alignment of the objects is precise? There are several methods for accurately aligning objects, but here are three quick ones: manual alignment, alignment from the Transform palette, and Paste in Front and Paste in Back.

Manual Alignment

The manual method of aligning is to select and drag an object to its target point. To use this method, activate Snap to Point in the View menu. As an object is being manually aligned, the cursor's appearance will change, signalling that the object has hit its target.

Selection Tool Icons

When aligning objects by hand, the appearance of the Selection tool's arrow is the identifying piece. When the selection arrow touches a segment (but not while clicking) of an unselected object, a small black square appears in its lower right corner. If the tool touches an anchor point, a hollow square appears. When the arrow touches a segment of a selected object, the arrow itself changes appearance, losing its stem. If the tool touches an anchor point of a selected object, the arrow changes appearance and a hollow square appears. This works best with selected objects if View>Show Bounding Box is showing in the View menu.

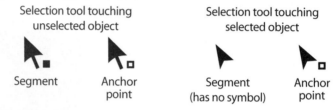

Aligning Anchor Points

To align an anchor point of one object with the anchor point of another object, you must click-hold the Selection tool on the anchor point of the object to be moved. Remember to choose View>Hide Bounding Box. Drag the object by its anchor point toward the target object with the objective of touching the arrow cursor to the target anchor point. The sign that exact alignment has been achieved is the cursor becoming hollow.

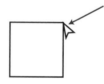

In this example, notice that the arrow takes on three different appearances as an object is dragged and aligned. The Selection tool was touched on the anchor point of the object, which was unselected to begin with. When the arrow cursor touched the object's corner a small hollow square appeared next to the arrow to indicate it was touching an anchor point (A). The anchor point was dragged to the right, at the same time the arrow cursor lost its stem (B). When the anchor point of the moving object matched the target anchor point, the arrow became hollow, showing that the objects have been aligned (C). Having View>Snap to Point selected assured that the anchor points would remain matched when the mouse button was released.

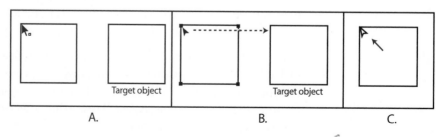

The bounding box can be distracting when working with anchor points. Make certain that the bounding box is not showing when aligning manually.

Aligning Segments

Aligning objects is not limited to placing one anchor point on top of another. Segments can also be accurately aligned but only to guides, not to anchor points or other segments. In the same way that the selection arrow becomes hollow when aligning anchor points, the arrow dragging an object by its segment will turn hollow whenever it touches a guide.

Transform Palette

The Transform palette, accessed in the Window menu, shows an object's position in terms the X, Y coordinates of a selected reference point. The icon on the left of the Transform palette shows nine reference points, which correspond to the eight anchor points and the center point of a selected object's bounding box.

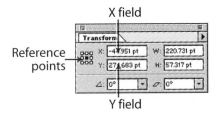

You can determine the X, Y position of an object by selecting it then clicking on a reference point in the Transform palette. The X and Y fields show the position of the corresponding point in the selected object's bounding box. By selecting the X and Y fields in the Transform palette, you can enter the desired X, Y position of the selected object. When applied, the object moves to the X, Y position entered in the fields.

Aligning Objects Manually

1. Create a new document set for CMYK Color Mode; leave it untitled and the Artboard set for default. Make certain you are in View>Preview mode, and the bounding box is not showing. Press Command/Control-R to show the rulers, and use File>Document Setup to change the Units to Inches. Notice how the ruler changes from points to inches. Be sure that Snap to Point is selected in the View menu.

2. Press the "D" key to set the stroke and fill to the default colors. With the Star tool, draw a star that is approximately 1-in. wide.

3. Hold the Option/Alt key and drag a duplicate star to the right. Hold the Shift key after the drag has begun to constrain the move.

4. Use the Selection tool to touch the top anchor point of the first star. Notice how the hollow little square appears to show you are touching an anchor point. Click-hold on this anchor point. Observe how the arrow does not change until you begin dragging the star to the right. Drag the star toward the duplicate and move the cursor around its top point. When the cursor makes contact with the target anchor point, it will turn hollow.

5. When the cursor arrow becomes hollow, let go of the mouse. The Snap to Point function will snap the moved anchor to the target point, aligning them exactly.

6. Since Illustrator has no "inline" paint feature, this is the only way to paint an object with an inline. Copying and positioning one object on top of another has a practical application frequently used by artists as the first step in creating an inline design.

7. To achieve the inlined star shown below, do this: Use the Selection tool to click on the top star and press Command/Control-2 to lock it. Click again on the star. The star on the bottom will be selected. Use the Stroke palette to change its stroke weight to 6 pt. Press Command/Control-Option/Alt-2 to unlock the top star, which will now be the selected star. Click the Swap Colors box in the Toolbox. This will give the top star a white stroke and black fill. Sitting on top of the star with the thicker stroke, the star with the 1-pt. white stroke will create the inline effect.

8. Select the two star paths and delete them. We will try other alignment techniques.

9. Press the "D" key to reset the stroke and fill to their default colors. From the left-side ruler, drag a vertical guide out to the middle of the page. From the ruler at the top of the document, drag a horizontal guide to the top area of the page.

10. With the Rectangle tool, draw a 1-inch square. Deselect the square.

11. Touch (but don't click) the Selection tool to the right-side segment of the unselected square. Note that the tool arrow has a stem. Single-click the object to select it. Touch the arrow to the same segment. Observe that the arrow's stem disappears.

12. Click-hold on this right segment to move the object. Move it toward the vertical guide. When the arrow touches the guide, notice that it becomes hollow.

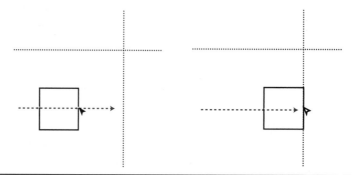

13. Dragging this same segment, move the cursor up to touch the horizontal guide. The cursor will not become hollow because you are not dragging the top or bottom (horizontal) segments of this square. Select the top segment and drag it to touch the horizontal guide. Now the cursor becomes hollow when it touches the guide.

14. Deselect the square. Click-hold the Selection tool on the top-right anchor point and drag to the vertical guide. Note that a dragged anchor point turns the cursor hollow when it touches a guide. Now drag the anchor point up to where the horizontal guide intersects with the vertical guide. Touch this intersection with the dragged anchor point. Note that the cursor becomes hollow, but with a small symbol inside it. This signifies that you have aligned the anchor point where two guides intersect.

15. Leave the square located at this point. Keep it selected.

16. From the Window menu, use Show Transform to access the Transform palette. Notice that the center reference point is selected. Click on the letter "X" in the palette to activate the X field and type "2". Press the Tab to activate the Y field. As soon as you press the Tab key, the square moves so its center is positioned at X: 2. Type "9" in the Y field and press Return/Enter.

Reference Point

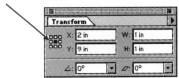

17. The center of the square is now positioned at the point where the ruler's 2-in. and 9-in. marks intersect.

18. Drag a duplicate of the square (holding Option/Alt) to the right. Select this duplicate. You notice that the numbers in X and Y fields are now different, showing its own location.

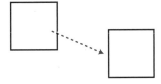

19. In the Transform palette, type "2" in the X field. Type "9" in the Y field. Press Return/Enter to apply.

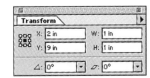

20. Where did this duplicate square go? You see only one square on the page.

This is because the duplicate is resting on top of the original square. Matching their X, Y settings has matched their positions. They are perfectly aligned.

Duplicating objects by dragging with the Option/Alt key is one of the most timesaving and useful features of Illustrator. It is a method that allows for rapidly duplicating and aligning objects. The Shift key constrains the drag, but must not be pressed until after the drag has begun.

21. Click on the duplicate square with the Selection tool and move it to one side to see this.

22. You have used guides and the Transform palette to align objects and observed how they operate. You have also learned how to recognize the symbols that show alignment. Close the document without saving.

Paste in Front and Paste in Back

An object can be copied and aligned with the original using Edit>Paste in Front or Edit>Paste in Back. This is done by selecting an object, copying it with Edit>Copy (Command/Control-C), then selecting one of the paste commands from the Edit menu. When you use the Copy command, the original item remains selected. When Paste in Front or Paste in Back is applied, the newly pasted object becomes the active selection.

In this example, the star was drawn with a black fill (A) then painted with 1-pt. white stroke, shown below in grey (B). It was copied, and then Command/Control-B pressed to paste the copy behind the original. The duplicate was painted with no fill and a 4-pt. black stroke. The duplicate's thick stroke juts out further than the 1-pt. white stroke of the original, creating an inline white border.

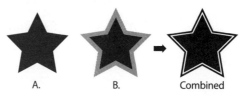

A.   B.   Combined

Duplicating Objects

There will be times when an object must not be moved, but a duplicate of the object must be created and aligned precisely with another image. The fastest way to duplicate any object in Illustrator is to drag the selected object to the desired position while holding the Option/Alt key.

When the mouse is released, a duplicate of the original will appear in the new position. Holding the Shift key once the dragging has begun will constrain the movement of the duplicate so it will be perfectly aligned (horizontally, vertically, or at 45°) with the original.

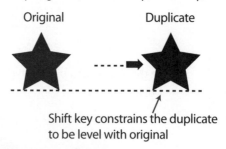

Original   Duplicate

Shift key constrains the duplicate to be level with original

Once a drag-duplication has been executed, the duplication and distance (or angle) it moved can be repeated, creating another duplicate, by pressing Command/Control-D.

Aligning and Distributing Objects

Controlling the space between objects, as well as how they're positioned relative to each other, can be a time-consuming process. Not all objects are easily aligned. Custom shapes, for example, don't have an easily discernible top, bottom, or center. Even primitive objects like stars, spirals, and polygons aren't easily aligned with other differently shaped objects. Even though they might be lined up based on mathematical attributes, they still might not look quite right.

Discrepancies in alignment and spacing become apparent in finished art work, so you should always pay attention to the relative positions of objects as you create them.

If you accidentally align a group of objects incorrectly (for example, they all wind up on top of each other), just Undo the process and try again.

Keep in mind that each alignment occurs immediately when selected and is cumulative. For example, aligning all the objects on their left edges, then on their top edges will pile them all up into a stack.

Sometimes the tops or bottoms of objects need to be lined up on one plane, and the space between them evenly distributed. Life would be simpler if, like a drill sergeant, you could just yell, "Line up to the left." In a manner of speaking, you can do this using the Align palette, which is accessed by choosing Window>Show Align.

Align Palette

Under the Window menu you will find several tools and palettes that can improve both the speed and accuracy with which you align or distribute objects. Both functions are available in the Align palette. To use the alignment options in this palette, simply select the objects you want to position, go to the palette, and click the appropriate button.

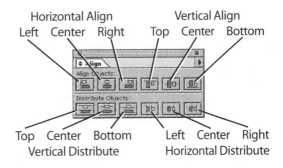

Here are descriptions of the Align and Distribute sections of the palette.

Align Objects

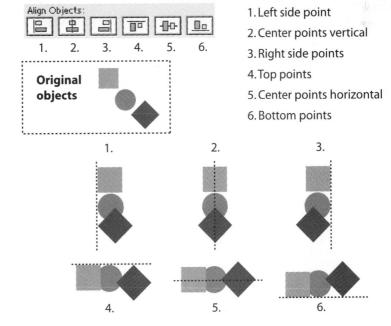

Aligns objects according to their:

1. Left side point
2. Center points vertical
3. Right side points
4. Top points
5. Center points horizontal
6. Bottom points

Distribute Objects

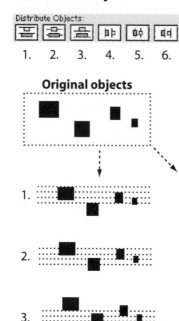

Distributes equal distance between objects:

1. Vertically using top points
2. Vertically using center points
3. Vertically using bottom points
4. Horizontally using left points
5. Horizontally using center points
6. Horizontally using right points

If multiple objects are to be aligned with other objects, you must first group the objects if you want to preserve their positions in relation to each other.

Aligning and Distributing Objects

1. Go to the **SF-Intro Illustrator** folder and open the document **Align Objects.AI**. There are three sets of objects, positioned differently on the page. Treat each set separately for this exercise.

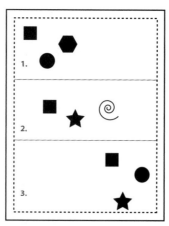

2. Go to Window>Show Align.

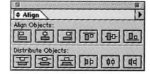

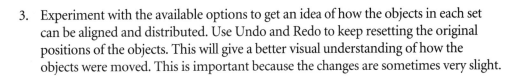

3. Experiment with the available options to get an idea of how the objects in each set can be aligned and distributed. Use Undo and Redo to keep resetting the original positions of the objects. This will give a better visual understanding of how the objects were moved. This is important because the changes are sometimes very slight.

In many cases you will not see much of a change. Drag guides to mark the edges and center points of the objects and you will see more clearly how they were arranged.

4. Close the file without saving.

Using Precision Alignment Techniques

1. From the **SF-Intro Illustrator** folder, open **Precision Alignment.AI**.

2. Use Document Setup to set the units to inches. Go to the Preferences>Guides & Grid dialog box to change the guides to black dots. Mark the edges of the object by dragging Ruler guides onto the page. If the Rulers aren't visible, press Command/Control-R to activate them. In the View menu, select Hide Page Tiling to give you a clean page.

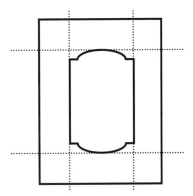

3. With the Selection tool, click the Default Colors icon in the Toolbox to reset the paint attributes. Work in Outline mode, so the painted objects won't distract you when maneuvering the objects.

4. Select the Rectangle tool and click the cursor on the point where the two guides intersect in the upper-left corner. A dialog box will appear. Type "0.4" for Width and Height, then click OK. A small square will be drawn, extending its origin from the point you clicked.

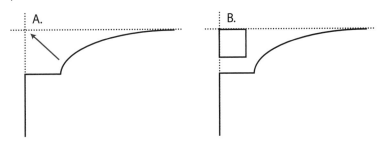

5. With the Selection tool, drag the upper right anchor point of the square to the right. Continue dragging the anchor point toward the guides until the cursor arrow turns hollow with a symbol in it, indicating that the anchor point has been moved to the intersection of the two guides. When this happens, hold down the Option/ Alt key and let go of the mouse. You have created a duplicate square that is aligned with the guides.

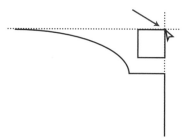

6. Select the two squares. Click-hold on the bottom segment of the first square made. Hold the Option/Alt key and drag both squares down (holding the Shift key after the drag has begun to constrain their movement) until they're aligned with the guides at the bottom of the artwork. You will know alignment has been made when the cursor becomes hollow. Select all four squares and use Object>Arrange>Send to Back.

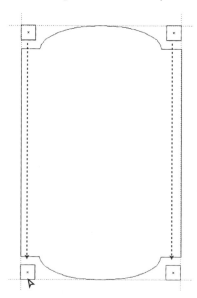

7. Go to Preview mode to see the objects as they are painted. Click on the large original object, that came in the file, to select it. Click on the Default Colors icon in the Toolbox. The fill will be white, and the stroke black. Click the Swap Colors icon in the Toolbox to reverse the paint attributes. Click on the Fill box to make it active.

8. In the Swatches palette, view the Show Color Swatches colors by Name View. Scroll to the Blue C: 100, M: 50 swatch and click it to apply to the fill. The object will now have a dark blue fill, and a white, 1-pt. stroke.

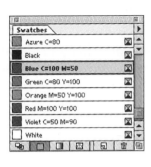

9. Press Command/Control-C to copy the image. Go to Edit>Paste in Back. A selected duplicate will be pasted behind this object. In the Toolbox, click the Swap Colors icon so that the dark-blue color will now be applied to the stroke. Go to the Window menu and access Show Stroke. In the Stroke palette, set the Weight to 6 pt. and press Return/Enter to apply.

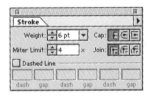

10. The thicker stroke of the duplicate will extend from the path, and the white stroke of the original will lie on top, creating a white "inline."

11. Your next task is to select these two painted objects. But, since they are exactly on top of each other, it's difficult to select both. If you click on the object, you will only select the topmost object. There is no way to go through the top object and get the one underneath, without tedious locking and unlocking. However, you can select both objects with the Selection tool by drawing a marquee that touches both objects. Marquee-select both objects.

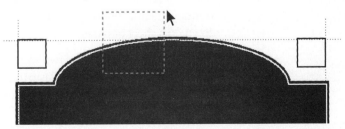

Many designers use this "inline" technique to create rules within borders, or multilevel borders.

Another example of two lines of different weights and colors being positioned on top of each other are the little hollow roads that you see on maps. By putting a thin light-colored path on top of a thicker, darker path, you create a "hollow" line.

12. Press Command/Control-G to Group the two objects. Press Command/Control-3 to hide the objects.

13. Press Command/Control-A to select the four squares. Click the Fill box in the Toolbox to make it active. From the Swatches palette, click the Blue C: 100, M: 50 swatch that was used for the larger object. Click on the Fill box and drag its dark-blue color to touch the Stroke box, setting both the fill and the stroke for this color. Use the Stroke palette to set the Weight of the stroke to 4 pt. Press Return/Enter to apply this to the squares.

14. You are going to use several of the methods you've learned so far. This is only to demonstrate the techniques, not to show the fastest way to create a design. Click on the first square you drew in the upper left. Use Edit>Copy to copy the square.

15. Go to Edit>Paste in Front. A selected duplicate will be pasted in front of the copied square. Keep the fill the same with this square, but change its stroke to 1 pt., white.

16. You are about to do a manual alignment by dragging on an object's anchor point. To avoid confusion, go to the View menu and select Guides>Hide Guides. You don't want guides making the cursor hollow prematurely. You want to know when the cursor touches an anchor point.

17. Go to the square you just painted. With the Selection tool, click-hold on the square's upper-left anchor point and drag it down to the square directly below it. You will know when they're aligned when the cursor arrow becomes hollow. When the object is aligned, press the Option/Alt key and let go of the mouse to make a duplicate.

18. We will do the squares on the other side a little differently, using the Transform palette. Select the top and bottom squares on the right side of the design. From the Window menu, choose Show Transform. Look at the X, Y numbers. Write them down on a sheet of paper.

19. On the left side, click on the two squares painted with the white stroke to select them. Go to Edit>Copy, then Edit>Paste them on the page. There is no need for Front/Back pasting because they are about to be relocated.

20. With the two pasted squares selected, go to the Transform palette and enter the numbers you wrote down into the X, Y fields. Press Return/Enter to apply the change.

21. The pasted squares will move on top of the two right side squares.

22. Go to the Object menu and choose Show All to make the large object visible again. Choose View>Guides>Show Guides.

23. At this point, you have used the various techniques of precision alignment we have addressed. The design is based on several objects (with different paint attributes) being positioned over and under each other.

24. The Align palette has not been used in this piece and it can help align randomly created or duplicated objects. Before going on, select all of the objects with Command/Control-A and press Command/Control-G to group them.

25. This design is eventually going to become a political poster. That means we will need to add a few stars and stripes. Deselect any selected objects. Go to the Toolbox and click on the Default Colors icon.

26. We'll begin with the red stripes. From the vertical ruler, drag a guide that is 0.5 in. from the left side of the page. Select the Rectangle tool and click its cursor on the point where this new guide intersects with the previous top guide. In the dialog box set the Width to 1.479 in. and Height to 6.887 in. Click OK. The rectangle will appear on the page.

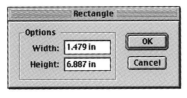

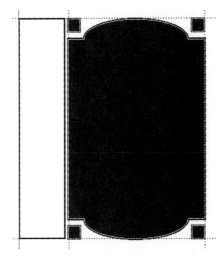

27. Select the Star tool in the Toolbox. Click its cursor on the rectangle. In the dialog box, set the Radius 1 to 0.45 in., Radius 2 to 0.25 in. and Points to "5". Click OK.

28. The Star will appear. Move it to the top of the rectangle, not quite touching the rectangle. Drag-duplicate four more stars by holding the Option/Alt key and dragging down. Don't worry that they don't line up.

Get into the habit of saving your work frequently using the simple Command/ Control-S keystroke. The more complex a document becomes, the more often you should save.

If you have been saving frequently and then make a mistake that would be difficult or time consuming to undo, you can close the document without saving, then reopen it, thereby deleting the mistake. You may lose a small amount of work since your last save, but this is often less disastrous than the mistake. At one time or another, almost every computer-graphic artist has accidentally deleted a large and important part of a document. Usually, this only happens once.

29. Marquee-select the rectangle and all the stars. In the Window menu, select Show Align. The Align palette will appear. Click on the Horizontal Align Center option. All the objects will line up by their centers.

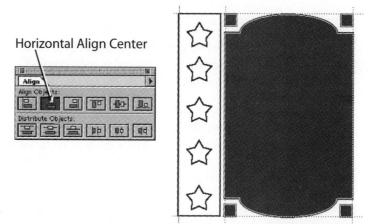

Horizontal Align Center

30. Select the bottom star and move it (holding the Shift key) to be just above the bottom of the rectangle, about the same distance the top star is from the top. Select the rectangle and choose Object>Lock. Select all of the stars. In the Align palette, click the Vertical Distribute Center option. The stars will distribute evenly between the top and bottom stars.

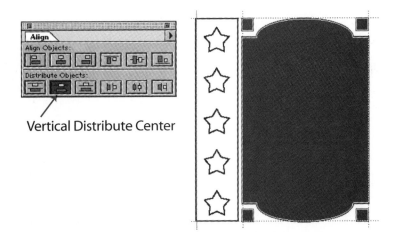

Vertical Distribute Center

31. Use Object>Unlock All to make the rectangle accessible. It will be selected. From the Window menu, choose Show Color to view the Color palette. In the palette, click on the Stroke box and then click the None icon in the palette. Click on the Fill box and drag the Magenta and Yellow sliders to 100%. The Cyan and Black values should be 0%. This will create a vivid red color that fills the rectangle.

Fill

None

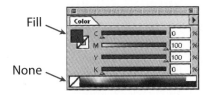

32. With the Selection tool, select all of the stars. Click the Default Colors icon in the Toolbox. Change the stroke to None. Marquee-select the stars and the rectangle. Press Command/Control-G to group them.

33. Drag a vertical guide that is .125 in. to the right of the large blue poster object.

34. Select the grouped stars and stripe by click-holding on the rectangle's left side segment. Drag the selected group to the other side of the page, adding the Shift key after the move has begun. You want the rectangle's left segment to touch the 1/8″ guide you just created. When the cursor turns hollow, the group will be in place. Now hold the Option/Alt key and let go of the mouse to duplicate the group.

35. To make sure that the three groups are aligned and distributed evenly, select them all. In the Align palette, click first on the Horizontal Distribute Center, then on the Vertical Align Center.

Vertical Align Center

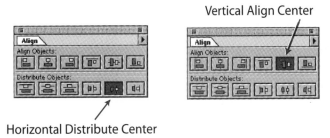

Horizontal Distribute Center

36. The design is finished and should look like this.

37. Use Save As to save the background in Illustrator format to your **Work in Progress** folder. Name the file "Political Poster.AI".

Chapter Summary

You have learned how to stack and align objects in Illustrator. You have been shown how to use the Lock, Hide, and Group features. You have learned three of the basic alignment techniques — manually aligning objects, using the Transform palette, and Pasting in Front or Back. You have used the Align palette and observed how it manipulates multiple objects into precise alignment.

PROJECT ASSIGNMENT #1

Assignment

You are a graphic designer working for an architectural firm. You have been hired to create a design for the front of a new and elegant country home. At this point they just want a design for the outside of the house, showing the front of the house as it might appear from the road. These types of drawings are often called "elevations" and are a common requirement for builders.

A review committee made up of staff members from the architectural firm as well as the people moving into the house will be reviewing your house design when you are finished. The architectural firm has indicated to you that the client wants to see three different house concepts with three different looks. The client is open to all design concepts but wants the front of the house to have at least the following specifications: five windows, one entrance door, a fence, a mailbox, a porch, and one two-car garage. The house should be two stories and have either brick, cedar shingle, or clapboard wood siding.

Applying Your Skills

To design the houses, you will need to use the following functions, methods, and features:

- Sketching a rough design for the three houses on paper, or creating three rough designs in Illustrator.

- Using primitive shapes alone combined in some manner with drawing tools to create different visual elements that effectively convey the overall shape of the houses.

- Using the Toolbox tools that draw primitive shapes to create the shapes and details for the house such as the windows and doors.

- Using the Pen tool in conjunction with the primitive shapes to create custom shapes that help convey the features of the house.

- Using alignment and grouping to help layout the house.

- Duplicating objects to provide visual interest and to assist in developing the houses.

Specifications

Execute the drawings on an 8.5- by 11-in. page with Landscape orientation. You can use as much of the page as you wish.

Note: Anyone can draw a simple house with a box and triangle for a roof with some smoke coming out, and a bird or two in the sky. The challenge here is to present the client with a series of solid designs that can then be used as the starting point for an actual dwelling. Elevation drawings are, at their core, a collection of simple primitive elements, all of which are at your disposal from the Toolbox.

Included Files

There are no files provided for this exercise. You might consider going to the Sunday Real Estate section of your local newspaper, where you'll see plenty of examples of the type of illustration you're required to create. That would provide you a good reference point from which to start.

Publisher's Comments

Architecture and building are specialty design environments and require far more skills than simply being able to develop an elegant front view of an expensive home. A thorough understanding of such disciplines as materials, building codes, safety concerns, stress factors, and mathematics are absolute necessities.

Designing a unique look and feel for an elegant country home is, however, something that many designers are well capable of — yet not often called upon to do.

The steps to developing a house design are relatively straightforward; you use rough shapes — rectangles, circles, arches, triangles, slopes, and curves — to sketch out the basic idea. Once you know where the design is going, begin adding details such as windows, doors, cornices, cupolas, garages, wind vanes, chimneys, and whatever else suits your design. Last, add the textures of the siding you have chosen.

You might also imagine what the buyer is like as a person — because someone's personality is often reflected in the items that they purchase, the homes they live in, and the decorations they select. Try to develop each of the three elevations so that they reflect a common personality, while appearing different.

REVIEW #1

CHAPTERS 1 THROUGH 8:

In Chapters 1 through 8, you learned the Illustrator environment —
how to manage documents, the grid and guides, and the viewing modes.
You learned about primitive shapes and paths, and how to create them;
how to create and edit type; painting objects; and how to use templates.
After completing the first half of this course, you should:

- Understand the basic elements of Illustrator's working environment —
  creating documents, opening and saving documents, the Artboard, the
  Toolbox, menus, palettes, and preferences.

- Know how to use and control the grid, guides, rulers, and the zero point;
  how to manage them in your document for accuracy and efficiency; and
  understand how to customize these elements for your own efficiency.

- Be comfortable with the viewing modes, and understand the importance of
  changing views in your artwork. You should be familiar with the creation of
  New Views, and using the New Window feature; know how to move around
  the document using the Navigator palette.

- Know how to create basic primitive shapes — squares, rectangles, circles,
  and ellipses. You should know how to set the origin point when drawing an
  ellipse or rectangle. You should also know how to use Illustrator's other
  tools such as the Twirl, Spiral, Star, and Polygon tools.

- Understand anchor points and segments — the two components of any
  Illustrator path. You also should be comfortable with using the Pen tool,
  and understand its use for creating both straight and curving paths.

- Be comfortable with using type in your layouts; understand the difference
  between point type and area type; know about the many typographic
  attributes that can be applied to type; know how to enlarge a text block and
  reveal hidden type that is overset.

- Understand Illustrator's painting features, and know how to use them to
  add colors, gradients, and patterns to objects in a document. You should
  also understand fills and strokes, and how to apply them; know how to use
  the Color palette, and how to create colors for storage in the Swatches
  palette.

- Be fully comfortable with manipulating objects — how to stack, reposition,
  align, arrange, or move them into the required position. You should also be
  familiar with precision alignment using manual aligning techniques and
  using the Transform palette. You should also know how to use the Align
  palette for vertical and horizontal aligning and distribution.

CHAPTER 9

ORGANIZING YOUR ART WITH LAYERS

CHAPTER OBJECTIVE:

To understand the concept of layers and how to use them in constructing a design. Learn to use the Layers palette to organize the objects in a document. In Chapter 9, you will:

- Learn the features in the Layers palette that help manage the layers and the objects in them.

- Learn how Illustrator stacks objects in layers and sublayers.

- Study and use the Layer Options dialog box.

- Learn how to manage the position of a layer in the Layers palette

- Observe and use sublayers.

- Learn how to reassign objects to other layers and sublayers.

- Learn how to lock and hide layers and sublayers.

- Learn how to toggle a layer between Preview and Outline viewing modes.

- Learn about layer templates, how to create them and how to customize them for best use with your document.

PROJECTS TO BE COMPLETED:

- Art Deco House (A)
- BearWear Business Cards (B)
- Wine and Cheese Invitation (C)
- Walking the Dogs (D)
- Broadway Bound (E)
- Joker's Wild (F)
- BearWear Label (G)

Organizing Your Art with Layers

In this chapter, we're going to explore the many different tasks that can be accomplished with the use of layers in a document. You can think of layers as the different floors in buildings. A building can have one or more floors. Each floor has its own elements — people, furniture, appliances. All of the stories together combine to make up the building.

In the same way, an Illustrator document may have one or more layers, with each layer containing its unique elements. The difference between a multistory building and a multi-layered document, is that you can view all of the layers in a document at one time, and it is much easier to add, remove, or rearrange in an Illustrator document than it is to add, remove, or rearrange the floors in a building.

Layer Basics

An Illustrator document can have any number of layers. Each layer is like an isolated sheet of paper laid on top of another. Objects drawn on one layer (or moved there) are totally separate from objects created on other layers. All elements on a layer can be created, deleted, painted, moved, copied, and modified without affecting the other layers. Each layer can be shown, hidden, locked, have viewing modes changed, be moved over or under other layers, and controlled in various ways to be described. Creating multiple layers in a single document has many advantages which will become apparent as you begin to create complex designs.

In this example of a pet shop flyer, the components have been divided into strategic elements, which determined the names of the layers — Headline, Art (the fish), Text, and Logo. Here's how the layers would look if they were on separate sheets of paper. When the layers are combined (shown on the bottom), the piece looks and prints like a single design unit.

Completed flyer

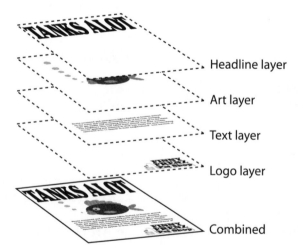

Headline layer

Art layer

Text layer

Logo layer

Combined

Certain types of drawings, like architectural or technical drawings, and some types of ads and designs can be easier to develop — and easier to modify — if you construct them using layers. The kind of complex work that calls for layers also calls for structure and preplanning.

Trying to reproduce artwork and illustrations you find lying around is a great way to develop your own skills. Just remember that published artwork is protected by copyright laws. Using it for practice is, we're certain, just fine with any professional artist.

Organizing the Elements

What goes where? The design may have a multitude of paths, objects, groups, placed images, and other elements. Creating a design should not be a random, thrown together process. All projects should be carefully thought out in advance. It's common sense that if you want to take a trip, you should have a map. If you know where you are going with the design, you should be able to map it out in a rough sketch, planning the piece.

The first step is to break down the design to its basic elements. How an artist organizes the elements of a design depends on individual style. Being too conservative with the number of layers used can add perhaps hours of work to the job — moving, hiding, and arranging objects that could be handled in seconds with layers. Likewise, using too many layers can slow down the process because it takes time keeping track of them all.

In this example, one designer might say the Coffee Du Jour ad contains only two basic design elements: the type (headline, body copy, logo tag-line), and the graphics (border around ad, thick rule at top of page, coffee cup art, logo at bottom). The type could be put on one layer, and the graphics on another.

To carry the breakdown further, the ad border and thick rule could have its own border layer. The headline and its subhead could be on one headline layer. The coffee cup art could be placed on an art layer; the body copy would be on its own text layer. The logo in the lower right corner, with its tag line, could be on its own logo layer. In essence, break the design down to its various elements on the page, and assign each element its own layer. When this is done, the layers would look like this in the Layers palette. Notice that each layer has been given a name that clearly identifies its contents.

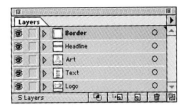

No object can be in an Illustrator document without being on a layer. Even if a document is newly created, its default layer is Layer 1.

Take time to name layers and sublayers as you create them. It will you save time in the long run as the number of layers in your document grows.

Layers work in a logical manner, one on top of another. You can shuffle their order, lock them, hide or delete them at any time.

Layers Palette

The control an artist has over layers depends on how well the Layers palette is understood and utilized. The Layers palette, accessed from Window>Show Layers is used to create layers, assign or move elements to specific layers, lock or hide specific layers, or toggle layers between Preview and Outline mode.

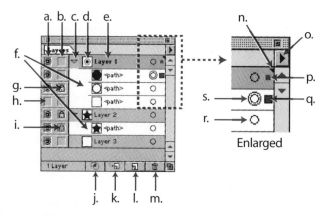

Enlarged

a. **Show/Hide button.** This button toggles the layer in and out of view.

b. **Lock/Unlock button.** This button toggles between locking and unlocking the layer. Locking makes objects on the layer inaccessible.

c. **Show Sublayers button.** This triangular button, toggles between listing the sublayers and not listing them.

d. **Image box.** This box shows a thumbnail view of all the objects on the layer and where they appear. Each sublayer has a thumbnail of its single object.

e. **Layer Name field.** A highlighted name field indicates that the layer or sublayer is currently active. Double-clicking in this field brings up the Layer Options dialog box where the layer can be named and some of its features customized.

f. **Sublayers.** By default a new sublayer is assigned to each object added to a layer.

g. **Padlock icon.** The Padlock icon indicates that the layer is locked.

h. **Hidden Layer.** When the Eye icon is missing, the layer is hidden.

i. **Sublayer Padlock icon.** This faded padlock icon appears for sublayers of a locked layer.

j. **Layer Mask icon.** Layer masking is an advanced Illustrator feature, and will be discussed in our advanced book.

k. **New Sublayer.** Clicking this button adds a new sublayer to the selected layer.

l. **New Layer.** Clicking this button creates a new layer. Keep in mind that the new layer will appear above the currently selected layer.

m. **Delete Selected Layer.** This option deletes a selected layer. When this icon is clicked, a message appears asking if you want to delete the selected layer. If you drag a layer directly to this icon, it will be deleted without the warning message.

Keep in mind that you can use Shift-Click and Command/Control-Click for selecting multiple items within variety of Illustrator's features, such as selecting layers or targeting buttons in the Layers palette.

Dragging a layer with objects to touch the New Layer button at the bottom of the palette will not only duplicate the layer, but also all the objects, directly on top of the originals.

n. **Select All Objects.** This tiny triangle appears in the name field of the active layer or sublayer. Double-clicking the arrow selects all of the objects that layer or selects the single object on that sublayer.

o. **Palette menu.** This triangular button, when clicked, shows the Layers palette menu, which offers additional options for customizing the layers.

p. **Selected Art icon (small).** This icon appears in the name field of a layer that contains one or more (but not all) currently selected objects. If the small Selected Art icon is dragged to another layer, the selected sublayer objects will be moved to the new layer.

q. **Selected Art icon (large).** The large icon appears in the name field of a layer where all of the objects on the layer are selected. The large Selected Art icon also appears on any sublayer containing a currently selected object. If the large Selected Art icon is dragged to a different layer, the selected object will moved to the new layer.

r. **Targeting button.** Clicking this button will select the object in a sublayer or all of the objects on a layer, targeting them for changes, such as applying a different color to the fill. Dragging the Targeting button to the targeting button of another object will set the *targeted* object with the fill and stroke (but not the effects) of the targeting object.

s. **Object Targeted.** The extra circle around the Targeting button indicates that the object is currently targeted. Suppose you want to apply a new style to one object in a layer. To do this, you can click on the Targeting button so it takes on the bull's-eye appearance, then click on the desired style in the Styles palette. The object will take on the new appearance.

Layers Palette Menu

In addition to the icons and buttons in the Layers palette, there are many options in the Palette menu accessed by pressing the triangle button to the right of the palette's name tab.

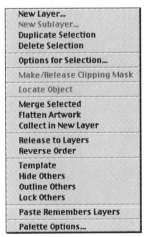

- **New Layer.** Creates a new layer.
- **New Sublayer.** Creates a new sublayer.
- **Duplicate Selection.** Creates a copy of the selected layer and its objects.

All new layers created appear directly above the layer selected at the time.

If you hold Option/Alt while clicking the New Layer button at the bottom of the Layers palette, the Layer Options dialog box for this new layer will appear.

- **Delete Selection.** Deletes the selected layer.

- **Options for Selection.** Brings up the Layer Options dialog box for the selected layer.

- **Make/Release Clipping Mask.** Layer masking is an advanced feature, which will be discussed in our Advanced Illustrator book.

- **Locate Object.** When an object is selected, and this option chosen, the Layers palette will immediately show and highlight the sublayer the object resides on.

- **Merge Selected.** Combines two or more selected layers. Multiple layers and sublayers can be selected by Shift-selecting adjacent layers or pressing the Command/Control key while clicking on the desired layers.

- **Flatten Artwork.** Combines all layers into one layer, defaulting to the selected layer.

- **Collect in New Layer.** Combines selected objects into a newly created layer.

- **Release to Layers.** Assigns individual layers to the sublayers on the selected layer that receives this option.

- **Reverse Order.** Inverts the order of the layers in the palette. The bottom layers go to the top and descend in sequence.

- **Template.** Converts a selected layer to a Template layer.

- **Hide Others.** Hides all layers other than the selected layer.

- **Outline Others.** Toggles to Outline view all layers other than the selected layer.

- **Lock Others.** Locks all layers other than the selected layer.

- **Paste Remembers Layers.** Keeps objects on their assigned layer, even though they have been cut and pasted. If this is toggled off, you can cut and paste an object from one layer to another.

  If Paste Remembers Layers is not selected, the use of Paste In Front or Paste In Back should be used with care. The cut object, when Pasted Front/Back to another selected object, will be assigned to the layer of the selected object.

- **Palette Options.** Selecting this option brings up a dialog box that allows you to customize the Layers palette's appearance. The size of the layer rows may be changed as well as the size of the thumbnail views of the objects.

The shortcut for accessing the Layer Options dialog box is to double-click the layer in the palette. The Layer Options dialog box relates only to the active layer in the palette.

A layer can be unlocked but still contain locked objects in some of its sublayers. In the same way, a layer can be set to "Show," but can still contain hidden objects. Locking a layer locks the entire layer and all of its objects; hiding a layer hides the layer and all of the objects it contains.

Layer Options

The Layer Options dialog box appears when New Layer or Options for Layer is selected in the Layers palette menu. The options in this dialog box control only the layer selected in the palette.

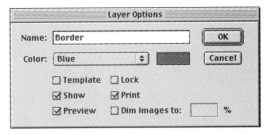

- **Name.** Assign a name to the layer that identifies its content.

- **Color.** This option allows you to change the color of edges, anchor points, and curve handles of selected objects on the layer. If you select an object, you will notice how it has a colored glow. This is known as the "edges, which appear to let you the object is selected. The View menu has an option called Hide/Show Edges, which turns this off. If turned off, however, it is almost impossible to determine if an object is selected.

- **Template.** This selection locks the selected layer and dims any placed raster images assigned to it.

- **Show.** Shows the objects on the layer. If unchecked, the layer becomes hidden.

- **Preview.** When this button is checked, the layer will appear in Preview mode. If it is unchecked, the layer will appear in Outline mode.

- **Lock.** When this button is unchecked, the layer is unlocked.

- **Print.** Determines whether the objects on the layer will print or not. You can use this option to suppress the output of layers containing elements such as notes or comments.

- **Dim Images.** Appears only when Template is checked and affects only placed images. This customizes how light or dark the template image appears.

Layer Levels

Layers are stacked in the same order that they appear in the layers in the palette list. The layer at the top of the list is in front of all other layers. As the list descends, the layers and their objects move to the back, respectively. As shown here, Layer 3 is in front of all others. Next is Layer 2, then Layer 4. The bottommost layer is Layer 1. All objects on these layers would be viewed in the corresponding front-to-back sequence.

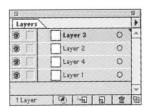

Changing Layer Levels

There will be many times when a layer (or sublayer) needs to be moved to another level. The layer is dragged up or down the layer list to the new level desired. When the mouse is click-held on the layer, a clenched fist (A) appears. The fist is dragged, relocating the layer to its new location. A black double-triangle appears and the bottom of the target layer becomes darkened when the layer meets the new location (B). In this example, Layer 4, at the top of the list, needed to be relocated to the bottom. It was clicked on, then dragged down to be below Layer 1 (C).

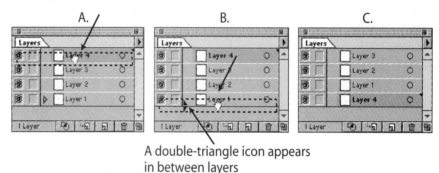

A double-triangle icon appears in between layers

Reassigning Objects on Layers

There are situations when an object should be above or below other objects; and yet, to relocate the layer it resides on would alter the positions of other art pieces. This lone object would best be assigned to a different layer. An object can be reassigned by selecting the object in the document then click-holding its Selected Art icon in the corresponding name field in the Layers palette. Dragging the icon to the desired location will reassign the object on the target layer.

In this example, the selected black circle shown is assigned to Layer 2. The Selected Art icon indicates that the circle is selected (A). It becomes necessary to reassign the square to Layer 1. The colored square is dragged up to Layer 1 (B). The black circle is now assigned to Layer 1.

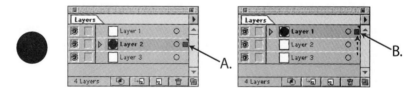

Tips on Layers

- If a layer or sublayer is active, and new items are created or placed, they default to that layer. Be aware of which layer is active before drawing objects.

- Layers can be moved up and down the list in the Layers palette.

- Objects can be reassigned to other layers by selecting them and dragging the Selected Art icon for that object to the new layer.

- The layer color (designated in the Layer Options dialog box) is the color of the edges and anchor points of selected paths. This can be changed if the edge color competes with a color in the design and is hard to differentiate.

- If a layer is locked, but remains the selected layer, you can't make changes to it or create new objects. You must select another unlocked layer to work on or unlock this layer.

- Be careful when deleting layers. If a message warns you that there are objects on the layer about to be deleted, reassign them before you delete the layer, unless you really want them deleted.

- Layers dragged to touch the New Layer button at the bottom of the palette will be duplicated, along with all of the objects on the layer.

- The size of the thumbnails in the Layers palette can be enlarged by using the Palette Options, found at the bottom the palette menu.

Keyboard Shortcuts

- Pressing the Command/Control key while clicking on the Show/Hide box toggles a layer between Outline and Preview mode. When the layer is in Preview mode, the pupil in the eye icon is dark, 👁. A "dilated" pupil, 👁, indicates that the layer is in Outline mode.

- If you want to keep one layer in Preview mode, and send all of the other layers to Outline mode, press Command/Control-Alt while clicking the Show/Hide box in the layer you desire to keep in Preview mode. All other layers will toggle to Outline mode. Note that the layer chosen to be viewed in Preview mode does not necessarily have to be the active layer.

  To return all layers to Preview mode, press Command/Control-Alt while again pressing the Show/Hide box for the layer in Preview mode.

- Pressing the Option/Alt key while clicking the Lock/Unlock box of a layer will unlock that layer and toggle between locking and unlocking all of the remaining layers. The layer being unlocked while the others are being toggled does not necessarily have to be the selected layer.

- A pair of adjacent layers can be selected by clicking on their name fields while holding the Shift key. A number of adjacent layers can also be selected by pressing the Shift key and clicking on the first and last desired layers. The two clicked layers and all layers in between will be selected.

- Any nonadjacent layers can be selected by pressing the Command/Control key and clicking on the desired layers.

- To select a layer by name, hold Command-Option/Control-Alt and click anywhere inside the Layers palette. A small black border around the palette's interior will appear. When you begin typing the layer's name its name field will be highlighted; click on the highlighted field to complete the selection process.

Working with Layers in a Design

1. Open **Tubing Turtle.AI** from the **SF-Intro Illustrator** folder. The objects in this document are the components of an ad. All of the components currently reside on one layer. Your task is to separate the objects onto different layers and arrange the objects into the ad.

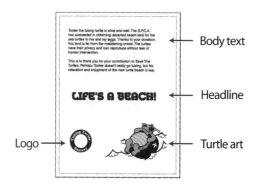

Body text

Headline

Logo

Turtle art

2. Choose Window>Show Layers. The Layers palette will appear. Click the New Layer button at the bottom of the palette three times to create three new layers. Double-click on Layer 1 and rename it "Headline." Move upward in the list, and rename the other layers: "Graphics," "Body Text," and "Background." The Layers palette should appear as follows.

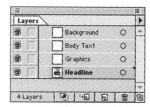

3. Click on the headline object in the document and note that the Selected Art icon appears in the Headline name field (formerly Layer 1). This headline object belongs on this layer, so leave it alone. We will relocate the other objects to their appropriate layers.

4. Select the Turtle Art piece in the document. Drag its Selected Art icon from the Headline layer to the Graphics layer. Click on the Tubing Turtle Society logo and drag its Selected Art icon to the Graphics layer. Select the block of body text and drag its Selected Art icon to the Body Text layer. Deselect the text object.

5. We will now create the background. Click on the Background layer. Since this is the active layer, any objects drawn on it will be assigned to this layer. Click-hold the Rectangle tool icon and select the Rounded Rectangle tool from the pop-out menu.

Be careful when dragging layers up and down the layer list. If one layer goes into another layer, it becomes a sublayer of the receiving layer.

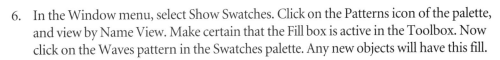

6. In the Window menu, select Show Swatches. Click on the Patterns icon of the palette, and view by Name View. Make certain that the Fill box is active in the Toolbox. Now click on the Waves pattern in the Swatches palette. Any new objects will have this fill.

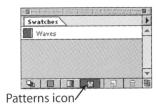

Patterns icon

7. Hold the Option/Alt key and click the Rounded Rectangle tool cursor on approximately the center of the document page. In the dialog box set the Width for 7 in., and the Height for 9 in. Click OK. The rounded rectangle, filled with the Waves pattern will be created. As the rectangle appears, it will obscure all of the other objects on the page. This is because the Background layer is at the top of the layer list. Being at the top, it is in front of all other objects.

8. Click on the Background layer and drag it down to the bottom of the layer list. Drag the Headline layer up to the top of the layer list. Position the Graphics layer underneath the Headline layer. Be very careful not to move the layers too quickly or you may assign one layer to another. When moving the layers, look for the small double-triangle to the right of the Lock button. Click the Lock button of the Background layer so it cannot be accidentally selected and moved.

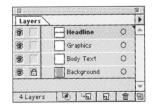

9. With the Selection tool, select each of the objects (headline, turtle, text, and logo) in turn and move them into place on the background, as shown.

Guides drawn on a layer are controlled by that layer. When you hide a layer, its guides are hidden, as well. You might want to create a separate layer called Guides if you want to view all of the guides on each layer.

10. We will add a little bit of halo to the headline. Click on the Headline layer to select it. Drag this layer down to touch the New Layer button at the bottom of the palette. You will see the new layer (marked "copy") appears above the Headline layer. We would like the halo to be behind the real headline, so drag the Headline Copy layer down directly underneath the Headline layer.

11. The Headline Copy layer possesses an exact duplicate (unseen to you) of the actual headline object. Click on the Headline layer's Show/Hide box to hide the headline object. When this is done, you will still see a black headline object. This is the duplicate on the Headline Copy layer.

12. Click the Target button on the Headline Copy layer. This will select the headline object on this layer. Select the Eyedropper tool in the Toolbox and, away from the page, click on the white background of the document. This is a shortcut to painting objects white. The headline will become white. Leave it selected.

13. In the Effect menu, select Blur>Gaussian Blur. In the dialog box that appears, set the Pixels for 8 and click OK. The white headline will blur slightly. Click on the Hide/Show box of the Headline layer to bring it back to view. It will sit on top of the halo, accenting it. Double-click on the Headline Copy layer and rename it "Halo".

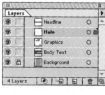

A locked layer can be hidden by clicking its Hide icon.

Dragging a layer to touch the New Layer button duplicates the layer and all objects assigned to it. The Palette menu also has Duplicate Selection, which does the same thing.

14. We will move on to the body-text object. Black type against this dark background is difficult to read, and we need to make the type pop out more visually. Click on the Target button of the Body Text layer. With the Eyedropper tool, click on the white background of the document to paint the text white. It still does not contrast well enough with the background to be easily read. Perhaps it needs a slight drop shadow. Select Undo in the Edit menu to undo the paint attribute you just applied.

15. With the Body Text layer selected, drag it down to touch the New Layer button at the bottom of the palette. The new layer, Body Text Copy, will appear above the dragged layer. Double-click on this copy layer and rename it "Body Text Shadow". Drag this copy layer down to be directly underneath the Body Text layer. Click the Show/Hide box of the Body Text layer.

16. On the Body Text Shadow layer, click the Target button to select the text object. Hold the Command/Control key and press the Right Arrow key once, and the Down Arrow key once. (Note: If you do not hold the Command/Control key, pressing the arrow keys will select the topmost sublayer in the Layers palette).

17. You have offset the body text copy slightly. Click the Hide/Show box of the Body Text layer to bring it back to view. Click the Target button of this layer to select the body text. It is still painted black. Select the Eyedropper tool and paint the text white. It will now appear with the drop shadow to accent it from the background.

18. The area to the left of the turtle looks somewhat blank and needs something to add attraction to the ad. Click on the Graphics layer. In the Layers palette menu, select the New Layer option. A new layer will appear above the Graphics layer. In its dialog box, name this layer "Sun".

19. We will use another technique to see the objects. The background will be too dark to see the thin path outlines, so click the Show/Hide box of the Background layer to hide it from view. You should still be on the Sun layer. Hold the Command/Control key and click the Show/Hide box of this layer to change it to Outline view. You will only see outline paths of objects on this layer. Select the Ellipse tool in the Toolbox and hold the Shift key while you draw a small 0.8-in. circle to the left of the turtle. The drawn object will appear on the Sun layer.

The image icon of a layer shows a composite of all its sublayers. Changing the appearance of an object on a sublayer changes its icon.

20. Choose Window>Show Color to access the Color palette. Use the palette menu to show CMYK color sliders. Select the Stroke box in this palette, and click the None button. Click the Fill box and move the cursor down to the color sampler at the bottom of the Color palette. (When the cursor is over the color sampler, it will take on an eyedropper appearance.) Click on the brightest yellow swatch of the sampler to paint the sun. Note: You will not see it turn yellow on the page, though the image icon on the Sun layer will turn yellow.

21. Hold the Command/Control key and click on the Show/Hide box of the Sun layer. This will bring it back to Preview mode. Now hold Command-Option/Control-Alt and click the Sun layer's Show/Hide box one more time. This will send all other layers into Outline view.

The objects on various sublayers can be selected by clicking their Target buttons while holding the Shift key.

22. Doing this is a convenient way to see a painted object more clearly without other painted objects obscuring the view. Hold Command-Option/Control-Alt and click the Show/Hide box again to bring the other layers back to Preview. Click the Show/Hide box of the Background layer to bring it back to view.

23. Since the sun radiates beams of light, we can make the sun more realistic by using Gaussian Blur. Drag the Sun Layer down to touch the New Layer button. The Sun Copy layer will appear. Double-click on this layer and rename it "Sunbeam". Drag the Sunbeam layer down to be directly underneath the Sun layer. Click the Target button of the Sunbeam layer to select the circle. From the Effect menu, select Blur>Gaussian Blur. Set it for 8 Pixels and click OK. The sun will now radiate a halo.

Though objects are Grouped, and are all selected when clicked on, the individual objects may be selected by clicking the Target buttons on their sublayer.

A handy aspect of guides having individual sublayers is that specific guides may be singled out and hidden by clicking their Hide icon.

24. You have created an attractive ad using layers. Save the document to your **Work in Progress** folder in case you want to review this design later. Close the file.

Sublayers

When an object is on a layer, you will note that to the left of the layer name and thumbnail is a triangular button. This button toggles between showing and not showing a list of the sublayers residing on the layer. Sublayers behave somewhat the same as we have been describing the layers of previous pages, but with some differences we will go into.

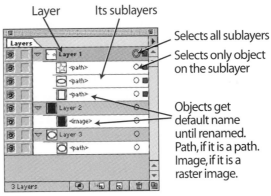

When you create a new document, and drag out guides, you will not see the sublayer button at first. Click on the page and this activates it.

- A single object, whether an open or closed path, or raster image, is a sublayer.

- A selected single path (sublayer) cannot be assigned to another sublayer by moving its Selected Art icon square.

- The Target button in the layer's name field selects all the objects in all of the sublayers. The Target button on a sublayer, however, will only select its single object.

- If a layer is dragged to another layer, it becomes a sublayer.

- A sublayer can be dragged and assigned to another layer.

- Sublayers can be restacked in sequence, in the same way that layers can be restacked.

- Double-clicking a sublayer name brings up a dialog box where it can be named.

Nesting Sublayers

A sublayer can have its own sublayers, which are created when two or more objects are grouped. Creating sublayers inside of sublayers is referred to as "nesting." The new nested sublayers can also have their own sublayers. Don't let it get out of hand, though.

In this example, Layer 1 has five objects, each in its own sublayer (A). Three of the sublayers were selected (B), and Object>Group was selected. The three sublayers combined into one (defaulting to the topmost sublayer selected) and marked as "group" (C) in the palette. The triangle button of this new sublayer was clicked and the three sublayers appeared (D). Even when grouped, objects maintain their individual one-object-per-sublayer status.

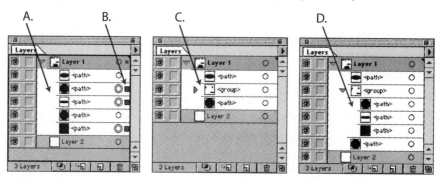

Guides and Layers

We have discussed the value of guides for accuracy in designing and developing your work. When a guide is created, Illustrator assigns it a sublayer and lists it in the Layers palette. If the layer or sublayer holding a guide is hidden, the guide is hidden as well. This could become a hindrance. The guides, however, can get very plentiful if you use them a lot. This means they can be very confusing to the eye when viewing the Layers palette.

If the guide sublayers get out of hand, we suggest putting them into their own layer named "Guides" and keep it located at the bottom of the layer list. Remember to click on this layer when drawing guides. We recommend making layer for guides whenever you create a new documents.

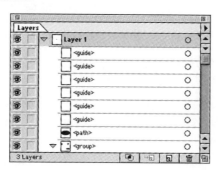 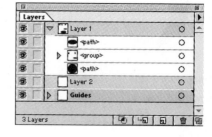

Working with Sublayers and Guides

1. Create a new document set for CMYK Color Mode; leave it untitled and the Artboard set for default.

2. In the View menu, set the view for Fit in Window so you can see the entire page with its objects and guides as they are created.

3. If the Layers palette is on the screen, use Window>Hide Layers to put it away. You will come back to this palette later.

4. Show the page rulers (Command/Control-R) if they are not visible. In the File>Document Setup dialog box, set the Units for Inches.

5. From the vertical and horizontal rulers, drag guides to mark the center of the page. Also, drag guides to mark margins that are 1 in. from the page's edge.

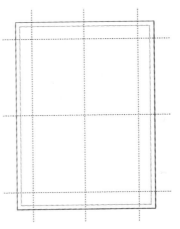

6. Click on the page. Use Window>Show Layers to view the Layers palette. You will at first see only Layer 1 with a triangle button. Click this button. You will see all the guides you created. They are inset on Layer 1, which means they are sublayers. If you use guides frequently, this can make the Layers palette a rather long list of layers and sublayers to scroll through.

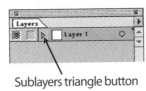

Sublayers triangle button

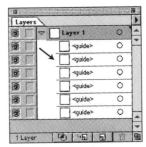

When clicked, shows all
sublayers of the layer

7. If the guides had their own layer, this would keep them out of the way of important layers. Click the sublayer triangle button again to remove the sublayers from view. Select the New Layer button at the bottom of the palette. Layer 2 will appear above Layer 1. Double-click on Layer 1 and rename it "Guides." Double-click on Layer 2 and rename it "Objects". Now we will go on to draw objects.

8. Make sure the Objects layer is active. Select the Ellipse tool in the Toolbox. Hold the Option/Alt key and single-click on the center of the page. Use the dialog box to create a circle that has a Width and Height of 2 in. Click OK.

9. Paint the circle with a black fill, and a stroke of None. Click the triangular sublayer button of the Objects layer. You will see the circle listed there as "<path>". Because the circle is still selected, the Target button on its layer has an added outline.

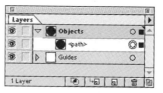

Sublayers stack on top of each other when objects are drawn in the same way that objects are stacked in the order they are added to a document— with the most recently added object on top. Relocating sublayers in the Layers palette accomplishes the same thing as restacking objects in a document using the paste options in the Object menu and the Object>Arrange options.

10. Deselect the circle. Click the Default Colors box in the Toolbox. Change the fill to None. Select the Rectangle tool, press the Option/Alt key, click the cursor on the center of the page. Drag the cursor while pressing the Shift key to draw a square from the center. Make the square big enough to enclose the circle. Observe how the sublayer of this path appears above the circle sublayer. Deselect the square.

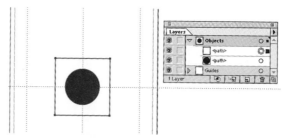

11. Use the Star tool to draw a star that covers both the square and circle. Fill the star with yellow from the Color palette sampler. Observe how the star appears as a sublayer above the other objects in the Layers palette. Deselect the star.

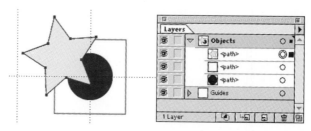

12. Drag the star sublayer down to be under the circle sublayer. Observe how the star object goes behind the square and circle on the page.

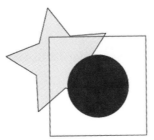
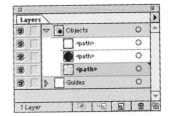

Multiple Target buttons may be selected by holding the Shift key or the Command/Control key while clicking them.

13. Double-click on the star's sublayer and, in the Options dialog box, rename it "Star". Do this for the other objects. Name the circle's sublayer "Circle", and the square sublayer "Square". Yes, each layer has an image icon, but these are not always very clear. Naming layers can avoid accidentally selecting a wrong one.

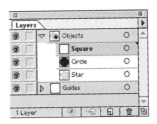

14. The layer Target buttons make it easy to select a specific object, especially in designs that are extremely complex. Click the Target button on the Star layer. Observe how the object becomes selected. Press the Shift key and click the Target buttons of the Circle and Square sublayers. All three objects will be selected. Press Command/Control-G to group the three objects. The grouped objects will become a nested sublayer named "<group>". Click the <group> sublayer button to see the three objects.

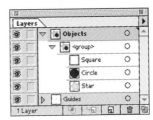

15. Click on the Objects layer. Select the New Layer button at the bottom of the palette. A new layer will appear above the Objects layer. This will be named Layer 3.

16. Use the Rectangle, Ellipse, Star, and Spiral tools to draw an object with each at the top the page. Click the sublayer button on Layer 3 to see the new objects listed as sublayers.

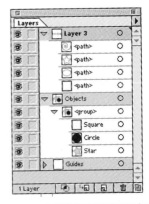

17. Double-click on these sublayers and rename them: "Spiral", "Star 2", "Oval", and "Box".

18. At the top of the page, select the new square and oval, then group them. Observe how the two sublayers combined into a nested sublayer. Deselect the objects.

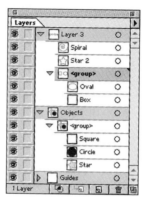

19. When you are working in a document page, selecting individual objects within groups of objects requires using the Direct Selection tool. Sublayers make it easy to do this just by clicking the Target button. While pressing the Command/Control key, click on the Target buttons of the grouped sublayers (Oval, Box, Square, Circle, and Star). Observe how their corresponding objects in the document become selected.

20. You can use sublayers to hide or lock objects singled out from within groups. Click the Show/Hide box of the Circle sublayer. Click the Lock/Unlock box of the Square sublayer. Attempt to select the square object with the Selection tool. It is locked. In the document, click on the large star object. It is part of this group, but you can still select it.

21. Click the Show/Hide box of the Circle sublayer to bring it back to view. Click the Lock/Unlock box of the Square sublayer to unlock it.

22. Hold the Command/Control key and click the Show/Hide box of the large star. This will send it to Outline viewing mode. Observe the star on the page. Click on the Show/Hide box again holding the same key to return it to Preview.

23. In Layer 3, the Box and Oval are grouped. Click on this "<group>" sublayer and drag it down to touch the Objects layer. It will relocate to be a part of this layer.

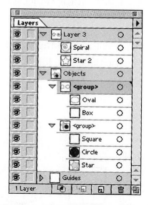

24. Click on the Objects layer. In the palette menu, select Collect in New Layer. The layer and all its sublayers will be nested to a new layer named Layer 4. You can see how versatile layers and sublayers are for relocating and altering objects.

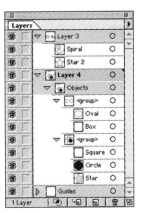

The Trash icon is useful for deleting layers or sublayers. The Palette menu also has Delete Selection, which does the same thing.

25. Click on Layer 3 and drag it down to touch the Trash icon. This will delete the layer and sublayers without a warning message.

26. In the palette menu, select Flatten Artwork. This will combine all layers into one layer, defaulting to the selected layer at the top of the list, which is Layer 4. You will see all the sublayers of the layer, including the guides. Click on the guide sublayer at the top of the list. Hold the Command/Control key and select the rest of the guide sublayers. Choose Delete Selection from the palette menu.

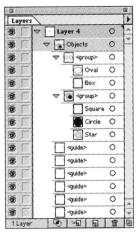

27. Click on the two remaining grouped sublayers and drag them to the Trash icon. All that remains is Layer 4. Can it be deleted? No, every document must have at least one layer to work on.

28. You have observed most of the functions of sublayers and how they increase the flexibility of layers, objects, and maneuvering them while developing a design. Close the document without saving.

Chapter Summary

You have observed how useful, if not indispensable, layers are to creating complex designs. You have learned how to use the Layers palette and identify its components. You have learned to organize layers by dragging them in the Layers palette. You have learned how to relocate selected objects to other layers, and change the order of layers. You have learned about Sublayers, and how they relate to their main layer. You have learned how to use keyboard shortcuts to manipulate layer features and have observed how guides are shown in the Layers palette.

Notes:

CHAPTER 10

ARTISTIC EFFECTS

CHAPTER OBJECTIVE:

To learn how drawing paths with the Pen, Rectangle, and Ellipse tools can create objects that when combined with others, or modified individually, produce artistic effects that would take considerable time to produce traditionally. In Chapter 10, you will:

- Learn about Operations and Filters and what defines them.
- Study and learn about Outline Path, Offset Path, Slice, Add Anchor Points, and Simplify, using and observing their path altering attributes.
- Learn about the Pathfinder palette, and how to use its features on objects.
- Learn about Illustrator's additional creative drawing tools such as the Pencil and Paintbrush tools.
- Learn about the Brush palette, its four categories of brushes: Calligraphic, Scatter, Art, and Pattern, and understand how to apply the brushes to paths.
- Observe and experience the usage of Filters and how they affect both vector and raster objects.

PROJECTS TO BE COMPLETED:

- **Art Deco House (A)**
- BearWear Business Cards (B)
- Wine and Cheese Invitation (C)
- **Walking the Dogs (D)**
- Broadway Bound (E)
- Joker's Wild (F)
- BearWear Label (G)

Remember, the difference between the Filter and Effect menu is that filters modify the object's original path, whereas effects do not.

Note that the fill of the original object affects the outcome of applying Outline Stroke: If the original path is filled with anything (color, gradient, pattern), it retains the original path, which can be deleted or used further. If the original object is filled with None, the original path is deleted when Outline Stroke is applied.

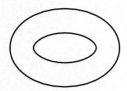

Outlined stroke shown. Original object had Fill set at None.

Artistic Effects

Drawing paths with the Pen, Rectangle, Ellipse, and other drawing tools can create objects that can be combined and modified to produce results to rival art produced in any traditional media and in less time. This chapter covers many of the Illustrator features that produce stand-alone special effects, and others that when combined with other effects will allow you to produce highly complex and professional designs. Many of these effects fall under the headings of Operations and Filters.

- **Operations.** An operation is a path-modifying effect that either cuts, combines, intersects, deletes, or expands paths to achieve the desired result.

- **Filters.** The Filter menu is filled with preprogrammed enhancements that affect the appearances of both vector and raster objects. Most supply a dialog box that allows you to customize the filter.

Operations

The Object menu has a Path option that offers several features related to manipulating paths. Five of these features are used for modifying paths: Outline Stroke, Offset Path, Simplify, Add Anchor Points, and Slice.

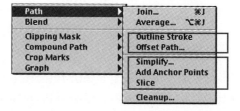

Outline Stroke

Outline Stroke is a very convenient way to add outer and inner paths to a selected object. This feature works directly from the thickness of the object's stroke and becomes especially noticeable on objects with heavy stroke weights. When Outline Stroke is applied to an object, the original path is duplicated along the inner and outer edges of the stroke.

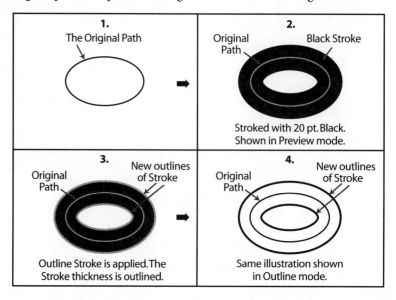

Offset Path

The path, regardless of its stroke attributes, is the starting point in this operation. Offset Path has a dialog box that allows specific increments to be set.

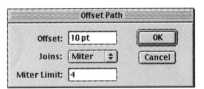

Positive numbers make the offset occur outside of the original path. Negative numbers offset the path inside. Here is an example of Offset Path, seen in Outline mode. The original path remains intact, and may be deleted or reused.

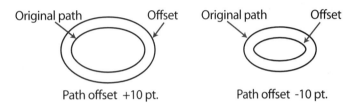

Path offset +10 pt.   Path offset -10 pt.

Outlining Strokes and Offsetting Paths

1. Create a new Untitled document set for CMYK Color Mode. Leave the Artboard Size set for default. Show the Color and Stroke palettes from the Window menu.

2. In the Stroke palette set the Weight at 3 pt. In the Color palette, click on the Stroke box, then click on the black color box in the lower right corner of the palette. Select the palette's Fill box and click a bright color from the Color Sampler.

3. Select the Ellipse tool from the Toolbox and draw an ellipse about $3'' \times 2''$ (A). Use the Selection tool to select the ellipse and press Option/Alt to drag a copy of the ellipse. Keep the ellipse copy selected and reset the stroke weight to 10 pt. (B). Choose Object>Path>Outline Stroke. Nothing apparent will happen to the selected object.

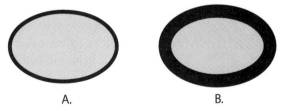

A.   B.

4. With this outlined object selected, select the Eyedropper tool from the Toolbox, and click on the original ellipse. This will apply the paint attributes, including the stroke weight, to the outlined paths. Go to Outline viewing mode to see the new paths.

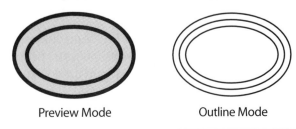

Preview Mode   Outline Mode

When working with object widths, the standard unit of measurement in printing and commercial art is the Point. Use either Document Setup or Preferences>Units of Measurement to set the units to Points when inches or picas appear in dialog boxes.

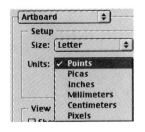

With Offset Path, negative offset numbers make a path inside the selected object. Positive numbers create an outside path.

5. Return to Preview mode. Click on the outlined object with the Selection tool and move it to the side. Observe the result. What you see are two objects: the original path and the outline stroke. Notice how the new object is transparent in its middle section.

Original Path   Outlined Stroke

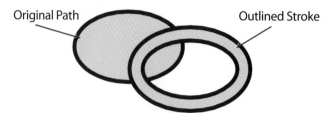

6. Select the original path and delete it. This will leave the outlined object.

7. Click on the smaller path with the Direct Selection tool to select only this path. Click on the Fill box in the Color palette and change the fill to any color in the Color Sampler. Observe the results. Even though you singled out the smaller path and tried to fill it with color, it remained white in its interior.

8. Why is this? The Outline Stroke feature does something to the two paths called Compounding (an advanced issue covered in ATC's Advanced Digital Illustration book). You do not have to understand this feature to turn it off and access the paths individually. Select the outline object with the Selection tool. Go to the Object menu and select Compound Path>Release. The smaller path will take the fill color of the larger path (A) Now click on the smaller path with the Selection tool (you no longer need the Direct Selection tool now that Compounding has been removed). Fill the smaller path with a lighter color from the Color Sampler. Observe how the two paths are now separate from each other (B).

A.   B.

9. Using Outline Stroke on objects gives you two paths to work with. The Offset Path feature offers only one extra path. We will now move on to see how this takes place. Select all the paths in the document and delete them.

10. Use the Star tool to draw a star (hold the Shift key to constrain). Click the Default Colors icon in the Toolbox to paint it. Set the Weight field in the Stroke palette for 15 pt., then apply this to the path.

11. We will use Outline Stroke to prepare the object before offsetting its path. Choose Object>Path>Outline Stroke. View the results in Outline mode to see the two new paths. Select the two inside stars with the Direct Selection tool (holding Option/Alt) and delete them. The largest star will remain. Select it with the Selection tool.

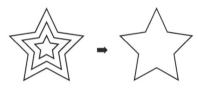

12. Use Object>Path>Offset Path to display its dialog box. Set the offset for -0.069 in. Click OK. The offset duplicate will appear inside the original. Click the original with the Direct Selection tool. Delete it, leaving the offset copy.

13. Select the offset copy and go back to Object>Path>Offset Path to display its dialog box. Set the offset for 0.2 in. Click OK.

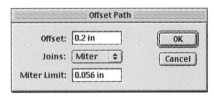

14. The Offset Path feature will create a new and large star path around the original. An Offset Path object needs no ungrouping or releasing of compound. The paths are separate and can be selected individually.

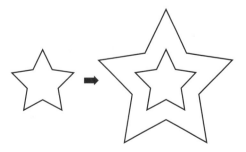

15. Close the file without saving.

Slice

Slicing allows one object to cut its contours into another, the way a cookie cutter would. The slicing object is placed on top of the target object. Then, with only the cutting object selected, Object>Path>Slice is applied. The target object appears with the cutting shape "drawn" into it. When that shape is deleted, the target object shows the contour of the object that was sliced out of it.

In this example, a star was placed over a square (A). The star was selected, and Object>Path>Slice applied. The portion of the star's path (shown in white) that remained after the slice took on the fill color of the square (B). We moved the star (C) to show the cut that was made into the square. Note how the star was cut off at the edge of the square (B and C).

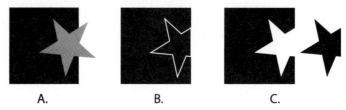

A.   B.   C.

Slice will only alter objects with if their paths are touching.

Simplify

The Simplify feature either adds or removes anchor points while altering the straight lines and curves set in its dialog box. Some interesting variations of a simple object can be obtained using Simplify. The lower the percentage number in the Curve Precision field, the fewer the number of anchor points; and vice versa. We suggest you create some paths and experiment with the features in the dialog box.

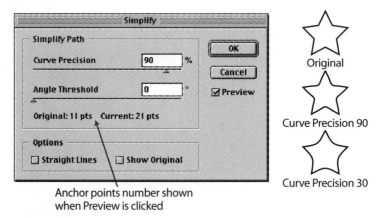

Anchor points number shown
when Preview is clicked

The Simplify feature is not a refining and fine-tuning function. It can remove or add anchor points, but the segments are also affected and require you to do the refining with the Direct Selection tool.

Add Anchor Points

The Add Anchor Points feature accessed in the Object>Path menu does not directly alter the appearance of an image. However, this feature is very convenient because there are many operations and filters that use anchor points as the takeoff point for executing their effects. Each time you apply Add Anchor Points, a new point appears at the halfway position between two existing anchor points.

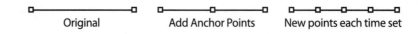

Original   Add Anchor Points   New points each time set

Slicing Paths, Simplifying Paths, and Adding Anchor Points

1. Create a new Untitled document set for CMYK Color Mode, and leave the Artboard Size set for default. Press the "D" key to make certain the fill and stroke colors are set for default. Set the stroke weight for 3 pt. in the Stroke palette. Select the Star tool and click its cursor on the page. In the dialog box that appears, set Radius 1 at 0.25, Radius 2 at 0.30, and Points at 11. Click OK. The star will appear. Use the Direct Selection tool to select and move several anchor points, making the star appear somewhat ragged.

2. With the Ellipse tool, draw an "egg" about 3 in. wide and 2 in. high. Move the distorted star to be on the top right of the ellipse.

3. Go to Object>Path>Slice. Select and delete the remaining part of the star. You have used Slice to create an interesting cracked egg object.

Delete star path

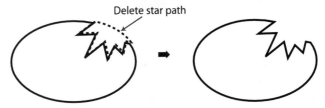

4. Use the Rectangle, Ellipse, Polygon and Spiral tools to draw some objects at the top of the page. Select each object and access the Simplify option from the Object>Path menu. In the dialog box, make sure Preview is checked so you will see the results on the selected path. Experiment with the settings and see how they affect the objects.

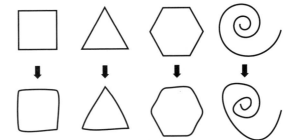

5. You have used some of Illustrator's operations.

6. Close the file without saving.

Pathfinder is one of the handiest operation features of Illustrator, having the ability to modify and create new objects with basic shapes, such as circles and squares.

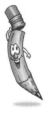

Some Pathfinder operations must be Ungrouped before the composite objects can be maneuvered or relocated.

Pathfinder Palette

The Pathfinder palette is accessed from the Window menu. There are many operations in the palette that work on two or more selected objects. They are very powerful and work quickly. These Pathfinder functions will save hours of time that would be spent drawing, redrawing, cutting, joining, and performing the many path-editing tasks that can be accomplished in seconds with Pathfinder.

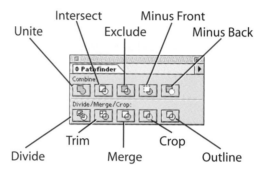

We are not going to describe each function and how it affects paths in detail, but we will show the effects, based on two original objects. Some of these operations will be demonstrated in the exercise that follows.

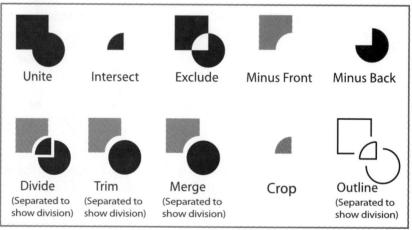

Using Pathfinder on Objects

1. Open the document **Pathfinder.AI** from the **SF-Intro Illustrator** folder. Set the view for Preview. Select the top rectangle and the star.

2. In the Pathfinder palette, click the Unite icon. Observe how all the interior paths are removed, leaving a single path outlining the two objects. Choose Edit>Undo (Command/Control-Z) to undo this operation.

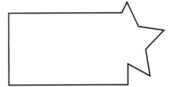

3. Click the next Pathfinder operation, Intersect. Observe how only the area of the star that intersected within the rectangle was retained. Undo this.

4. Click the next Pathfinder operation, Exclude. You will not see anything apparent happen. They have been grouped. Ungroup the two, and move the star outside the rectangle to the right. Observe how the intersecting piece has been excluded. Select Undo three times to reset the objects to their original shape.

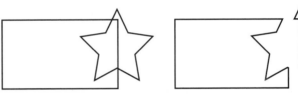

What Pathfinder creates   Separated to show division

5. Move down to the gray rectangle and star. Select both objects. Click the next Pathfinder operation, Minus Front. Notice how the front object, the star, has been removed, cutting its shape into the rectangle. Undo this.

What Pathfinder creates

6. Click the next Pathfinder operation, Minus Back. Observe how the rectangle, which was in back, has cut its shape into the star. Undo this.

7. Click Pathfinder's Divide icon. Ungroup the resulting object. Move its sections to the right to see how it was divided. Select Undo three times to go back to the original.

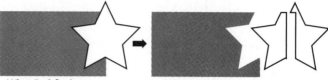

What Pathfinder creates Separated here to show division

8. Click the next Pathfinder operation, Trim. The star will cut its shape into the rectangle, but there is still a star outline, as shown below. Undo this.

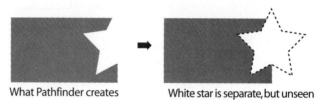

What Pathfinder creates White star is separate, but unseen
(shown here)

9. Click the next Pathfinder operation, Merge. The effect is identical to Trim. Even the unpainted star still remains. Undo this.

What Pathfinder creates The white knock-out
is made by a white path (shown)

10. Click the next Pathfinder operation, Crop. The intersected portion of the star will remain, but an unpainted section is also there. Undo this.

11. Click the next Pathfinder operation, Outline. The result is an empty portion of the rectangle where the star was located. If you choose Outline mode, you will see the outlines of the star.

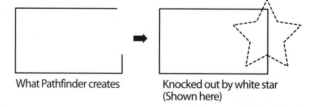

What Pathfinder creates Knocked out by white star
(Shown here)

12. You have used the Pathfinder operations and observed how they affect selected paths. We recommend that you experiment with the features in the Pathfinder palette so you will understand and remember their effects when you need to modify objects.

13. Close the file without saving.

Creative Drawing Tools

Other than the Pen, Rectangle, and Ellipse tools that draw paths suitable for modifications, there are two more tools that are used to make creative paths in Illustrator: the Pencil and Paintbrush tools. Though they create paths in a different way, the Pencil and Paintbrush tools are both used in a freehand style of drawing, much like using a pencil or paintbrush held by hand.

Pencil Tool

The Pencil tool gives you the freedom of drawing movement that you get with paper and pencil. Though a line made with the Pencil tool does not much resemble a vector path as it is being drawn, as soon as the Pencil cursor is released, the line becomes a path with anchor points and editing handles at each curve. A line drawn with this tool can be modified using any of Illustrator's features that apply to paths.

Drawing a Closed Path

The Pencil tool can be used to draw a closed path by following a specific sequence of steps. Begin by dragging the Pencil cursor on the page to create the desired path. Press the Option/Alt key before releasing the cursor. The path will close as soon as the cursor is released. Once an open path has been drawn, it can be converted to a closed path as described below.

Editing a Path with the Pencil Tool

The curves in a path drawn with the Pencil tool can be edited using the anchor point handles in the same way that any vector path can be modified. In some situations, this kind of precision drawing is not needed or desired. A path can be lengthened with the Pencil tool by clicking the Pencil cursor on one of the path's end points and continuing the drawing.

An open path can be converted to a closed path by clicking with the Pencil tool on any anchor point or segment in the path, then drawing a line and releasing the cursor directly on top of a segment or anchor point anywhere in the original path. In this example, a path was drawn (A). With the path selected, the Pencil cursor was clicked on the endpoint and the line continued to a segment in the original path (B). When the cursor was released, the "tail" left from the original path was absorbed into the newly created closed path (C).

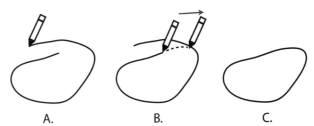

A.   B.   C.

Smooth Tool and Eraser Tool

In the Pencil tool pop-out menu, you will find two very useful path-editing tools: the Smooth tool and the Eraser tool.

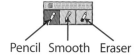

Pencil Smooth Eraser

These tools can be used to edit any vector path, regardless of which tool was used to create the path. The Smooth tool, when dragged over anchor points on a selected path will smooth jagged corners, more and more, as it is applied.

The Eraser tool is designed to delete portions of any segment of a selected path and to sever segments. The tool's cursor is clicked on any existing anchor point or segment of a path then dragged along the path to shorten the segment. As the Eraser tool deletes segments in a path, it also deletes the anchor points associated with those segments. However, the tool cannot be used to simply delete individual anchor points along a path.

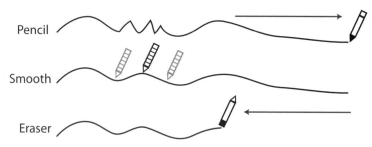

Tips on the Smooth and Eraser Tools

- Neither of these tools will affect a path unless the path has first been selected.

- Single-clicking on any existing anchor point or segment and dragging toward the path shortens a segment.

- Double-clicking on a segment severs the path and deselects one of the newly created segments.

- Single-clicking on a segment or anchor point and immediately releasing the cursor severs the path, but leaves the new endpoints of the two new paths connected. To disconnect the anchor points, you must select one of the new paths with the Selection tool and drag the selected path away. If you leave the two endpoints connected, and use the Direct Selection tool to reshape one of the segments, you can create the appearance of the stroke having been split but not severed.

To quickly select a path while the Eraser tool is active, hold down the Command/Control key while clicking on the desired path with one of the selection tools.

To toggle between the Eraser tool and the Smooth tool, hold down the Option/Alt key.

Before using the Paintbrush tool, or applying Brushes to drawn paths, make certain that the Fill box in the Toolbox is set for None. Otherwise, the paths painted with brush strokes will fill in and obscure the image.

Filled with None

Filled with Gray

The Scatter brush objects that appear are quite large for basic paths. You might want to reduce their size, which can be done by double-clicking on the Brush in the Brushes palette. This brings up an options dialog box where the size percentage can be changed.

Paintbrush Tool

The Paintbrush tool works in the same freehand style as the Pencil tool. The attributes of the strokes created by the Paintbrush tool are determined by whatever brush swatch has been selected from the Brushes palette or the Brush Libraries found in the Window menu.

Illustrator's brushes are grouped into four categories: Calligraphic, Scatter, Art, and Pattern.

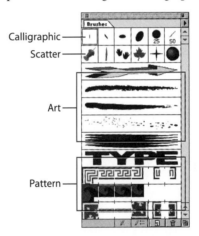

Calligraphic

This brush stroke is a continuous flow that simulates the effect of an actual calligraphy pen. The strokes are constructed of various thicknesses and endcaps.

Scatter

The Scatter brush stroke does what the name implies. It scatters objects along the stroke of the drawn path.

A freeform closed path can be drawn with the Paint-brush tool in the same way as a closed path is drawn with the Pencil tool. The key to success is following the correct sequence: Begin drawing the path with the Paintbrush tool then press the Option/Alt key before releasing the tool's cursor.

Changes made in any of the Brush Options dialog boxes are applicable only to the brushes in the document where the changes are made. They will not be set permanently so that all future documents will retain these modifications. If these changes are made in the Adobe Illustrator Startup document, however, the modifications will be available in all Illustrator documents. You may recognize that this is also true of the Styles and Swatches palettes.

Art

An Art brush stroke is a single object, such as a pointing arrow, that extends the length of a path from beginning point to end point.

These brush objects bend and twist along with the contours of the path.

Pattern

Attractive borders can be drawn with the Pattern brush stroke, when applied to open or closed paths.

Brush Libraries

In addition to the brush strokes available in the Brushes palette, Illustrator provides Brush Libraries, which can be accessed from the Window menu. The keystrokes, buttons, and palette menus for the Brush Libraries palettes function much in the same as the other library palettes.

Brush Libraries ▶	Animal Sample
Show Swatches	Arrow Sample
Swatch Libraries ▶	Artistic Sample
Show Layers	Border Sample
Show Actions	Calligraphic
Show Links	Default
	Default_CMYK
Show SVG Interactivity	Default_RGB
Show Transform	Floral Sample
Show Align	Object Sample
Show Pathfinder	Other Library...

The Pattern brushes can be applied to any object, whether circle, rectangle, polygon, or open path.

As with any of its powerful features, we can only scratch the surface of these drawing. If you desire to truly understand and gain proficiency with these tools, you must devote time to experimenting with them on your own.

The Calligraphy brushes are highly effective when you want to achieve the look of a calligraphy pen tip.

Each of the brush strokes from the various Brush Libraries fall into the same categories (art, scatter, calligraphic, and pattern) as the brush strokes on the Brushes palette. Here are six of the Brush libraries you can use.

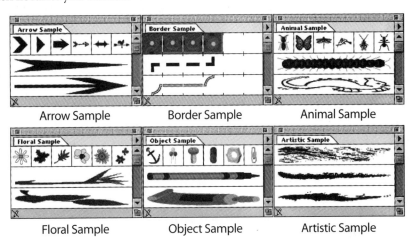

Arrow Sample   Border Sample   Animal Sample

Floral Sample   Object Sample   Artistic Sample

Applying Brush Strokes to Paths

There are two methods for applying a brush stroke to a path: One method is to select a brush stroke from one of the Brush Libraries or from the Brush palette, then activate the Paintbrush tool and draw a path. The stroke will be applied to the path as you draw. This method is only useful when drawing freeform paths.

The other method for applying a brush stroke to a path is to select a path that already exists then click on a brush stroke from one of the brush palettes. Any path, regardless of its origin, can be painted with a brush stroke. This means that brush strokes can be applied to paths created with any of the drawing tools or paths created with such tools as the Star and Rectangle tool. In these examples, Pattern brush strokes were applied to closed paths to create borders.

Editing Paths Containing Brush Strokes

We refer to the path that supports a brush stroke a "spine." The spinal path, like other paths, can be edited, modified, and extended to alter a brush's appearance.

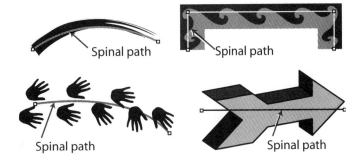

Spinal path   Spinal path

Spinal path   Spinal path

In this example, the short path (A) did not show enough of the brush. The spine was extended with the Pen tool, and showed more objects (B).

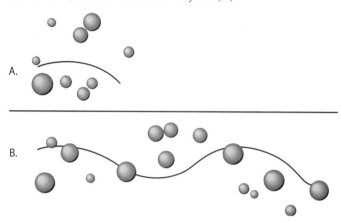

Editing Brush Strokes

Any brush stoke can be applied to a path which can then be edited, and the brush stroke itself can be converted to a path, and then edited. This makes the possibilities for creating artistic effects with Illustrator's features almost unlimited.

Customizing Brushes

Each of the four types of brush — Art, Scatter, Pattern, and Calligraphic — has an options dialog box for customizing a brush stroke. You have your choice of different ways to access the options dialog box for a brush stroke: double clicking on the brush stroke's swatch in the Brushes palette, clicking on the Options of Selected Stroke icon at the bottom of the Brushes palette, or selecting Brush Options in the palette menu.

This is an example of how the options in the dialog box can be applied. The six Calligraphic pen tips provided by Illustrator may have the right shape but may be too large for your purposes. The tip diameter can be changed in the Calligraphic Brush Options dialog box.

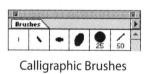

Calligraphic Brushes

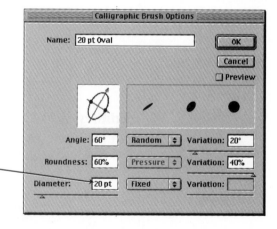

Editing Brush Strokes as Objects

If you apply a brush stroke, such as the Push Pin, to a path, you are restricted to the positions of the objects as applied. Let's suppose you would like to relocate specific objects in the brush stroke. As it is, the brush strokes assigned to a path are merely an "appearance." They are not tangible paths that can be selected. Before a brush stroke can be edited, it must be extracted from the spine on which it resides.

The "diameter" of a brush can be customized to a certain extent without changing the settings in the Brush Options dialog box. Use the Weight setting in the Stroke palette to alter the point size. The default weight is 1 pt. If you change the stroke weight to 0.5 pt., the diameter of the brush will be 50% of its default. Setting the stroke weight at 2 pt. would result in a 200% increase in diameter.

Experimenting with the many drawing tools is an education in itself. You will be able to see what you can create, how the tools work, and what you can expect from the tools.

This is done by selecting the spine and choosing Object>Expand Appearance. This converts the brush stroke to a path or group of paths. Though the spinal path still exists, it is no longer associated with the brush-stroke objects.

The brush-stroke objects are grouped and may need to be ungrouped using Object>Ungroup (Command/Control-Shift-G) before they can be edited or moved as individual objects. To move individual objects without ungrouping, the Direct Selection tool is used to select and relocate them.

In this example, the Push Pin brush was applied to the line (A). Because the brush stroke is an appearance and not an object, in Outline view push pins were not visible (B). When Object>Expand Appearance was applied, the push pins become paths that were selected with the Direct Selection and moved (C).

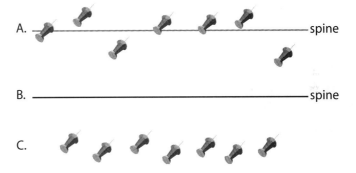

Using the Pencil and Paintbrush Tools

1. Create a new document set for CMYK Color Mode, leave it untitled and the Artboard Size set for default. In the Toolbox, click on the Default Colors icon, then set the Fill box for None. You will have a 1-pt. black stroke.

2. Select the Pencil tool and experiment with dragging it onto the page to draw paths. Click the Pencil tool on one of the endpoints and drag it to the right of the path. You will see how the tool can be used to extend a path.

3. Now draw a path that is very jagged. Keep the path selected.

4. Select the Smooth tool in the Pencil tool pop-out menu. Drag the tool over some of the anchor points of the path. Notice how it smooths the jagged curves.

5. Select the Eraser tool. Drag it on some of the anchor points of the path. Notice how it erases anchor points and segments.

6. Keep this path selected.

7. Choose Window>Show Brushes. Click on any of the brushes in the palette to see how your selected path takes on the brush stroke.

8. When you're through experimenting, delete this path.

9. Click on the Paintbrush tool in the Toolbox.

10. In the Brushes palette, click on the Charcoal brush stroke. Drag the Paintbrush tool on the page. Experiment with quick strokes, slow strokes, and long, drawn out strokes.

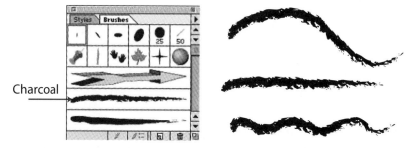

Charcoal

11. Click on each of these drawn paths, one at a time, with the Selection tool, and select a different brush stroke from the Brushes palette for each one. Observe how simple it is to apply brush strokes to paths.

12. Use the Direct Selection tool to click on any single path you drew to view its anchor points. Select different points and drag to relocate the path. Click on the control handle of any curve and modify its shape. Observe how these changes alter the effects of the Brush appearance on the path. When you are through experimenting with these paths, delete them.

13. With the Rectangle tool, draw a 5-in. by 3-in. rectangle on the page. One at a time, click on each of the Pattern brushes to apply their borders to the rectangle. When you are finished applying the brush strokes, select all the rectangles and delete them.

14. With the Pen tool draw a single horizontal path about 5 in. long, holding the Shift key to constrain it. With this path selected, click on the variety of Scatter brushes in the Brushes palette.

15. Observe how the objects are "scattered" along the line.

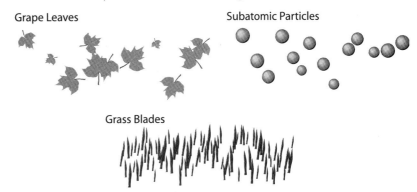

Grape Leaves

Subatomic Particles

Grass Blades

16. Leave the path painted with the Subatomic Particles brush stroke. With the path selected, choose Object>Expand Appearance. The particles will be extracted from the brush stroke and reside on the page as path objects. With the objects still selected, choose Object>Ungroup.

17. Go to Outline mode and you will see the spinal path and the paths of the particles. Use the Direct Selection tool to select the spine, and delete it.

18. Return to Preview mode. With the Selection tool, select and move the particles around into a different pattern.

19. Expanded brushes turn into paths that can be edited. They can be moved, deleted, or painted in the same manner as any other paths in Illustrator. Select some of the particles, open the Color palette, and use the Color Sampler to experiment with assigning different colors to the fill and stroke of the objects.

20. Choose Edit>Select All (Command/Control-A) to select all the objects on the page, and delete them. Make certain that the Fill box of the Toolbox is set for None and the Stroke is set for Black. Click on the Paintbrush tool in the Toolbox.

21. In the Brushes palette, click on any of the Calligraphic brushes and experiment with drawing on the page. Try different calligraphic tips, and observe how the objects look as you are drawing them and after you release the mouse. Draw shapes, then write words, and notice how clean the edges of the strokes look.

22. Select all of the objects on the page and delete them. Double-click on the far right Calligraphic brush, which is an example of a large calligraphy pen.

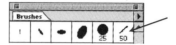

23. In the Calligraphic Brush Options dialog box, set the Diameter at 7 pt. Click OK.

24. With the Paintbrush tool, write different words, write your name, and experiment with this pen tip.

25. You have experienced and observed the many features of the Pencil and Paintbrush tools, and how the Brushes palette can be used to affect the appearance of paths drawn with these tools.

26. Close the document without saving.

Filters

Filters are preprogrammed operation, that modify elements of a drawing to create specialized visual effects. In an instant, filters perform tasks that would prove very complicated if performed using Illustrator's basic tools and commands. There are two categories of options in the Filter menu: filters that can be applied only to vector paths and filters that can be applied only to raster (bitmap) images. Though each category has filters with the same names that create similar visual effects, the filters are not interchangeable. Filters that cannot be applied to a selected object are grayed out in the menu.

Filters are applied by selecting an object then choosing an option from the Filter menu. As with many of Illustrator's features, many (but not all) filters can be edited from within a corresponding dialog box.

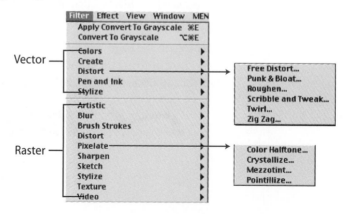

The Preview button in most Filter dialog boxes is a convenient way to see how an effect will look before applying it to the path.

Most of the Raster filters work only on RGB. A few work on Grayscale and CMYK. When a raster object is selected but a filter name is grayed in the section of the Filter menu that applies to raster images, it means the color model of the selected object is not correct.

Raster Object Filters

The raster filters become available only when raster objects, such as TIFF, JPG, GIF, PICT, BMP, and others, are selected. These can be either raster objects that were placed in the document, or paths drawn in the document that were Rasterized by the Rasterize feature.

Vector Path Filters

Filters for vector paths can be applied to objects drawn within Illustrator, as well as on vector path objects imported from other drawing programs, as long as they are imported into the Illustrator document with their paths intact. This example shows how a simple ellipse can become an advertising bug using a series of filters.

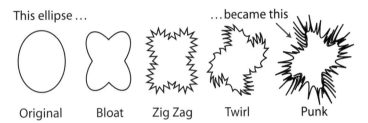

This ellipse …   …became this

Original   Bloat   Zig Zag   Twirl   Punk

We will observe and practice with some of Illustrator's vector path filters.

Zig Zag Filter

To turn a straight line into a zigzag line, select the path and choose Filter>Distort>Zig Zag. This will bring up a dialog box where you can customize the zigzag appearance.

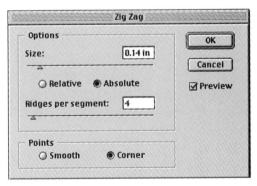

- **Size.** Designates the total height of the zigzag peaks.

- **Absolute/Relative.** Determines the height of the peaks in points or in a percentage. Absolute sets the height of the peaks at the number of points entered in the Size field. Relative sets the height of the peak as a percentage of the length of the original path (the shorter the path, the shorter the peaks).

- **Ridges.** Sets the number of zigzags that will appear on the selected path. The higher the number of ridges, the closer together the zigzag peaks will be.

- **Points.** Designates the shape of the zigzag peaks: Smooth button sets rounded peaks. The Corner button sets pointed peaks.

- **Preview.** Allows you to see how the path's appearance will change before the filter is actually applied.

Here are some samples of the Zig Zag filter.

All paths set for Size = 12   Ridges = 24

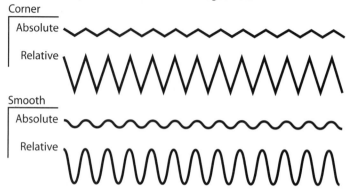

Creating Effects with the Zig Zag Filter

1. Create a new document set for CMYK Color Mode, leave it untitled and the Artboard Size set for default. Click the Default Colors box in the Toolbox. In the File> Document Setup dialog box set the Units to Inches.

2. With the Pen tool, draw a line segment about 1.5 in. long, holding the Shift key to constrain the path to 45°.

3. Choose Filter>Distort>Zig Zag. Set the Size to 30 pt., keep the Absolute button selected, and set the Ridges to 12. Select the Corner button and the Preview button. Click OK.

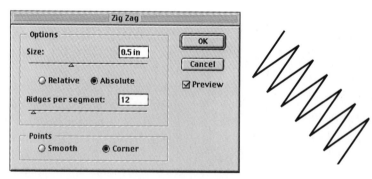

4. With the path selected, choose Window>Show Swatches. Click on the Gradients button at the bottom of the palette. View the palette by Name View.

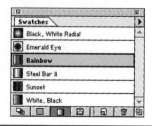

Once you have applied a hatch effect to an object, this object turns into a "masked" path holding the hatch. When an object becomes a mask, it looses its original paint attributes. In the event that you want this object later, even if you don't think you will need it, we recommend making a copy of your original path before applying the hatch.

Some experimenting should be performed to see how the Hatch menu affects the Hatch effect, and vice-versa. The other features control the density, rotation, and scaling of the hatch, which can offer a wide range of possible effects.

5. Fill the zigzag with the Rainbow gradient. Observe how the open path connects the fill from endpoint to endpoint. The result should look similar to this.

6. Delete this object. Keep the document open for the next exercise.

Pen and Ink Filter

Illustrator's Pen and Ink feature allows you to create the rough dry-brush look associated with art rendered by hand. Selecting the Hatch Effects option from the Filters>Pen and Ink menu brings up a dialog box with a sizeable list of artistic effects.

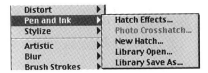

You could create your own hatch effects by drawing an enormous number of short paths and applying various strokes to them, or you can choose from Illustrator's almost unlimited options in the Hatch Effects dialog box. The options in Hatch Effects field describe the lengths and contours of the paths that make up the hatching, and the Hatch field describes the strokes that have been applied to the paths.

When these options are selected, the appropriate fields display attributes of the hatching that can be modified. The Preview button is a valuable time saver because it allows you to see the hatching as you select and modify it before applying it to an object in a document. The gray scale to the right of the Preview button allows you to set the light-dark value of the hatching.

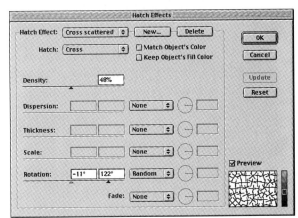

If you have created a hatch effect that you want to save, you can add it to Illustrator's premade hatches. This is done by selecting and copying (Command/Control-C) the effect you have created then choosing Filter>Pen and Ink>New Hatch. This brings up a dialog

The Hatch filters can get rather messy, so be careful. Use the Preview button in their dialog boxes to see the effects before applying them.

box where you can click on New to bring up a field for naming the new hatch. When the name has been assigned, the copied effect is then added by clicking the Paste button.

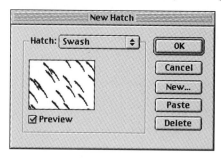

Applying Pen and Ink Hatch Effects

1. Continue in the open document from the last exercise. Click the Default Colors icon in the Toolbox.

2. With the Rectangle tool, draw a 3-in. square on the page. Paint it with a bright fill color and a contrasting 8-pt. stroke, then copy it.

3. Choose the Filter menu and select Pen and Ink>Hatch Effects.

4. In the dialog box, make certain that Preview is selected. Click on the Hatch Effects menu and select Cross scattered. In the Hatch menu, select the Cross option. Observe how the Preview looks.

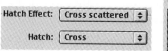

The masses of paths and strokes in a single applied hatch effect takes up large amounts of memory on your hard drive. You will know this is happening when there are long pauses between selecting a command and seeing the results on the screen. Using the Preview function in the Hatch Effects dialog box allows you to avoid some of this memory slow-down as you select the hatch you want.

5. In the Hatch Effects dialog box, select the Match Object's Color button, then select the Keep Object's Fill Color button and compare the results in the Preview box. Notice that both buttons cannot be selected at the same time. Deselect both buttons.

6. Select Dots from the hatch menu. Observe how this changes the Preview. Click on different buttons in the Grayscale bar to the right of the Preview box to see what happens to the dots.

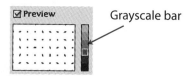
Grayscale bar

7. Change the Hatch Effect to Stipple Medium, select Match Objects Color, and tryout different grayscale buttons in the Grayscale bar. Now select Keep Object's Fill and tryout different grayscale settings.

8. Change the Hatch to Cross. Observe how the Cross hatch changes the appearance of the Stipple Medium hatch effect.

9. Change the Hatch back to dots. Click OK. Notice how the stroke and fill colors of your original square have disappeared. You cannot select the path again and apply a stroke. That is why we had you copy the original square. Click on this Pen and Ink object and choose Edit>Paste in Front. Change the Fill box to None so the pasted square has no fill.

10. Close the document without saving.

Free Distort Filters

The Filter>Distort>Free Distort filter will shear and skew (pull and stretch) an object or group of objects, allowing you to shape objects in the design to satisfy many different requirements — such as perspective or distortion.

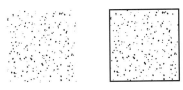

In this example, the object was selected, then Filter>Distort>Free Distort was chosen bring up the dialog box. The anchor points in the dialog box were used to stretch and pull the object adding perspective to the image. When OK was selected, the distortion was applied to the object.

Using Free Distort

The objective is to fit the Tropical Suites logo on one side of the cube.

1. Use File>Open to navigate to the **SF-Intro Illustrator** folder and open the student file **Free Distort.AI**.

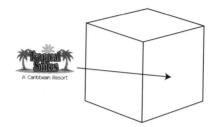

2. Select the Tropical Suites logo. Go to Filter>Distort>Free Distort.

3. The Free Distort window shows the outlines of the logo. Each of the four corners of this object are the working points to be moved.

4. Move the corners to achieve the angle that will make the logo fit the cube.

5. When the distorting is finished and you are satisfied with the results, click OK to apply these changes to the selected logo.

6. Moved the distorted logo to fit on the cube. All shearing was performed in Free Distort and not with the Shear tool.

7. Close the document without saving.

Roughen

The Roughen filter can give some very wild and explosive qualities to an object. It is a good idea to have the Preview button clicked in its dialog box so the effects can be seen before clicking OK. When controlled, Roughen gives some very attractive contours to an object.

Roughen

Scribble and Tweak

Filter>Distort>Scribble and Tweak adds some rough contours to a path that could resemble the scribbling of a child or the artistic strokes of a chalk or pastel pencil. It is best to have the Preview button selected so you can see the effects as you use the Horizontal and Vertical sliders to alter the settings.

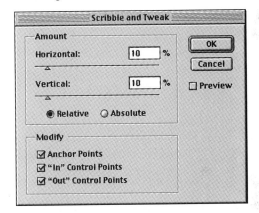

Making an Object Look Rough Drawn

1. From the **SF-Intro Illustrator** folder, open the file **UTA Caribe Island.AI**. We will add a border around this Caribbean logo.

2. Make certain that Preview viewing mode is selected. Click the Default Colors box in the Toolbox, then change the fill to None.

3. Use the Pencil tool to draw a path around the logo, pressing Option/Alt before releasing the cursor to close the path.

4. Choose Filter>Distort>Scribble and Tweak. With Preview button clicked in the dialog box, experiment with the settings to see how the object gets distorted. Finally, set the Horizontal for 4, the Vertical for 6 and click OK. Observe how the object was scribbled and tweaked. Undo this effect.

5. With the border still selected, choose Filter>Distort>Roughen. With Preview clicked in the dialog box, experiment with the settings to see how they affect the object.

6. Finally, set the Size to 2, the Detail to 3, and Points to Smooth. Click OK. Observe how the Roughen filter affected the path.

7. Paint the path with a fill of C: 0, M: 25, Y: 50, K: 0 and no Stroke. Send the path to the back. Observe how you have added an extra dimension to the logo.

8. Close the document without saving.

Punk & Bloat

Filter>Distort>Punk & Bloat will move the anchor points in or out from the line of the selected path. In the Punk & Bloat dialog box, the slider indicates how much effect is applied. Bloat requires moving the slider to the right (positive numbers). To Punk an object, move the slider to the left. Keep Preview checked to see the effect before clicking OK.

Punk

A -20% punk was applied to this rounded corner rectangle. Observe how the anchor points of the rounded corner extrude from the path. Also, notice how the straight lines of the original became curved.

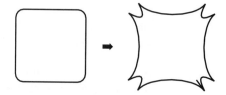

Bloat

The Bloat filter rounds the segments connected to the anchor points of the selected path. It is best to experiment with the filter on various objects to see how it looks. Some samples are shown below:

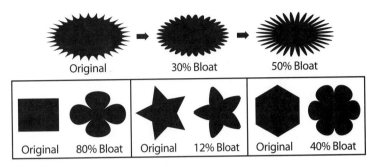

Using Punk and Bloat

1. Create a new document set for CMYK Color Mode, leave it untitled and the Artboard Size set for default. Choose Outline mode.

2. With the Ellipse tool, draw an oval. Keep the oval selected.

3. Choose Object>Path>Add Anchor Points. Add anchor points two more times to have enough points for this example.

4. Choose Filter>Distort>Punk & Bloat. Move the slider to the left or type "-20" into the field. Click Preview to see how it will look. Click OK. Observe how the anchor points were extended from the path.

5. Return to the Punk & Bloat dialog box. Type "29" in the box. Click OK. Observe how the Bloat filter rounded off the anchor points.

6. Close the document without saving.

Creating rounded edge stars is very easy with Bloat. If you are drawing a starfish, this is an excellent filter.

Trim Marks

Trim marks on the page show the printer where to trim the paper with their cutting device. Illustrator has a filter that applies trim marks. The objects to receive the trim marks must be selected, then the Filter>Create>Trim Marks option is selected. Illustrator then applies trim marks to the imaginary bounding box area of the selected objects. In this example, the multiple objects had a bounding box. The Trim Marks option was applied and shows this area by their marks.

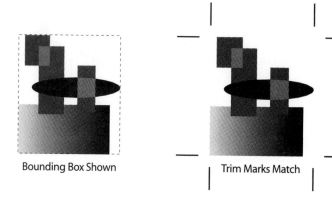

Bounding Box Shown   Trim Marks Match

The Trim Marks filter produces trim mark paths with the Registration color applied to the stroke. If the file was then saved as an Illustrator EPS, placed in a publishing program (such as PageMaker or QuarkXPress), the trim marks would appear on each plate of a separation. This is not true of the Crop Marks option from Object menu. They are not the same thing. This Crop Marks feature sets a bounding box around the image for use only by the Illustrator Separation Setup dialog box. This is covered in the ATC Illustrator: Advanced book.

Creating Trim Marks

1. Open the file **Trim Marks.AI** from the **SF-Intro Illustrator** folder.

2. Choose Edit>Select All.

3. Choose Filter>Create>Trim Marks. This will set Trim Marks for the bounding box of all the selected objects.

4. Close the document without saving.

Complete Project D: Walking the Dogs

USING GRADIENTS

CHAPTER OBJECTIVE:

To learn about gradients and the visual effects they create. To understand Illustrator's specialized tools for creating and customizing gradient fills. In Chapter 11, you will:

- Learn about linear and radial gradients.
- Study and understand the Gradient palette.
- Learn how to paint objects with gradients.
- Learn how to create a new gradient.
- Learn how to modify colors in a gradient with the Gradient tool.
- Understand the multicolored gradient and how to create one.
- Learn how to change gradient angles using either the Gradient palette or the Gradient tool.

PROJECTS TO BE COMPLETED:

- Art Deco House (A)
- BearWear Business Cards (B)
- Wine and Cheese Invitation (C)
- Walking the Dogs (D)
- **Broadway Bound (E)**
- Joker's Wild (F)
- BearWear Label (G)

Using Gradients

Variations in color shades is a critical component in complex drawings. One color divided into tints and shaded tones can give the impression of having many colors. It is an artistic tool used by many designers. The most effective use of this shading can be seen in gradients, which can which can produce a wide variety of effects — from realistic drawings, to subtle backgrounds, color shifts, and special effects in type.

Illustrator provides specialized tools to create gradients, though their overuse can result in complex drawings that might prove difficult to print. We mention this because it's very tempting to use gradients profusely since they're so easy to apply and are very dramatic in their appearance. This chapter introduces the many aspects of gradients and their use in Illustrator. In this illustration, every path is filled with a gradient. This is to show you the many effects that gradients can produce.

Look at the banners and buttons used on the Internet. There is hardly one that does not use gradients to give the impression of 3-D surfaces and contours.

Linear and Radial Gradients

There are only two types of gradients, but they can be used to create an endless variety of 3-D effects.

- **Linear.** Bands of color blend from one shade or color to another. There can be multiple colors in the gradient, but they all travel in the same direction at the specified angle.

- **Radial.** This type of gradient radiates from the center shade or tint out to the edges giving an object its round appearance. Radial gradients can have multiple colors in them.

Linear   Radial

You can apply linear and radial gradients to create the illusion of contoured and solid objects.

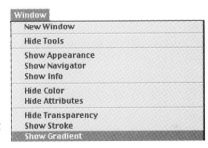

Linear gradient   Radial gradient

Gradient Palette

Whatever the gradient effect desired, it can all be created and modified in one place — the Gradient palette. Knowing how to effectively and efficiently use the Gradient palette is the secret to creating beautiful, awe-inspiring designs. The Gradient palette is accessed in two ways: by clicking the Gradient icon in the Toolbox under the Fill/Stroke boxes or by selecting Show Gradient from the Window menu.

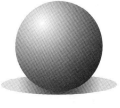

Gradient

The features of the Gradient palette are simple but powerful. You should understand the effects that they have on a gradient. Here is the Gradient palette shown with descriptions of its many features.

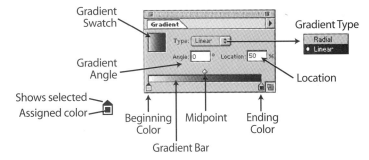

Gradient Swatch
Gradient Type
Gradient Angle
Location
Shows selected Assigned color
Beginning Color
Midpoint
Ending Color
Gradient Bar

- **Gradient Swatch.** Shows how the gradient will look when applied.

- **Gradient Angle.** Changes the angle at which a linear gradient fills the object. By default, a linear gradient fills an object with vertical bands.

- **Midpoint Slider.** By default, this slider appears midway between two color sliders. This slider can be moved to adjust the color range between colors. Gradients can show more of one color and less of the other by moving this slider.

Metallic surfaces are also easy to create with Gradients. Illustrator provides a metallic gradient in the Swatches palette. It's called Steel Bar II.

- **Gradient (Color) Sliders.** These sliders mark the beginning color and ending color in a gradient. The top triangle of a slider appears black if it is selected for modification. The interior of the boxes take on the colors that are applied to them.

- **Location.** Shows the location percentage of the selected color box or midpoint.

- **Gradient Type.** This pop-up menu provides a choice between a Linear or Radial gradient.

Painting Objects with Gradients

There are several ways to apply gradients to objects. Gradient swatches can be dragged or clicked from the Swatches palette, Color palette, Gradient palette, or from the Toolbox.

- If an object is selected, clicking the Gradient icon in the Toolbox will fill the object with the current gradient and bring up the Gradient palette at the same time.

- When the Fill box in the Color palette has a gradient, dragging this swatch to any selected or unselected objects will paint them with the gradient.

- If an object is selected, clicking the gradient swatch in the Gradient palette will paint the object.

- Dragging the gradient swatch from the Gradient palette will apply a gradient to both selected and unselected objects.

- It does not matter if the Stroke box of the Toolbox is active when selecting a gradient for a fill. Strokes cannot receive a gradient, so the Toolbox automatically switches over to the Fill box and applies the gradient.

Painting Objects Using the Swatch Palette

There are three ways to view the gradient swatches in the Swatches palette: Name View, Small Swatch, and Large Swatch. The Name View displays swatches in a list along with the gradient name. Small Swatch view shows the same small swatches as Name View, but without the name. Large Swatch shows the most detail of what the gradient looks like.

When first choosing the Gradient palette, you may not see much.

Use the palette menu to Show Options, and the entire Gradient palette will appear.

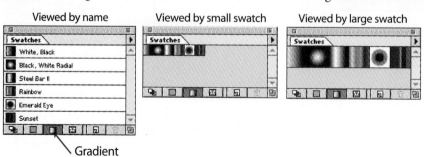

Viewed by name   Viewed by small swatch   Viewed by large swatch

When the Swatches palette is set to Gradient, an object can be selected and the desired gradient swatch clicked in the palette, painting the object.

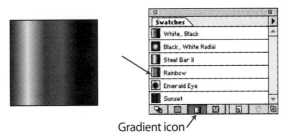

Gradient icon

Creating a New Gradient

Illustrator provides a few gradients to get you started. In the Gradient palette you can build customized gradients to suit your exact needs.

The first decision to be made is whether the gradient should be linear or radial. The Type pop-up menu in the palette gives you this choice. The minimum number of colors for a gradient is two. The color boxes under the gradient bar can receive colors from various sources. The fastest way to apply color is to drag swatches to touch the color box. This can be done from the Swatches palette, the Color palette, or the Fill/Stroke boxes of the Toolbox.

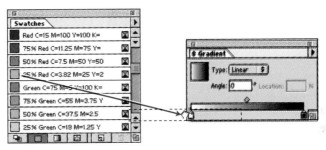

You can apply a color from the Swatches palette to a color box by clicking on the color box to select it, then click the color swatch in the Swatches palette while holding the Option/Alt key.

The Color palette will not allow this. If the Gradient palette is selected, and the Color palette clicked on to drag colors, the gradient's color boxes disappear.

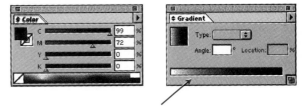

Once the beginning and ending sliders have had new colors applied to them, the gradient swatch in the palette will show what the gradient looks like. The midpoint slider can be moved to the left or right to adjust how much of each color will show.

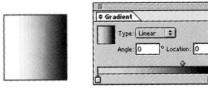

Perhaps you wish to see more of the gradient bar in the Gradient palette. It defaults at a minimal strip. If you enlarge the palette with the sizing handle in the lower right corner, the gradient bar will become bigger.

Creating a Linear Gradient

1. Create a new document set for CMYK Color Mode, leave it untitled and the Artboard Size set for default.

2. Access the Gradient palette, through Window>Show Gradient. In the palette menu select Show Options to view the entire palette. Click on the gradient bar to see the color boxes underneath it. Leave the gradient type set to Linear.

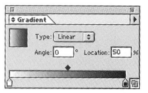

3. Access the Swatches palette from Window>Show Swatches. Click on the Show Color Swatches icon at the bottom. In the palette menu, select Name View. Go back to the palette menu and select Sort by Name, to alphabetize the colors.

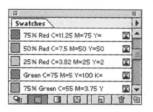

4. Scroll down the list of colors until you find the color Blue C: 100, M: 50. Drag the color swatch to the ending color slider.

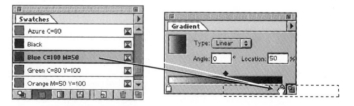

5. Scroll down to the bottom of the color list. You will find the color Yellow. Drag its swatch to the beginning color slider. Leave the gradient Angle at 0.

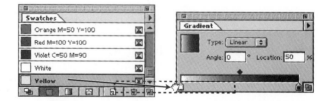

6. Drag the midpoint slider back and forth to see how this affects the color ranges between colors. Observe how the gradient swatch in the palette changes as this is moved, showing how the gradient will appear. Leave the midpoint set at around 40%. It is difficult to move the slider to round numbers. Highlight the number in the Location field and type "40". Press Return/Enter to apply.

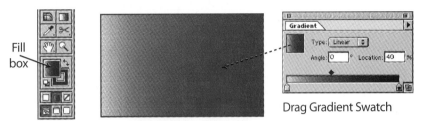

7. Click the Default Colors box in the Toolbox. Select the Rectangle tool and draw a rectangle. Click the Stroke box in the Toolbox to make it active. Drag the swatch from the Gradient palette to touch the rectangle. Observe how the Fill box in the Toolbox took on the gradient swatch, not the Stroke box. The Gradient icon under the Fill/Stroke boxes will also take on the gradient.

Fill box

Drag Gradient Swatch

8. Try to click on the Swap Colors icon in the Toolbox. Notice that it will not respond. This is because gradients cannot be applied to strokes. In the Gradient palette, change the Gradient Type to Radial. Observe how the rectangle looks.

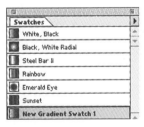

9. Return the Type to Linear. From the Gradient palette, drag the Gradient Swatch over to the Swatches palette. A new gradient will appear called New Gradient Swatch 1.

10. Double-click on the New Gradient Swatch 1. The Swatch Options dialog box will appear, but no options will be available except to rename the gradient. Type "My Gradient" for the name, and click OK. Observe how the name now appears in the Swatches palette.

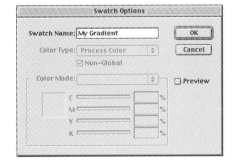

11. You have now created a custom gradient that is accessible to paint objects you draw in this document. Close the document without saving.

You can reset the gradient in the Gradient palette back to the default colors of black and white. Hold the Command/Control key and click either the Gradient icon underneath the Fill/Stroke boxes in the Toolbox or the gradient swatch in the Gradient palette.

Multicolored Gradients

The Gradient palette defaults to two colors that can make a gradient. The color sliders under the gradient bar are the foundation of a gradient. They will duplicate when moved while holding the Option/Alt key. In this example, the black color box was duplicated to the middle of the gradient bar (A). The white color box was duplicated between the two black boxes (B). More duplication was performed on the color boxes (C).

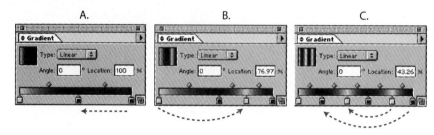

The color sliders are not restricted to their original locations. Here, the gray color sliders was moved between the black and the white sliders (A). It was dragged to the right. The swatch showed the color changes (B).

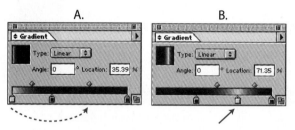

To delete color sliders, drag them out of the Gradient palette at the bottom. The white box in this example needed to be removed. It was dragged out of the palette. The gradient adjusted to compensate for its loss.

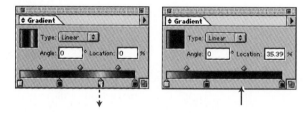

Creating a Multicolored Gradient

1. Create a new document set for CMYK Color Mode, leave it untitled and the Artboard Size set for default. Access the Gradient and Swatches palettes from the Window menu. Click the Default Colors box in the Toolbox. With the Rectangle tool, draw a rectangle. Deselect it.

2. In the Gradient palette, drag the beginning color slider to the right, holding the Option/Alt key. In the same way, duplicate this copy you just made. Keep duplicating until you have five color sliders in the palette. Space the sliders out evenly under the gradient bar.

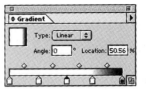

3. From the Swatches palette set for Name View, experiment with dragging color swatches over to the color sliders in the Gradient palette. Use your own judgment and tastes. Create a multicolored gradient.

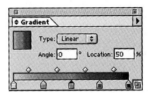

4. Drag the swatch from the Gradient palette to touch the unselected rectangle. It will take on the customized gradient. Click on the rectangle with the Selection tool.

5. In the Gradient palette, delete one of the color sliders. Notice how the rectangle changed its gradient as you deleted the color. This happens only if an object is selected and painted with the gradient you are altering. Deselect the rectangle.

6. Delete another color box from the Gradient palette. Notice how the fill in the rectangle remains the same.

7. Click on the rectangle to select it. Observe how the older version of the gradient appears in the Gradient palette.

8. You have created and modified a multicolored gradient. Keep the document open for the next exercise.

Modifying Colors in a Gradient

We have shown how to apply colors to the color boxes in the Gradient palette. How are the individual colors of a gradient modified? Here is where the Color palette comes into play.

When a color slider in the Gradient palette is selected, the "cap" of the slider becomes black. This means that any color changes made in the Color palette will affect that color box only. When the color slider is selected, a Slider icon appears in the Color palette. It is best to change the Color palette's menu to CMYK (assuming you are in a CMYK document). This shows how versatile gradients are for controlling their appearance with colors, color sliders, and the Color palette.

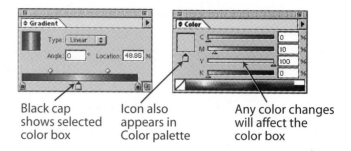

Black cap
shows selected
color box

Icon also
appears in
Color palette

Any color changes
will affect the
color box

Adjusting Gradient Colors

1. Continue working in the open document. Make certain that the Gradient and Color palettes are on screen.

2. Click on the rectangle you drew earlier. Its gradient will appear in the Gradient palette. Click on one of the color boxes to select it. Its cap will turn black.

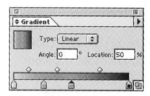

3. In the Color palette, notice that a Slider icon has appeared. Drag any of the CMYK sliders to adjust the color to have a different look. Use your imagination. You can even click on the color sampler in the Color palette to pick random colors.

Double-clicking a color box under the gradient bar will immediately show the Color palette, if it is not already on the screen.

4. Click on each color slider in the Gradient palette and change its color with the Color palette.

5. Observe how the rectangle fill changes as you modify the gradient.

6. Close the document without saving.

Changing Angles of Gradients

Learning how to change the angle and direction of a blend is very important — especially when attempting to create shading effects. In the Gradient palette, a number may be entered in the Angle field to change the Linear gradient's direction.

Gradient angle typed here

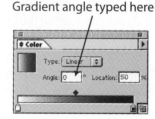

The Angle field in the Gradient palette works only on the Linear gradient. Return/Enter must be pressed to apply angle changes to selected objects.

Not sure just what angle you are dragging the Gradient tool? Use the Info palette from the Window menu (Show Info). It will give you exact angles and dimensions as you drag.

After customizing a gradient angle, if you forget what angle is was set for, click on the object in question and look at the Gradient palette. The number in the Angle field will reflect the new angle applied.

Add new color boxes by clicking the Gradient palette directly underneath the gradient bar.

Gradient Tool

Another way to change the angle of a linear gradient is by dragging the Gradient tool (accessed in the Toolbox) across a selected object that is already painted with a gradient fill. The angle of the gradient is determined by where the Gradient tool cursor is first clicked before dragging and where the mouse button is released after the drag. The cursor is click-held at the point where the gradient is to start, then dragged to the point where the gradient is to end.

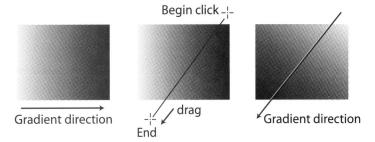

A gradient can be applied to an individual object, and the Gradient tool can change its angle. But what if several single objects need to look as if one gradient were flowing through them? The Gradient tool takes care of this. Several objects can be painted with what looks like one gradient. They are all selected, then the Gradient tool is dragged across them at one time. The tool will adjust them all from the beginning of the drag to the end.

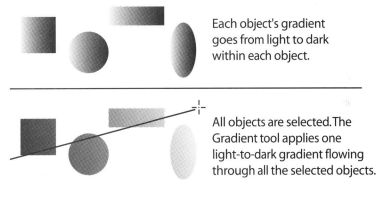

Each object's gradient goes from light to dark within each object.

All objects are selected. The Gradient tool applies one light-to-dark gradient flowing through all the selected objects.

Applying Radial Gradients with the Gradient Tool

The first click is the beginning color. The ending color is applied where the mouse button is released. Getting the right effects from a radial gradient requires some experimenting.

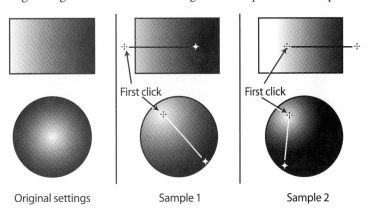

Original settings   Sample 1   Sample 2

Practicing with Gradients

1. Open the file **Gradient Practice.AI** from the **SF-Intro Illustrator** folder. The document has several objects that use gradients to represent texture, 3-D contours, and colors. It's supplied to you as unpainted paths. Use the image below as a guide. Select the paths and apply gradients, changing their angles to achieve this look. Use your imagination for selecting the colors. Use the standard Swatches palette gradients or make your own. Close without saving.

Chapter Summary

You have learned about the many applications and effects that gradients can be used for. You have learned about the Gradient palette, and how it is used to create, customize and modify gradients. You have observed the difference between the two gradient types — Linear and Radial. You have experienced how to paint objects with gradients, and how to apply a new gradient. You have created multicolored gradients, and used the Color palette for applying and adjusting gradient colors. You have learned how to change gradient angles using either the Gradient palette or the Gradient tool.

Project E: Broadway Bound

CHAPTER 12

TRANSFORMATION TOOLS

CHAPTER OBJECTIVE:

To learn how to modify shapes using Illustrator's transformation tools. To learn the tools and methods for transforming object paths by reflection, rotation, shearing, and scaling. In Chapter 12, you will:

- Learn how to use the Rotate, Reflect, and Scale tools manually and with their dialog boxes.

- Learn about the origin point or axis of a transformation.

- Understand how to transform an object using its bounding box.

- Understand how to use the Free Transform tool to transform an object.

- Learn keystroke shortcuts to use for transforming objects.

PROJECTS TO BE COMPLETED:

- Art Deco House (A)
- BearWear Business Cards (B)
- Wine and Cheese Invitation (C)
- Walking the Dogs (D)
- Broadway Bound (E)
- **Joker's Wild (F)**
- BearWear Label (G)

When using the Direct Selection tool, to select objects for transformation, take care that the entire object is selected. To make certain you are selecting all of the desired paths, press the Option/Alt while clicking with the Direct Selection tool. This will assure that the entire object is selected and not just a portion of it. This is not a problem when using the Selection tool.

When several objects are selected, the default origin point goes to the exact center of the bounding box for all the objects combined.

Transformation Tools

Developing a drawing efficiently requires more than just being able to draw shapes — there is also the need to apply transformations, such as scaling, rotating, or reflecting. To help with this process, Illustrator provides powerful tools that stretch, grow, shrink, rotate, and mirror the shapes created.

Transformation Basics

The visual results of the various transformations are different, but they all have two things in common: every transformation occurs either along a horizontal or vertical axis or from an origin point; and transformations can be performed manually or using a dialog box.

Axis

The transformations Move and Reflect (create a mirror image) take place along an axis. That is to say the selected object moves on an imaginary horizontal or vertical line, or at an angle to the vertical line. In both of these transformations the object's position changes, but not its shape.

Origin Point

The Rotate transformation turns an object around an origin point. The Shear (stretch) and Scale (enlarge or shrink) transformations are used to pull a selected object from an origin point to change its shape or size. The origin point of each transformation defaults to the center of the selected object or objects, but this origin point can be repositioned before the transformation is performed.

In this example, the original square was selected and the Rotate tool clicked in the Toolbox. The tool's cursor was single-clicked to the right of the square, setting the origin point. The selected object was then rotated around the origin point by dragging on the object.

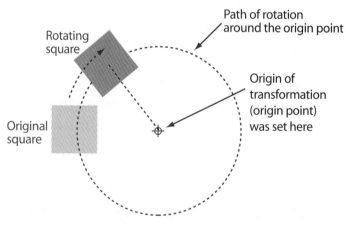

If the default origin point is acceptable, then the transformation tool is dragged on the object. For quick transformations, such as scaling an object, the default origin point works well.

The transformation tool dialog box can be accessed in three ways:

1) Double-clicking on the tool in the Toolbox

2) Holding Option/Alt key, then clicking the tool cursor on the page.

3) Selecting the tool in the Toolbox, then pressing Return/Enter.

If an object is selected, and the transformation tool double-clicked in the Toolbox, the tool's dialog box will appear. If the dialog box is accessed this way, the transformation is restricted to the default origin point, which is the center of the object.

In the following example, the oval was selected and the Rotate tool chosen in the Toolbox. The origin point crosshair appeared in the default center of the object (A). The crosshair cursor was clicked on the top of the oval to begin the manual rotation. The crosshair cursor turned into an arrowhead (▶) shape (B). The oval was then dragged, which rotated it around the center origin point (C).

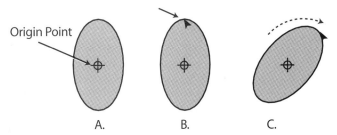

Origin Point

A.   B.   C.

Manual Transformation

Manually transforming a selected object involves dragging objects or their anchor points with a transformation tool cursor. To do this requires clicking on the specific transformation tool in the Toolbox, such as the Rotation tool, moving the tool's cursor to the object, then dragging to perform the necessary transformation.

Dialog Box

Clicking the transformation tool's cursor on the page places the origin point where the cursor was clicked. Holding the Option/Alt key while clicking the cursor positions the origin point and opens a dialog box where the transformation can be specified.

Each dialog box offers specifications appropriate to the transformation tool. The standard features are Objects, Patterns, Copy, and Preview. Objects means that, if selected, only the object itself will be transformed. Patterns will apply the transformation to any patterns filled in the object. Copy, an alternative to OK, will perform the transformation on a copy of the object. Preview shows how the specifications will affect object before OK is clicked.

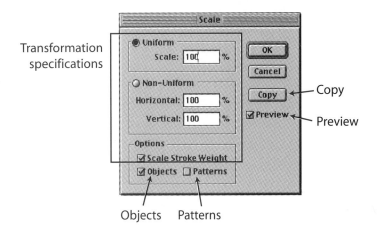

Transformation specifications

Copy

Preview

Objects   Patterns

If an object is selected, a transformation tool selected in the Toolbox, and the crosshair clicked on the page, while holding the Option/Alt key, the tool's dialog box will appear. The advantage to this method is that where the tool crosshair is clicked on the page is where the origin point is set. Any settings made in the dialog box will transform from this point.

Holding the Option/Alt key as you manually Rotate an object will duplicate it.

Rotate Tool

At times, objects need to be twirled or angled at specific angles. The Rotate tool is used to revolve objects. In Illustrator, rotating an object can be performed by two different methods: manual rotating, and dialog box settings.

Manual Rotation

The Rotate tool crosshair cursor is single-clicked (without holding any keys) on the page to set the origin point, that is, the point around which the object will rotate (A). The cursor is dragged becoming an arrow tip, which is used to manually rotate the object (B).

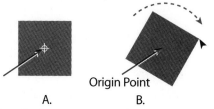

Origin Point

A.   B.

Rotating with the Dialog Box

To rotate a selected object using the dialog box, double-click on the Rotation tool in the Toolbox. The center of the object becomes the origin point.

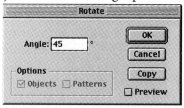

To set a custom origin point with the dialog box, click on the Rotation tool in the Toolbox, then hold the Option/Alt key. The cursor is clicked on or around the object to set an origin point. The dialog box will appear. The rotation angle is typed in, and OK clicked. If a rotated copy is desired, click Copy.

Changing the Origin Point Manually

The origin point does not have to be set on top of the object rotated. There are times that an object (or group of objects) need to be rotated based on an origin point at a different part of the page. If you click the Transformation tool cursor elsewhere on the page, pressing no key, you will reset the origin point for the manual transformation to come.

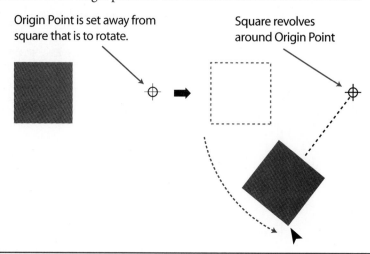

Origin Point is set away from square that is to rotate.

Square revolves around Origin Point

The Shift key plays a role in rotation. Hold it down while you're rotating, and you will constrain the rotation to 45-degree increments.

Positive numbers set for the Angle in the Rotate dialog box will revolve counter-clockwise. Negative numbers make an object rotate clockwise.

Many shapes are constructed from identical objects rotated around a central point. Can you think of any shapes that are built this way?

Using Rotate

1. Create a new document set for CMYK Color Mode, leave it untitled and the Artboard Size set for default.

2. With the Star tool, draw a star approximately 1 in. wide, while holding the Shift key. Fill the star with Black, and set a stroke of None. Click on the Rotate tool in the Toolbox. The origin point crosshair will appear in the center of the star.

3. With the tool cursor, click-hold on the top point of the star and pull to the right to rotate it. When you have rotated it slightly to the right, release the mouse.

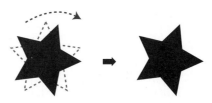

4. Undo the transformation (Command/Control-Z). With the star still selected, click the Rotate cursor at the lower right of the star to set a different origin point. Click the cursor on the top point of the star and drag to the right to rotate it. As you drag, observe how the star is rotating around the origin point set in the lower right. When you are through, undo this.

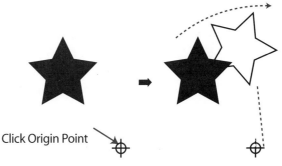

5. With the star selected, double-click on the Rotate tool in the Toolbox. The dialog box will appear. Type "45" for the Angle. Click Preview in the dialog box and watch the selected star rotate. Press Copy and a duplicate rotated star will appear.

6. Undo the last rotation. Click the Rotate tool cursor to the right of the star, holding the Option/Alt key as you click. Type "22.5" for the Angle then click OK.

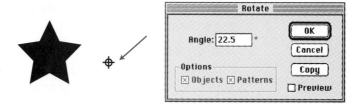

Observe how the star rotates the set angle (relative to the vertical axis) and around the origin point you clicked.

7. Close the file without saving.

Reflect Tool

One of the drawbacks to manually transforming an object is that you can't tell how much, in mathematical terms, that you transformed it. If you access the dialog box of the tool after performing a manual transformation, the settings in the box will reflect the action just performed.

The Reflect tool mirrors a selected object either horizontally, vertically, or at a specified angle. To access the Reflect dialog box, either double-click the Reflect tool in the Toolbox, or click the Reflect tool cursor on the page while holding down the Option/Alt key.

Holding the Option/Alt key and clicking on the page brings up the tool dialog box where you set the axis across which the object will reflect. The rule is to click the cursor on the page where the axis is desired. The Vertical, Horizontal, or Angle axis of the reflection is then selected in the dialog box. When OK is clicked, the object will mirror across the set axis.

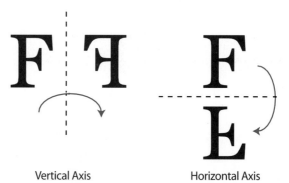

Vertical Axis   Horizontal Axis

A practical use of reflecting is to create a wine glass. In this example, half of the glass was drawn (A). It was reflected and copied on a vertical axis specified in the dialog box (B). The anchor endpoints at the center top of each half of the glass were selected with the Direct Selection tool, then Object>Path>Join (Command/Control-J) was chosen to create the shape (C).

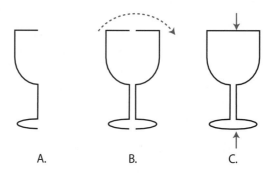

A.   B.   C.

Holding down the Shift key as you Scale an object will keep the transformation proportional.

Transformations, such as rotating and scaling, can also be repeated by pressing Command/Control-D to create interesting designs. Copying an object while you rotate it, for example, allows you to create symmetrical groups of objects — such as the numbers on a clock, the stars circling the head of a whipped prize fighter, or the points on a compass.

Using the Reflecting Dialog Box

1. Create a new document set for CMYK Color Mode, leave it untitled and the Artboard Size set for default. Click on the Default Colors icon in the Toolbox. Use the Rectangle tool to draw a 1-in. square (A).

2. Use the Delete Anchor Point tool (in the Pen tool pop-out menu) to delete the lower right anchor point to make a triangle (B). Select the triangle.

3. Select the Reflect tool. Hold the Option/Alt key, and click the crosshair cursor to the right of the triangle. In the dialog box, choose the Vertical axis, then click Copy (C).

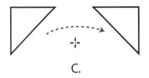

A.   B.   C.

4. Select the two triangles. Select the Reflect tool, then, while pressing the Option/Alt key, click the crosshair cursor below the two triangles (D). In the dialog box, choose Horizontal axis, then click Copy. The two triangles will reflect and duplicate across the axis (E). You've now reflected the object both vertically and horizontally.

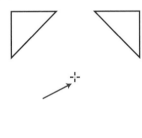

D.   E.

5. Close the document without saving.

Scale

When the dialog box method is used, a scaled object is sized based on one of two types of scaling: Uniform or Nonuniform. Uniform keeps vertical and horizontal dimensions proportional. Nonuniform separates horizontal from vertical and allows each to be sized individually.

Uniform   Non-uniform

Horizontal

Vertical

Manual Scaling

When scaling by hand, the Scale tool cursor turns into a crosshair which is used to click the origin point for the scaling (A).

Once the origin point is clicked, the cursor turns into an arrow. The arrowhead cursor is used to drag the object (B). If the Shift key is held down while dragging, the object will scale uniformly, keeping proportional dimensions (C).

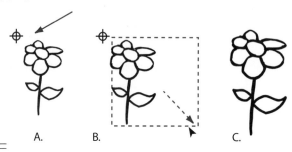

A.   B.   C.

Scaling Objects

1. Create a new document set for CMYK Color Mode, leave it untitled and the Artboard Size set for default. Click on the Default Colors icon in the Toolbox. With the Rectangle tool, draw a 2-in. square. Choose View>Preview mode.

2. Double-click on the Scale tool in the Toolbox. Notice that a crosshair automatically appears in the exact center of the square. The Scale dialog box will also appear. Set the scaling for Uniform, then type "50" in the Scale field. Click OK. Observe how the square's reduction is centered on the origin point set by the crosshair.

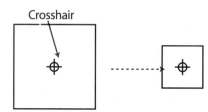

Crosshair

3. Now, click the crosshair cursor on the upper-left corner of the square, while holding the Option/Alt key.

4. The Scale dialog box will appear. Set the scaling for Non-Uniform, and set the Horizontal to "75", and Vertical to "125". Click Preview in the dialog box and you will see the square take on these dimensions. The Preview feature is handy for seeing transformations before you apply them. Click OK.

5. Click the crosshair on the upper right corner of the rectangle (A). Move the cursor to the lower left corner (B).

A.

B.

You should be in the habit of holding down the Shift key whenever you stretch something — unless you deliberately want to distort the object horizontally or vertically.

Be careful! The handles on the bounding box could be mistaken for anchor points. We recommend that the Bounding Box not be active, except when needed.

6. Without holding the Shift key, drag the mouse around to see how the object changes its dimensions, stemming from the origin point set in the upper right corner. Now, hold the Shift key and observe how the scaling becomes Uniform. This must be used carefully when manually scaling for proportional purposes. You have to keep control over this by visual observation while the object is scaling.

7. When you are satisfied with the manual scaling you have performed, release the mouse button.

8. Close the document without saving.

Transformations Using the Bounding Box

All objects, whether selected individually or as a group of objects, have an imaginary rectangular boundary that marks the extreme perimeter of one or more selected objects. The following examples show boundaries around objects of various sizes and shapes.

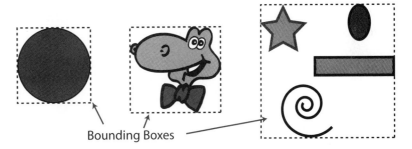

Bounding Boxes

When View>Show Bounding Box is selected, Illustrator provides bounding boxes with handles that can be used for performing transformations manually. Keep in the mind the object must be selected with the Selection tool (the Direct Selection tool does not activate bounding boxes).

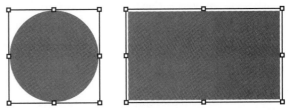

Using the bounding box can be tricky. The transformation that you perform depends on where you move the Selection tool arrow.

Rotating

When the cursor touches directly outside a handle, the Rotation tool becomes active. The mouse is then dragged on that handle to rotate the object.

Scaling

When the cursor is touched directly on top of the handle, the Scale tool becomes active. The mouse is then pulled on that handle to scale the object.

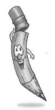

Reflecting

If the side, top, or bottom handles are dragged across their opposite handle, the object becomes reflected, mirroring the object and its fill.

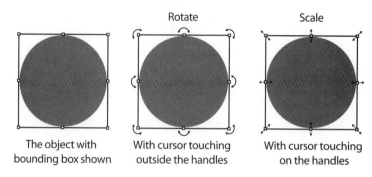

The object with bounding box shown | With cursor touching outside the handles | With cursor touching on the handles

Rotate

Scale

If the object is filled with a linear gradient, the gradient reverses its linear angle.

Manual Reflecting

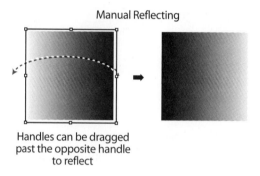

Handles can be dragged past the opposite handle to reflect

Free Transform Tool

As we've shown, Illustrator's Bounding Box feature can be used to rotate, scale, and reflect an object. The Free Transform tool can perform these transformations in addition to shearing (distorting) an object. The Free Transform tool also allows you to relocate the origin point from the object's center. Both tools are very convenient shortcuts to making transformations without a lot of tool clicking and/or dialog boxes.

The bounding box can be toggled on and off by choosing View>Show/Hide Bounding Box or with the Command/Control-B keystroke. The Free Transform tool is located in the Toolbox. The keyboard shortcut to activate it is to press the "E" key.

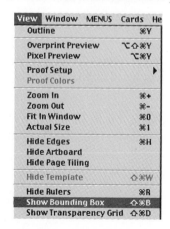

Free Transform Tool

The Shear tool is found in the pop-out menu for the Reflect tool.

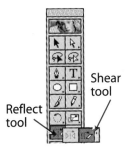

Shear tool

Reflect tool

You can shear an object manually then fine-tune the transformation by bringing up the dialog box. The increments of the last angles will be present. Use the dialog box with these numbers to then fine-tune the shearing.

Shear

Shearing distorts an object by skewing it at various angles. The Shear tool provides a quick way to create the illusion of perspective in a drawing. It's also very useful for creating shadow effects. Shearing can be done either manually, or with the dialog box.

Manual Shearing

Shear works like the other transformation tools. Achieving the desired visual effect with shearing depends on where the origin point is established and where the object itself is clicked before dragging it. The best location for the origin point is somewhere off center.

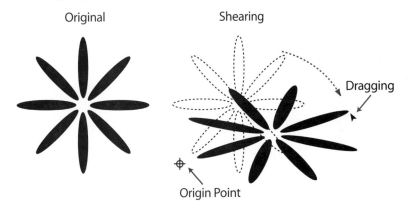

Original Shearing Dragging Origin Point

Be certain to set the origin point manually. Often you will get the best results from shearing if you set the origin point at one of the four corners of an object's bounding box (A) and to drag from the corners of the box (B).

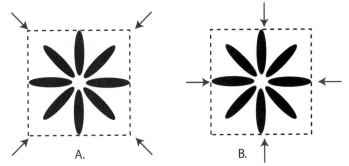

A. B.

Dialog Box

With the dialog box, the angle of the shear is typed into the desired box. As with the other transformation tools, the dialog box is accesses by holding Option/Alt while single-clicking the Shear tool on the document page. Keep in mind at the same time that you click the cursor to open the dialog box, you are setting the location of the origin point. Even though the origin point can be relocated, it is useful to click where you want the origin point to be located because this location will appear in the dialog box.

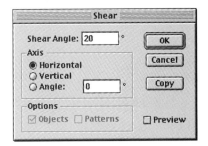

When the origin point is in the center of an object, the effects from dragging the object with the Shear tool can be unpredictable. We recommend that you avoid shearing from an object's center.

We also recommend saving your document right before you begin shearing. That way you can reverse any serious mishaps by closing without saving, then reopening the document. Also, Illustrator's Undo feature may become a valued friend when you are transforming an object with the Shear tool.

These are some examples of shearing with the dialog box.

Original   20% Horizonal   20% Vertical

Photos can be sheared for creative effects.

Original   Horizontal   Angled

Shearing Text

Lets suppose a logo is needed for a racing team, and they want the letters of the name to show extreme showing speed. You can use the Shear tool to achieve this effect.

In the example below, the first text block (A) was set as normal text. With the block selected by the Selection tool, the Shear tool was activated and Option/Alt-clicked to set the origin point at the lower left baseline of the block and open the dialog box. In the dialog box that appears, the Angle was set for 20% Horizontal. OK was then clicked (B). Using the Shear dialog box kept the text baseline constrained, whereas manually shearing the text may have pulled the baseline out of its horizontal alignment.

A.   TYPE THAT IS NORMAL

B.   *TYPE THAT IS SHEARED*

Shearing an Object

1. Open **Shearing Flower.AI** from the **SF-Intro Illustrator** folder and select the flower with the Selection tool.

2. Click-hold on the Reflect tool in the Toolbox to access the Shear tool.

You can perform any number of transformations on an object in order to achieve a desired visual effect. For instance, an object may be copied, rotated, then sheared to create a shadow for another object.

3. Single-click the crosshair at the bottom left of the flower.

4. An arrow cursor will now appear. Position the cursor near on the top-right corner of the flower and pull slightly to the right. Be careful not to pull too far too fast. Shearing has "explosive" qualities when overdone. Observe how the Shearing affected the flower. Experiment with movements of the tool.

5. Close the document without saving.

Creating a Shadow with Shearing

1. Create a new document set for CMYK Color Mode, leave it untitled and the Artboard Size set for default.

2. Click the Type tool cursor on the page. Type the word "REFLECTION". Highlight the word and use the Character palette to set the Font to ATC Cozumel and the Size to 48 pt. Press Return/Enter to apply.

REFLECTION

3. Click on the text block with the Selection tool. Choose View>Outline mode, then select Type>Create Outlines. The letters will automatically be grouped.

4. Click on the Reflect tool in the Toolbox. Hold the Option/Alt key and click the tool's cursor underneath the "R." In the Reflect dialog box, click the Horizontal field, then click Copy. Illustrator will reflect and copy the outlines across the horizontal axis determined by the position of the origin point.

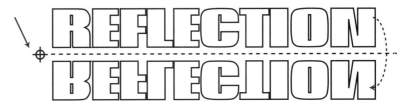

5. Select the Shear tool, and click the crosshair at the top left corner of the duplicate's "R." Drag the bottom right corner of the duplicate to Shear.

6. The idea is to shear the duplicate to create a shadow, as if the sun were in the far distance, shining on the word "REFLECTION."

7. When satisfied with the sheared duplicate, move it into place, touching the baseline of the original text create the shadow effect. Choose Preview mode. Paint the shadow by clicking the Gradient button below the Fill/Stroke box, and set the stroke to None. Select the white, black gradient fill in the Swatches palette. Notice how each letter has an individual gradient. We want the gradient to flow through all the letters as one gradient.

8. With the gradient-filled object selected, access the Gradient tool in the Toolbox (just above the Scissors tool). Click-hold its cursor under the duplicate. Drag the tool to a position just above shadow object, holding the Shift key to constrain. Release the mouse button.

9. You have used Shear to create a reflection of an object.

10. Close the file without saving.

Chapter Summary

You have learned about the tools and techniques for transforming objects for visual effect. You have learned how to perform manual and dialog box transformations, and observed the axis and origin point, which are the foundations of transformation. You have observed the four most basic forms of transformations: Reflecting, Scaling, Rotating, and Shearing. You have learned about the bounding box and Free Transform tool, and how they act as shortcuts to performing some transformations.

Complete Project F: Joker's Wild

Shearing is a great technique, but can result in an object's becoming overly distorted. Try using the dialog box and entering a figure the Preview button clicked in the dialog box. That way you can gradually determine which setting provides the look you're seeking to achieve.

CHAPTER 13

WORKING WITH IMAGES

CHAPTER OBJECTIVE:

To understand how to incorporate and manage external images within Illustrator documents. To become familiar with the graphic formats that can be placed into your design. In Chapter 14, you will:

- Learn how to place and manage images in Illustrator.
- Study and learn the Links palette and its palette menu.
- Understand the Document Info feature.
- Understand missing links and how they affect the design.
- Learn how to identify placed EPS and raster images.
- Learn how to export images from an Illustrator document.
- Learn how to embed images using the Links palette menu.

PROJECTS TO BE COMPLETED:

- Art Deco House (A)
- BearWear Business Cards (B)
- Wine and Cheese Invitation (C)
- Walking the Dogs (D)
- Broadway Bound (E)
- Joker's Wild (F)
- BearWear Label (G)

Working with Images

There is a lot to learn about working with images. Color correction, proper scanning resolution, and a host of other technical issues all crop up when you're attempting to produce high-quality images. The popularity of the Internet and so many surfers using and sending raster images makes Illustrator an almost indispensable program for creating or converting images to the Web.

While we cannot cover all of these in issues in depth here, it is important to know how to import, export, and modify these images using Illustrator document features. Whatever is created or imported into the document can be saved and exported.

What Can Illustrator Do with Images?

The Illustrator program is very versatile in how it creates, converts, and manages vector objects and raster images. There are many variables as to how objects (vector) or images (raster) can be imported and exported from documents. We will give you some examples of what can be done.

- On the most basic level of how raster images are created in Illustrator, first, the image is created as vector paths and type. The objects are exported to an external raster image (TIFF), leaving the original objects in the document intact. If modifications are to be made to the paths at a later date, they will still be in vector format in the original document.

- A raster image is placed in a document, and Illustrator tools are used to draw vector paths using the imported image in the design. The document is then saved as Illustrator EPS for placing in other programs.

- An Illustrator document is used to create a design with vector paths. The paths are then rasterized (an Illustrator function) into a single raster image. Illustrator raster filters are used to enhance this image. An external raster image is placed into the document and combined with the rasterized image by selecting the two and rasterizing them into a single raster image. More Illustrator filters enhance this image, and more vector paths are created to complement the piece.

- An external raster image is placed in the document and turned into a template. This dimmed image is traced with a variety of Illustrator's drawing tools. The placed image is released from being a template, bringing it back to its 100% viewing quality. This image is selected with the vector paths and combined into one raster image. Raster filters are applied to this new image, then the document is exported to a GIF format for use on the Web.

This just scratches the surface of what can be done. We will cover the basics of working with images so you will know what can and can't be done.

Illustrator can create its own raster images, or import them from outside sources. It can even combine several raster images into new ones. The list goes on and on.

Placing Graphics

The Place command allows you to import graphics into an Illustrator document. There are two types of graphic files that can be placed into an Illustrator document. The first category are vector graphics — such as an Illustrator EPS or an EPS file created in another application. The second category is raster, or bitmap images, such as TIFF, JPEG, GIF, PICT, or BMP — typically created with image editing applications such as Adobe Photoshop. The file type dictates what you can do with the graphic once it's been placed into your drawing.

Place Dialog Box

When external images need to be imported into a document, it is best to use the Place option found in the File menu. The Place dialog provides controls that determine the relationship between the document and the original (source) image.

External images can be brought into the Illustrator document by methods such as drag-and-drop, or cut and paste (shown later in this chapter). Importing images in this manner will not give you the linking option. The images will be automatically embedded in the document.

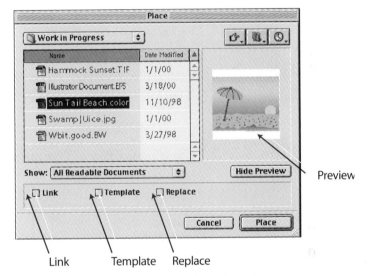

Macintosh Place Dialog Box

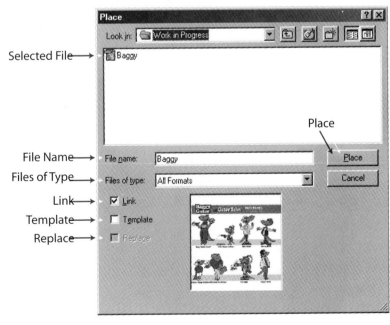

Vector and raster placed images have their idiosyncrasies. This chapter covers most of the things to look out for.

Windows Place Dialog Box

Anything created or imported into an Illustrator document can be exported to an external raster image. If you want the document objects to be used for an Internet Web image, the Save For Web option in the File menu should be used.

- **Link.** Creates a connection between the placed external image and the document it is placed in. If linked, images inside the document will be updated to modifications made to the external file. Choosing not to link embeds the image (makes it an editable component of the document).

- **Template.** When selected, places the image on a separate template layer, dimming the image.

- **Replace.** If an image is selected in the document, this option becomes available to be replaced by an updated version or a completely different image.

- **Preview.** Shows a thumbnail preview of the image in the selected file. The Macintosh version has the Show/Hide Preview choice. With Windows, the Preview is standard in the dialog box.

- **Show Files of Type.** Displays the type of file you want to see — EPS, AI, BMP, and so on.

The Macintosh **Show** menu allows the choice of All Documents, which is all existing files in a folder; All Readable Documents shows just the file types that Illustrator can access. Under these headings, you can select more specific file types to view, thus limiting the size of the list of file names you must view to find the one you want.

The Windows' **Files of Type** menu either shows All Formats, or specific file types to narrow the file list.

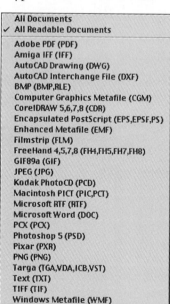

Macintosh

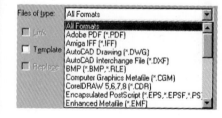

Windows

Other Image Import Methods

We stress using File>Place to import images, but there are other methods of introducing an external image into an Illustrator document.

Drag and Drop

If a Photoshop or Illustrator document possessing an image is open while the target Illustrator file is active, the selected image can be dragged from one document to another. In this example a Photoshop document is open, showing its image on the screen. An Illustrator document is also open, showing its document page. The Photoshop image is selected and dragged into the Illustrator file. This method can also be used for dragging images and objects between Illustrator documents.

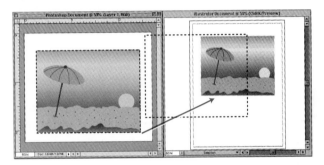

Cut and Paste

Depending on the program, such as PageMaker, an image may be cut or copied to the clipboard memory. This image can then be pasted to the open Illustrator document.

The Links Palette

In the Links palette you can manage any linked image in an Illustrator document — images can be linked, embedded, updated, replaced, and substituted.

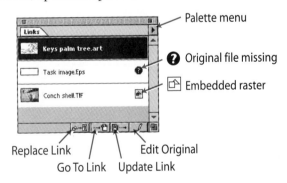

- **Replace Link.** Works with linked and unlinked images. It allows you to reassign another external image to the link, that is to say, the selected image in the Links palette is replaced in the document with a new image. Even embedded images can be replaced and linked to a new external file.

- **Go To Link.** Selects and shows mid-screen the actual image in the document that is highlighted in the Links palette.

- **Update Link.** Updates the image in the document with the modified external Link. Illustrator asks in a warning message if you want this updating performed.

- **Edit Original.** Opens the linked image in the program that created it.

What actually is "embedding?" The embedded image is saved, with all its file information, into the Illustrator document. Embedding greatly enlarges the file size of the document, which has to retain all the extra information.

If you are linking placed images, do not move the original image from the folder or Desktop where you retrieved it from. Also, do not rename it or delete it. Illustrator keeps track of where it obtained the file and its name. You will get error messages if the Illustrator document cannot find the linked file.

Links Palette Menu

The Links palette menu offers more features for managing images in a document. Any image, whether linked, unlinked, rasterized in the document, or embedded, can be relinked, replaced, or updated with the Links palette.

Disabling warnings in the Preferences has its drawbacks. If a linked image has had its original modified, Illustrator will warn you when the document opens. That is, unless you have disabled the warnings.

- **Go To Link.** Brings the selected image to the middle of the screen for viewing.

- **Update Link.** If you want to immediately update a link to a modified external image, this option will bring the image selected in the Links palette up to date.

- **Edit Original.** Launches the application that created the linked image, opening the image in that program for further modifications.

- **Replace.** Allows you to assign a different or modified image to the selected link. Rasterizing an image in the Illustrator document will embed it, breaking all links. If this is done, use Replace Link to reassign a link.

- **Embed Image.** Breaks the links to an image, embedding it into the document.

Link Information

In the Links palette menu, the Information option provides important information about the linked image as well as giving specifications for any transformations that have been performed on the image.

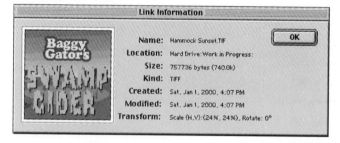

When sending an Illustrator EPS file to the commercial printer, make certain that you also send any linked images the EPS might possess.

Missing Links

If the original linked graphic has been moved from where Illustrator first found it, a warning message will appear when the document opens. If No is clicked, the document will still open, but the missing image will show as an empty bounding box.

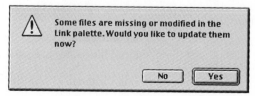

The Extract function of the warning dialog box will only duplicate missing EPS images. If the missing image is a raster format, the preview of this file is embedded into the document.

In the graphic or commercial art profession, templates are almost indispensable. You will constantly come upon new clients who do not have a tangible copy of their logo except on a printed piece of paper. Often your task is to reproduce this logo in the computer. If you have the equipment, you can scan the logo and use it as a template.

If scanning does not yield a clear enough image, consider asking your client to submit a CD containing photograph of the logo. The raster image on a CD can be placed in your document and converted to a template.

If Yes is clicked, another dialog box will appear, which his offers several options to deal with the missing image problem.

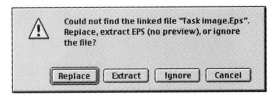

- **Replace** will display a dialog box to find the original or substitute another image.

- **Extract** creates a duplicate image with the name of the missing file. This image will have no preview, though, and should be opened by the original application to save it with a preview. The Links palette can be used to relink to this file.

- **Ignore** will allow the document to open, but an empty bounding box will be substituted for the missing graphic.

Creating Templates

As a drawing program, Illustrator uses the word "template" in the classic art sense, meaning a guide from which to create artwork, such as taking a rough sketch and laying a piece of tracing paper over it. Through the slightly transparent tracing paper, the sketch is subdued, but visible enough to trace its lines or contours. The Layers palette menu has a Template option that turns a selected layer into a dimmed image that can be used to trace with drawing tools such as the Pen tool.

In this example, the grayscale raster image was turned into a template. The subdued gray allows the artist to draw paths that follow the contours without being confused by the lines of the art at 100% black.

The grayscale TIFF image
was placed in the document

Template was clicked in the Layers
palette menu, turning the image to gray

Illustrator templates work in the same way. The image formats that can be converted to templates are vector EPS and raster images from practically any source — scans or graphics created in other applications, such as Photoshop or Illustrator EPS. This can include GIF, JPEG, and BMP.

To import a vector path created in a program other than Illustrator, the file must be saved in an EPS format before it is placed. Vector paths in an Illustrator document, however, can be rasterized, making them immediate candidates to be turned into a template.

When an image on a layer is turned into a template, it is dimmed to 50% visibility (by default) and automatically locked so it cannot be accidentally moved or modified. The dimming percentage, as well as other aspects of the template, can be altered in the Layer Options dialog box.

There are two ways to convert artwork into a template in Illustrator: using the Layers palette or the File>Place dialog box.

Layers Palette Menu

The Layers palette has a Template option that converts a placed image into a template. There are three features of a layer that change when it becomes a Template layer: The Show/Hide Eye icon is replaced with the Template icon, 🔃; the layer becomes locked; and the layer name remains the same, but becomes italicized.

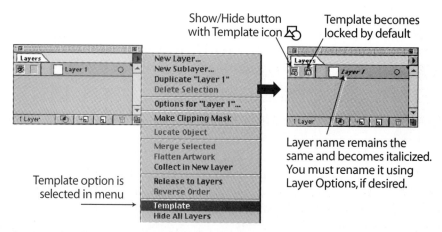

Show/Hide button with Template icon 🔃

Template becomes locked by default

Template option is selected in menu

Layer name remains the same and becomes italicized. You must rename it using Layer Options, if desired.

When the Template layer is double-clicked, its Layer Options dialog box appears. Only four items are available for changes: The Template button toggles the contents of the layer back to objects, the Dim Images button and Percentage field allow you to set the appearance of the template object; and the color field allows you to change the color of the selection lines. The other buttons in the dialog box are grayed, indicating that they cannot be activated. If the Lock button in the dialog box is checked and grayed, this indicates that the template is locked and cannot be changed in the dialog box. The Layer palette has to be used to unlock the Template layer.

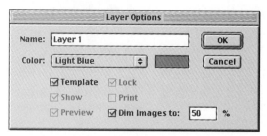

Placing Images

An image can be placed into a document using File>Place. The dialog box that appears has a Template option that will place an object into a document as a template. Once a file is selected in the dialog box, check the Template button and click OK.

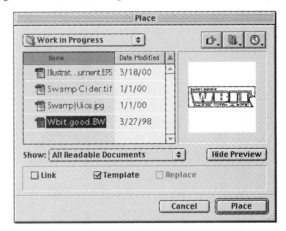

When the place method is used to create a template, the Template icon replaces the Show/Hide icon, and the layer name defaults to the name of the placed file. The type of file that is being placed determines whether the template is automatically locked. Raster images are not locked, but a placed vector EPS image will create a locked template.

Placed raster image (TIFF)   Placed vector EPS image

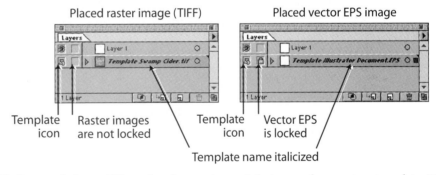

Template   Raster images   Template   Vector EPS
icon   are not locked   icon   is locked

Template name italicized

The file formats behave differently when an image is being used to create a template. We stress that you stay with raster images, preferably Grayscale TIFF. The most commonly used file formats are: 1-bit line art Grayscale, Raster, and vector EPS.

- **Raster.** Bitmapped images that run the range of formats from TIFF, GIF, JPEG, PDF, BMP, PCX, PIXAR, PNG, as well as a raster EPS saved in a photographic program. Any of these can become templates.

- **Vector.** Encapsulated PostScript (EPS) images created by such programs as Illustrator or FreeHand. **Important note:** the vector EPS image will not dim unless it is Linked in the Place dialog box.

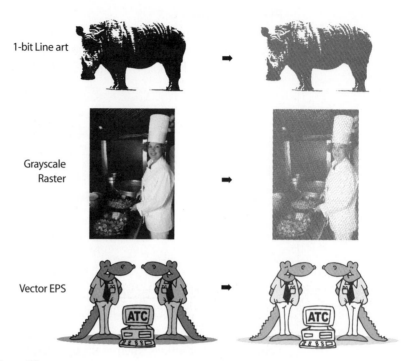

1-bit Line art

Grayscale Raster

Vector EPS

Template Tips

- Templates cannot be made using vector paths within the document. They will not dim. The paths must be rasterized first.

- Clicking the Template option in the Place dialog box creates the Template layer directly underneath the layer selected at the time the template is placed. Template layers do not automatically appear at the bottom of the layer list.

- Only the Template option in the Place dialog box will automatically make a new layer. Otherwise, you must create a new layer yourself and use the Layers palette menu to turn this layer into a Template.

- If Layer 1 is the only layer available, do not turn it into a template layer from the palette menu. It will lock, and there will be no other layer to begin work on. Create a new layer, drag it to the bottom of the layer list, then choose Template from the palette menu.

- A placed vector EPS image will automatically lock the template, but it must be linked from the Place dialog box before it will dim.

- When linking a vector EPS file, you will see this warning message. *Do not* embed the image for use as a template. Templates are not for printing, so this warning does not pertain to creating templates.

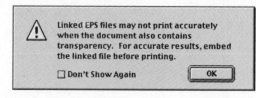

- Templates can be unlocked and moved to a better location for tracing if desired.

Creating Template Layers

1. Create a new document set for CMYK Color Mode. Leave it untitled and the Artboard Size set for default.

2. Select Show Layers from the Window menu. The new document will have Layer 1 in the Layers palette. If you place an image on this layer and turn it into a locked template, you will not have an accessible working layer. Click the New Layer icon at the bottom of the palette. Layer 2 will appear above Layer 1. Drag Layer 2 down and release it below Layer 1 in the layer list. Leave Layer 2 selected.

3. From the File menu, use the Place option to navigate to the **SF-Intro Illustrator** folder and select the 1-bit image **Face.TIF** and click Place. In the Place dialog box, make certain the Template and Link options are not selected.

4. The image will be assigned to Layer 2. In the Layers palette menu, select Template.

5. Layer 2 will turn into a locked template layer, with the image dimmed. Double-click on Layer 2 and rename it "Template Layer" in the Layer Options dialog box.

 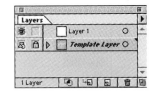

6. Click the Show/Hide button of Layer 2, marked by the Template icon. The dimmed image will be hidden from view. Observe that the name goes back to normal, not italics, indicating that there is no visible template. Click again on the Show/Hide box to bring the Template back to view.

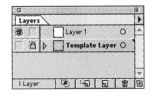

7. Click on the Lock/Unlock button. The box shows no Padlock icon, indicating that the template is unlocked. Move the image to the upper center of the page. Click on the Lock/Unlock button to lock the template again.

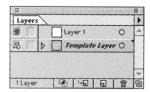

8. Double-click on the Template Layer. In the Layer Options, replace the "50" with "35" in the Dim Images field. Click OK. The image will become dimmed to 35% opacity.

9. Select the Template option in the palette menu to toggle the layer back to its original unlocked state. The image will return to its 100% black appearance.

10. You have observed the many features of manually converting an image to a template using the palette menu. You will now go on to use the Place feature to create templates in a different manner.

11. Drag the Template layer down to the Trash icon at the bottom of the Layers palette. Keep this document for the next exercise.

Using Place to Create a Template

1. In the same document, you will have one layer remaining as the working layer. Use File>Place to navigate to the **SF-Intro Illustrator** folder and select the color photo **Hammock Sunset.TIF**. In the Place dialog box, select the Template option. Click Place.

2. The image will automatically be assigned to a new unlocked layer directly underneath Layer 1. The word "Template" will be added to the italicized name.

3. In the palette menu, click on Template to uncheck it. Notice how the layer appearance has changed. The Show/Hide icon has returned, the name of the layer is not italicized. The word "Template," though, remains in the layer name. Click the Lock/Unlock button.

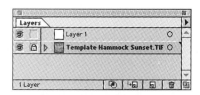

4. Return to the palette menu and select Template. The layer will become a template again. Use the File menu to and select Place. What's the matter? The Place option is gray? That's because you are still on the template layer, which is locked. A locked layer cannot receive images. Click the Lock/Unlock button on this layer to unlock it. Delete the Hammock Sunset photo and then choose File>Place.

5. In the Place dialog box, return to the **SF-Intro Illustrator** folder. Make certain that the Link option is selected and the Template option is not checked. Select the **Thermidor.EPS** file in the list of files. Click Place.

6. The image will be placed on the selected Template layer. It will automatically become dimmed. When Placing a vector EPS image for use as a Template, remember always to Link it. Otherwise, it will not become dimmed.

7. You have observed placing objects to create Template layers.

8. Close the document without saving.

Placing a Vector EPS

A vector EPS is created with programs such as Illustrator or FreeHand, and saved as an EPS file format. EPS files can be placed into programs that accept this format, such as InDesign, PageMaker or QuarkXPress. They can also be placed into Illustrator documents. The question of linking now comes into focus.

To Link or Not to Link

When a vector EPS image is Placed, it has some very important differences between its linked and unlinked files. These differences can play an important part of getting the document to output properly. One of the things you don't want to happen is to get a phone call from your printer saying that a Linked image cannot found. The printing job would be held up until this could be addressed. Here are the ramifications of linking or not linking a placed image.

A linked EPS image is easy to recognize in Outline view because of the diagonal lines in its bounding box.

If there are any text blocks in the placed EPS image, parsing will break up the text block into bits and pieces of many little text blocks. The quickest way to get these back into one text block is to cut them all out of the document and paste them into a single text block.

Link

When an image is linked in the Place dialog box, the actual image does not go into the document. A placeholder image will appear with diagonal lines in a bounding box. We could call this a substitute. It represents the external image you are Placing.

Any modifications you make to the placed image will be applied to the image output when the document is printed. While sending the PostScript language of the document to the printer, the Illustrator document will draw information about the image from the original. The document must be able to find the original when printing. The linked EPS image can be easily recognized by the diagonal lines in the preview, which is a very course 72 dpi representation. This is the screen preview acting for the external original.

Linked Illustrator EPS

 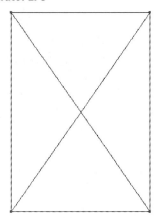

Seen in Preview view   Seen in Outline view

Despite the fact that the original EPS image is made up of vector paths, the linked image will be a solid, single object having no paths that can be edited. Though you cannot alter the image as you would a vector path, you can perform some transformations on the image as a whole, and you can apply masks. (Masks are paths used to hide parts of images. This complex subject is covered in the ATC Illustrator Advanced course.) When transformations, such as rotating or reflecting are performed on a linked vector EPS, the image may seem to behave like a raster image, however do not try to apply any raster filters because they will not work with a vector EPS image.

As we have shown, the vector EPS image cannot be seen in Outline view. There is, however, a slight exception to this. The File>Document Setup dialog box has an option called Show Image in Outline, meaning that the placed EPS image will show a rough screen representation of the image while in Outline viewing mode.

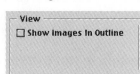

In Outline mode the image is not pretty. It does, however, give you some idea of the image for placement and identification.

Placing Unlinked Vector EPS Images

An unlinked image is embedded in the file, becoming a part of the document. When a raster image is embedded in the document, nothing unusual happens to the image. It is different with a vector EPS. All unlinked EPS files are parsed as they are being brought into the document. Parsing means that the image is being translated into Illustrator vector format. The vector paths are imported and still intact when the image is placed into the document.

A linked EPS image may be embedded from the Links palette menu, cutting off any connection with its external original. Embedding an EPS image also removes its file name from the Links palette.

The parsed images all have a bounding box around them. If this bounding box is not needed any more, you may select it with the Direct Selection tool (holding Option/Alt) and delete it.

Linked Illustrator EPS.
Shown in Preview mode.

Same file embedded.
Shown in Outline mode.

Placing a Raster Image

A raster image is a bitmapped image, such as a photograph or art created in other graphic programs. Placed raster images can be transformed only with Scale, Rotate, Reflect, and Shear. They can also be modified by the Rasterize feature, and have raster filters applied to them.

Once a vector EPS image has been embedded and parsed into a document, it is impossible to use Replace Link to connect it with any outside source.

There are no precautions to be taken with linking or unlinking raster images. The only factor to keep in mind is the final output of the document, and whether the images are CMYK or RGB. If the document is going to a commercial printer, the color mode must be CMYK. If the images are going to be saved for the Web, the color mode must be RGB.

This is an important aspect to keep in mind when you first create the document. The New Document dialog box allows you to decided whether to set the Color Mode as CMYK or RGB.

Placing Images into Illustrator

1. Create a new document set for CMYK Color Mode, leave it untitled and the Artboard Size set for default. In File>Document Setup, make certain that Show Images in Outline is *not* checked. Use the View menu to go to Preview viewing mode.

2. Choose File>Place and make certain that the Link option is selected. Navigate to the **SF-Intro Illustrator** folder and place the TIFF graphic, **Girl in Hat.TIF**.

3. Return to the same folder and place the image **Girl in Hat.EPS**. Move this raster EPS file to the right of the previous image so they are side-by-side. Select them both. Observe how their previews are different. The EPS image is not as clear as the TIFF. The EPS image also has the diagonal lines in its bounding box. Deselect the images to see how the EPS diagonal lines disappear.

TIFF image   EPS image

4. Choose View>Outline mode and observe how the bounding boxes look.

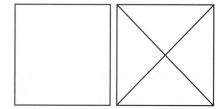

5. Activate the option File>Document Setup>Show Images in Outline. Remain in Outline mode. Observe how this feature makes the images look.

TIFF image   EPS image

6. From the Window menu, select Show Links to bring up the Links palette. Observe how the two images are listed with a thumbnail and their file name.

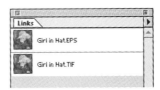

7. Click on the **Girl in Hat.TIF** image, and in the palette menu, select Embed Image. Nothing visible happens to the image itself, but look at the Links palette. The Embed icon will appear to the right of the name. Return to Preview mode.

8. Use File>Place to navigate to the **SF-Intro Illustrator** folder again and select the **Tropical Suites.EPS** logo. Select the Link option and click Place. You will possibly receive a warning that suggests embedding the EPS file into the document. This is not pertinent at this time. Click OK to continue.

Observe how rough an Illustrator EPS screen preview looks. Choose Outline mode. Make certain that File>Document Setup>Show Images in Outline is still checked. Notice that in Outline mode the image appears coarse but is still identifiable.

Preview mode   Outline mode

9. Hold the Option/Alt key and drag a duplicate of this file to the side.

10. Examine the Links palette to verify that the same file is now listed twice.

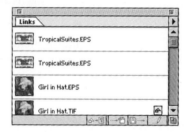

11. Click on the duplicate image you dragged. In the Links palette menu, select Embed Image. Observe how the image becomes parsed back to its original vector path format. The object will no longer be listed in the Links palette. Deselect all objects.

The original   The duplicate embedded and parsed

12. Click on the bounding box of the Tropical Suites embedded object with the Direct Selection tool (holding Option/Alt) and delete it. The remaining Tropical Suites objects are vector paths that can be painted and modified. Select all the paths of this duplicate and delete them.

13. Click the Tropical Suites name in the Links palette. At the bottom of the Links palette, click the Edit Original icon.

14. The Tropical Suites document will be opened by Illustrator. With the Direct Selection tool click on the two palm trees while holding the Shift key. Paint them with a different color selected from the Swatches palette. Save the document, then close it.

15. Back in the working document, wait a few seconds and a warning will appear telling that some files in the Link palette were modified, and asks if you want to update them. For this exercise, click No.

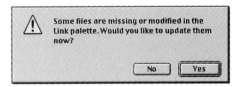

16. Click on the Update Link icon at the bottom of the Link palette. This will update the image to take on the color changes. Select and delete the Tropical Suites image from the document.

17. Click on the **Girl in Hat.TIF** selection in the Links palette. This image was embedded earlier. At the bottom of the palette, click on the Go to Link icon. Observe how the image is selected and brought to the middle of the screen. Click on the icon to the left of Go to Link, which is Replace Link. In the dialog box, make certain that Link is selected. Navigate to the **SF-Intro Illustrator** folder and choose **Hammock Sunset.TIF**. Make certain that Link is selected. Click Place.

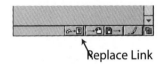

Replace Link

18. Observe how the **Girl in Hat.TIF** image was replaced with the new photo in the Links palette.

19. You have observed how the placing objects and managing their linking can be handled in Illustrator.

20. Close the document without saving.

Exporting Illustrator Documents

When exporting the document to a raster image, all the objects in the file will be included in the image, regardless of whether they are Hidden or Locked. Anything in the document will be present in the exported image. To export the file is simple. The Export option from the File menu is selected. Where the decision-making comes into play depends on what file format you choose from the Export menu. You should have a very good idea of where the image will be used, whether in commercial press printing or in another layout program. The Export dialog box has a Format drop-down menu that shows a variety of file formats to choose from.

Exported files are saved outside of the Illustrator document, as an individual raster file, to whichever folder or directory you choose. The objects and images in the document are untouched. They can then be modified and Export chosen again.

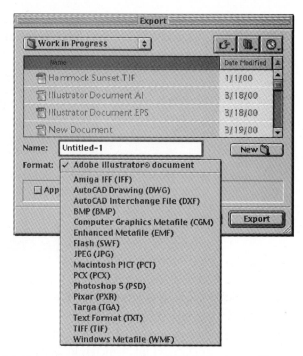

Depending on which format you choose, its specific dialog box will appear (with default settings for the most basic output). The settings may be customized.

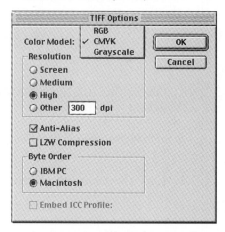

Macintosh TIFF Options dialog box

We will jump into an exercise concerning exporting, and explain the settings of three of the most standard formats (TIFF, JPEG, and BMP) as we move along.

Exporting and Placing Images

1. Create a new document set for CMYK Color Mode, leave it untitled and the Artboard Size set for default.

2. Click the Default Colors box in the Toolbox. Change the stroke to None. Click on the Fill box to make it active.

3. Select the Rectangle tool and draw a 2-in. square on the page.

4. From the Window menu, show the Swatches palette. Click on the Patterns button at the bottom of the palette. Select Name View in the palette menu. Click on the Clown Attack pattern to apply this to the Fill of the square. You will see the square look like it has been filled with various colored balloons.

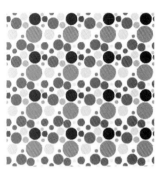

5. In the File menu, select Export. In the Export dialog box that appears, open the **Work in Progress** folder save the exports here. To do this, name the exported file "Clown Balloons.TIF". Select the Format menu and choose TIFF (TIF). Click Export.

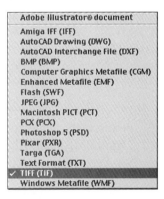

6. The TIFF dialog box will appear. Despite the fact that the document is a CMYK color model, we can export the image as RGB. Set the Color Model to RGB.

7. In the Resolution options, notice that Other can be customized. Select Medium, which is a midway resolution. Check the Anti-Alias option. In the Byte Order section click either IBM PC or Macintosh, depending on what platform you are using. Click OK. The file will be saved separately to the **Work in Progress** folder. The Illustrator document will remain intact.

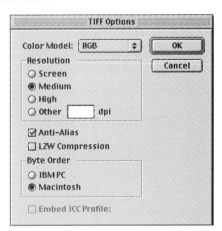

8. Go back to the File>Export option and in the Export dialog box, name the file "Clown Attack.JPG". In the Format menu, select JPEG (JPG). The JPEG Options dialog box will appear. Set the Image Quality to 5 Medium. The Color Model should be CMYK, leave the Method set for Baseline (Standard), change the Resolution Depth to Medium to coincide with the Image Quality. Do not check Anti-Alias or Imagemap. Click OK. The JPEG file will be saved externally.

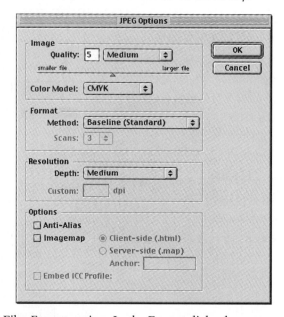

9. Return to the File>Export option. In the Export dialog box, name the file "Clown Export.BMP". From the Format menu, select BMP. Click Export.

10. The BMP feature first brings up the Rasterize dialog box. Set the Color Model for Grayscale. For the Resolution choose Screen (72ppi), and check Anti-Alias. Click OK.

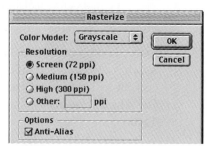

11. The BMP export also has an extra options dialog box. Click the Windows option (Macintosh people do this, too) and leave the depth set for 8 bit. Don't select the Compress button. Click OK. The BMP file will be saved.

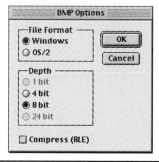

12. You have succeeded in exporting three of the most commonly used file types. Now let's see what they look like.

13. In the File menu, select Place. In the dialog box, navigate to the **Work in Progress** folder and select **Clown Balloons.TIF**. Do not Link the file. Click Place.

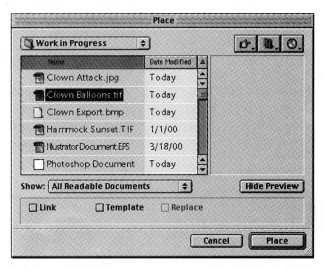

14. The image will appear in the document. Click on it with the Selection tool and relocate it to the upper left corner of the page.

15. Use File>Place to go back to the **Work in Progress** folder and Place the second file you created, **Clown Attack.JPG**. Select Link in the Place dialog box to link it. Click Place. When the image appears in the document, move it up to the right of the first placed image.

16. With File>Place, return to the **Work in Progress** folder and place the third file you created, **Clown Export.BMP**. Select Link to link the file. Click Place.

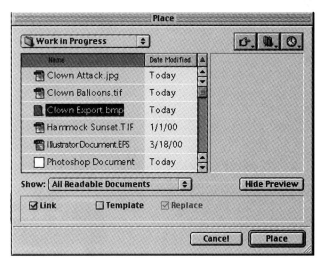

17. Move the BMP file up to the right of the JPEG image. The three placed images should be lined up across the top of the page.

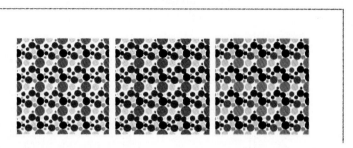

18. With the Zoom tool, draw a marquee on the gap between the TIFF and JPEG images to enlarge them. We want you to see the difference between Anti-Alias and non-Anti-Alias. The TIFF image (shown on left below), when you exported it, had Anti-Alias clicked. Anti-Alias smooths the edges of nonwhite objects in the image. Look at the right image below. The JPEG image received no Anti-Alias and is very jagged. If you want to retain the clarity of objects in your exports always click Anti-Alias.

 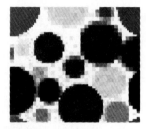

19. Select the View>Fit in Window option to change the view. Use the Hand tool to move the page so the three objects are centered on the screen.

20. Select Show Links from the Window menu. The Links palette will appear showing the three placed image names. The **Clown Balloons.TIF** selection will have an icon to the right of the name indicating it was embedded. The thumbnails to the left of the name show what the image looks like.

21. Click on the **Clown Export.BMP** selection. Use the palette menu to select Embed Image from the options.

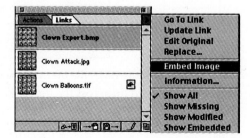

22. The **Clown Export.BMP** selection will now also have the Embedded icon.

23. Click on the **Clown Balloons.TIF** selection. The first button at the bottom of this palette is the Replace Link icon. Click on this button.

24. The Place dialog box will appear for you to choose another object to replace the selection with. Click the **Clown Export.BMP** item in the list of files and click on the Link button to link the image. Click Place.

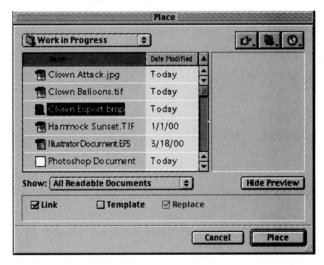

25. In the Links palette, the selected TIFF file will be replaced with the BMP file. It is linked, so there will be no embedded icon. Keep this item selected.

26. The palette menu also has a Replace Link option, though you will only see "Replace…" Select this item from the menu, then use the Place dialog box that appears to select the **Clown Balloons.TIF** image to replace the BMP file. Do not Link this replacement file.

27. Select the **Clown Attack.JPG** in the Links palette and use the palette menu to embed it. All three items will have the Embed icon.

28. We will now show you other things that can be done with placed images. Click on the TIFF image at the far left. In the File menu select the option called Document Info. A Document Info palette will appear. In the palette menu, choose Embedded Images to get information about this kind of image.

29. You will see that type is listed as CMYK. This is odd, because you exported the image as an RGB. The answer is that when the image was placed into a CMYK document, its color model was changed. Also, note that there is no information about the file format of the image, whether it is TIFF, JPEG, or BMP. This is why we always advise adding an extension to file names (tif, jpg, bmp, and others).

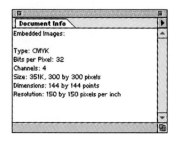

30. Separately, click on the next images and observe their information. The grayscale image is also listed as a CMYK. The black color is the "K" in CMYK. Since grayscale is actually a black image, it fits into the CMYK scheme and will separate on the black plate during printing. Close the Document Info palette.

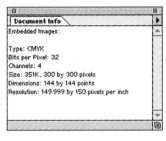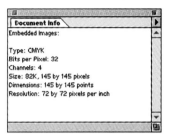

JPEG   Grayscale

31. You have used the Export and Place dialog boxes to export and import images into the document. You have also used the Links palette to relink, embed and update images. Close the document without saving.

Chapter Summary

You have learned the two basic file types that can be placed in an Illustrator document. You have learned to use the Place dialog box to place images. You now know the qualities of linking and unlinking images. You have seen the differences between vector and raster images. You have used the Links palette to manage links, using it to embed images, and update links. You have also observed and used the placing techniques that go with creating templates. You have learned the various ways an image may be used as a Template, and the idiosyncrasies of the file formats when used.

Complete Project G: BearWear Label

If you are going to use Illustrator filters on the placed images, keep in mind that most of the filters will only work with RGB. Only Blur, Pixelate, and Sharpen will work when the colors are CMYK or Grayscale.

Notes:

Color Separation and Printing

Chapter Objective:

To learn how to prepare a document for output to a printer. To gain a general knowledge of commercial printing conditions and operations. To know the color specifications of artwork and how they are reproduced in the printing process. In Chapter 14, you will:

- Learn the two ways to print your artwork — as a black-and-white composite or as color separations.

- Learn about registration marks, and how to use them in a document.

- Understand the Print dialog box and its printing features.

- Understand how to use Separation Setup to prepare print separations.

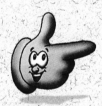

Projects to be Completed:

- Art Deco House (A)
- BearWear Business Cards (B)
- Wine and Cheese Invitation (C)
- Walking the Dogs (D)
- Broadway Bound (E)
- Joker's Wild (F)
- BearWear Label (G)

Color Separation and Printing

Performing color separations is the final step in preparing a color document to be printed. The better you understand what happens to the colors in your document once it leaves your hands, the better chance there is that the final printing will go without a hitch.

Color Separation

The yellow in CYMK process colors is a specific ink called "Process Yellow."

The term "color separation" refers to the way color inks are separated onto individual plates for printing. In Chapter 7, Painting Objects, you learned about the two types of color models used in most commercial printing: process (CMYK) colors and spot colors. Regardless of which model you use to create your artwork, when it gets to press, the color inks will be separated onto individual plates.

Process colors take four separate plates, cyan, magenta, yellow, and black; a spot color requires one plate. Each plate is created with dots of various sizes and spacing determined by the percentages (or color density) that were set in the Color and Swatches palettes when the color was created in Illustrator. This limited number of plates with variously sized and spaced dots produce the multitude of colors, tints, and shades seen on the final printed page.

Composite Proofs

Many people think that "K" in CYMK is used for black to avoid its being confused with blue, or cyan. Actually, the "K" stands for Key, and refers to the black plate that carries most of the details in many images. This plate can be used to register the entire separation if necessary — hence the term Key Plate.

We will discuss how to perform color separations in a minute, but first, let's look at what the printer does with those separations. Color plates are created from the electronic file and each color is printed separately as a "proof" along with one "composite proof" of the combined colors. These initial proofs do not require using the full presses and provide an inexpensive way for you and the printer to make sure the final printed product will have the desired appearance.

Each proof will show the full range of ink densities (color percentages), which appear as tints of the color. This example was a two-color job — black and blue. All the objects in the Illustrator document were painted with one or the other of these two colors and their tints. Notice the blue tint that was used to represent steam coming off the hot coffee.

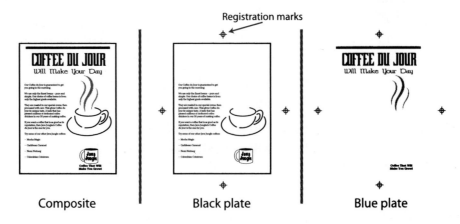

Composite   Black plate   Blue plate

Registration marks. We will show you how to create the registration marks used by the printer to align the color separations so they print in precisely the correct position.

Spot colors are often used for clients working on a budget yet desiring some color in their jobs to add interest. Spot colors are easy to make, separate, and print, Process printing is very expensive, by comparison.

If a client has four-color process printing in the budget, it is not unusual for a fifth plate to be added with a spot color. This is because the printing the fifth color is not significantly more expensive than printing four colors. Be aware that these decisions must be made before the project begins.

Deciding Who Will to Do Color Separations

Illustrator files can be separated using different sources which come down to two choices: You can separate the file using Illustrator's Separation Setup; or you can save the file as an Illustrator EPS, place it in a layout program, such ass PageMaker, InDesign, or QuarkXPress and use that program's features to do the separating. We give an in-depth look at separating with Illustrator's Separation Setup later in this chapter.

Outsourcing Your Files

Most output bureaus do not use Illustrator as their separating program. They will probably ask you to save the file as Illustrator EPS so they can place the file and separate the colors using a different software program. Before turning your files over to an outside source for color separation, there are some final steps to preparing your files, such as adding registration marks. If you have all your ducks in a row, spot colors named correctly and color models set accurately, the job should separate flawlessly.

Registration Marks

All color separations require registration marks so the colors from each plate will be positioned accurately with the other colors on the page. These marks appear on each color plate in the same location so that when the job is printed, the press proofs can show whether or not the colors are "in register" (correctly positioned).

The registration mark is made up of two crossing segments with a circle positioned at their junction. Registration marks can be applied two ways: drawing them as an object in the document, or choosing Printer's Marks in the Separation Setup dialog box.

Adding Registration Marks Manually

When registration marks are added to a document as drawn objects, the strokes should be painted a special color called Registration, accessed in the Swatches palette. When this color is applied to an object, it will appear on all color plates during separation.

When positioned on the page with the artwork, where should the registration marks be located? If the artwork is small enough to fit on the page with trim marks, the best place for registration marks is centered between the trim marks at the top, bottom, and sides.

Another good method for positioning registration marks manually is to draw a box around the artwork with the Rectangle tool, leaving some extra space around the art work, then turning the box into a guide. The registration marks can go at the top, bottom, and sides of the box.

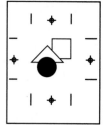
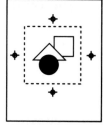

With Trim Marks   Around bounding box guide

If the artwork bleeds off the edges of the page, or even if it takes up the majority of the page not leaving room for registration marks, print at a reduced size while proofing. When your artwork is sent out for high-resolution output to be printed, the film or paper your service provider will use is larger than the letter size of your job, and big enough to hold any marks outside the page size. If this is the case, don't consider creating the marks manually. The provider's output software can apply the marks directly.

Preparing to Print

In order to print anything from Illustrator, you must use the File>Print option to bring up the Print dialog box. Depending on your platform, Macintosh or Windows, the dialog boxes will vary somewhat, though the basic settings you need are available in both.

Macintosh

The Macintosh Print dialog box is preset for the most basic print output — a black-and-white composite. In the upper-left corner of this dialog box there is a General setting on a pop-up menu. If clicked on, this menu shows other features that allow you to customize the output.

Depending on your printer, this dialog box may look slightly different than the one shown in this example. If you make no changes to the settings, and click on Print, a black-and-white composite of the art job will be printed. If, however, you want to print separations, you must click on the General menu and choose the Adobe Illustrator 9.0 selection.

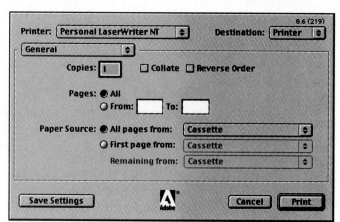

If you are creating your own registration marks, do so for Spot color separations that will be done by outside parties. If you are doing the separations yourself, you can use Illustrator's Separation Setup, which has its own Printer's Marks. Do not make registration marks for Process separation jobs. The companies doing these separations have highly sophisticated equipment and software that already has registration capabilities.

If all you are requiring is a printed example of your artwork, just select Print from the File menu, and in the appearing dialog box, click the Print button. It is as simple as that. If, however, you are requiring modifications of the output, such as printing several copies of the art on one sheet of paper, you need to investigate the many options found in the dialog box's pop-up menu.

The Adobe Illustrator 9.0 Print window shows further options to be used when printing an Illustrator document. The Output menu pops up to give the choice of Composite or Separate. Setting the specifications for a separation requires clicking the Separation Setup button. If you try to switch the Composite selection to Separate and find that Separate is gray, make sure that a PPD has been selected in Separation Setup.

Pop-up Menu   Separation Setup

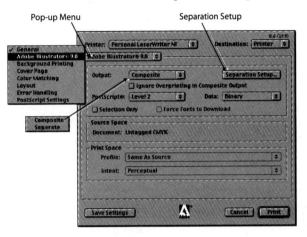

Windows

The Windows Print dialog box is slightly different than the Macintosh. In the upper right corner is the Properties menu, which is similar to the General menu of the Macintosh Print dialog box. It is here that you can select the Adobe Illustrator 9.0 option, though, with Windows, you do not need this for separations. The Separation Setup button is in the lower right of the Print dialog box. There is also an Output field which must be set for Separation using its pop-up menu if separations are to be made.

Properties - pop-up menu quivalent to the Macintosh "General" menu

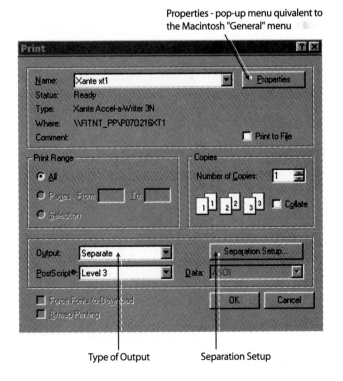

Type of Output   Separation Setup

Separation Setup

Illustrator can print its own color separations (process or spot), though they must be configured using the Separation Setup option. This can be accessed in two ways:

- **File menu.** Accesses the Separation Setup option from the File menu.

- **Print.** Selects Print from the File menu and shows its dialog box and the Separation Setup option is chosen.

When the Separation Setup option is first selected, its features will appear gray. In order to get this dialog box functional you must select a PPD (PostScript Printer Description). This can be found in either the Extensions>Printer Descriptions folder (Macintosh), or in the Windows>System>*.ppd directory (Windows). Once a PPD is selected, the dialog box features will appear black.

Macintosh

The Illustrator folder where the application resides has a Utilities folder. In this folder is Sample PPDs folder that has a General printer description.

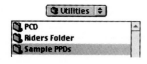

Windows

If you have a printer, and have its driver installed into the system, you should be able access the Separation Setup options. If you must choose a PPD, use Windows>System>.ppd to gain access to the available PPD's.*

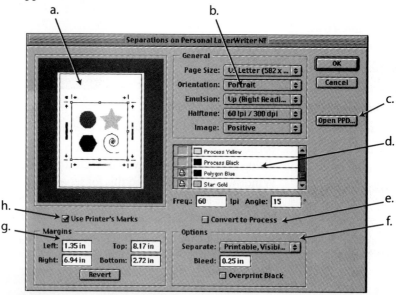

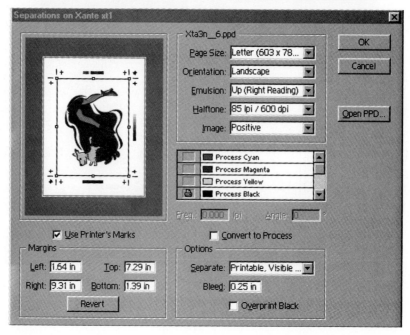

Descriptions of the marked sections:

a. **Preview window** shows the image and Printer's Marks (if selected).

b. **Page Size** is the size of the paper to be printed on.

   Orientation is either Portrait (vertical) or Landscape (horizontal).

   Emulsion refers to printing film and whether or not the emulsion is Right Reading Up or Right Reading Down.

   Halftone sets the halftone resolution of the separations.

   Image controls output to be positive or negative images.

c. **Open PPD** allows the selection of a Postscript Printer Description (PPD). Select the one that is compatible with the target printer.

d. **Color Print Selectors.** This window allows selection of the colors that are to print. The symbols at the left of each color name are very important to know. The small icon shaped like a printer indicates that the color next to it will print. This icon can be clicked on or off, to control whether the color will print.

   If Convert to Process is clicked, the spot colors will receive a process icon, which means they will be included in the separations as process colors. The process color will be close to the spot color you selected but it will not be exactly the same. The spot color names will be dimmed to show they are no longer available as spot colors.

e. **Convert to Process** affects spot colors and includes them in a process color separation, broken down to their CMYK color values. If Convert to Process is not selected, the spot colors become available.

f. **Printable Layer** selector. This option allows you to designate which objects will print, determined by the layers they are assigned to.

   Printable Visible Layers refers to any objects that are on layers that are not hidden. In order for the layer to print, the Print option must be selected for that layer in the Layer Options menu.

   Visible Layers only prints objects on visible layers. Objects on hidden layers will not print.

   All Layers will print all objects residing on all layers.

g. **Left, Right, Top, Bottom.** This is the distance from the bounding box round the artwork to the edge of the paper. If more or less room is needed around the bounding box, the amount of space can be entered into these fields.

h. **Use Printer's Marks.** These are both trim marks and registration marks, determined by the bounding of the image. If more room is desired, the handles of the bounding box in the preview window can be moved on all four sides.

The Printer's Marks found in the preview of the Separation Setup window can be dragged away from the art, giving it breathing room.

Making a Spot Color Separation

1. From your **Work in Progress** folder, open **Wow Logo.AI**.

2. Select Print from the File menu. Leave the Print dialog box at its default settings. You are going to print a black-and-white composite of the logo. If your computer is hooked up to a printer, click Print/OK.

3. In a matter of minutes, the composite proof of the WOW logo will be printed.

4. We will now go on to print a spot color separation. You did not make registration marks for this logo because you are going to separate it yourself from Illustrator, and the Separation Setup has its own marks.

5. Go back to the File menu and select Print.

   Macintosh
   In the Print dialog box, click on the General menu and select Adobe Illustrator 9.0.

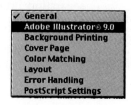

   Click on the Separation Setup button. If a PPD has not been selected, all the separation options will be gray. Click Open PPD. Go to the appropriate folder where your Printer Descriptions reside (System>Extensions>Printer Descriptions), and select the PPD for your laser printer. If the options of this dialog box are black, continue on to step number 6.

   Windows
   In the File menu, select Print. In the dialog box that appears, click on the Separation Setup button in the lower right of the window.

6. All the options of the Separations Setup window should now be accessible.

7. Make certain that Use Printer's Marks is selected. In the Preview window, click on the bounding box handles and enlarge the area around the WOW logo. Click on the logo image in this Preview window and move it around to observe that you can customize the position of the image.

This exercise is primarily about printing separations. There are some printers, however, that will not perform separations. Your printer must be set up for PostScript in order to do this. Check with the printer's handbook to see if it will do separations.

8. Using the other features and options of this dialog box, make these settings: Set Orientation to Portrait; set Emulsion to Up (Right Reading); Leave Halftone set as it is; set Image for Positive to see positive images in the printout; make certain that Convert to Process is not clicked.

The two spot colors at the bottom of Color Print Selector list will be: PMS 185 2X CVC, and PMS 273 CVC. They should have the printer icons next to them. If not, click to make the icons appear. Make sure no other color names have a printer icon next to them. The Separation Setup dialog box should look similar to this sample. Click OK.

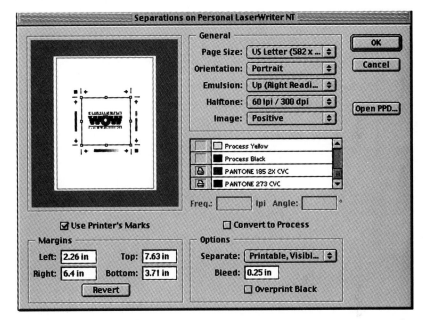

9. You will be back at the Print dialog box. Use the Output pop-up menu to change from Composite to Separation. Click Print/OK.

10. When the job prints, observe how the two colors are printed separately with trim and registration marks on each printout.

11. Observe also how the spot colors printed as black on the page. When the job is taken to a commercial printing service, this image will be used to create a negative for producing a plate. The spot colors will be applied to their respective printing plates. When the two colors combine on the page, the logo will be printed correctly.

12. Close the document without saving.

The small icon that looks like a printer is the symbol telling you that the color it is next to will print.

Chapter Summary

You have learned about registration marks, and know when to use them. You have been shown the Print dialog box and learned about its most important features for printing either composites or color separations. You have worked with Separations Setup and observed how it manages process-color and spot-color separations.

Notes:

PROJECT ASSIGNMENT #2

Assignment

A farm in Northern California is introducing a new line of seasoned vinegars in four flavors: garlic, thyme, cilantro, and basil. They want a contemporary logo to go along with this new line of products.

The client is a family-owned company with more than fifty years' experience in organic farming and the manufacture of bottled and canned foods are sold to a largely regional market. They're looking to introduce a modern look that's still able to convey a feeling of tradition, longevity, and commitment to the highest quality. They have a few professionally produced images of the flavoring agents that you can use if you want to.

Applying Your Skills

To develop the labels, you will need to use the following functions, methods, and features of Adobe Illustrator:

- Using type and outlined-type elements combined with appropriate shapes and Pathfinder functions to create a new logo for the client.

- Importing the copy supplied by the client for use on each of the four labels.

- Copying and pasting the nutritional information supplied on to the four labels and positioning it properly on the new designs.

- Using gradients and custom process colors to build subtle color and interest into each of the labels in the series.

- Using rotation and other transformations to position type and graphic elements vertically and horizontally to meet the requirements of the design.

- Selecting images from the files we've supplied and placing them into the labels, complete with whatever framing or outlining method you decide to choose for the labels.

- Printing test separations and a composite proof, along with the appropriate images and typefaces prior to packaging the job for delivery to a service provider.

Specifications

Each label will wrap around three sides of a bottle, and must be ten inches wide and five inches high. Each label must incorporate the supplied text, the nutrition label, and an image. Name each vinegar appropriately and use the same graphic treatment for all of the titles.

The labels are to be produced as a four-color process job, with no additional spot colors. Subtle colors and pastel shades are preferred, but don't limit your creativity — the client might like something surprising.

Included Files

We have supplied a full compliment of images and support files for this project. You must use these text and graphics.

There are various CMYK images supplied in TIFF format. You only need to use four of them, so you have some flexibility in your selections. There is also a text file containing the copy for the Celtic Farms label, called Copy for CF Labels.TXT. Lastly, use the Nutrition Label.AI file containing the information required by the FDA for food products. Make sure it's on all four labels.

Publisher's Comments

Labels are a true contemporary artistic venue — you can see the work of some of the nation's finest artists on food, record labels, and other forms of packaging. Many of the top awards in the graphics industry are awarded for unique and compelling packaging. Labels like the ones you're required to execute in this project are but one form.

This project is typical of many real-world assignments in that the client has supplied certain images that they feel are right for the look and feel they're trying to accomplish. Although you might have picked something different, it's up to you to incorporate what they're supplying with your own imagination to come up with something that will not only please the client but will help the product fly off the shelves.

This is ultimately the true purpose of the assignment — to make people notice your client's products in a sea of similar packages. A unique and compelling design that really stands out is the answer to this challenge.

REVIEW #2

CHAPTERS 9 THROUGH 14:

In Chapters 9 through 15, you learned how to manipulate and duplicate objects; how to align and distribute objects; how to organize art with layers, and use the features of the Layers palette. You also learned how to draw paths with the Pen, Rectangle, and Ellipse tools to create artistic effects. You learned about Operation and Filters, and their importance in the creative environment. You learned about gradients, transformations, how to work with placed images, and finally, you learned about outputting files. After completing the second half of this course, you should:

• Know about layers and sublayers, and how they apply to your design. You should understand the stacking order of objects on a layer; the features of the Layers palette; modifier keys; the Layer Options dialog box; and the importance of the priority of the levels as they appear in the Layers palette.

• Be comfortable with creating artistic effects with Illustrator operations and filters, and what settings are needed to achieve them; know how to use the Pathfinder palette; have learned about the Pencil tool and how to use its Eraser and Smooth tool; and the Paintbrush tool and know about its four categories of brushes in the Brush palette; know how to create and apply Styles, and use the Styles palette; know how the Appearance palette is indispensable when working with the objects altered from the Effect menu.

• Understand gradients, and the wide variety of effects they add to your design; know the difference between Linear and Radial gradients. You should also know how to use the Gradient tool and the Gradient palette to change angles of gradients. You should also know how to modify the colors in a gradient using the Color palette.

• Know how to transform shapes: how to rotate, reflect, scale and shear, both with dialog boxes and manually. You should understand the origin point, its relationship to the selected objects, and how to set it. You should also understand the concept of the bounding box and its in transformations.

• Know how to incorporate external images into Illustrator documents. You should understand Link info, Missing Links, know how to identify placed images, and know how to embed images from the Palette menu. You should also know how to place images as templates, and how the template images behave depending on their linked and unlinked status.

• Understand that you must have a general knowledge of the output process. You should know about color models; the two ways to print your document; understand the difference between process and spot colors; and understand registration marks.

Project A: Art Deco House

The Art Deco period of the '30s left us with some very attractive and easily recognizable architecture. This project is an illustration reflecting this art style. It is not an architectural rendering, so exactness of perspectives and angles is left to artistic license. The artist wanted to create an appealing illustration that could be used in many situations as clip art or generic art. It is a black and white work, so tonal screen percentages of black will be relied on in painting the objects.

Getting Started

1. Use File>Open to navigate to the **SF-Intro Illustrator** folder and select **Deco Building.AI**. Save As the document with the same name to your **Work in Progress** folder. The document has a template of the final art placed on the page for you to trace.

The final thickness of the strokes is 5 pt. If you attempt to trace the template in Preview mode, these thick rules would obscure the template as you click the Pen tool. In Outline mode, the thin segment lines are hard to see against the background of the template. We suggest that you work in Preview mode, drawing lines with a fill of None, and a 1-pt. black stroke. We have included a square to the left of the template, called the generic square. It is painted with a fill of None, and a 1-pt. black stroke. Clicking this square with the Selection tool changes the Fill and Stroke boxes in the Toolbox to these settings.

Where should you click the Pen tool on the template? Remember, the segments are in the center of a stroke, with half the stroke on either side of the segment. You should then make your clicks in the center of the thick stroke in the template. When the thicker 5-pt. stroke is applied later, the line will fit almost perfectly.

Click in middle of template
Stroke thickness

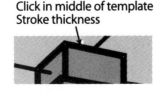

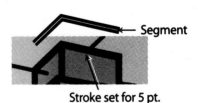

Segment

Stroke set for 5 pt.

For proper alignment, there will some cases of aligning anchor points. First, Snap to Point should be checked in the View menu. When a single anchor point is selected and dragged with the Direct Selection tool, the cursor becomes hollow when it touches an anchor point of another path. Snap to Point also allows dragged anchor points to snap to guides, turning hollow when they touch the guide.

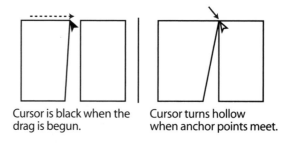

Cursor is black when the drag is begun.

Cursor turns hollow when anchor points meet.

Starting at the Top

1. We will begin at the top of the building, with the tower. To look at this piece in the template, the most probable approach would be to draw two rectangles and adjust their anchor points to fit the template, and each other. Here are the two rectangles, butted up to each other (A). Notice what takes place. When using thick strokes, the edges jut out, creating an odd-looking effect. Beveled Joins do not help (B). Neither do Rounded Joins (C) Even adjusting the Miter didn't help much. How does one approach fixing this problem?

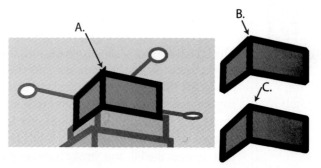

2. The answer is to do something you will sometimes finding yourself doing in digital illustration — cheat. Rather than two rectangles, you will draw one closed path. Click the generic square with the Selection tool. Select the Pen tool and click the shape around what would be two rectangles. With this technique, there are no butting corners that cause the jutting effect.

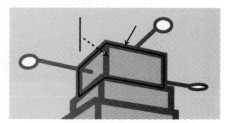

3. A single extra segment is needed to fit the corner of this path. Hold the Shift key to constrain the Pen tool and draw the vertical segment. Position the segment at the corner where the two rectangles are butting up to each other. Use the Direct Selection tool to move the anchor points, and watch for the hollow cursor when the anchor points match. Select the two objects and Object>Group. Leave the stroke set for 1 pt. for now.

4. With the top part of the tower drawn, go on to draw the piece underneath it the same way. Make sure you add the connecting cheat piece. Deselect all paths.

5. The projecting lamps are next. Click the Default Colors box in the Toolbox to set the fill for white, with a black stroke. Use the Pen tool to draw the rods as single segments. Use the Ellipse tool to draw the oval lights. Hold the Option/Alt key to start the ellipse from the center. This will help it fit to the template better as you draw. Select the rods and light. Select Window>Show Stroke to access the Stroke palette. Change the rods and lights to a stroke of 3 pt. with rounded caps. Select the rods and lights of the center and right side lamps. Send them to the back be choosing Object>Arrange> Send to Back. Deselect the lamps.

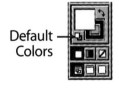

Default Colors

3 pt.   Rounded Caps

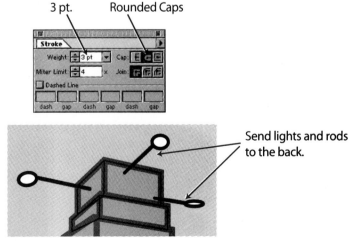

Send lights and rods to the back.

6. The objects that align at the bottom of the building must conform to an angled perspective line. Click on the generic square with the Selection tool. With the Pen tool, draw a line from the bottom left corner of the building to the bottom right. Press Command/Control-5 to turn the line into a guide. This is so that future paths can be modified to align with the guide. Remember, when dragged anchor points touch a guide, the cursor becomes hollow. This is very important for achieving exact alignment.

7. Now the front of the building can be drawn. Select the Rectangle tool and drag downward originating from the upper left corner of the front (A). Drag so that it completes a rectangle, ending just below the door. With the Direct Selection tool, click on the top right anchor point of the rectangle to select it. Holding the Shift key to constrain, move the anchor point down to match the template. Click on the bottom right anchor point to select it. Holding the Shift key to constrain, move the anchor point down to touch the guide you created. Leave this piece at 1 pt. for now.

A.   B.

8. The lines inside this rectangle are individual segments drawn with the Pen tool. Select the Pen tool and draw the segments to match the template. Deselect the paths.

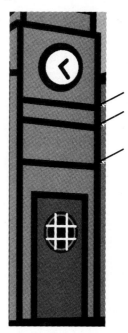

9. The next piece is the left side of the tower. This is created using another trick of avoiding the jutting lines. The object is going to be behind the tower front rectangle. Draw this piece with an extra anchor point at the top right corner. This will eliminate the abrupt corner edge. Send this object to the back with Object>Arrange>Send to Back. Save your changes made so far.

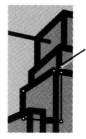

The Clock

1. The clock is made by selecting the Ellipse tool and drawing the larger ellipse first (A), then the smaller (B). Do not hold the Shift key so the ellipses are not circles. The clock hands are actually a single path, made by three consecutive clicks with the Pen tool. Click the generic square and draw the paths now (C).

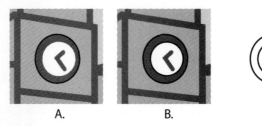

A.	B.	C.

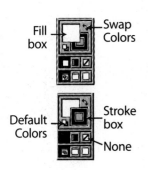

Fill box — Swap Colors

Default Colors — Stroke box — None

2. To paint the clock parts, go to Outline view. In Preview mode, the objects will get in each other's way as they are painted. Select the larger clock ellipse first. It is currently painted with a fill of None, and stroke of black. It needs to be filled with black, and stroked with None, the reverse of its colors. Click the Swap Colors icon in the Toolbox to switch these paint attributes. This ellipse will be filled black, and stroked with None.

3. Select the smaller ellipse, which should be filled with white, stroked with None. Click the Default Colors icon in the Toolbox which paints the ellipse with a white fill, with black stroke. To remove the stroke, click the Stroke box in the Toolbox, then click the None icon, which applies None to the stroke.

4. The clock hands are filled with None, and stroked with 3-pt. black. Select the clock hands path. Use the Window menu to Show Stroke, bringing up the Stroke palette. If you do not see all of the palette shown here, use the palette menu to Show Options. Set a 3-pt. stroke weight. Click on the Rounded Caps icon. The clock should now be drawn and painted. Deselect the paths. Return to Preview mode.

3 pt.   Rounded Caps

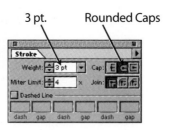 

5. Press Command/Control-S to save your changes so far.

The Door

1. The door is a rectangle drawn to match the template; its anchor points will be adjusted with the Direct Selection tool. Click the generic square with the Selection tool. In the Stroke palette, change the stroke weight to 1 pt. Select the Rectangle tool and draw the door. Select the individual anchor points of the rectangle with the Direct Selection tool and adjust them to fit the template.

2. The window on the door is built from two ellipses and four segments. Draw the larger ellipse first, then the smaller, followed by the segments. Select the four segments and Object>Group them. We will now go on to paint the paths.

3. Go to Outline viewing mode. Select the larger ellipse. In the Window menu, select Show Color to view the Color palette. Use the palette menu to show the CMYK colors. Click the Fill box in the palette. Click the black color swatch in the bottom right corner. Click the Stroke box. Click the None box for no stroke. Press Return/ Enter to apply.

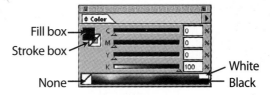

4. Select the smaller ellipse. Click the Fill box in the Color palette, then click the None icon. In the Stroke palette, change the weight to 1.5 pt. Click the Stroke box in the Color palette. Set the C, M, Y fields to "0". Set the K to 50%. Press Return/Enter to apply this.

5. Select the 4-segment group. In the Color palette, click the Fill box, then click the None icon. Click the Stroke box, then click the white icon. In the Stroke palette, set the weight for 2 pt., with Rounded Caps. Press Return/Enter to apply. The door window should look like this. We will now paint the door.

6. Click on the door rectangle. In the Color palette, click on the Fill box. In the K field, type "50", and press Return/Enter to apply. In the Stroke palette, change the weight to 5 pt. and apply. The door and window should look like this — filled with 50% black, and stroked with a 5-pt. black line.

7. Press Command/Control-S to save your changes so far.

Finishing the Tower

1. The tower portion of the art is finished. Select the tower closed paths that have remained 1 pt. and paint them with a fill of 30% black using the Color palette as on the previous paths. In the Stroke palette, change the stroke to 5 pt. The single 1 pt. connecting segments are also 5-pt. black strokes. Press Command/Control-A to Select All objects in the document. Press Command/Control-3 to Hide them. This will make the next drawing easier to work with.

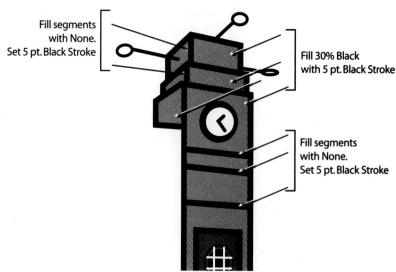

Fill segments with None. Set 5 pt. Black Stroke

Fill 30% Black with 5 pt. Black Stroke

Fill segments with None. Set 5 pt. Black Stroke

2. Click the generic square to set the colors. The column to the left of the tower is made with the extra anchor point to avoid a jutting corner (A). The covering rectangle is drawn with the Rectangle tool to match the template, and its anchor points adjusted. To its right, another rectangle is drawn and adjusted, (B). Fill these paths with 30% black, stroked with a 5 pt. black. A smaller rectangle shadow (C) is drawn and painted with a fill of 100% black, and stroke of None. Deselect the rectangle path.

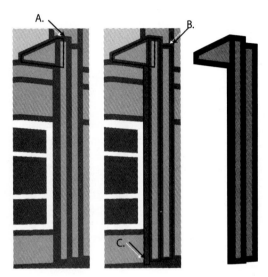

3. The column on the right side of the tower is made by drawing two rectangles and adjusting them to the guide at the bottom. Paint the two rectangles with a fill of 30% black and a stroke of 5 pt. black. To show the shadowed side of the taller column, a small filler piece is drawn. Paint the filler piece with 100% black, stroked with None. The filler piece anchor points will now have to be adjusted so that the piece butts up evenly to the corner of the taller column. When finished, select the three pieces and Object>Group them, then deselect. Press Command/Control-S to save your changes so far.

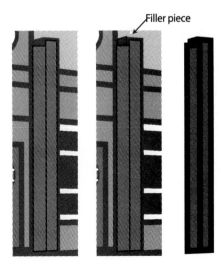

Filler piece

The Corner Windows

1. Click the generic square. Begin the left window side by drawing a closed path with the Pen tool to mark the white background of the windows (A). Draw the accenting bars of the building's exterior (B). Draw the window panes, matching the template. Fill the window background with white and give it a stroke of None. Paint the accenting bars with a fill of None, and a 5-pt. black stroke. The window panes are filled with black and stroked with None (C).

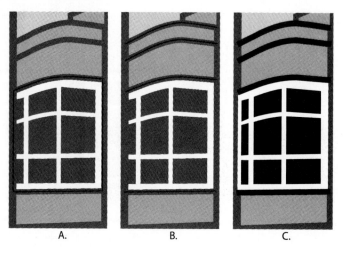

A.   B.   C.

2. To finish the right side, begin by drawing the white background piece of the window. It is a rectangle that is adjusted to fit the angled segments (A). The window panes are drawn next with the Pen tool to fit the template (B). Next, draw the four accenting bars, which are the top curving piece, with three other segments. Paint the window panes with a fill of black, and stroke of None. Select the white background rectangle and paint it with a fill of white, and stroke of None. Paint the accenting bars with a fill of None, and stroke of 5-pt. black, with Rounded Caps. Select all these paths and Object>Arrange>Send to Back. Go back to the Object menu and select Show All to bring the hidden paths back to view. Deselect all paths.

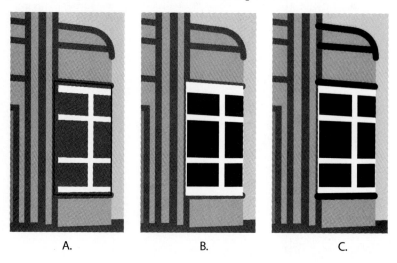

A.   B.   C.

3. Let's look at the entire piece drawn so far, but without the template. Templates can be hidden. Use the Window menu to select Show Layers. In the Layers palette, the template resides on its own layer, which controls whether it is viewed or not. We want to hide the template to see the paths better. On the far left side of the template layer is an eye icon. This represents Show/Hide. When clicked, the layer will become hidden. Click the icon now. The template on the page will be hidden from view.

Hide

4. You will now see the paths you've drawn more clearly. Most of the closed paths have been painted with a fill of 30% black.

5. Let's bring the Template back to view. Click again on the same Show/Hide box you clicked to hide the template. The graphic icon will reappear, and so will the template. Press Command/Control-S to save your changes so far.

Finishing the Building

1. Finishing the rest of the building does not require a lot of other closed paths or path modifications. Click the generic square. Use the Pen tool to draw a single closed object around the remainder of the building. Paint this path with a fill of 50% black, and a stroke of None. Send the path to the back with Object> Arrange>Send to Back.

2. Press Command/Control-S to save your changes so far.

The Final Touches

1. The final touches are the parking lot, the surrounding border, and the background color. With the Pen tool, draw a closed path that will act as the black parking lot. Paint this path with a fill of 100% black and a stroke of None. Leave this path in front of the building.

2. The surrounding border and background color are made from one rectangle that has been duplicated. Use the Rectangle tool to draw the border around the art. Paint the rectangle with a fill of None, and stroke of 10 pt. black. Use the Edit menu to Copy the rectangle. Use Edit>Select All to select all paths. Choose Edit>Paste in Back to paste the copy of the rectangle in back of all other objects. Paint the copy with a fill of 20% black, and stroke of None.

3. The Deco Building is complete and should look similar to this.

4. Save your last changes and close the document.

Notes:

Project B: BearWear Business Cards

As a graphic designer or commercial artist, sooner or later you will get an assignment to create business cards for a paying client. Business cards are not to be taken lightly. The quick printing shop on the corner can produce business cards for a phenomenally low price, but the artist preparing the art has to be exacting in measurements and alignment, if the card is to look in any way professional.

Setting up the Layout

1. Use File>New to create a new document. In the New Document dialog box, set for CMYK Color Mode, name the file "BearWear Card.AI", and leave the Artboard Size set for default. Save As the file to your **Work in Progress** folder using the Adobe Illustrator Document format. In File>Document Setup, set the Units for Inches. Press Command/Control-R to see the rulers. In the Edit>Preferences>Guides & Grid, change the guides to dots that are colored black. This will make them more visible.

2. From the rulers, drag guides to mark the page. The vertical guide should go to the 4.25-in. mark on the horizontal ruler to show the center of the page. A horizontal guide should be dragged down to mark the 8.5-in. mark on the vertical ruler. The intersection of where the horizontal guide crosses the vertical guide will be the center of the business card.

4.25"

8.5"

3. From the Window menu, select Show Transform. The Transform palette will allow you to relocate objects to exact X,Y positions.

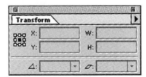

Default Colors

4. Click the Default Colors icon in the Toolbox. Select the Rectangle tool in the Toolbox and click its cursor anywhere at the top of the page. In the Rectangle dialog box, set the Width for 3.5 in. and the Height for 2 in. Click OK.

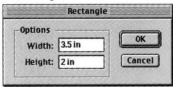

5. A rectangle the size of a business card will appear. We will now relocate it to the top center mark. The top horizontal guide is set for 8.5 in. The vertical center guide is set for 4.24 in. With the rectangle selected, in the Transform palette set the X field for 4.25 in. and the Y for 8.5 in. Make sure the Reference Point in the palette is set for Center. Press Return/Enter to apply this.

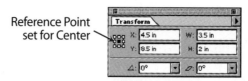

Reference Point set for Center

6. The rectangle will move its center point to the X,Y location you specified.

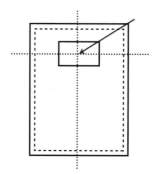

7. Now you need to set guides that are 1/8″ inside the business-card border. The Grid is set up for 8 units per inch, so it will be faster to use it. In the View menu, select Show Grid. You will see a grid appear in the background, but did you notice something else? The business card is filled with white. This keeps you from seeing the Grid.

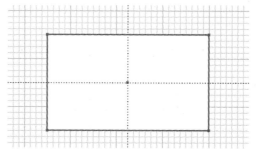

8. What if you go to Outline view? Do this now. You can see the rectangle and guides more clearly, but the Grid has disappeared. The answer is to remove the white fill from the rectangle. With the rectangle still selected, click on the Fill box in the Toolbox, then click the None box. Now the rectangle will be transparent, and the Grid becomes visible.

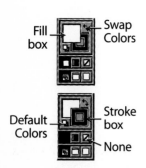

Fill box — Swap Colors

Default Colors — Stroke box — None

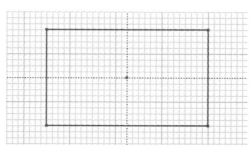

9. In the View menu, select Snap to Grid. Using the Grid as a matrix (the small squares are 1/8″ in size), drag guides to mark a margin 1/8″ edge of the card. Unless a bleed is called for (where a background color or image is printed to the outer edge), this is the closest the type or images should come to the border. Do not overstep this boundary. Use the View menu to Hide Grid and toggle off the Snap to Grid feature.

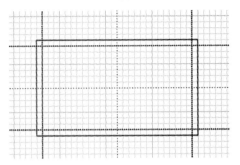

10. With the rectangle selected, press Command/Control-2 to Lock it. This will avoid any accidental selecting and moving of the card's edges. We can now proceed to set type on the business card.

11. Press Command/Control-S to save your changes so far.

Selecting a Typeface

1. Press "T" to select the Type tool. If the Character palette is not visible, press Command/Control-T. Use the palette menu to Show Options if all of the palette features are not present. Click the Type cursor on the page to the right, away from the business card guides.

2. Type the word "BEARWEAR." Highlight the text with the Type tool.

3. Click the pop-up menu to the far right of the Font fields. A list of available fonts will appear. Scroll through it until you select ATCBahama, then release. This font gives an appearance of down-to-earth, solid craftsmanship. Change the size to 50 pt., the leading to Auto (which will be 60 pt.).

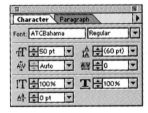

4. In choosing a font, it often helps to actually see your copy set in several different fonts to choose the best for the job. Highlight the BEARWEAR word and Edit>Copy. Click the cursor at the end of the word, make a line return, then Paste the word on the second line. Continue making line returns and pasting the word until you have six lines of type, with the same BEARWEAR word. This is to make examples of different typefaces seen on the same word.

5. The first line of type is set with the font ATCBahama. Highlight the second line and change it to ATCFreeport. Select the third line of type and make it ATCMonsoon. Make the fourth line ATCMargarita Bold, the fifth line ATC Holiday, and the sixth line ATCMango.

BEARWEAR

BEARWEAR

BEARWEAR

BEARWEAR

BEARWEAR

BEARWEAR

Combining Fonts

Combining fonts can create visual interest in a logo if it's not overdone. Warning: this can look too busy or amateurish unless the fonts are well-suited to each other. In this case, we combine two stylized fonts.

1. The two fonts you will combine, after considering the other possibilities, are ATCBahama and ATCMonsoon. Together they convey an impression of solid dependability, combined with a subtle flair for design.

2. Delete all the lines of type except the one set in ATCMonsoon. Using the Type tool, select the last four letters, "WEAR." Change their Font to ATCBahama. As you will see, the "WEAR" letters are larger than the "BEAR."

BEARWEAR

3. With the four letters still highlighted, change the size of the "WEAR" to 43 pt., the horizontal scale to 85%, and apply.

Making Further Modifications

1. Computerized typesetting is very efficient, but the automatic spacing is not always the best possible. Manual kerning allows you to reposition the letters by adjusting the space between them.

2. Highlight all the letters of the type block and press the Left Arrow key once, while holding the Option/Alt key. This will tighten the tracking to -20 pts.

3. The rest of the letter spacing will have to be performed with kerning between what are called "kerning pairs" or the space between two letters. Click the Type tool cursor between any two letters that you want to kern. Holding the Option/Alt-Shift keys, press the Left Arrow key to close up the space, or press the Right Arrow key to widen the space between two letters. Do this now to adjust the letters to look this way.

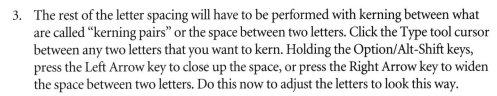

Positioning the Logo

1. Select the text block with the Selection tool. In the Type menu, select the option Create Outlines to convert the text to path outlines. When a text block is converted to outlines, the letters are immediately grouped. Leave them grouped. We will call this the "logo group."

2. Double-click on the Scale tool in the Toolbox. In the Scale dialog box, set the Uniform percentage to 50% and click OK. We now want to center the logo group, and position it just above the card's horizontal center guide.

3. Show the Transform palette if it is not currently on the screen. In the X field, type "4.25" so it will vertically center. In the Y field, type "8.75". This Y setting is 1/4″ above the 8.5-in. horizontal center. Press Return/Enter to apply these settings.

4. The BearWear logo will be centered in the upper portion of the card. Press Command/Control- ; (semicolon) to hide the guides to see the card without guide distractions.

5. Press Command/Control- ; again to toggle the guides back to view. Press Command/Control-S to save your changes so far.

Creating the Body Type

1. Select the Type tool in the Toolbox, and click the cursor on the center of the card.

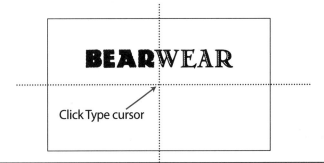

Click Type cursor

2. In the Character palette set the Font to ATC Cabana Bold, set the size to 10 pt., leading to Auto, tracking to -20, vertical and horizontal scales to 100%, baseline shift to 0. From the Paragraph palette, set the alignment for Align Center. Type these words on two lines in the same text block:

Heathcliff Hollingsworth

Vice President

3. Highlight only the word "Vice President" and change its font style to Normal and the size to 9 pt. Deselect the text block.

4. Click the Type cursor on the left vertical 1/8″ guide. Set the alignment for Align Left. Type these words on two lines in the same text block:

17230 Rustic Way South

Belleview, WA 98115

5. Select the text block with the Selection tool and position it so the baseline of the bottom line rests on the horizontal 1/8″ guide.

6. With the Selection tool, drag the text block over to the right side of the card while holding the Shift key to constrain the move. When on the right side, press the Option/Alt key and let go of the mouse to duplicate the block. Set its alignment for Align Right. Position it so the right margin of the text block touches the vertical 1/8″ guide. The baseline should have remained in place as the Shift key was held during the drag. Highlight the top line of this text. Type the telephone number "(555) 517-0809". Highlight the second line and type the email address: "hhollings@bearwear.com".

7. The business card is finished. All that remains to be done is to duplicate the card and add trim marks for the printer. Use Object>Unlock All to unlock the business card rectangle. Save your changes made so far.

The Final Touches

1. Use Edit>Select All to select all the components of the card. Press Command/Control-G to group them. This is a precaution you should always take when moving several elements of a design at one time. They can be ungrouped later.

2. With this group selected, go to the Object menu and select Transform>Move. In the Move dialog set Horizontal for "0" (zero), the Vertical for "-2". Click the cursor in the Distance field and it will automatically reflect the necessary changes for Distance and Angle. Click Copy.

3. The original rectangle will duplicate a distance of two inches at a 90° angle. This exact measurement and alignment will butt the two groups up to each other (A). Press Command/Control-D twice to Transform Again, making two more exactly aligned cards underneath (B).

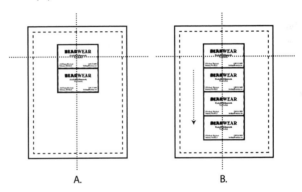

A.   B.

4. Press Command/Control-S to save your changes so far.

Making the Trim Marks

The business cards have been set up this way to save money. This layout of four business cards is referred to as "four-up." If the printer were to have to print 500 cards separately, then cut the 500 cards individually, you would have quite a labor charge to pay. The borders of the cards butted up to each other reduces the number of cuts needed to trim the cards and could accommodate various names in one print run.

1. Select the four groups of cards. In the Filter menu, select Create>Trim Marks. Trim marks will appear at the top and bottom corner of the selected items. We need to create horizontal trim marks for where the cards butt up to each other.

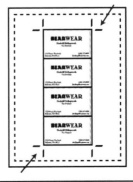

2. Deselect the trim marks. Press the letter "A" to access the Direct Selection tool. Hold the Option/Alt key and click on the top left trim mark, add the Shift key and click the top right trim mark (A). Go to Object>Transform>Move and set the Horizontal field for "0" (zero), and the Vertical field for "-2". Click Copy. The two selected paths will duplicate downward. Press Command/Control-D twice to create two more copies (B). These will tell the printer where to make the horizontal cuts between cards.

A.

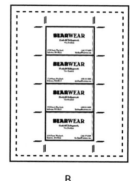

B.

3. Select View>Guides>Clear Guides. Select the four card borders with the Direct Selection tool and set their stroke to None. The final cards should look like this.

4. Save and close the document.

Project C: Wine and Cheese Invitation

Creating the Wine Glass Shape

1. Use File>Open to navigate to the **SF-Intro Illustrator** folder and open **WineGlass.AI**. A template of the wine glass is supplied for you to trace with the Pen tool. Choose Save As to save the file as an Adobe Illustrator Document to your **Work in Progress** folder. Name the file "Wine & Cheese.AI".

2. Zoom in on the bottom of the wine glass to begin tracing. Click on the Default Colors icon. Change the fill to None. Select the Rectangle tool in the Toolbox.

3. You will see that the bottom piece the glass sits on is part of a rectangle. Draw a rectangle and position it to match the template. When in place, select the Direct Selection tool and single-click the top segment of the rectangle, then press the Delete key once to delete it.

4. Select the Pen tool, which will be the one tool you will use to draw the entire wine glass.

5. Single-click the Pen tool on the far left endpoint of the rectangle to continue drawing the shape of the glass. Click-hold on the same anchor point and drag a curve control handle (A). Let go of the mouse. Moving to the right, in the middle of the curve, click-drag a smooth point anchor point (B). Single-click again just above this point to make an endpoint. Select the Direct Selection tool and click on the smooth point to see the control handles. Use these handles to adjust the curve to fit the template (C).

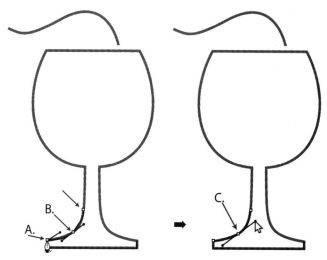

6. Select the Pen tool and single-click on the endpoint. Click-hold on the same point to pull out a smooth point control handle (A). Single-click the next point upward (B). Click-hold on this point to drag a control handle. Moving up the curve in the template, click-drag a smooth point (C), then click at the top of the glass to make the endpoint. Select the Direct Selection tool and click on the anchor points just drawn and adjust their curve handles to fit the template.

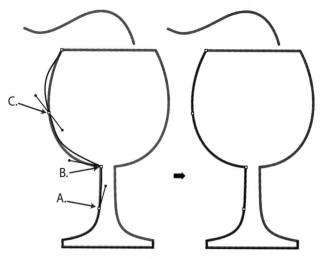

7. Select the Pen tool and single-click on the endpoint. Hold the Shift key to constrain to 90° and single-click on the right side of the wine glass (A). Click-drag on this anchor point to pull out a curve handle. Moving down, click-drag a smooth point (B) for the middle of this curving piece, then click an endpoint where the curve meets the stem of the glass. With the Direct Selection tool, click on each anchor point and adjust its curve handles to fit the template.

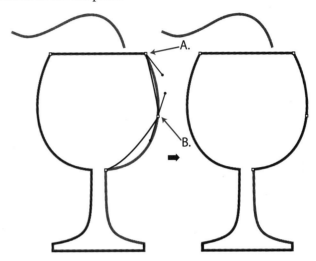

8. Select the Pen tool and single-click on the endpoint. Click-drag on this anchor point to pull out a curve handle (A). Single-click (B) to make an anchor point leading into the next curve. Click-drag on this same point to pull out a curve handle. Move to the middle of the curve and click-drag a smooth point (C). Finally, the last click will be on the far right endpoint of the rectangle, to close the path. With the Direct Selection tool, click on each anchor point and adjust its curve handles to fit the template. The wine glass is finished.

9. You will now trace the template path above the wine glass.

10. With the Pen tool, click on the right end of the template piece and drag (A). Move to the middle of the piece and click-drag a smooth point (B), making a final click on the left end of the template piece. With the Direct Selection tool, click on each anchor point and adjust its curve handles to fit the template.

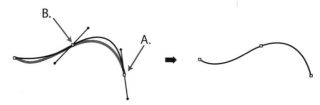

11. The wine glass and the object depicting the wine's bouquet are finished.

12. Press Command/Control-S to save your changes so far.

Placing Type in a Shape

1. Below the template is a block of tongue-in-cheek "chatty interoffice memo" type we have supplied to fill the wine glass with. Be forewarned that the settings of this text are not those that will fit the wine glass shape perfectly. We will only tell you that the font is our ATC Cabana, and that the best alignment setting for fitting text to a shape is Align Left. The rest you will have to figure out for yourself. Select the text block with the Selection tool. Press Command/Control-C to copy the text.

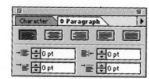

2. In the Toolbox, click-hold the cursor on the Type tool to see its optional tools. Choose the second option, the Area Type tool.

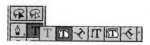

3. Click the crossbar of the tool's cursor anywhere on the wine glass path. The black stroke of the wine glass will disappear as the object becomes a text path. The text cursor is in the wine glass shape. Press Command/Control-V to Paste the type.

4. The text will be pasted inside the wine glass shape. Use the template to help fit the shape of the glass. Experiment with point size and leading first. These are the first two basics of "copy fitting."

5. As you experiment, you will probably not see all the type that was copied from the text block. Compare it with the text block if you have any questions. This means some type fitting must be done. The idea of the fitting is to have the text look as much like this example as possible. It should fit the contours of the wine glass.

Been a long week? Join the staff in the
reception area at 5 PM this Friday. Have
a glass of wine and hors d'oeuvres, let your
hair down, and meet our new interns Jessica
and Robert. We'd like to make them feel like
they're a part of our friendly PredaCorp family.
Word is, George Tirebiter is on the verge of the
big four-oh, and we want to lend him our hearfelt
support as he goes gently into that good night. Just
kidding, George! In other PredaCorp family news,
Betsy "Church Lady" Mogensen will very soon be
taking her maternity leave. How many does this
make now, Betsy? Four, five? Those breeders!
They're the Salt of the Earth. Speaking of
which, who was it who dubbed our new
subterranean wing "salt mine"?
Fess up, whoever it was!
Uh-
oh!
I'm
in a
very
nar-
row
space
and I
can't
seem to
finish that
thought…be here Friday!

6. Once you have made your initial adjustments to the size and leading, and the text is just about where way you want it, you can fine-tune your design by utilizing the tracking and kerning features of Illustrator. Tracking is the spacing between a range of selected letters. Kerning is adjusting the spacing between two letters. The keyboard shortcut for kerning and tracking is to hold the Option/Alt key and press the Left Arrow key to tighten, or the Right Arrow key to widen the spacing.

7. Use kerning and tracking to adjust the letter spacing so that the type fits the wine glass shape, and you can see all the type in the glass.

8. Save your changes made so far.

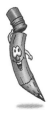

Do not resort to using the Horizontal Scale feature of the Character palette unless it is a required appearance of the design. Kerning and Tracking can fit the letter spacing, and not distort the appearance of the letters.

Fine-tuning the Text

There are variety of text formats, such as ASCII and ANSI, that specific characters should be scrutinized to make sure they are correctly styled. A case in point is the quotes and apostrophes. Most fonts have two sets of these characters. The characters that appear as the text is first being typed will look like this:

"Standard Quotes"

Some designers cringe at the thought of this type of quotation mark being in their artwork. The alternative set of quotes are called either Smart Quotes or Typographer's Quotes. They are very elegant and look like this:

"Typographer's Quotes"

There are two ways to achieve these quotes and other attractive typographer's characters: Illustrator's Type>Smart Punctuation or using keyboard commands. We cannot tell you all the various key commands because different fonts have different alternate characters. We can tell you, however, that, as a standard, the Typographer Quotes are achieved by pressing the following keys:

Beginning quote " Option/Alt-[(left bracket)

Ending quote " Option/Alt-Shift-[(left bracket)

Beginning apostrophe ' Option/Alt-] (right bracket)

Ending apostrophe ' Option/Alt-Shift-] (right bracket)

1. For this exercise we will show you the Illustrator Smart Punctuation feature found in the Type menu. Select the Type tool and click its cursor inside the wine-shaped text block and press Command/Control-A to Select All. The Smart Punctuation only works on text highlighted by the Type tool.

2. From the Type menu, select Smart Punctuation. In the dialog box that appears, note all the default alternate characters marked to be found and replaced. Do not change any of these settings. You will notice the Smart Quotes option is clicked. Click OK.

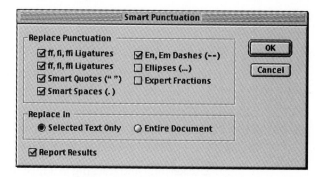

There will be a few seconds in which it makes its changes, then a window will appear telling you how many changes were made. Click OK.

3. Use the Zoom tool to zoom in closer and look at the quotation marks and apostrophes. They have been changed.

4. The only other symbol that needs to be replaced is the ellipsis in the last line of the text "thought . . . be there Friday!" After the word "thought" the three periods are typographically incorrect. There is a keyboard command that makes the true ellipsis (…) symbol. This is made by holding the Option/Alt key and pressing the semicolon key.

5. Use the Zoom tool to zoom in close to the "thought . . ." part of the sentence. Highlight and delete all spaces and periods between the words "thought" and "be." Insert the Type tool cursor before the word "be" and press Option/Alt-; (semicolon). The single ellipsis symbol will appear to look like this:

thought…be there Friday!

6. You have now used a variety of typographic features and controls to fit the text to the shape of the wine glass. Save your changes made so far.

Creating the Wine Bouquet

1. You will now move on to the path representing the wine's bouquet above the glass. Keep in mind that the type settings have been adjusted to fit the previous type, and it will be best to reset most of the settings in the Type Character palette. Set the font to ATCCozumel, size to 32 pt., leading to Auto, tracking to 0, kerning to Auto, both vertical and horizontal scales to 100%, and baseline shift to 0.

2. This time, you will use a different Type tool option, the Path Type tool.

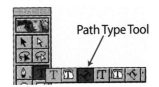

Select this tool and click its cursor on the bouquet path, near the center of the object. If the cursor appears under the path, making your type appear upside down, use the Selection tool to click on the Type I-beam and drag it upward. A shortcut for flipping text to the other side of a path is to double-click on the I-beam cursor with the Selection tool.

3. Type in all caps: "WINE & CHEESE". Use the Selection tool to pull the I-beam to move the type along the path, until the right side ends just above the type in the glass.

4. Select this text block with the Selection tool, and choose Create Outlines in the Type menu. Use the Direct Selection tool to select the letters in WINE, and go to the Swatches palette. Use its palette menu to Sort by Name. Make certain the Fill box is active in the Toolbox. Click on the color Violet C:50 M:90.

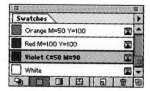

5. Select the ampersand, and click on the color Azure C:80.

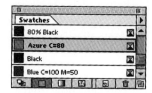

6. Select the word CHEESE, and click on the color Orange M:50 Y:100.

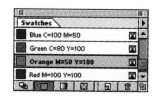

7. The wine glass, interoffice party memo is finished. To see the job without the distraction of the template, use the Window menu to Show Layers. In the Layers palette, click on the Wine Glass Template layer and drag it down to the Trash icon at the bottom of the palette. This will delete the template.

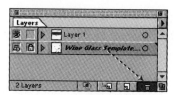

8. The wine glass job should look similar to this example.

Been a long week? Join the staff in the
reception area at 5 PM this Friday. Have
a glass of wine and hors d'oeuvres, let your
hair down, and meet our new interns Jessica
and Robert. We'd like to make them feel like
they're a part of our friendly PredaCorp family.
Word is, George Tirebiter is on the verge of the
big four-oh, and we want to lend him our heartfelt
support as he goes gently into that good night. Just
kidding, George! In other PredaCorp family news,
Betsy "Church Lady" Mogensen will very soon be
taking her maternity leave. How many does this
make now, Betsy? Four, five? Those breeders!
They're the Salt of the Earth. Speaking of
which, who was it who dubbed our new
subterranean wing "salt mine"?
Fess up, whoever it was!
Uh-
oh!
I'm
in a
very
nar-
row
space
and I
can't
seem to
finish that
thought…be here Friday!

9. Save your changes and close the document.

Project D: Walking the Dogs

The Walking the Dogs artwork is a carefree and fun example of how Illustrator's features can be used to create cartoon images. The cartoon drawing will be placed in a magazine done with four-color printing. To produce this artwork you will use the Paintbrush and Pencil tools along with the features in the Effect menu to enhance the background of the piece. You will use a systematic approach to naming the custom colors you create, which will help you efficiently manage the colors in the project.

Setting Up the Document

1. Use File>Open to navigate to the **SF-Intro Illustrator** folder and open the file **Walk the Dogs.AI.** Save As the document to your **Work in Progress** folder as an Adobe Illustrator EPS (EPS) file, naming it "Walk the Dogs.EPS."

2. The document has a template you can use to create your artwork. There is also an object you will use to create a custom Brush stroke.

Creating the Colors

1. Use Window>Show Swatches to view the Swatches palette by the Show Color Swatches icon at the bottom. Use the palette menu to select Name View, showing the percentages of the CMYK colors. Some of the standard Illustrator colors have names, such as Azure, Blue, Green, and Orange, although they are not used. You will create your own custom colors for this design.

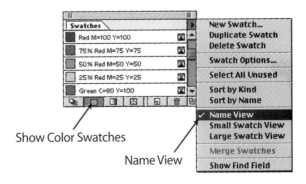

Show Color Swatches

Name View

Why would you global status to a custom color? As most commercial artists will agree, clients have a tendency to change their minds. If a great number of objects are painted with a custom color that is a certain shade, if this color is modified later on, you will have to select each painted object and modify it individually. If the color is global, merely changing the appearance in the Swatch Options dialog box will apply the new appearance to all objects painted with the global color.

2. Access the Color palette from Window>Show Color. Click on the Fill box in this palette. Set the magenta (M) for 50%. The cyan, yellow, and black percentage field should be set at 0 (zero). Drag the Fill box swatch from the Color palette over to the Swatches palette. A New Color Swatch will appear in the Swatches palette. If you don't see it immediately, scroll down to the bottom of the color list.

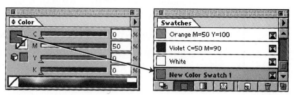

3. Double-click on the New Color Swatch name. The New Swatch dialog box will appear. Change the name to "Pink." Leave the Color Type set to Process Color. Click the Global button to select it. The CYMK sliders should show the 50% magenta swatch you dragged to the Swatch palette. You have made a global process custom color. Click OK.

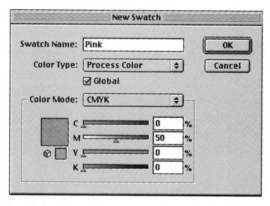

4. By the same method of setting the CMYK colors in the Color palette, then dragging the swatch to the Swatches palette for a New Color Swatch, create the following custom colors.

Brown	C:50, M:85, Y:100, K:0
Red	C:0, M:100, Y:100, K:0
Purple	C:45, M:90, Y:0, K:0
Light Blue	C:80, M:5, Y:0, K:0
Gold	C:0, M:35, Y:100, K:0

The Paintbrush Tool

1. We will start by customizing a special brush stroke for the Brushes palette. These strokes are primarily drawn with the Paintbrush tool. To keep this tool from erasing its own paths, double-click on the Paintbrush tool icon in the Toolbox. In the Paintbrush Preferences dialog box, make sure the option Keep Selected is unchecked.

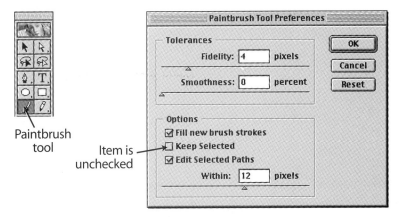

Paintbrush tool

Item is unchecked

When Keep Selected is checked in the Paintbrush Preferences (it is by default), you will find that drawing a brush stroke too close to a previous, still selected, brush stroke will delete this previous stroke. The small "X" symbol next to the cursor will tell the status. If the Paintbrush cursor has no symbol, it is too close to the previous, selected stroke and will delete it. You must either deselect the previous stroke, or move the cursor further away from this selected stroke for the "X" to appear. Unchecking Keep Selected eliminates the need to deselect path to avoid accidentally deleting it.

2. Access the Brushes palette with Window>Show Brushes. You will now create a custom Brush. In the working page's upper-left corner, select the black object with the Selection tool and drag it into the Brushes palette. A New Brush dialog box will appear. Click the New Art Brush option, then click OK.

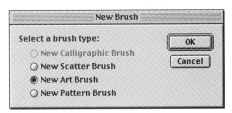

3. The Art Brush Options dialog box will appear. Name the brush stroke "Tapered Stroke." Change the Size>Width to 40%, then click OK. The Tapered Stroke brush strokes will now be present in the Brushes palette. If it is not near the other Art brush strokes, drag it up to be with them.

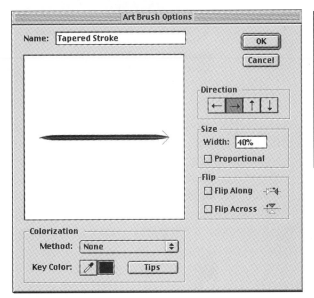

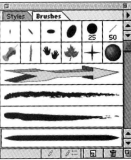

4. Select the object used to create this brush stroke and delete it. In the Toolbox, click on the Paintbrush tool. Click the Tapered Stroke brush in the palette. You will use this brush stroke to draw various paths in the design. Make certain the Fill box is set for None before using the Paintbrush tool. Save your changes made so far.

Putting on the Dog

1. In the Layers palette, double-click on Layer 1. In the Layer Options dialog box that appears, rename the layer "Dogs." Click OK.

2. Let's start drawing the first dog, named Boda. Use the Paintbrush tool to create the strokes of Boda's head. Her whiskers are made up of four separate brush strokes. This is because the Paintbrush tool, at certain thicknesses of line, does not do tight corners well. If the whisker piece were drawn as one path, the corners would be squared off and unattractive. Draw the nose with the Pen tool and paint it with a black fill, no stroke. The nose highlight is an ellipse painted with a white fill and no stroke. The eye is built from an ellipse drawn by the Ellipse tool, and an eyebrow shape drawn by the Pen tool. They are closed paths positioned to overlap slightly. In the Pathfinder palette, use Unite to combine them. The eye is painted with a black fill and no stroke.

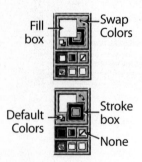

The Pathfinder palette only works with closed paths. Make sure your paths are closed before using any of Pathfinder's options.

3. Deselect all paths. Click the Swap Colors box in the Toolbox to change colors. Draw the rest of Boda with the Paintbrush tool. Her tummy and part of her tail should be separate curving pieces. The collar is drawn with the Pen tool, painted with a fill of Brown, and no stroke. The white circles on the collar are drawn with the Ellipse tool, holding the Option/Alt key to draw the circles from the center. Paint them with a white fill and no stroke. Draw the collar ring connected to the leash with the Ellipse tool and paint it with no fill and a 2-pt. black stroke.

4. Boda's furry coat color is drawn with the Pencil tool. Click the Default Colors box, then change the fill to None. Select the Pencil tool and draw paths for her coat. Make sure you hold the Option/Alt key as you finish the path so it will be closed. Paint the coat objects with a Gold fill and no stroke. Use Object>Arrange> Send to Back to position them behind the black outlines. Deselect any selected paths.

5. You will draw the second dog, named Chase, the same way you drew Boda. Click the Default Colors box, then change the fill to None. Use the Paintbrush tool to draw the outlines of Chase's body. His nose and its highlight are both ellipses. Paint the nose with a black fill and no stroke. Give the highlight in the nose a white fill and no stroke. Create the eye by drawing an ellipse and an eyebrow shape. Position them to overlap each other. Select both ellipses in the nose then choose Pathfinder>Unite to combine them. Position the eye and the nose to match the template. Deselect all paths.

6. Click the Default Colors box, then change the fill to None. Draw Chase's coat with the Pencil tool. When the closed objects are created, select and paint them with a fill of Brown, and no stroke. Send these selected paths to the back with Object>Arrange> Send to Back. Go to Boda and drag her collar ring down to Chase, holding the Option/Alt key to duplicate it.

7. Deselect all paths. Click the Default Colors box, then change the fill to None. Draw Chase's color spots with the Pencil tool, making them closed paths. Paint the paths with a black fill and no stroke. Deselect all paths.

8. Set the fill for None, and the Stroke for 4 pt. Brown. For each dog leash, use the Pen tool to draw a single curving segment. Adjust the curves to fit the template.

9. Click the Show/Hide icon of the Dogs layer to hide it. Save your changes.

Ladies Apparel Dept.

1. We will move on to drawing the lady's boots, fishnet hose, and skirt. In the Layers palette, create a new layer. Rename the layer "Lady." Drag this layer under the Dogs layer. Click the Default Colors box, then change the fill to None. Use the Paintbrush tool to draw the black outlines of the legs and boots. The skirt is a closed path drawn with the Pen tool. Select these objects and lock them.

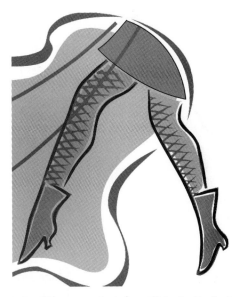

2. The fishnet lines are created with a slightly different technique. Click the Default Colors box, then change the fill to None. Select the Pen tool and draw all the criss-cross lines. Keep in mind that these lines are single segments, not closed paths. When finished, select all these lines and Object>Group them. Deselect this group.

Locking objects painted with Brush strokes does not exclude them from being affected when a change is made in their Brush Options dialog box. If Apply to Strokes is clicked, all stroked paths painted with the brushes will be affected; even Locked paths.

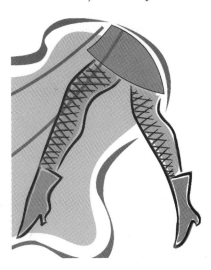

3. In the Brushes palette, double-click on the Tapered Stroke brush you created. In the Art Brushes Options dialog box, change the width to 25%. Click OK. A warning will appear asking if this change should be applied to the strokes, or to leave them as they are. Click ~~Leave Strokes.~~ APPLY TO STROKES

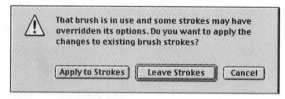

4. Now select the fishnet group you just made. Click on the Tapered Stroke brush in the Brushes palette to select it. All the selected crisscross lines will take on the 25% Tapered Stroke.

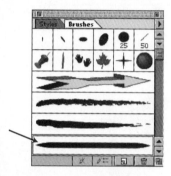 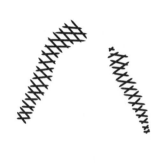

5. Make certain that the Stroke box is active in the Toolbox and that the fill is set to None. In the Swatches palette, click on the Pink color you made to paint the stroke of the crossed lines. Send them to the back with Object>Arrange>Send to Back. Deselect the group.

6. Use Object>Unlock All to unlock the locked paths. Set the Stroke box in the Toolbox for None. Click on the fill box. From the Swatches palette, drag the Red color swatch to touch the skirt to paint it.

7. Click the Default Colors box, then change the fill to None. With the Pencil tool, draw closed paths for the fishnet background. Select both background paths and paint them with a Light Blue fill and no stroke. Send them to the back and deselect.

8. Click the Default Colors box, then change the fill to None. With the Pencil tool, draw closed paths that will hold the color of the boots. Select both paths and paint them with a fill of Red and no stroke. Send them to the back and deselect.

9. Let's look at the design so far. Click the Show/Hide icon of the Dogs layer to show Boda and Chase. All that needs to be done to finish the work is to draw the background object, and the wavy paths around it.

10. Create a new layer and rename it "Background." Drag this layer to position it directly below the Lady layer. Click on the Show/Hide icon of the Dogs and Lady layers to hide them.

11. Save your changes made so far.

Finalizing the Design

1. Deselect all objects. Click the Default Colors box and change the fill to None. With the Pencil tool, trace the large color object in the template. Remember to hold the Option/Alt key to create a closed path. Don't paint this object just yet. The wavy objects around this background are also closed paths drawn with the Pencil tool. Draw these objects and paint them with a Red fill and no stroke. Deselect the wavy objects.

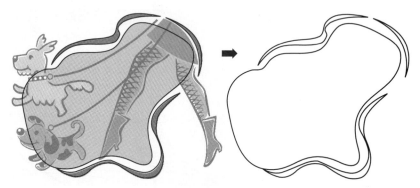

2. Select the large object you just drew. In the Window menu select Show Styles. From the Styles palette, click the Soft Red Highlight style. The object will take on a red radial gradient fill with a black drop shadow.

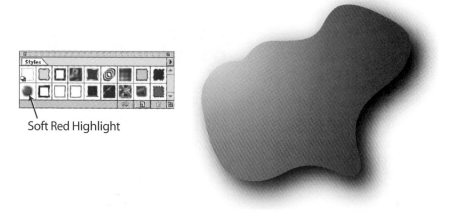

Soft Red Highlight

3. Be aware that the red gradient color is not the Red custom color you created. It is also too bright for the background. We need to change it to a color that better complements the rest of the objects. From the Window menu, select Show Gradient. The Gradient palette will appear. Click on its gradient swatch to show the beginning and ending gradient sliders underneath the gradient bar.

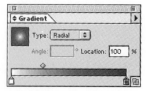

4. Bring up the Swatches palette if it is not on the screen. Click the Show Color Swatches icon at the bottom of the Swatches palette to see the process colors. Scroll down the color list until you see the Purple you created. Drag this color to touch the ending gradient slider in the Gradient palette. This will change the gradient's color from red to Purple. Press Command/Control-3 to Hide this gradient-filled object.

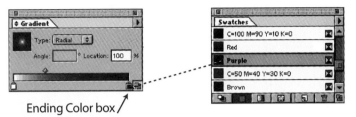

Ending Color box

5. We will now work on the wavy objects that surround this large path. Holding the shift key, select all three wavy objects. In the Effect menu, choose the Stylize>Feather option. Make no changes in the dialog box that appears. Click OK. The wavy objects will take on a feathery aspect that looks like they were Filled with gradients.

6. The thin wavy objects with the feathering do not seem to have much contrast with the white background of the document. Let's add a shadow. Go back to the Effect>Stylize menu and select Drop Shadow. In the dialog box make no changes. Click OK. The wavy objects will take on the offset shadows.

BLACK

7. Use the Object menu to Show All, which will bring the gradient object back to view. The design is finished. Click on the Show/Hide icons on the hidden layers to bring their objects back into view. Observe your work and save these changes.

Finalizing the Document

1. The template is no longer needed. Drag the Template layer to the Trash icon at the bottom of the Layers palette.

2. Click on the Dogs layer. In the Layer palette menu, select Flatten Artwork. This will combine all the paths and objects into the selected layer.

3. In the Swatches palette, click on the Show All Swatches icon at the bottom of the palette. Use the Swatches palette menu to choose Select All Unused. All unused attributes will become selected. Drag them down to the Trash icon at the bottom of the palette to delete them.

4. The artwork and preparation is complete. Save your changes and close the document.

Project E: Broadway Bound

Broadway Bound is a flyer advertising a coming theatrical show. The fliers will be on display in the "Coming Events" counter in the theatre lobby. Printed on one side only, on 100-lb. enamel paper, the job will be a four-color process piece. The trim dimensions of the job are 4.25 in. by 7.25 in., with a 1/8 in. bleed.

Setting Up the Document

1. Use File>Open to navigate to the **SF-Intro Illustrator** folder and open the student file **Broadway Bound.AI**. A template of the design is supplied for you to trace with the drawing tools. In your **Work in Progress** folder, save the file as "Broadway Bound.EPS" using the Adobe Illustrator EPS (EPS) format. Use Document Setup to set the Units to Inches.

2. To draw lines on a template, it is best to work in Preview mode, with the paths set for no fill and a 1-pt. black stroke. How can you have this specific paint attribute stored for immediate access? By using Styles. Create your own Style for this purpose, the following way.

3. Use Window>Show Styles to access the Styles palette. With the Rectangle tool, draw a small square to the left of the Template. Click on the Default Colors in the Toolbox to paint it. Change the fill to None. With the square selected, click the New Style button at the bottom of the Styles palette. The new style will appear as a swatch on the palette. We will refer to this as the Drawing style. Whenever you want to use any drawing tools with no fill and a 1-pt. black stroke, simply click this style and the paint attributes will change to this. Enlarge the palette to see all the styles, plus the new one. Delete the square you drew.

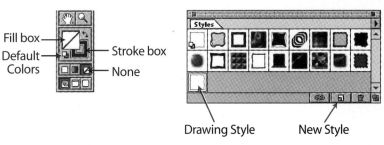

Fred's Foot

1. Use the Window menu to Show Layers. In the Layers palette, double-click on Layer 1 and rename it "Feet." This will be the layer that holds both Fred's and Ginger's feet.

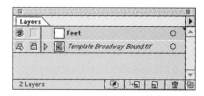

2. Select the Pen tool. Draw the pant leg and its highlight as closed paths by consecutive clicks of the Pen tool. The top of the path extends past the skirt in the template. The extending connecting points will not be seen behind the skirt, but it is important that the parts that will be seen are drawn accurately (A). Draw the highlight on the front of the pant leg with straight-line clicks. Paint the pant leg with a black fill and no stroke. Paint the highlight with a white fill and no stroke. For the shoe, draw a curving path that is connected up above the pant leg area. Paint this with a black fill and no stroke. The white portion of the shoe is a curving path painted with a white fill and no stroke. Draw the highlight on the toe with curving segments, and paint it with a white fill and no stroke (B).

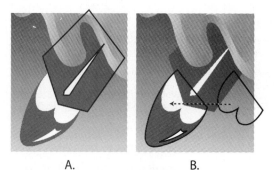

A.   B.

3. Select the shoe pieces and send them to the back with Object>Arrange>Send to Back. The pant leg and shoe should look like this.

4. Select all these drawn paths and apply Object>Group. Press Command/Control-3 to hide the group. Save your changes made so far.

Ginger's Foot

1. Ginger's foot is made up of the shoe, heel, a highlight, and foot. Click on the Drawing style to set the colors. With the Pen tool, draw the shoe, draw the highlight, then the heel.

2. Paint the shoe and heel with the following gradient. Select these two paths. Click the Color and Gradient icons under the Fill and Stroke boxes of the Toolbox to show their palettes. In the Gradient palette, click on the gradient swatch to show the beginning and ending gradient sliders. Click the ending slider to select it. A black cap will mark it as selected. In the Color palette, adjust the CMYK sliders to create a color made up of: C:0, M:100, Y:100, K:0, which will be a bright red.

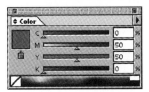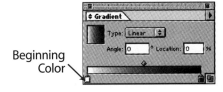

3. Click the beginning slider in the Gradient palette. In the Color palette set the Magenta and Yellow sliders for 50%. Make sure the Angle is set for 0 in the Gradient palette. Press Return/Enter to apply. Give the shoe and the heel no stroke.

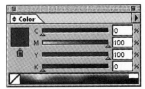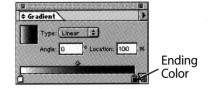

4. Select only the heel path and send to back with Object>Arrange>Send to Back. If the top curve of the heel path needs adjustment, make this so that there is no separation showing between the two objects. Select the highlight path and click the Default Colors in the Toolbox, which will give the highlight a white fill, then change the stroke to None.

5. Select these shoe pieces and Group them. Press Command/Control-3 to hide the group. We will continue with the foot piece. Click the Drawing style to continue.

6. Use the Pen tool to draw the foot with a series of curves. At its top, the connecting segment that extends above the skirt in the template can be a straight line because it won't be seen behind the skirt. The bottom of the foot should extend past the shoe's shape in the template. Curve these lines to contour with the shoe. Send the foot path to the back with Command/Control-Shift-[(left bracket).

7. You will paint the foot with a flesh-color gradient. In the Gradient palette, click on the Ending Color slider. In the Color palette, set the CMYK sliders for: C:10, M:10, Y:29, K:0.

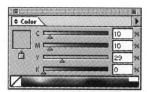 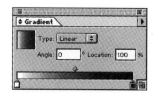

8. Click on the beginning gradient slider and set the Color palette for: C:10, M:55, Y:55, K:0. Set the midpoint slider for "70", to have more of the darker color. Change the foot's stroke to None.

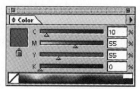 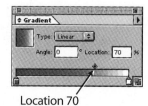

Location 70

9. Use Object>Show All to bring the shoe piece group back to view. Ginger's foot and shoe should look like this.

10. Click the Show/Hide icon of the Feet layer to hide both of the foot objects.

11. Save your changes made so far.

Ginger's Skirt

1. In the Layers palette, create a new layer and name it "Skirt."

2. Click the Drawing style to draw the bottom of the skirt. To create the illusion of an under layer of fabric, use the Pen tool to draw curves that make a closed path.

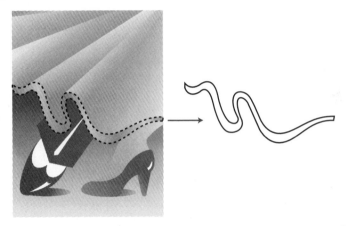

3. You will create a gradient to fill this path is a series of two alternating colors. Select the skirt edge just drawn. To make the gradient, drag the beginning slider, holding the Option/Alt key to duplicate it. Repeat this so that there are five extra sliders between the beginning and ending sliders. In the Color palette, set the CMYK colors of Color A and drag the color swatch to touch the sliders marked A. In the Color palette, set the CMYK colors of Color B and drag the color swatch to touch the sliders marked B. Change the stroke of this piece to None.

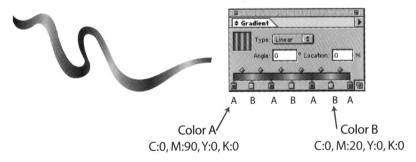

Color A
C:0, M:90, Y:0, K:0

Color B
C:0, M:20, Y:0, K:0

4. Press Command/Control-3 to Hide this edge piece.

5. Save your changes made so far.

Skirt Folds

1. To create the skirt folds, you will use the Divide feature in the Pathfinder palette. Begin by clicking the Drawing style. With the Pen tool, draw a single closed path that will be the outline of the skirt (A). Now draw single open-path segments that define the folds of the skirt. Make certain that the beginning and ending anchor points of these segments touch the path that outlines the skirt (B), otherwise Pathfinder's Divide feature will not work. Select the closed path and all the segments.

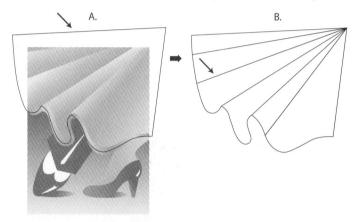

A.   B.

2. Choose Window>Show Pathfinder. In the palette that appears, click the Divide icon. This will create six separate closed paths that were determined by the segments. We separate them here to show you the individual closed paths. They will not look like this on your screen.

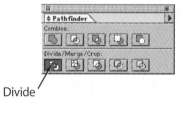

Divide

3. Save your changes made so far.

Painting the Skirt Folds

1. The skirt will be painted with a custom gradient. You will change the gradient's angle using the Gradient tool to give the impression of a single piece of softly flowing fabric. The edge of the skirt, drawn earlier, will eventually be stacked on top to cover any flaws along the bottom contours.

2. Use the Color palette to create colors for a gradient that has a beginning color of C:0, M:20, Y:0, K: 0 and an ending color of C:0, M:90, Y:0, K:0.

Once the custom color has been built in the Color palette, drag the color swatch to the appropriate slider in the Gradient palette.

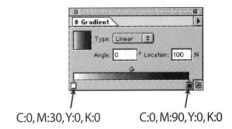

C:0, M:30, Y:0, K:0   C:0, M:90, Y:0, K:0

3. After the new gradient has been made, make certain the Fill box is active in the Toolbox. From the Gradient palette, drag the new gradient swatch over to touch and paint the first fold from the right. This will paint the fold with the new gradient. Press the "I" key to access the Eyedropper tool. Hold the Option/Alt key and the tool becomes the Paint Bucket tool. Use this tool to click on all the other "folds" to paint them with the gradient.

4. Now click on the first fold you painted with the Direct Selection tool to select it, and use the Gradient tool to adjust the angle of the gradient to go in the direction of the up and down movement of the folds. Keep in mind that the first click of the Gradient tool will paint the color assigned the beginning gradient slider. After you drag the Gradient tool and let go of the mouse, the darker ending color ends the gradient. Do this with each fold, one at a time. Once the folds have their gradients adjusted, use to Selection tool to click on this entire fold object to select it.

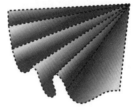

5. Use Object>Show All to bring back the skirt edge that was hidden earlier. Bring it to the front with Object>Arrange>Bring to Front. Select all the skirt folds plus the edge object. Apply Object>Group (Command/Control-G). Deselect the group.

6. Save your changes made so far.

Touch-ups

1. Click the Show/Hide icon of the Feet layer to show both Fred and Ginger's feet. Click on the feet layer to make it active. Click the Drawing style to continue. At Fred's toe, draw an ellipse that matches the shadow in the template. For the ellipse fill, apply the White, Black gradient in the Swatches palette. Apply a stroke of None. In the Gradient palette, set the angle of this gradient to "-180". Hold the Option/Alt key and drag the ellipse (holding the Shift key to constrain after the drag has begun) to make a shadow for Ginger's foot. Select these two foot shadows and send them to the back with Object>Arrange>Send to Back. Deselect the ellipses.

2. In the Layers palette, click the Show/Hide icon of the Skirt layer to hide the skirt. Click the Drawing style. With the Rectangle tool, draw a rectangle to match the dimensions of the template image. Paint this rectangle with the White, Black gradient and no stroke. Set its angle for 90 in the Gradient palette. Send the rectangle to the back with Object>Arrange>Send to Back.

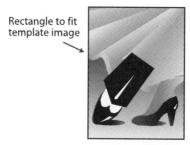 

Rectangle to fit template image

Paint with gradient

3. The tonal range of the gradient should be adjusted to give more of an impression of a darker room. With the rectangle selected, drag the Gradient tool cursor (be sure to hold the Shift key to constrain the angle) from below the bottom to just above the middle, then let go of the mouse.

Drag Gradient tool up

4. Save your changes made so far.

Trimming Off Loose Ends

1. In the Layers palette, click the Show/Hide icon to show the Skirt layer. The skirt folds extend outside of the rectangular template image. We will trim off the overlapping paths using Pathfinder. Select and copy the gradient-filled rectangle with Edit>Copy or Command/Control-C. Deselect this rectangle.

2. Click the Show/Hide icon of the Feet layer to hide its objects. Click on the Skirt layer to make it active. In the Layers palette menu, make sure Paste Remembers Layers is not checked. This is so the copied gradient rectangle, created on the hidden Feet layer, can be pasted and relocated to the Skirt layer. Select the skirt group and go to Edit>Paste in Front to paste the copied rectangle exactly in position in front of the skirt. Paint the pasted rectangle with no fill and no stroke. Select and copy this unpainted rectangle.

3. Press Command/Control-A to Select All the paths. Click the Crop icon in the Pathfinder palette. All paths of the folds outside of the rectangle will be deleted.

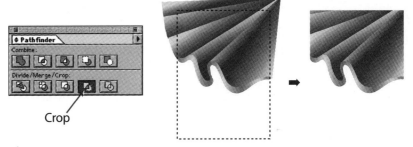

Crop

4. Click on the Show/Hide icon of the Feet layer to bring its objects back to view. The artwork is now complete. Select all the objects and Paste in Front the above copied rectangle to frame the objects. You will use this later. Deselect this rectangle.

5. The template is no longer needed. Drag the Template layer down to the Trash icon. Click on the Skirt layer. In the palette menu, select Flatten Artwork. This will combine all the objects into one layer. Select all the objects in the document group them (Command-Control-G) them. Save your changes made so far.

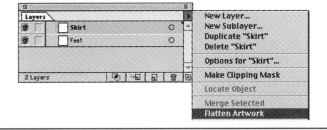

Creating the Background

1. In the Layers palette create a new layer and name it "Background." Drag it below the Skirt layer. Keep the Background layer active.

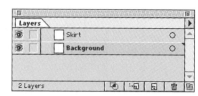

2. Select the Rectangle tool and click the tool's crosshair cursor anywhere on the dancing art group. In the dialog box set the Width to 4.75 in., the Height to 7.25 in. Click OK. Paint the rectangle with a black fill and no stroke.

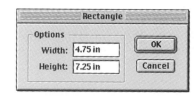

3. Position the rectangle under the dancing art. The objects need to be centered horizontally. Select the two objects, then access the Align palette. Click the Horizontal Align Center option. The objects will become spaced equally on both sides.

Horizontal Align Center

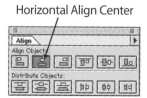

4. The dancing art group needs to be positioned the same distance down from the top of the rectangle as from the sides. There is no alignment feature that can do this. We will use the Measure tool and the Move dialog box. Go to Outline mode to see the paths better. In the Window menu select Show Info. Select the Measure tool by clicking on the Hand tool to pop out its optional tools. Deselect all objects. Single-click the Measure tool on the right edge of the dancing art rectangle. Click again on the right edge of the black rectangle. Observe the Info palette. The W: field will show the distance clicked. Your distance will perhaps be different from ours. Write down your distance number for reference.

Measure Tool

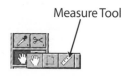

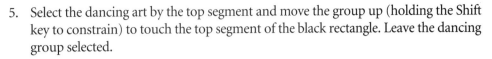

5. Select the dancing art by the top segment and move the group up (holding the Shift key to constrain) to touch the top segment of the black rectangle. Leave the dancing group selected.

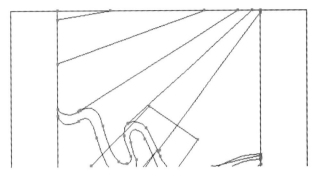

6. In the Object menu, select Arrange>Move. In the Move dialog box, set the Horizontal to "0" and the Vertical to your Measure tool distance. Put a negative symbol in front of your number to send the object downward. Click the cursor in the Distance field and you will see the numbers set themselves to your specifications. Click OK.

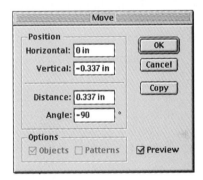

7. The dancing group will move down the distance you set. The top and side distances will now be equal.

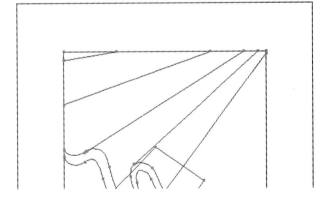

8. Go back to Preview viewing mode. Save your changes made so far.

Adding Type

1. In the Layers palette, create a new layer and name it "Type." Move it to the top of the layer list. Click on the Lock/Unlock icon of the Skirt and Background layers to lock them.

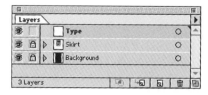

2. Select the Type tool and click in the area of the skirt. Type these words on two separate lines.

BROADWAY <return>

BOUND

3. Highlight the text and press Command/Control-T to access the Character palette. Set the font to ATC Kiwi, size to 34 pt., leading to 41 pt., tracking to -20, vertical scale to 70%, horizontal scale to 75%, baseline shift to 0. In the Paragraph palette, set the alignment for Align Center.

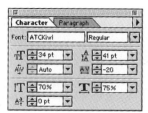

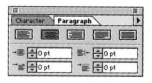

BROADWAY

BOUND

4. With the Type tool, highlight the "B" of "Broadway" and change its size to 56 pt. Change its baseline shift to -4. Highlight the "B" of "Bound" and change its size to 48 pt. and its baseline shift to -4.

5. The spacing between letters needs some kerning. Click the Type cursor between any two letters that need kerning. Hold the Option/Alt key and press the Left Arrow key to decrease the spacing, or the Right Arrow key to increase spacing.

BROADWAY

BOUND

6. When you are finished with the kerning, the headline is complete. Click on the Selection tool (from the Toolbox) and the text block will automatically be selected. In the Type menu, select Create Outlines. This converts the text to outline paths, as well as groups the objects.

7. Position this group in the area of the skirt. Unlock the two locked layers. Select the "BROADWAY BOUND" headline, the dancing art group, and the black background rectangle. In the Align palette, click the Horizontal Align Center option. The three objects will be centered horizontally.

Horizontal Align Center

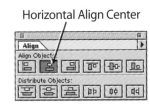

8. Select the Direct Selection tool. Holding the Option/Alt key, click on the last un-painted rectangle that you pasted in front of the dancing art group. In the Object>Path menu, select Offset Path. In the dialog box, set the Offset for 0.125 in. and click OK. A duplicate rectangle will appear around the dancing art group. Paint the duplicate with a fill of None and a 1-pt. white stroke.

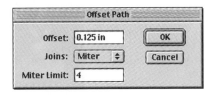

9. Go to Outline view so the black text you will now type won't be hidden against the black rectangle. The type still has its previous settings applied to the fields in the Character palette. Go to the Character palette and make sure you are viewing all the options, including vertical and horizontal scale. Hold the Command/Control key and single-click each icon of each option in the palette. This will reset the fields to their original default status. Select the Type tool. Click its cursor in the area under the dancing art group. Type these words on the separate lines shown:

> A Musical Review <return>
>
> Featuring songs & dances from <return>
>
> the most memorable Broadway musicals <return>
>
> March 19, 2000 <return>
>
> Ruth Eckerd Hall, Clearwater

10. Highlight all the text and paint it with a white fill. Access the Type>Character palette. Set the font to ATC Seagull Regular, the size to 18 pt., leading to Auto, tracking to -20, vertical scale to 80%, horizontal scale to 75%, baseline shift to 0.

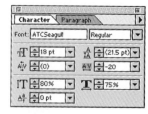

11. Highlight the phrase "A Musical Review" and change its size to 24 pt. Highlight the words "March 19, 2000, Ruth Eckerd Hall, Clearwater," and change their size to 20 pt.

12. Highlight all words from "Featuring" to "Clearwater." Hold the Option/Alt-Shift keys, and press the Down Arrow key three times. Highlight the words "March 19, 2000, Ruth Eckerd Hall, Clearwater," and hold the same keys. Press the Down Arrow key twice. This will increase the baseline shift spacing between the lines without affecting the leading.

13. Select all the objects in the document. In the Align palette, click the Horizontal Align Center option to center them all horizontally. The piece is complete except for setting the trim marks and the bleed. Save your changes made so far.

Trim Marks and Bleed

1. Click the Background layer in the Layers palette to make it active. Select the black rectangle background on the page. In the Filter menu, select Create>Trim Marks. The filter will draw trim marks that will be used by the printer when cutting the final piece after printing.

2. The black ink of the background will need to be trimmed at the edge of the piece, which means there must be a bleed applied. The black background must extend past the trim marks at least 1/8″. With the black background rectangle still selected, go to Object>Path>Offset Path. In the dialog box that appears, set the Offset for "0.125". Press OK. A duplicate rectangle will appear 1/8″ outside of the original. It will be filled with black, the same as the original.

Offset Path		
Offset: 0.125 in	OK	
Joins: Miter	Cancel	
Miter Limit: 4		

3. The job is finished. The file is an EPS (Encapsulated PostScript) file that may be given to a commercial printer for four-color process printing. Save your changes and close the document.

Notes:

Project F: Joker's Wild

The Joker's Wild project is a good example of using the time-saving operations in Illustrator, such as Pathfinder, the Styles palette, and the Effect menu. Much of the drawing and painting of this work would take a longer time to produce without these features. The Joker card is a fun project that will teach you a lot.

Joker's Wild

1. Use File>Open to navigate to the **SF-Intro Illustrator** folder and open the student file **Jokers Wild.AI**. There is a template of the design that you can use for placement and drawing the various objects. Save As the file with the same name in Adobe Illustrator Document format to your **Work in Progress** folder.

2. Use View>Show Rulers to view the page rulers. Go to Preferences>Guides & Grid and change the guides to the Black color, with dotted lines. Drag a vertical guide to the card that divides the Joker in half, going down the center of his body.

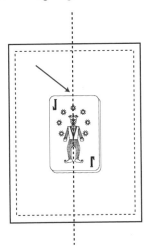

Creating the Colors

1. From the Window menu, show both the Color and Swatches palettes. In the Swatches palette, click the Show Color Swatches button at the bottom of the palette. View the swatches by Name View, selected from the palette menu.

2. In the Color palette, use the palette menu to set the colors for CMYK. Create the following Process colors (listed below) with the CMYK sliders. As each color is created, drag the color swatch from the Color palette to the Swatches palette. Double-click each new color swatch and name it appropriately. In the Swatch Options dialog box, make the color global. Make certain the color is process and not spot.

Yellow: C:0, M:0, Y:100, K:0

Purple: C:45, M:100, Y:0 K:0

Red: C:0, M:100, Y:100, K:0

Flesh: C:0, M:20, Y:20, K:0

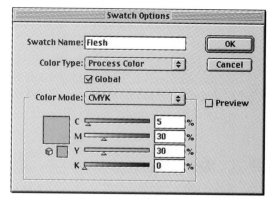

3. To draw lines on a template, it is best to work in Preview mode with the paint attributes set for no fill and a 1-pt. Black stroke. You can have this specific paint attribute stored for immediate access by using the Styles palette. Create your own style for this purpose the following way.

4. Use Window>Show Styles to access the Styles palette. Click on the Default Colors in the Toolbox. Change the fill to None (A). In the Stroke palette, make certain that the weight is set for 1 pt. With the Rectangle tool, draw a small square to the left of the template. Select the rectangle and drag it into the Styles palette. The new style will appear (B). We will refer to this as the Drawing style. Delete the square you drew.

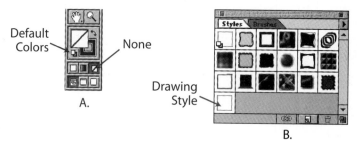

5. Whenever you want to use any drawing tools with no fill and a 1-pt. Black stroke, simply click this style and the paint attributes will change to this. This cuts out the steps of clicking the Default Colors, changing the no fill, and assigning a 1-pt. Black stroke. Make certain no objects are selected at the time you click this style.

Drawing the Joker's Head

1. From the Window menu select Show Layers to view the Layers palette. Double-click on Layer 1. In the Layer Options, rename the layer "Joker." Zoom in closely to the Joker's head. Click on the Drawing style to set the colors. With the Pen tool, click first on the vertical guide where it touches the bottom of the crown in the template. Move the mouse up to the top of the crown and hold the Shift key as you click again.

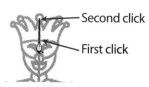

The idea of this design is to draw only the Joker parts on the left side of the vertical guide. When the left side is complete, a copy of the Joker paths will be reflected to the right side.

2. Continue drawing the curves of the crown, finishing by clicking on the first anchor point to close the path.

3. With the Ellipse tool draw the three circles to match those in the template. Paint the crown path with a fill of Purple, leaving a 1-pt. Black stroke. Deselect the path. Paint the circles with a Yellow fill, keeping the 1-pt. Black stroke.

4. When drawn, select the crown and circles. Press Command/Control-3 to Hide them.

5. The cheek and jaw are next to be drawn. Click on the Drawing style to set the drawing colors. With the Pen tool, draw the jaw first, then the cheek. The cheek can overlap the jaw, so exact fitting of the paths where they touch will not be required. After the cheek and jaw are drawn, fill them with the Flesh color, keeping the 1-pt. Black stroke. Make sure the cheek overlaps enough so as not to reveal the jaw's top segment. When the two paths are painted, group them (Command/Control-G). Send the group to the back with Object>Arrange>Send to Back. Press Command/Control-3 to hide this.

Jaw   Cheek   Combined

6. Click on the Drawing style to set the drawing colors. Draw the eye and mouth with the pen tool, then adjust the curves to fit the template. The nose is a modified circle. Draw the circle, then select its right anchor point with the Direct Selection tool and delete it. Select the top and bottom endpoints with the Direct Selection tool, then apply Object>Path>Join.

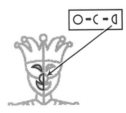

7. Paint the objects with the following fills: eye, Purple; nose, Red; and mouth, White. Keep their 1-pt. Black strokes.

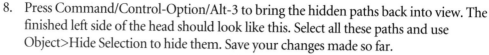

8. Press Command/Control-Option/Alt-3 to bring the hidden paths back into view. The finished left side of the head should look like this. Select all these paths and use Object>Hide Selection to hide them. Save your changes made so far.

Drawing the Chest

1. Click on the Drawing style to set the drawing colors. You will create the chest pieces using the Pathfinder>Divide operation. First, use the Pen tool to draw the closed shape of the left chest piece (A). Now draw three individual segments that divide the piece (B). Make certain that segments' anchor points touch the chest segments, otherwise, the coming divide operation will not work. With the Selection tool, select the segments and the chest piece. Show the Pathfinder palette from the Window menu. Click on Pathfinder's Divide option. The objects will divide into four pieces, shown separated here (C). Paint the objects with the following fills: a, Flesh; b, Red; c, Yellow; d, Purple. Keep their 1-pt. Black strokes (D). Select the pieces and send them to back with Object>Arrange>Send to Back. Press Command/Control-3 to hide them.

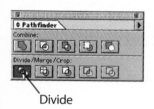

Divide

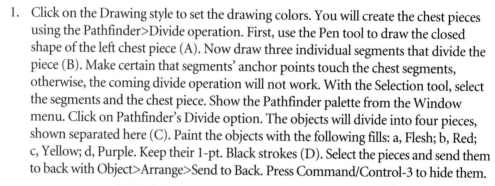

A.   B.   C.   D.

2. Click on the Drawing style to set the drawing colors. Off to the left of the template, use the Ellipse tool to draw a small 0.05-in. circle. Paint the circle with a Yellow fill, and a 1-pt. Black stroke. Holding the Option/Alt key, drag a copy of the circle, directly underneath. Hold the Shift key, after the drag has begun, to constrain the move. Once the duplicate is made, press Command/Control-D 10 times to repeat this duplication. There should be 12 circles.

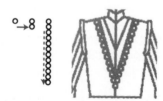

3. Select all the circles and group them. With the Selection tool, move the group over to the template so that the top circle matches the template's top circle. Select the Rotate tool in the Toolbox. Single-click the crosshair on the center of the top circle. Drag on the bottom circle to rotate the group to match the template.

4. Fine-tune the position of the group with the Selection tool. Keep in mind that matching the template exactly is not mandatory. Press Command/Control-3 to hide the circles.

5. To create the shoulder piece, draw a series of curves with the Pen tool. Paint this object with a Yellow fill, leaving the 1-pt. Black stroke. Hide the shoulder piece with Object>Hide Selection. Save your changes made so far.

Creating the Arm and Hand

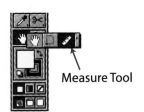

Measure Tool

1. The arm of the Joker uses the Measure tool for information. Access the Info palette from the Window menu. Select the Measure tool in the Toolbox. Click on the two farthest areas where the arm paths will extend (A). At the bottom of the Info palette the "D" refers to the distance between clicks. It will be approximately 0.807 in., so we'll round this off to 0.80 in. Again, with the Measure tool, click on the width of one of the bands in the arm (B). It will be approximately 0.049 in. Round that to 0.05 in.

A.

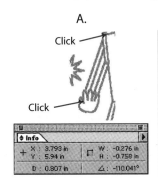

Click

Click

Click

◆ Info		
X : 3.793 in		W : −0.276 in
Y : 5.94 in		H : −0.758 in
D : 0.807 in		∠ : −110.041°

B.

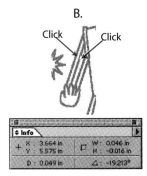

Click   Click

◆ Info		
X : 3.664 in		W : 0.046 in
Y : 5.575 in		H : −0.016 in
D : 0.049 in		∠ : −19.213°

2. Click on the Drawing style to set the drawing colors. Select the Rectangle tool. Off to the left of the template, click the tool cursor on the page. In the dialog box, set the Width for 0.05 in., and the Height to 0.8 in., which are the distances you measured. Click OK. The rectangle will appear.

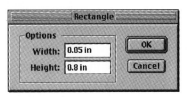

3. Use the Object menu to access Transform>Move. In the dialog box, set the Horizontal field for 0.05 in. and the Vertical field for 0 in. Click the cursor into the Distance field and you will see the necessary increments appear for Distance and Angle. Click Copy. The duplicate will appear to the right of the original. Press Command/Control-D (Transform Again) to repeat the object's move and duplication you just performed. This will create a third rectangle. Select the three rectangles and group them.

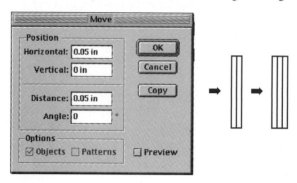

4. Move the group over to the template so the bottom left corner is where the sleeve in the template ends (A). Select the Rotate tool and single-click its crosshair on the rectangle's bottom left corner (A). Drag on the top of the group to rotate the rectangles to match the template (B).

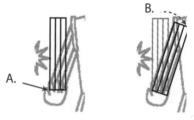

5. With the Direct Selection tool, click on the two outer rectangles and fill them with Red. Click on the middle rectangle and fill it with Purple. Leave their stroke set at 1 pt. Black. Select the group and send it to the back with Object>Arrange>Send to Back. Hide the group with Object>Hide Selection. Click the Drawing style.

6. Select the Pencil tool from the Toolbox and trace the hand in the template. Hold the Option/Alt key as you finish the hand to make it a closed path. Fill it with the Flesh color. Leave the stroke set for 1 pt. Black. Hide the hand with Object>Hide Selection.

7. You will now create the Joker's pants by using Pathfinder's Divide feature on the paths. Click the Drawing style to set the drawing colors. With the Pen tool, draw the outline of the left pant leg (A). Use the Pen tool to draw separate paths to match the stripes in the template (B). Make certain that the segments touch the pant leg path.

Pencil Tool

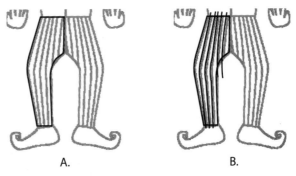

A.   B.

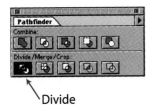

Divide

8. Select the pant leg and all stripe paths. Access the Pathfinder palette from the Window menu. Click on the Divide option. This operation will combine the stripes with the pant leg, creating separate closed paths (shown here separated). Click on each stripe object with the Direct Selection tool and paint it. Starting from the left, alternate the colors Red and Purple in the stripes, beginning with Red. Select the painted pant leg with the Selection tool and send it to the back with Object>Arrange>Send to Back.

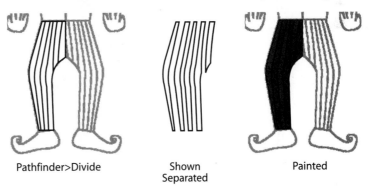

Pathfinder>Divide   Shown   Painted
                          Separated

9. Select the Pencil tool from the Toolbox and trace the foot in the template. Make sure it is a closed path. Fill the path with the Yellow color, leaving the stroke set at 1 pt. Black.

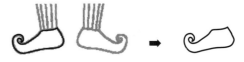

10. The Joker's left side is now complete. Press Command-Option-3/Control-Alt-3 to Show All the hidden pieces. Click the Show/Hide icon of the Template layer to Hide it. The Joker should look like this.

Preparing objects for the Pathfinder>Divide operation has one exacting aspect. All the paths that are to be divided must touch another path. Segments must touch (or overlap) at their ending points. As in the case of this leg piece, the segments overlap the pant shape at either end of the segment path. At the minimum an ending anchor point must touch the path that is to be divided.

11. Use Edit>Select All to select the Joker paths. Press Command/Control-G to group the paths. Select the Reflect tool in the Toolbox and click the crosshair on the vertical center guide, while holding the Option/Alt key. In the Reflect dialog box, select Vertical for the Axis, and click Copy. With the reflected duplicate selected, go to the Filter menu and select Colors>Invert Colors.

12. The inverted right side should look like this.

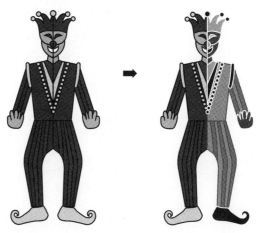

13. The Joker is complete. Let's give him some shading to stand on. Select the Ellipse tool and clicking its cursor between the Joker's heels, holding the Option/Alt key to draw an oval from its center. Paint the oval with a 50% Black fill and no stroke. From the Effect menu, choose Stylize>Feather. Set the Feather Radius for 0.2 in the dialog box. Click OK. The object will feather slightly. Send the oval behind the Joker with Object>Arrange>Send to Back.

14. Save your changes made so far.

Creating the Stars

1. Click on the Show/Hide icon of the Joker layer to hide it. Click on the Show/Hide square of the Template layer to bring it back to view. Click the New Layer icon in the Layers palette to create a new layer. Double-click on the layer and rename it "Stars."

2. Click on the Drawing style to set the drawing colors. You will set the number of points for the stars, then create stars the same size as the stars in the template. To do this, select the Star tool from the Toolbox. Click the crosshair off to the side of the template. In the dialog box, make no changes except setting the Points to 10. Now, any star drawn will have ten points. Click OK. When the star appears, delete it.

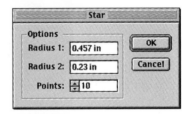

3. With the Star tool crosshair, click on the center of the top template star and drag a star. You do not have to hold any keys to make it draw from the center. It does this automatically. You will be able to rotate the star as it is drawn. Once the star fits the template, let go of the mouse.

4. Holding the Option/Alt key, drag-duplicate the first star to match all the other stars in the template. Use the Rotate tool to fine-tune how well they fit the template. Remember, you do not have to be exact with templates. They are just sketchy representations.

5. You will now add some special effects to the stars. Select the star at the top. Fill it with the Red color you created. From the Effect menu, select Stylize>Outer Glow.

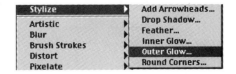

6. In the dialog box all the settings are correct, but the color of the glow can be customized. Click on the Color swatch next to the Mode field.

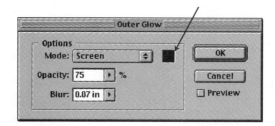

7. The Color Picker will appear. To the right of the dialog box, set these colors. C:95, M:91, Y:2, K:0. Click OK. This will set the color of the glow.

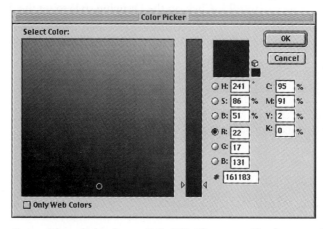

8. Back in the Outer Glow dialog box, click OK. The star will take on a glow that gives it a slight 3-D effect.

9. Deselect this star. Now select all the other six stars. Press the "I" key to change to the Eyedropper tool. Click the tool on the top star that received the Outer Glow effect. All the other stars will take on the color and glow effect. Now click on one star at a time with the Direct Selection tool and select a different fill color for each star.

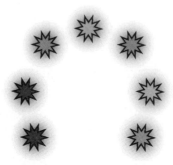

10. Save your changes made so far.

Creating the Card and Shadow

1. Click on the Show/Hide icon of the Stars layer to hide it. Create a new layer, and rename it "Card." Drag the Card layer down below the Joker layer. We will continue drawing on this Card layer, so make certain it is the active layer.

2. Click on the Drawing style to set the drawing colors. Select the Rounded Rectangle tool, click-hold its crosshair on the upper-left corner of the template and drag a rectangle to fit the card. Leave the card selected and press the "D" key to apply the default colors. The selected rectangle will have a center point. Mark this point with vertical and horizontal guides dragged from the rulers.

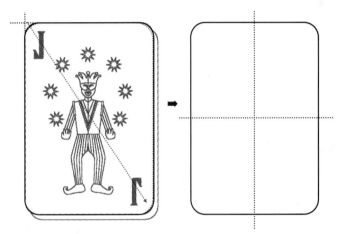

3. Go to the Effect menu and select Stylize>Drop Shadow. In the dialog box leave all settings as they are. Click the Color button to select it. It will default to Black. Click the Preview button so you can see this drop shadow appear on the card. Click OK to apply the drop shadow to the card.

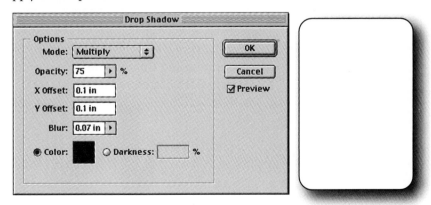

4. Save your changes made so far.

Creating the Type

1. Click the Show/Hide icon on the Card layer to hide it. Click the Stars layer. Create a new layer which will appear above the Stars layer. Rename the new layer "Type".

2. Press Command/Control-T to show the Character palette. Use the palette menu to show the options if you do not see all the features shown here. In the Font field, select ATC Tequila; set the Size to 66 pt.; and make certain the rest of the options are set to default, that is, Tracking to 0, Baseline Shift to 0, and Vertical and Horizontal scales at 100%.

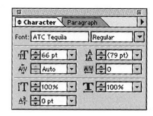

3. Select the Type tool in the Toolbox. Click its cursor to the left of the "J" in the template. Type the letter "J".

4. Select the text block with the Selection tool, then choose Type>Create Outlines. Apply a Black fill and stroke to the letter outlines. Choose Show Stroke from the Window menu. In the Stroke palette, set the weight at 6 pt. Also select the Rounded Join option. Press Command/Control-C to Copy this path.

Rounded Join

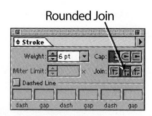

5. The path will have a 6-pt. Black stroke (A). Press Command/Control-F to paste the copied path in front. Give this pasted path a 2-pt. White stroke and a Rounded Join (B). Press Command/Control-F to paste the object in front one more time. Paint this pasted path with a Red fill and no stroke (C).

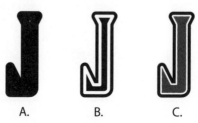

A.   B.   C.

6. Select all three of the letter paths and group them. Position the "J" group to fit the template in the top left.

7. Select the Rotate tool in the Toolbox; while holding the Option/Alt key, click its crosshair on the center point marked by the guides. In the dialog box, set the angle for 180° and click Copy. The duplicate will appear at the bottom of the card. Fine-tune the letter to fit the template.

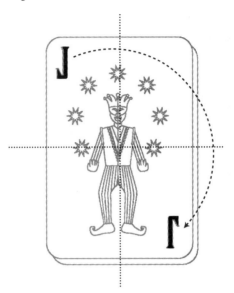

8. Save your changes made so far.

Viewing the Finished Card Design

1. In the Layers palette, click on the Show/Hide icons to show the hidden layers. Drag the Template layer to the Trash icon at the bottom of the palette. You will now combine the layers into one. Click on the Type layer, then use the palette menu to select Flatten Artwork.

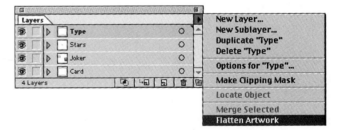

2. All the layers will combine into one, defaulting to the selected Type layer.

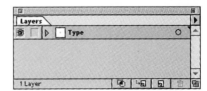

3. The finished art should like the sample below.

4. Save your changes and close the document.

Project G: BearWear Label

The BearWear clothing tag is a fun and casual piece, using path editing, gradients, and a placed photograph. It is also a good example of an art job that will be die cut to a special shape after the four-color process printing is finished. It is a one-sided print job, requiring no trim marks because the die will do all the cutting. All images and colors, called "live matter," will bleed over the edges, so the use of guides is essential to make sure there is a 1/8" bleed on all sides.

Setting Up the Basic Elements

1. Create a new document set for CMYK Color Mode, leave it untitled and the Artboard Size set for default. In File>Document Setup, set the Units for Inches. Save this new document to your **Work in Progress** folder in Adobe Illustrator EPS (EPS) format. Name the file "BearWear Label.EPS". Use Document Setup to set the Units of measurement to Inches.

2. Press Command/Control-R to see the rulers. From the rulers, drag guides to mark the center of the page. Place a vertical guide at the 4.25-in. mark to show the center of the page. Drag a horizontal guide down to the 5.5-in. mark. Press the "D" key to activate the Default Colors feature in the Toolbox. Change the Fill box to None.

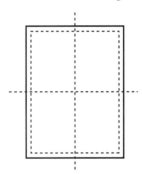

3. Select the Rectangle tool and, holding the Option/Alt key, click its crosshair on the center of the page marked by the guides. In the dialog box that appears, enter 4 in. in the Width field and 3.5 in. in the Height field. Click OK. A rectangle will appear with its center positioned over the center point marked by the guides.

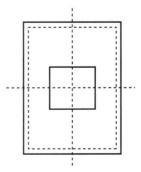

4. Hold the Option/Alt key and click the Rectangle tool on the vertical center guide slightly above the first rectangle. In the dialog box, set the Width to 4 in. and Height to 0.75 in. Click OK. A smaller rectangle the same width as the first, will appear. Select it and move it down (holding the Shift key to constrain the move) so its bottom segment is aligned exactly on the top segment of the first rectangle. Drag the ruler Zero Point to the upper left corner of the smaller rectangle. Drag vertical guides to mark the left and right sides of the rectangles.

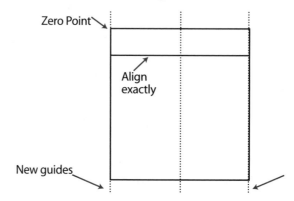

5. To angle the side of the small rectangle, drag guides that are 5/8″ inside the rectangle's sides (A). With the Add Anchor Point tool (a Pen tool option), click on the small rectangle's top segment where the 5/8″ guide touches it (B).

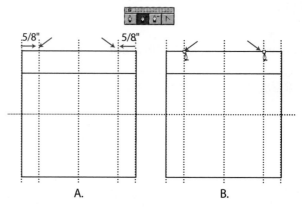

6. In the Pen tool pop-out menu, select the Delete Anchor Point tool. Click it on the top-left and top-right corner anchor points of the small rectangle (A). This will create a trapezoid (B).

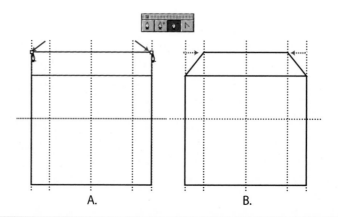

7. The trapezoid needs to be reflected and copied. Select the trapezoid, choose the Reflect tool in the Toolbox, and holding the Option/Alt key, click the cursor on the center page marked by the guides (A). This will set the origin point, and show the Reflect dialog box. Set the Axis for Horizontal, then click Copy. The trapezoid will mirror a copy below the large rectangle (B). With the Selection tool, fine-tune the reflected duplicate so its top segment is aligned exactly with the bottom segment of the large rectangle. The Shift key will help constrain the piece while moving it. Deselect the trapezoid.

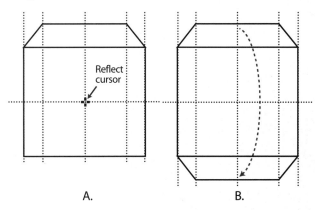

A. B.

8. Choose View>Unlock Guides. Select and delete all guides except those marking the center of the page. Lock the guides again. Save your changes made so far.

Creating the Gradient

If the full Gradient palette is not visible with all its options, use its palette menu to select Show Options. If the beginning and ending sliders are not showing, click on the gradient swatch in the upper left of the palette, and the sliders will appear.

1. The top and bottom trapezoids need to be filled with a gradient. If the Color and Gradient palettes are not on the screen, use the Window menu to show them. Position them next to each other in the document. In the Gradient palette, click on the ending gradient slider to select it. In the Color palette, use the CMYK sliders to create the color C:35, M:45, Y:100, K:0. This will set the color on the gradient slider.

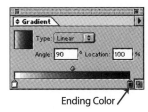
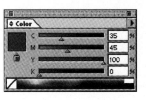

Ending Color

2. Click on the beginning gradient slider to select it. In the Color palette, use the CMYK sliders to create the color: C:0, M:20, Y:40, K:0. This will set the new color on the gradient slider.

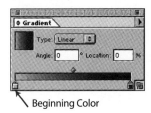
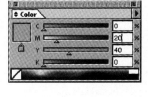

Beginning Color

3. The gradient color is complete. Click the Fill box in the Toolbox to make it active. From the Gradient palette, drag the gradient swatch to touch the top trapezoid. Drag the gradient swatch again to touch the bottom trapezoid. They will be filled with the custom gradient.

4. Select the top trapezoid with the Selection tool. Go to the Gradient palette and set the Angle for "90". Above the gradient bar is the Midpoint slider. Move this slightly to activate the Location box. Type "65" in the Location box and press Return/Enter to apply. The Midpoint slider will move to the right. Select the bottom trapezoid. In the Gradient palette, change the angle to "-90". Make sure the Location is set for "65". The two rectangles will be painted with this gradient. For now, to see the objects better, leave their Strokes set for Black. This will be changed later in the exercise.

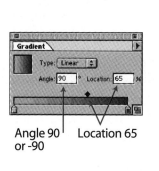

Angle 90
or -90   Location 65

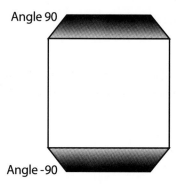

Angle 90

Angle -90

5. Save your changes made so far.

Setting Up Layers

1. The basic elements that shape the label are now drawn, painted, and in position. The next objects you add will need their own layers to keep the pieces organized.

2. If the Layers palette is not on the screen, choose Window>Show Layers. The layer you have been working on is Layer 1. Double-click this layer, and rename it to "Background".

3. Create three new layers. Name them, "Photo," "Type," and "Die Cut."

4. Drag the layers to be in the following order in the layer list, starting at the top: Type, Background, Photo, and Die Cut. Click on the Background layer to continue.

5. Save your changes made so far.

The type objects to be in the job cannot be positioned too close to the edge or they will be cut off by the die cut. It is necessary, before going further, to create guides that show where the die will cut.

Setting Guides for the Bleed

1. The paths of the rectangle and two trapezoids must touch and be precisely aligned. Use the Zoom tool to zoom in very close to the corners where the paths meet. Go to Outline mode to see only the segments and anchor points. Make sure Snap to Point is selected in the View menu. Use the Selection tool to move a path by its anchor point closer to another path. The Selection arrow turns hollow, indicating a perfect alignment.

2. When you have finished aligning the objects, go back to Preview mode. Select the three objects with the Selection tool and copy them (Command/Control-C).

3. In the Layers palette, click on the Die Cut layer to make it active. Click the Show/Hide icon of the Die Cut layer while holding the Option/Alt key. This will hide all other layers, except the Die Cut layer.

4. Paste the copied objects in front (Command/Control-F). These border copies will be pasted exactly in the same location as the originals. Click on the Default Colors box in the Toolbox, then change the Fill box to None.

5. Choose Window>Show Pathfinder. Click on Pathfinder's Unite option. All the interior segments will be deleted, leaving the outline of the three objects as one closed path. In the Object menu, select Path>Offset Path. Set the Offset for -0.125 in. (-1/8 in.) and click OK.

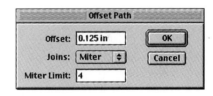

6. A copy will appear 1/8″ in from the edge of the original. Select the original united path with the Direct Selection tool, and delete it. Select the offset path and press Command/Control-5 to make guides. The selected path will become a guide that designates the cutting path of the die cut.

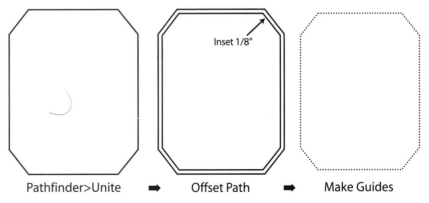

Pathfinder>Unite ➡ Offset Path ➡ Make Guides

7. Save your changes made so far.

Photograph

1. In the Layers palette, hold the Option/Alt key and click again on the Show/Hide icon of the Die Cut layer. This will bring all other layers back into view. The die cut guide will allow you to keep objects from being cut off by the die. Make sure all objects that you don't want trimmed off are within the die-cut guide.

2. Click on the Photo layer to make it active. In the File menu, select Place and navigate to the **SF-Intro Illustrator** folder. Select the file **Bear.TIF**. Click the Link option to link the photo. Click Place.

3. Position the bear photo on top of the large rectangle. It will almost fit, but don't be too critical about the sides. The photo should not show any gaps between it and the trapezoids. In the next step, you will be fitting type. To make it easier to see the type, dim the photo by keeping the Bear layer selected and choosing the Template option from the palette menu. This will both dim and lock the bear photo.

4. Save your changes made so far.

Modifying the Logo

1. Click on the Type layer to continue. Use File>Open to navigate to the **Work in Progress** folder where you saved the BearWear business card created earlier in the file called **BearWear Card.AI**. Open this document. Hold the Option/Alt key and with the Direct Selection tool click on the "B" in the BearWear logo of the top card. Only the "B" outline will be selected. Continue holding the Option/Alt key and click again on the "B" outline. This will select the entire logo group. Copy this logo. Close the business card document without saving.

BEARWEAR

2. Back in the working document, paste the logo and position it on the page below the bottom trapezoid. Double-click the Scale tool icon in the Toolbox to bring up the Scale dialog box. Set the Uniform percentage for 115%, and click OK. The logo needs to be painted. Keep it selected.

3. In the Color palette click on the Fill box to make it active. Use the palette menu to set the color sliders to CMYK. Use the sliders to create a brown color using C:50, M:85, Y:100, K:0. Press Return/Enter to apply the color to the logo.

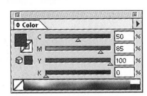

4. Hold the Option/Alt key and drag a marquee with the Direct Selection tool around the "WEAR" letters. In the Object menu, choose Compound Paths>Release. The interior paths will now be available to be painted separately. Go to Outline view to see the paths more clearly. Use the Direct Selection tool to select all the decorative interior paths of the "WEAR" letters. Do not select the central interior paths of the "A" and "R." From the Color palette, fill the decorative paths with Y: 75% and no stroke. Do not color the two central paths.

Select interior decorative paths

Don't select

5. With the decorative interior paths still selected, cut them with Edit>Cut (Command/Control-X).

6. Use the Direct Selection tool to drag a marquee around the remaining "WEAR" letters while holding Option/Alt. In the Object menu, choose Compound Paths>Make. This will compound the selected objects, making the central interior paths transparent.

7. Press Command/Control-F to paste the decorative paths back in place.

8. Use the Selection tool to marquee the entire BearWear logo and the painted decorative paths. From the Object menu, select Group to group the paths.

Centering the Logo

1. You will now center the logo on the bottom trapezoid using settings in the Transform palette. Click on the bottom trapezoid. It should show a center point. If the trapezoid's center point is not visible, use the Attributes palette from the Window menu to select the Center Point option to show the center point. Use the Window menu to bring up the Transform palette. Make certain the reference point in the palette is set for Center. Since the label started out being centered on the page, the X field should show 4.25 in. and the Y should be set at roughly 3.3 in. Make a note of your own settings (which may differ slightly from ours) and use them in the next step.

Center Point

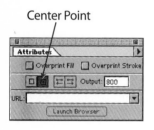

2. Select the BEARWEAR logo. We want the logo to center vertically on the trapezoid, but we want its bottom to rest on the horizontal center. In the Transform palette make sure the bottom center Reference Point selected. Now enter the X,Y settings you made note of above. Press Return/Enter to apply the settings. The logo should now be centered on the trapezoid with its bottom on positioned on Y-coordinate listed in the Transform palette. Use the Down Arrow to nudge the logo down to fit the top portion of the trapezoid. Be sure to keep the logo within the boundaries of the die cut guide. Deselect all objects.

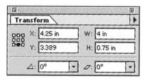

3. Save your changes made so far.

Creating the Text

1. The type above the bear will be text applied to a path. The paths will be two circles. Click the Default Colors icon in the Toolbox, then change the fill to None. Select the Ellipse tool, and click its cursor near the bear. In the dialog box, set the Width and Height to 2.657 in. Click OK. Use the Selection tool to position the circle's left anchor point on the top of the bear's head (A). Double-click the Scale tool in the Toolbox. Change the Uniform percentage to 75%. Click Copy. A smaller circle will appear inside the larger (B).

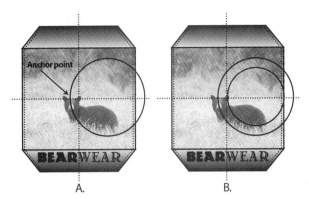

A.   B.

2. In the Layers palette, click the Lock/Unlock icon of the Background layer to lock its objects. This will keep unwanted objects from being selected or moved.

3. In the Toolbox, click-hold on the Type tool icon to bring up the pop-out menu. Select the Path Type tool. Click its cursor on the path of the larger circle just above the left anchor point.

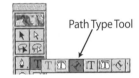

Path Type Tool

4. The black stroke of the circle will disappear as it becomes a text path. Enter the text as seen below.

"Does a Bear Dress Up"

5. Highlight the text. Press Command/Control-T to access the Type>Character palette. Set the Font to ATC Cabana, Weight to Bold, and Size to 24 pt. In the Paragraph palette, set the alignment for Align Left.

6. The type will curve on the circular path (A). Deselect this text path. (Clicking anywhere on the work page while holding Command/Control key will deselect the text and "reset" the Path Type tool so you can enter text in a new location.) Click the Path Type tool on the smaller circle to convert it to a text path. Enter the text as seen below.

"in the Woods?"

They will have the same settings as set on the former text path (B). Don't worry about how the text fits the design at this point. The type sizes now need to be changed.

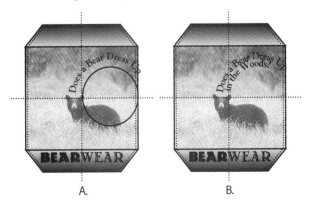

A.   B.

7. Highlight the letter "U" in "Up," and change its size to 23 pt. Move to the left. Set the next letter, "s," to 22 pt. Go backwards through the text letter by letter, making each consecutive one a point less (21, 20, 19, and so on) than the previous point size. Do this until you have changed the "D" in "Does."

8. Now perform the same size-changing scheme on the "in the Woods?" phrase. Starting with the "d" in "Woods," make it 23 pt., and move to the left, reducing each consecutive letter's size by one point. The idea of this design technique is to make the words look as if they are thoughts coming out of the bear's head.

9. Change to Outline mode to see the text paths more clearly. Click on the first text path and you will see its I-beam. Drag this to the left so the first word is near the top of the bear's head. If the type jumps underneath the text path, use Undo, and try again. It is very tricky working with text on a path. When the text is in position, click on the second text path and move its I-beam so the question mark is to the left of the descender in the word "Up." Go back to Preview mode.

The Shadow of Your Thoughts

1. When the two text paths are in place, select them with the Selection tool. Go to Type>Create Outlines to turn the text into path outlines. Keep them selected. Access the Color palette if it's not on screen. Set the CMYK sliders for: C:0, M:0, Y:20, K:0, to paint the letters.

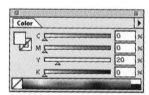

2. In the Effect menu, select Stylize>Drop Shadow. In the dialog box change the Blur to "0.03 in." In the Y Offset field, insert a minus symbol before the default number. It should be "-0.1 in." Click the Color button, which defaults to coloring the shadow black. Leave all other options as they are. Click OK.

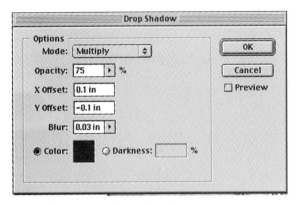

3. The drop shadow will appear on the selected type.

4. Save your changes made so far.

The Final Touches

1. Unlock the Background layer in the Layers palette and select it. At the top of the label, you must create a black circle to show the printer where to punch the hole for the string that hangs the label. To do this, click on the top trapezoid and you will see its center point (A). Drag a horizontal guide to mark this point. Select the Ellipse tool and, holding the Option/Alt key, click the cursor on the point where the horizontal guide meets the vertical center guide (B). In the dialog box, set the Width and Height to 0.185 in. Click OK. Paint the circle with a fill of Black and no stroke.

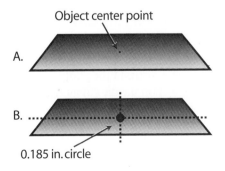

2. Select the two trapezoid objects and change their stroke to None. Select the first large rectangle you drew and delete it. In the Layers palette, click on the Photo layer and use the palette menu to toggle the Template option off, returning the photo to its full color. Choose View>Guides to hide the guides and observe your work.

3. Click on the Background layer to make it active. The rules that bridge the fine line where the photo butts up to the trapezoids must be created.

4. You could draw these rules with the Pen tool. This would require drawing, measuring, aligning, and guides to get the rules accurately placed. Whereas, there are already some rules sized and aligned exactly where they should be. This is the segment of the trapezoids that touches the photo.

5. Click on the Lock icon of the Photo layer to lock it. With the Direct Selection tool, click on the segments of the trapezoids that touch the photo. You're selecting only the segments, not the entire path. Copy the segments.

6. With the Selection tool, click on both of the trapezoids, while holding the shift key. Press Command/Control-F to Paste the segments In Front. Change the fill of the segments to None. In the Stroke palette, change the weight of the segments to 3 pt.

7. Make sure the Stroke box is active in the Toolbox. Set the Swatches palette to Show Color Swatches and view by Name View. Scroll down the list until you see the color named Yellow. Click on this color to paint the Stroke.

8. Unlock the Photo layer. Save your changes made so far.

Finalizing the Cutting Die

1. Select View>Guides to Show Guides. Go to Outline mode to notice the die cut guide without the photo image. Hold the Command/Control-Shift keys and double-click on the die cut guide. This will return it to a path. In the Layers palette, move the Die Cut layer up to the top of the list.

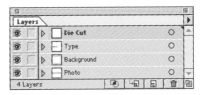

2. Deselect the die cut path. Make sure the Swatches palette is on the screen. Choose Window>Swatch Libraries and select Pantone Uncoated. Notice that each swatch in this palette has a triangle with a dot in it, indicating that the swatch is a spot color.

3. In the palette menu, select Show Find Field. In the field that appears at the top of the palette, begin typing the word "Black," and immediately "Pantone Black 2 2X CVU." At the same time the swatch for this color will be selected in the palette. Click on the selected swatch and it will automatically be added to the Swatches palette.

4. Select the Die Cut path. In the Toolbox, make sure the Fill box is set for None. Click on the Stroke box to make it active. Click on the Pantone Black 2 2X CVU swatch in the Swatches palette to apply this color to the stroke. When the job is color separated, the printer will do a four-color separation for the process colors and add a fifth plate for the spot color, which will print the Die Cut path on an individual plate. This will be sent to the company that will make a die from this art.

5. To make sure that the selected Die Cut path doesn't "knock" through all the colors underneath it, go to the Window menu and select Show Attributes. In this palette, click on the Overprint Stroke option. Deselect the Die Cut path.

6. Clear the guides and view your final work. The BearWear label is finished.

Die Cut

7.   When the label is trimmed it should look similar to the sample below.

8.   Save your changes and close the document.

Achromatic

Having no color; therefore, completely black or white or some shade of gray.

Acrobat

This program by Adobe Systems, Inc. allows the conversion (using Acrobat Distiller) of any document from any Macintosh or Windows application to PDF format, which retains the page layout, graphics, color, and typography of the original document. It is widely used for distributing documents online because it is independent of computer hardware. The only software needed is a copy of Acrobat Reader, which can be downloaded free.

Adaptive Palette

A sampling of colors taken from an image, and used in a special compression process usually used to prepare images for the world wide web.

Additive Color Process

The additive color process is the process of mixing red, green, and blue light to achieve a wide range of colors, as on a color television screen. See Subtractive Color.

Adjacent Color

The eye will respond to a strong adjacent color in such a way as to affect the perception of the particular color in question. That is, a color having different adjacent colors may look different than it does in isolation. Also referred to as metamarism.

Adobe Systems Incorporated

A major software developer responsible for the creation of the PostScript page description language (see PostScript), used in almost all graphic arts environments. PostScript resides in a printer or Raster Image Processor (see Raster Image Processor) and is used to convert graphics from the screen to high-resolution output. Adobe also develops the highly popular Photoshop, Illustrator, PageMaker, and Premiere graphics and video applications, in addition to a range of others.

Adobe In-RIP Trapping

A trapping system that is active at the RIP, rather than on the desktop computer. It allows for more complex trapping than trapping routines built into Adobe programs. In-RIP trapping is a feature of the Adobe PostScript 3 page-description language.

Adobe Multi-line Composer

Justification routine that makes hyphenation and line-ending decisions based on the parameters of a pre-efined number of lines of type.

Adobe Single-line Composer

Justification routine that makes hyphenation and line-ending decisions based on the parameters of a single line of type.

Algorithm

A specific sequence of mathematical steps to process data. A portion of a computer program that calculates a specific result.

All Signature Folding Dummy

A folding dummy in which all of the signatures that make up the job are used to determine the page arrangement for each signature. Also known as a Job Worksheet.

ANSI

American National Standards Institute, the recognized standards-making body for the United States. ANSI code is used by some Windows computers for addressing text.

Anti-Aliasing

A graphics software feature that eliminates or softens the jaggedness of low-resolution curved edges.

Archival Storage

The process of storing data in a totally secure and safe manner. Archiving differs from backup in that it's meant to be used to restore entire systems or networks, rather than providing quick and easy access to specific files or folders.

Art

Illustrations and photographs in general; that is, all matter other than text that appears in a mechanical.

Artifact

Something that is artificial, or not meant to be there. An artifact can be a blemish or dust spot on a piece of film, or unsightly pixels in a digital image.

Ascender

Parts of a lower-case letter that exceed the height of the letter "x". The letters b, d, f, h, k, l, and t have ascenders.

ASCII

The American Standard Code for Information Interchange, which defines each character, symbol, or special code as a number from 0 to 255 (8 bits in binary). An ASCII text file can be read by any computer, and is the basic mode of data transmission on the Internet.

ATM (Adobe Type Manager)

A utility program which causes fonts to appear smooth on screen at any point size. It's also used to manage font libraries.

Backing Up

The process of making copies of current work or work-in-progress as a safety measure against file corruption, drive or system failure, or accidental deletion. Backing up work-in-progress differs from creating an archive (see Archiving) for long-term storage or system restoration.

Banding

A visible stair-stepping of shades in a gradient.

Banner

A large headline or title extending across the full page width, or across a double-page spread.

Baseline

The implied reference line on which the bases of capital letters sit.

Bézier Curves

Curves that are defined mathematically (vectors), in contrast to those drawn as a collection of dots or pixels (raster). The advantage of these curves is that they can be scaled without the "jaggies" inherent in enlarging bitmapped fonts or graphics.

Bindery Marks

Marks that appear on a press sheet to indicate how the sheet should be cropped, folded, collated, or bound.

Binding

In general, the various methods used to secure signatures or leaves in a book. Examples include saddle-stitching (the use of staples in a folded spine), and perfect-bound (multiple sets of folded pages sewn or glued into a flat spine).

Bit (Binary Digit)

A computer's smallest unit of information. Bits can have only two values: 0 or

1. This can represent the black and white (1-bit) pixel values in a line art image. Or in combination with other bits, it can represent 16 tones or colors (4-bit), 256 tones or colors (8-bit), 16.8 million colors (24-bit), or a billion colors (30-bit). These numbers derive from counting all the possible combinations (permutations) of 0 or 1 settings of each bit: 2 x 2 x 2 = 16 colors; 2 x 2 x 2 x 2 x 2 x 2 x 2 x 2 = 256 colors; 2 x 2 x 2 x 2 x 2 x 2 x 2 x 2 x 2 x 2 x 2 x 2 x 2 x 2 x 2 x 2 x 2 x 2 x 2 x 2 x 2 x 2 x 2 x 2= 16.8 million colors.

Bitmap Image

An image constructed from individual dots or pixels set to a grid-like mosaic. Each pixel can be represented by more than one bit. A 1-bit image is black and white because each bit can have only two values (for example, 0 for white and 1 for black). For 256 colors, each pixel needs eight bits (2^8). A 24-bit image refers to an image with 24 bits per pixel (2^{24}), so it may contain as many as 16,777,216 colors. Because the file must contain information about the color and position of each pixel, the disk space needed for bitmap images is usually quite significant. Most digital photographs and screen captures are bitmap images.

Bitmapped

Forming an image by a grid of pixels whose curved edges have discrete steps because of the approximation of the curve by a finite number of pixels.

Black

The absence of color; an ink that absorbs all wavelengths of light.

Blanket

The blanket, a fabric coated with natural or synthetic rubber wrapped around the cylinder of an offset press, transfers the inked image from the plate to the paper.

Bleed

Page data that extends beyond the trim marks on a page. Illustrations that spread to the edge of the paper without margins are referred to as "bled off."

Blend

See Graduated fill.

Blind Emboss

A raised impression in paper made by a die, but without being inked. It is visible only by its relief characteristic.

Blow up

An enlargement, usually of a graphic element such as a photograph.

Body Copy

The text portion of the copy on a page, as distinguished from headlines.

Border

A continuous line that extends around text; or a rectangular, oval, or irregularly-shaped visual in an ad.

Bounding Box

The imaginary rectangle that encloses all sides of a graphic, necessary for a page layout specification.

Brightness

1. A measure of the amount of light reflected from a surface. 2. A paper property, defined as the percentage reflection of 457-nanometer (nm) radiation. 3. The intensity of a light source. 4. The overall percentage of lightness in an image.

Bullet

A marker preceding text, usually a solid dot, used to add emphasis; generally indicates that the text is part of a list.

Byte

A unit of measure equal to eight bits (decimal 256) of digital information, sufficient to represent one text character. It is the standard unit measure of file size. (See also Megabyte, Kilobyte, and Gigabyte).

Calibration

Making adjustments to a color monitor and other hardware and software to make the monitor represent as closely as possible the colors of the final printed piece.

Calibration Bars

A strip of reference blocks of color or tonal values on film, proofs, and press sheets, used to check the accuracy of color registration, quality, density, and ink coverage during a print run.

Callout

A descriptive label referenced to a visual element, such as several words connected to the element by an arrow.

Camera Ready

A completely finished mechanical, ready to be photographed to produce a negative from which a printing plate will be made.

Cap Line

The theoretical line to which the tops of capital letters are aligned.

Caps

An abbreviation for capital letters.

Caps and Small Caps

A style of typesetting in which capital letters are used in the normal way, while the type that would normally be in lower case has been changed to capital letters of a smaller point size. A true small-caps typeface does not contain any lower-case letters.

Caption

The line or lines of text that identify a picture or illustration, usually placed beneath it or otherwise in close proximity.

CCITT

International Coordinating Committee for Telephone and Telegraphy. A lossless compression method appropriate for black-and-white images.

CD-ROM

A device used to store approximately 600MB of data. Files are permanently stored on the device and can be copied to a disk but not altered directly. ROM stands for Read-Only Memory. Equipment is now available on the consumer market for copying computer files to blank CD-ROMs.

Center marks

Press marks that appear on the center of all sides of a press sheet to aid in positioning the print area on the paper.

Character Count

The number of characters (letters, figures, signs or spaces) in a selected block of copy. Once used to calculate the amount of text that would fit on a given line or region when physically setting type.

Choke

See Trapping

Chroma

The degree of saturation of a surface color.

Cromalin

A single-sheet color proofing system introduced by DuPont in 1971 and still quite popular in the industry. It uses a series of overlaid colorants and varnish to simulate the results of a press run.

Chromaticity Diagram

A graphical representation of two of the three dimensions of color. Intended for plotting light sources rather than surface colors. Often called the CIE diagram.

Cicero/Didot Point

The cicero is a unit of horizontal distance slightly larger than the pica, used widely in continental Europe. A cicero equals 0.178 inches, or 12 Didot points.

Clipboard

The portion of computer memory that holds data that has been cut or copied. The next item cut or copied replaces the data already in the clipboard.

Clip Gallery

A Publisher tool for previewing and inserting clip art, pictures, sounds, video clips, and animations. You can add new clips to the Gallery from other programs or from a special Microsoft site on the World Wide Web.

Cloning

Duplication of pixels from one part of an image to another.

CMS

See Color Management System

CMYK

Acronym for cyan, magenta, yellow, and black, the four process color inks which, when properly overprinted, can simulate a subset of the visible spectrum. These colors form the subtractive primaries. See also color separation.

Coated

Printing papers having a surface coating (of clay or other material) to provide a smoother, more even finish with greater opacity.

Cold Type

Type produced by photographic or digital methods, as opposed to the use of molten metal.

Collate

To gather separate sections or leaves of a publication together in the correct order for binding.

Collate and Cut

Multiple signatures that are stacked then cut to be later placed in sequential order, drilled, and placed in three-ring binders.

Color Balance

The combination of yellow, magenta, and cyan needed to produce a neutral gray. Determined through a gray balance analysis.

Color Cast

The modification of a hue by the addition of a trace of another hue, such as yellowish green, pinkish blue, etc. Normally, an unwanted effect that can be corrected.

Color Chart

A printed chart of various combinations of CMYK colors used as an aid for the selection of "legal" colors during the design phase of a project.

Color Control Strip

A printed strip of various reference colors used to control printing quality. This strip is normally placed outside the "trim" area of a project, as a guide and visual aid for the pressman.

Color Conversion

Changing the color "mode" of an image. Converting an image from RGB to CMYK for purposes of preparing the image for conventional printing.

Color Correction

The process of removing casts or unwanted tints in a scanned image, in an effort to improve the appearance of the scan or to correct obvious deficiencies, such as green skies or yellowish skin tones.

Color Gamut

The range of colors that can be formed by all possible combinations of the colorants of a given reproduction system (printing press) on a given type of paper.

Color Key

An overlay color proof of acetate sheets, one for each of the four primary printing inks. The method was developed by 3M Corporation and remains a copyrighted term.

Color Management System

A process or utility that attempts to manage color of input and output devices in such a way that the monitor will match the output of any CMS-managed printer.

Color Model

A system for describing color, such as RGB, HLS, CIELAB, or CMYK.

Color Overlay

A sheet of film or paper whose text and art correspond to one spot color or process color. Each color overlay becomes the basis for a single printing plate that will apply that color to paper.

Color Picker

A function within a graphics application that assists in selecting a color.

Color Proof

A printed or simulated printed image of the color separations intended to produce a close representation of the final reproduction for approval and as a guide to the press operator.

Color Scheme

A defined set of colors that is associated with a publication.

Color Separation

The process of transforming color artwork into four components corresponding to the four process colors. If spot colors are used, additional components may be created containing only those items that will appear in the corresponding spot color layer. Each component is imaged to film or paper in preparation for making printing plates that correspond to each ink.

Color Sequence

The color order of printing the cyan, magenta, yellow, and black inks on a printing press. Sometimes called rotation or color rotation.

Color Space

Because a color must be represented by three basic characteristics depending on the color model, the color space is a three-dimensional coordinate system in which any color can be represented as a point.

Color Temperature

The temperature, in degrees Kelvin, to which a blackbody would have to be heated to produce a certain color radiation. (A "blackbody" is an ideal body or surface that completely absorbs or radiates energy.) The graphic arts viewing standard is 5,000 K. The degree symbol is not used in the Kelvin scale. The higher the color temperature, the bluer the light.

Color Transparency

A positive color photographic image on a clear film base that must be viewed by transmitted light. It is preferred for original photographic art because it has higher resolution than a color print. Transparency sizes range from 35mm color slides up to 8x10in. (203x254mm).

Colorimeter

An optical measuring instrument designed to measure and quantify color. They are often used to match digital image values to those of cloth and other physical samples.

Column

A vertical area for type, used to constrain line length to enhance design and readability.

Column Rule

A thin vertical rule used to separate columns of type.

Combination Signatures

Signatures of different sizes inserted at any position in a layout.

Commercial Printing

Typically, printing on high-capacity, high-resolution presses. High-resolution commercial printing processes include offset lithography, flexography, gravure, and screen printing. Offset printing is the most widely used commercial printing process.

Comp

Comprehensive artwork used to present the general color and layout of a page.

Compose

To set copy into type, or lay out a page.

Composite Proof

A version of an illustration or page in which the process colors appear together to represent full color. When produced on a monochrome output device, colors are represented as shades of gray.

Compression

A digital technique used to reduce the size of a file by analyzing occurrences of similar data. Compressed files occupy less physical space, and their use improves digital transmission speeds. Compression can sometimes result in a loss of image quality and/or resolution.

Compression Utility

A software program that reduces a file's size for storage on a disk. If a compressed file is too large to fit onto a single disk, the compression utility compies it onto multiple disks. See Stuffit.

Condensed Type

A typeface in which the width of the letters is narrower than that of the standard letters of the font. Condensed type can be a designed font, or the effect may be approximated by applying a percentage of normal width by a formatting command.

Continuous Tone

An image such as an original photograph in which the subject has continuous shades of color or gray tones through the use of an emulsion process. Continuous tone images must be screened to create halftone images in order to be printed.

Contrast

The relationship between the dark and light areas of an image.

Copyright

Ownership of a work by the originator, such as an author, publisher, artist, or photographer. The right of copyright permits the originator of material to prevent its use without express permission or acknowledgment of the originator. Copyright may be sold, transferred, or given up contractually.

CorelDRAW

A popular drawing program originally designed for the Windows environment, but now available also as a Macintosh program. CorelDRAW is known to create files that can cause printing and/or output problems in many prepress environments.

Creep

The progressive extension of interior pages of the folded signature beyond the image area of the outside pages. Shingling is applied to correct for creep.

Crop Marks

Printed short, fine lines used as guides for final trimming of the pages within a press sheet.

Cropping

The elimination of parts of a photograph or other original that are not required to be printed.

Crossover

An element in a book (text, line art, or other graphic) that appears on both pages of a reader spread crossing over the gutter.

Custom Printer Description File

A file containing information specific to a type of output device; used in conjunction with a standard PPD file to customize the printing process.

Data Source

A file where you store all addresses or other information for customers, friends and family, or merchants you do business with. Before you can merge a publication, you must connect your publication to a data source. See also Mail Merge.

DCS

Acronym for Desktop Color Separation, a version of the EPS file format. DCS 1.0 files are composed of five PostScript files for each color image: cyan, magenta, yellow, and black file, plus a separate low-resolution FPO image to place in a digital file. In contrast, DCS 2.0 files have one file that stores process color and spot color information.

Default

A specification for a mode of computer operation that operates if no other is selected. The default font size might be 12 point, or a default color for an object might be white with a black border.

Densitometer

An electronic instrument used to measure optical density. Reflective (for paper) and transmissive (for film).

Descender

The part of a lower-case letter that extends below the baseline (lower edge of the x-height) of the letter. The letters y, p, g, and j contain descenders.

Desktop

1. The area on a monitor screen on which the icons appear, before an application is launched. 2. A reference to the size of computer equipment (system unit, monitor, printer) that can fit on a normal desk; thus, desktop publishing.

Desktop Publishing (DTP)

Use of a personal computer, software applications, and a high-quality printer to produce fully composed printed documents. DTP is, in reality, an incorrect term these days. In the early days of Macintosh and PostScript technology, the term Desktop Publishing inferred that the materials produced from these systems was somehow inferior (as opposed to professional publishing). Now, the overwhelming majority of all printed materials — regardless of the quality — are produced on these systems, up to and including nationally famous magazines, catalogs, posters, and newspapers

Dictionary

A collection of words, used by page layout programs to determine appropriate spelling and hyphenation.

Die Line

In a digital file, the outline used to mark where cutting, stamping, or embossing the finished printed piece will occur. Uses to create a particular shape, such as a rolodex card.

Digital

The use of a series of discrete electronic pulses to represent data. In digital imaging systems, 256 steps (8 bits, or 1 byte) are normally used to characterize the gray scale or the properties of one color. For text, see ASCII.

Digital Camera

A camera which produces images directly into an electronic file format for transfer to a computer.

Digital Proofs

Digital proofs are representations of what a specific mechanical will look like when output and reproduced on a specific type of printing press. The difference with a digital proof is that it is created without the use of conventional film processes and output directly from computer files.

Dingbat

A font character that displays a picture instead of a letter, number or punctuation mark. There are entire font families of pictographic dingbats; the most commonly used dingbat font is Zapf Dingbats. There are dingbats for everything from the little airplanes used to represent airports on a map, to telephones, swashes, fish, stars, balloons — just about anything. Also, a printer's typographical ornament.

Direct-to-plate

Producing printing plates directly from computer output without going through the film process.

Disk Operating System

Software for computer systems that supervises and controls the running of programs. The operating system is loaded into memory from disk by a small program which permanently resides in the firmware within the computer. The major operating systems in use today are Windows95/98 and WindowsNT from Microsoft, the Macintosh OS from Apple Computer, and a wide range of UNIX systems, such as those from Silicon Graphics, SUN Microsystems, and other vendors.

Dithering

A technique used in images wherein a color is represented using dots of two different colors displayed or printed very close together. Dithering is often used to compress digital images, in special screening algorithms (see Stochastic Screening) and to produce higher quality output on low-end color printers.

Document

The general term for a computer file containing text and/or graphics.

Dot Gain

The growth of a halftone dot that occurs whenever ink soaks into paper. This growth can vary from being very small (on a high-speed press with fast-drying ink and very non-porous paper) to quite dramatic, as is the case in newspaper printing, where a dot can expand 30% from its size on the film to the size at which it dries. Failure to compensate for this gain in the generation of digital images can result in very poor results on press. Generally speaking, the finer the screen (and therefore, the smaller the dot) the more noticeable dot gain will be.

Double-page Spread

A design that spans the two pages visible to the reader at any open spot in a magazine, periodical, or book.

Downloadable Fonts

Typefaces that can be stored on disk and then downloaded to the printer when required for printing.

DPI (Dots Per Inch)

The measurement of resolution for page printers, phototypesetting machines and graphics screens. Currently graphics screens use resolutions of 60 to 100 dpi, standard desktop laser printers work at 600 dpi, and imagesetters operate at more than 1,500 dpi.

Drop Shadow

A duplicate of a graphic element or type placed behind and slightly offset from it, giving the effect of a shadow.

Draw-type Pictures

Object-oriented images or vector graphics) Pictures created from a series of instructions that tell the computer to draw lines, curves, rectangles, and other objects. See Bitmap Image.

Drum Scanner

A color scanner on which the original is wrapped around a rotary scanning drum. See Scanner.

DSC

Acronym for the Adobe Document Structure Conventions, designed to provide a standard order and format for information so applications that process PostScript, such as PressWise, can easily find information about a document's structure and imaging requirements. These conventions allow specially formatted PostScript comments to be added to the page description; applications can search for these comments, but PostScript interpreters usually ignore them. TrapWise requires that the PostScript in incoming files is formatted using conventional DSC comments, so certain functions may not work properly if the file is not DSC-conforming.

Duotone

The separation of a black-and-white photograph into black and a second color having different tonal values and screen angles. Duotones are used to enhance photographic reproduction in two-three-or sometimes four-color work. Often the second, third, and fourth colors are not standard CMYK inks.

Dye

A soluble coloring material, normally used as the colorant in color photographs.

Dye Transfer

A photographic color print using special coated papers to produce a full color image. Can serve as an inexpensive proof.

Electronic Form

An interactive form in a Web site, filled out by readers and then sent back to the owner of the Web site or stored on a Web server.

Electrostatic

The method by which dry toner is transferred to paper in a copier or laser printer, and liquid toners are bonded to paper on some large-format color plotters.

Element

The smallest unit of a graphic, or a component of a page layout or design. Any object, text block, or graphic might be referred to as an element of the design.

Elliptical Dot Screen

A halftone screen having an elliptical dot structure.

Embedding

1. Placing control codes in the body of a document. 2. Including a complete copy of a text file or image within a desktop publishing document, with or without a link (see Linking).

Em Dash

A dash (—) that indicates the separation of elements of a sentence or clause.

Em Space

A space that is of equal width in points to the point size. An em space in 10 point type is 10 points wide.

Emulsion

The coating of light-sensitive material (silver halide) on a piece of film or photographic paper.

En Dash

A dash (–), half the width of an em dash, that often replaces the word "to" or "through," such as 9–5 or Monday–Friday.

En Space

A space that is equal to half the width of an em space.

EPS

Acronym for encapsulated PostScript, a single-page PostScript file that contains grayscale or color information and can be imported into many electronic layout and design applications.

EPS (Encapsulated PostScript)

Acronym for file format used to transfer PostScript data within compatible applications. An EPS file normally contains a small preview image that displays in position within a mechanical or used by another program. EPS files can contain text, vector artwork, and images.

Expanded Type

Also called extended. A typeface in which the width of the letters is wider than that of the standard letters of the font. Expanded type can be a designed font, or the effect may be approximated by applying a percentage of normal width by a formatting command.

Export

To save a file generated in one application in a format that is readable in another application.

Extension

A modular software program that extends or expands the functions of a larger program. A folder of Extensions is found in the Macintosh System Folder.

Film

Non-paper output of an imagesetter or phototypesetter.

Film Assembly

See Stripping.

Filter

In image editing applications, a small program that creates a special effect or performs some other function within an image.

First Signature Folding Dummy

A folding dummy that determines the page arrangement for a single signature layout template. This template can then be applied to a job that requires multiple signatures, and PressWise will correctly impose all the pages based on the numbering sequence and binding method specified by the first signature.

Flat

Individual film assembled onto a carrier readied for contacting or platemaking. Referred to as a cab in gravure printing.

Flat Color

Color that lacks contrast or tonal variation. Also, flat tint.

Flatbed Scanner

A scanner on which the original is mounted on a flat scanning glass. See Scanner.

Flexographic Printing

A rotary letterpress process printing on a press using a rubber plate that stretches around a cylinder making it necessary to compensate by distorting the plate image. Flexography is used most often in label printing, often on metal or other non-paper material.

Floating Accent

A separate accent mark that can be placed under or over another character. Complex accented characters such as in foreign languages are usually available in a font as a single character.

Flop

To make a mirror image of visuals such as photographs or clip art.

Folder

1. The digital equivalent of a paper file folder, used to organize files in the Macintosh and Windows operating systems. The icon of a folder looks like a paper file folder. Double-clicking it opens it to reveal the files stored inside. 2. A mechanical device which folds preprinted pages into various formats, such as a tri-fold brochure.

Folding dummy

A template used for determining the page arrangement on a form to meet folding and binding requirements. See also All signature folding dummy and First signature folding dummy.

Font

A font is the complete collection of all the characters (numbers, uppercase and lowercase letters and, in some cases, small caps and symbols) of a given typeface in a specific style; for example, Helvetica Bold.

Font Subsetting

Embedding only part of a font. If you use only a small number of characters from a font, say for drop caps or for headlines, you can embed only the characters you used from the font. The advantage of font subsetting is that it decreases the overall size of your file. The disadvantage is that it limits the ability to makes corrections at the printing service.

Font Substitution

A process in which your computer uses a font similar to the one you used in your publication to display or print your publication. Although the substitute font may be similar to the original font, your publication will not look exactly as you intended; line breaks, column breaks, or page breaks may fall differently, which can affect the entire look and feel of the publication.

Force Justify

A type alignment command which causes the space between letters and words in a line of type to expand to fit within a line. Often used in headlines, and sometimes used to force the last line of a justified paragraph, which is normally set flush left, to justify.

Form

The front or back of a signature.

Four-color Process

See Process Colors

FPO

Acronym for For Position Only, a term applied to low-quality art reproductions or simple shapes used to indicate placement and scaling of an art element on mechanicals or camera-ready artwork. In digital publishing, an FPO can be low-resolution TIFF files that are later replaced with high-resolution versions. An FPO is not intended for reproduction but only as a guide and placeholder for the prepress service provider.

Frame

In desktop publishing, (1.) an area or block into which text or graphics can be placed; (2.) a border on .

FreeHand

A popular vector-based illustration program available from Macromedia.

Full Measure

A line set to the entire line length.

G (Gigabyte)

One billion (1,073,741,824) bytes (230) or 1,048,576 kilobytes.

Galley Proof

Proofs, usually of type, taken before the type is made up into pages. Before desktop publishing, galley proofs were hand-assembled into pages.

Gamma

A measure of the contrast, or range of tonal variation, of the midtones in a photographic image.

Gamma Correction

1. Adjusting the contrast of the midtones in an image. 2. Calibrating a monitor so that midtones are correctly displayed on screen.

Gamut

See Color Gamut

GASP

Acronym for Graphic Arts Service Provider, a firm that provides a range of services somewhere on the continuum from design to fulfillment.

GCR

An acronym for Gray Component Replacement. A technique for adding detail by reducing the amount of cyan, magenta, and yellow in chromatic or colored areas, replacing them with black.

GIF

An acronym for Graphics Interchange Format. A popular graphics format for online clip art and drawn graphics. Graphics in this format look good at low resolution.

GIF, Animated

A series of GIF graphics that functions like a film loop, giving the appearance of animation. See GIF.

Global Preferences

Preference settings which affect all newly created files within an application.

Glyph

Any character of a font.

Gradient Fill

See Graduated fill.

Graduated Fill

An area in which two colors (or shades of gray or the same color) are blended to create a gradual change from one to the other. Graduated fills are also known as blends, gradations, gradient fills, and vignettes.

Grain

Silver salts clumped together in differing amounts in different types of photographic emulsions. Generally speaking, faster emulsions have larger grain sizes.

Graininess

Visual impression of the irregularly distributed silver grain clumps in a photographic image, or the ink film in a printed image.

Gray Balance

The values for the yellow, magenta, and cyan inks that are needed to produce a neutral gray when printed at a normal density.

Gray Component Replacement

See GCR

Grayscale

1. An image composed in grays ranging from black to white, usually using 256 different tones of gray. 2. A tint ramp used to measure and control the accuracy of screen percentages on press. 3. An accessory used to define neutral density in a photographic image.

Greeking

1. A software technique by which areas of gray are used to simulate lines of text below a certain point size. 2. Nonsense text use to define a layout before copy is available.

Grid

A division of a page by horizontal and vertical guides into areas into which text or graphics may be placed accurately.

Grind-off

The roughing up at the back (or spine) of a folded signature, or of two or more gathered signatures, in preparation for perfect binding.

Gripper Edge

The leading edge of a sheet of paper, which the grippers on the press grab to carry the paper through a press.

Group

To collect graphic elements together so that an operation may be applied to all of them simultaneously.

GUI

Acronym for Graphical User Interface, the basis of the Macintosh and Windows operating systems.

Gutter

Extra space between pages in a layout. Sometimes used interchangeably with Alley to describe the space between columns on a page. Gutters can appear either between the top and bottom of two adjacent pages or between two sides of adjacent pages. Gutters are often used because of the binding or layout requirements of a job — for example, to add space at the top or bottom of each page or to allow for the grind-off taken when a book is perfect bound.

H & J

Hyphenation and Justification. Parameters used by a page layout program to determine how a line of text should be hyphenated, or how its inter-word and inter-character space should be adjusted.

Hairline Rule

The thinnest rule that can be printed on a given device. A hairline rule on a 1200 dpi imagesetter is 1/1200 of an inch; on a 300 dpi laser printer, the same rule would print at 1/300 of an inch.

Halftone

An image generated for use in printing in which a range of continuous tones is simulated by an array of dots that create the illusion of continuous tone when seen at a distance.

Halftone Tint

An area covered with a uniform halftone dot size to produce an even tone or color. Also called flat tint or screen tint.

Hanging Punctuation

A margin alignment technique where the punctuation falls outside the margins, making the edges of the text appear more even.

Hard Drive

A rigid disk sealed inside an airtight transport mechanism that is the basic storage mechanism in a computer. Information stored may be accessed more rapidly than on floppy disks and far greater amounts of data stored.

High Key

A photographic or printed image in which the main interest area lies in the highlight end of the scale.

High Resolution File

An image file that typically contains four pixels for every dot in the printed reproduction. High-resolution files are often linked to a page layout file, but not actually embedded in it, due to their large size.

Highlights

The lightest areas in a photograph or illustration.

Home Page

The first page readers encounter when opening a Web site.

Hot Spot

An area on an object containing a hyperlink. An entire object can be a single hot spot, or an object can contain multiple hot spots.

HSL

A color model that defines color based on its hue, saturation, and luminosity (value), as it is displayed on a video or computer screen.

HSV

A color model based on three coordinates: hue, saturation and value (or luminance).

HTML

An acronym for HyperText Markup Language. The language, written in plain (ASCII) text using simple tags, that is used to create Web pages, and which Web browsers are designed to read and display. HTML focuses more on the logical structure of a page than its appearance. HTML is used to mark, or code, the content of your design (text, graphics, sounds, and animation) so that it can be published on the Web and viewed with a browser.

Hue

The wavelength of light of a color in its purest state (without adding white or black).

Hyperlink

An HTML tag directs the computer to a different Anchor or URL (Uniform Resource Locator). The linked data may be on the same page, or on a computer anywhere in the world. A hyperlink can be a word, phrase, sentence, graphic, or icon. A hyperlink can also cause an action, such as opening or downloading a file.

Hyphenation Zone

The space at the end of a line of text in which the hyphenation function will examine the word to determine whether or not it should be hyphenated and wrapped to the next line.

ICC Profile

Using a format designed by the International Color Consortium, the profile

describes the colorspace used to create the document, based on the gamut of

the color device referenced.

ICM

An acronym for Image Color Matching. Many, but not all, printer and monitor manufacturers use the Image Color Matching standard. ICM gives you a better idea of what the final colors in your publication will look like.

Icon

A small graphic symbol used on the screen to indicate files or folders, activated by clicking with the mouse or pointing device.

Illustrator

A vector editing application owned by Adobe Systems, Inc.

Imaging

The process of producing a film or paper copy of a digital file from an output device.

Imagesetter

A raster-based device used to output a computer page-layout file or composition at high resolution (usually 1000 - 3000 dpi) onto photographic paper or film, from which to make printing plates.

Import

To bring a file generated within one application into another application.

Imposition

The arrangement of pages on a printed sheet, which, when the sheet is finally printed, folded and trimmed, will place the pages in their correct order.

Indent to Here

A special character that, when activated, causes all subsequent lines in a paragraph to indent from the left margin to that point.

InDesign

A page layout program from Adobe Systems.

Indexed Color Image

An image which uses a limited, predetermined number of colors; often used in Web images. See also GIF.

Indexing

In DTP, marking certain words within a document with hidden codes so that an index may be automatically generated.

Initial Caps

Text in which the first letter of each word (except articles, etc.) is capitalized.

Intensity

Synonym for degree of color saturation.

International Paper Sizes

The International Standards Organization (ISO) system of paper sizes is based on a series of three sizes A, B and C. Series A is used for general printing and stationery, Series B for posters, and Series C for envelopes. Each size has the same proportion of length to width as the others. The nearest ISO paper size to conventional 8-1/2 x 11 paper is A4.

Internet

An international network of computer networks, which links millions of commercial, educational, governmental, and personal computers. See World Wide Web.

Island Spread

A spread that includes more than two pages.

ISO

The International Standards Organization.

Internet Service Provider (ISP)

An organization that provides access to the Internet for such things as electronic mail, bulletin boards, chat rooms, or use of the World Wide Web.

Jaggies

Visible steps in the curved edge of a graphic or text character that results from enlarging a bitmapped image.

JPG or JPEG

An acronym for Joint Photographers Experts Group. A compression algorithm that reduces the file size of bitmapped images, named for the Joint Photographic Experts Group, an industry organization that created the standard; JPEG is a "lossy" compression method, and image quality will be reduced in direct proportion to the amount of compression. JPEG graphics produce resolution for color photographics than a GIF format. See GIF.

Justified Alignment

Straight left and right alignment of text — not ragged. Every line of text is the same width, creating even left and right margins.

Kelvin (K)

Unit of temperature measurement based on Celsius degrees, starting from absolute zero, which is equivalent to - 273 Celsius (centigrade); used to indicate the color temperature of a light source.

Kerning

Moving a pair of letters closer together or farther apart, to achieve a better fit or appearance.

Key (Black Plate)

In early four-color printing, the black plate was printed first and the other three colors were aligned (or registered) to it. Thus, the black plate was the "key" to the result.

Keyline

A thin, often black border around a picture or a box indicating where to place pictures. In digital files, the keylines are often vector objects while photographs are usually bitmap images.

Kilobyte (K, KB)

1,024 (210) bytes, the nearest binary equivalent to decimal 1,000 bytes. Abbreviated and referred to as K.

Knockout

A printing technique that represents overlapping objects without mixing inks. The ink for the underlying element does not print (knocks out) in the area where the objects overlap. Opposite of overprinting.

L*a*b

The lightness, red-green attribute, and yellow-blue attribute in the CIE Color Space, a three-dimensional color mapping system.

Landscape

Printing from the left to right across the wider side of the page. A landscape orientation treats a page as 11 inches wide and 8.5 inches long.

Laser Printer

A high quality image printing system using a laser beam to produce an image on a photosensitive drum. The image is transferred to paper by a conventional xerographic printing process. Current laser printers used for desktop publishing have a resolution of 600 dpi. Imagesetters are also laser printers, but with higher resolution and tight mechanical controls to produce final film separations for commercial printing.

Layer

A function of graphics or page layout applications in which elements may be hidden from view, locked, reordered or otherwise manipulated as a unit, without affecting other elements on the page.

Layout

The arrangement of text and graphics on a page, usually produced in the preliminary design stage.

Leaders

A line of periods or other symbols connecting the end of a group of words with another element separated by some space. For example, a table of contents may consist of a series of phrases on separate lines, each associated with a page number. Promotes readability in long lists of tabular text.

Leading ("ledding")

Space added between lines of type. Usually measured in points or fractions of points. Named after the strips of lead which used to be inserted between lines of metal type. In specifying type, lines of 12-pt. type separated by a 14-pt. space is abbreviated "12/14," or "twelve over fourteen."

Letterspacing

The insertion or addition of white space between the letters of words.

Library

In the computer world, a collection of files having a similar purpose or function.

Ligature

Letters that are joined together as a single unit of type such as œ and fi.

Lightness

The property that distinguishes white from gray or black, and light from dark color tones on a surface.

Line Art

A drawing or piece of black and white artwork, with no screens. Line art can be represented by a graphic file having only one-bit resolution.

Line Screen

The number of lines per inch used when converting a photograph to a halftone. Typical values range from 85 for newspaper work to 150 or higher for high-quality reproduction on smooth or coated paper.

Linking

An association through software of a graphic or text file on disk with its location in a document. That location may be represented by a "placeholder" rectangle, or a low-resolution copy of the graphic.

Lithography

A mechanical printing process used for centuries based on the principle of the natural aversion of water (in this case, ink) to grease. In modern offset lithography, the image on a photosensitive plate is first transferred to the blanket of a rotating drum, and then to the paper.

Lossy

A data compression method characterized by the loss of some data.

Loupe

A small free-standing magnifier used to see fine detail on a page.

LPI

Lines per inch. See Line Screen.

Luminosity

The amount of light, or brightness, in an image. Part of the HLS color model.

LZW

The acronym for the Lempel-Ziv-Welch lossless data- and image-compression algorithm.

M, MB (Megabyte)

One million (1,048,576) bytes (220) or 1,024 Kilobytes.

Macro

A set of keystrokes that is saved as a named computer file. When accessed, the keystrokes will be performed. Macros are used to perform repetitive tasks.

Mail Merge

The process of combining a data source with a publication to print a batch of individually customized publications.

Margins

The non-printing areas of page, or the line at which text starts or stops.

Mask

To conform the shape of a photograph or illustration to another shape such as a circle or polygon.

Masking

A technique that blocks an area of an image from reproduction by superimposing an opaque object of any shape.

Master

Underlying pages or spreads containing elements common to all pages to which the master is applied.

Match Print

A color proofing system used for the final quality check.

Mechanical

A pasted-up page of camera-ready art that is to be photographed to produce a plate for the press.

Medium

A physical carrier of data such as a CD-ROM, video cassette, or floppy disk, or a carrier of electronic data such as fiber optic cable or electric wires.

Megabyte (MB)

A unit of measure of stored data equaling 1,024 kilobytes, or 1,048,576 bytes (1020).

Megahertz

An analog signal frequency of one million cycles per second, or a data rate of one million bits per second. Used in specifying computer CPU speed.

Menu

A list of choices of functions, or of items such as fonts. In contemporary software design, there is often a fixed menu of basic functions at the top of the page that have pull-down menus associated with each of the fixed choices.

Metafile

A class of graphics that combines the characteristics of raster and vector graphics formats; not recommended for high-quality output.

Metallic Ink

Printing inks which produce an effect of gold, silver, bronze, or metallic colors.

Midtones or Middletones

The tonal range between highlights and shadows.

Misregistration

The unwanted result of incorrectly aligned process inks and spot colors on a finished printed piece. Misregistration can be caused by many factors, including paper stretch and improper plate alignment. Trapping can compensate for misregistration.

Modem

An electronic device for converting digital data into analog audio signals and back again (MOdulator-DEModulator). Primarily used for transmitting data between computers over analog (audio frequency) telephone lines.

Moiré

An interference pattern caused by the out-of-register overlap of two or more regular patterns such as dots or lines. In process-color printing, screen angles are selected to minimize this pattern.

Monochrome

An image or computer monitor in which all information is represented in black and white, or with a range of grays.

Monospace

A font in which all characters occupy the same amount of horizontal width regardless of the character. See also Proportional Spacing.

Montage

A single image formed by assembling or compositing several images.

Mottle

Uneven color or tone.

Multimedia

The combination of sound, video images, and text to create a "moving" presentation.

Nested Signatures

Multiple signatures that are folded, gathered, and placed one inside another, and then saddle-stitched at the spine.

Nesting

Placing graphic files within other graphic files. This unacceptable practice often results in errors in printing.

Network

Two or more computers that are linked to exchange data or share resources. The Internet is a network of networks.

Neutral

Any color that has no hue, such as white, gray, or black.

Neutral Density

A measurement of the lightness or darkness of a color. A neutral density of zero (0.00) is the lightest value possible and is equivalent to pure white; 3.294 is roughly equivalent to 100% of each of the CMYK components.

Noise

Unwanted signals or data that may reduce the quality of the output.

Non-breaking Space

A typographic command that connects two words with a space, but prevents the words from being broken apart if the space occurs within the hyphenation zone. See Hyphenation Zone.

Non-reproducible Colors

Colors in an original scene or photograph that are impossible to reproduce using process inks. Also called out-of-gamut colors.

Normal Key

A description of an image in which the main interest area is in the middle range of the tone scale or distributed throughout the entire tonal range.

Nudge

To move a graphic or text element in small, preset increments, usually with the arrow keys.

Object-oriented Art

Vector-based artwork composed of separate elements or shapes described mathematically rather than by specifying the color and position of every point. This contrasts to bitmap images, which are composed of individual pixels.

Oblique

A slanted character (sometimes backwards, or to the left), often used when referring to italic versions of sans-serif typefaces.

Offset

In graphics manipulation, to move a copy or clone of an image slightly to the side and/or back; used for a drop-shadow effect.

Offset Lithography

A printing method whereby the image is transferred from a plate onto a rubber covered cylinder from which the printing takes place (see Lithography).

OLE

An acronym for Object Linking and Embedding. When you add an object to a publication as a linked object, you can use another program while you're in Publisher to make changes to the object. But unlike an embedded object, a linked object can be easily updated to match changes made to the original document (called the source document) in your source program. Likewise, any changes you make to the linked object in your publication will also appear in the source document (and any other documents that are linked to that object).

Online Publishing

Preparing documents for viewing on monitors, such as through CD distribution or the Internet.

Opacity

1. The degree to which paper will show print through it. 2. Settings in certain graphics applications that allow images or text below the object whose opacity has been adjusted, to show through.

Opaque Inks

Inks which are not designed to interact with other inks. Their pigment is so dense that, when they overprint another color ink, there is no interaction between them.

OPI

Acronym for Open Prepress Interface. 1. A set of PostScript language comments originally developed by Aldus Corporation for defining and specifying the placement of high-resolution images in PostScript files on an electronic page layout. 2. Incorporation of a low resolution preview image within a graphic file format (TIF, EPS, DCS) that is intended for display only. 3. Software device that is an extension to PostScript that replaces low-resolution placeholder images in a document with their high-resolution sources for printing.

Optical Disks

Video disks that store large amounts of data used primarily for reference works such as dictionaries and encyclopedias.

Orphan

A single or partial word, or a partial line of a paragraph appearing at the bottom of a page. See widow.

Output Device

Any hardware equipment, such as a monitor, laser printer, or imagesetter, that depicts text or graphics created on a computer.

Overflow Area

Where Publisher stores text that will not fit in a text frame or chain of connected text frames, or in a cell of a table whose size is locked. You cannot see text that's stored in the overflow area.

Overlay

A transparent sheet used in the preparation of multicolor mechanical artwork showing the color breakdown.

Overprint

A printing technique that lays down one ink on top of another ink. The overprinted inks can combine to make a new color. The opposite of knockout.

Overprint Color

A color made by overprinting any two or more of the primary yellow, magenta, and cyan process colors.

Overprinting

Allowing an element to print over the top of underlying elements, rather than knocking them out (see Knockout). Often used with black type.

Package

Prepare a document for delivery to a service provider by putting the document file, together will all linked files in one folder. Fonts may or may not be included in the package, based on the licensing parameters.

Page Description Language (PDL)

A special form of programming language that describes both text and graphics (object or bit-image) in mathematical form. The main benefit of a PDL is that makes the application software independent of the physical printing device. PostScript is a PDL, for example.

Page Layout Software

Desktop publishing software such as InDesign used to combine various source documents and images into a high quality publication.

Page Proofs

Proofs of the actual pages of a document, usually produced just before printing, for a final quality check.

PageMaker

A popular page-layout application produced by Adobe Systems.

Palette

1. As derived from the term in the traditional art world, a collection of selectable colors. 2. Another name for a dialog box or menu of choices.

Panose

A typeface matching system for font substitution based on a numeric classification of fonts according to visual characteristics.

Pantone Matching System

A system for specifying colors by number for both coated and uncoated paper; used by print services and in color desktop publishing to assure uniform color matching. One of the most widely used color-matching systems in commercial printing.

Parallel Fold

A folding method in which folds of a signature are parallel.

Pasteboard

In a page layout program, the desktop area outside of the printing page area, on which elements can be placed for later positioning on any page.

PCX

Bitmap image format produced by paint programs.

PDF (Portable Document Format)

Developed by Adobe Systems, Inc. (and read by Adobe Acrobat Reader), this format has become a de facto standard for document transfer across platforms.

Perfect Binding

A binding method in which signatures are "ground off" at the spine of the book and then bound with adhesive, so each page is glued individually to the spine.

Perspective

The effect of distance in an image achieved by aligning the edges of elements with imaginary lines directed toward one to three "vanishing points" on the horizon.

Photoshop

The Adobe Systems image editing program commonly used for color correction and special effects on both the Macintosh and PC platforms.

Pi Fonts

A collection of special characters such as timetable symbols and mathematical signs. Examples are Zapf Dingbats and Symbol. See also Dingbats.

Pica

A traditional typographic measurement of 12 points, or approximately 1/6 of an inch. Most DTP applications specify a pica as exactly 1/6 of an inch.

PICT/PICT2

A common format for defining bitmapped images on the Macintosh. The more recent PICT2 format supports 24-bit color.

Pixel

Abbreviation for picture element, the smallest element capable of being produced by a monitor, scanner, or other light-transmitting device. If a pixel is turned on it has color. If it is turned off it appears as a blank space. Pixels can vary in size from one monitor to another. A greater number of pixels per inch (ppi) results in a higher resolution.

Plug-in

A program that works within a primary program to extend the features of the core program.

PMS

See Pantone Matching System

PMT

Photo Mechanical Transfer - positive prints of text or images used for paste-up to mechanicals.

PNG

Portable Network Graphics format that uses adjustable, lossless compression to display 24-bit photographs or solid-color images on the Internet or other online services.

Point

A unit of measurement used to specify type size and rule weight, equal to (approximately, in traditional typesetting) 1/72 inch. Note: Font sizes are measured completely differently from leading, even though they're both specified in points, and the only way you can verify font size on your hard copy is by measuring it against the designated sizes you'll find on an E-scale.

Polygon

A geometric figure consisting of three or more straight lines enclosing an area. The triangle, square, rectangle, and star are all polygons.

Portrait

Printing from left to right across the narrow side of the page. Portrait orientation on a letter-size page uses a standard 8.5-inch width and 11-inch length.

Positive

A true photographic image of the original made on paper or film.

Posterize, Posterization

The deliberate constraint of a gradient or image into visible steps as a special effect; or the unintentional creation of steps in an image due to a high LPI value used with a low printer DPI.

Postproccssing Applications

Applications, such as trapping programs or imposition software, that perform their functions after the image has been printed to a file, rather than in the originating application.

PostScript

1. A page description language developed by Adobe Systems, Inc. that describes type and/or images and their positional relationships upon the page. 2. An interpreter or RIP (see Raster Image Processor) that can process the PostScript page description into a format for laser printer or imagesetter output. 3. A computer programming language.

PostScript Printer Description file

(PPD) Acronym for PostScript Printer Description, a file format developed by Adobe Systems, Inc., that contains device-specific information enabling software to produce the best results possible for each type of designated printer.

PPI

Pixels per inch; used to denote the resolution of an image.

Preferences

A set of defaults for an application program that may be modified.

Preflight Check

The prepress process, in which the printing service verifies that fonts and linked graphics are available, traps your publication, makes color corrections or separations, and sets final printing options.

Prepress

All work done between writing and printing, such as typesetting, scanning, layout, and imposition.

Prepress Proof

A color proof made directly from electronic data or film images.

Press Sheet

In sheet-fed printing, the paper stock of common sizes that is used in commercial printing.

Primary Colors

Colors that can be used to generate secondary colors. For the additive system (i.e., a computer monitor), these colors are red, green, and blue. For the subtractive system (i.e., the printing process), these colors are cyan, magenta, and yellow.

Printer Command Language

PCL — a language, that has graphics capability, developed by Hewlett Packard for use with its own range of printers.

Printer Driver

The device that communicates between your software program and your printer.

Printer Fonts

The image outlines for type in PostScript that are sent to the printer.

Process Colors

The four transparent inks (cyan, magenta, yellow, and black) used in four-color process printing. A printing method in which a full range of colors is reproduced by combining four smitransparent inks. Process-color printing is typically used when your publication includes full-color photographs or multicolor graphics, and when you want the high resolution and quality that printing on an offset press provides. See also Color separation; CMYK.

Profile

A file containing data representing the color reproduction characteristics of a device determined by a calibration of some sort.

Proof

A representation of the printed job that is made from plates (press proof), film, or electronic data (prepress proofs). It is generally used for customer inspection and approval before mass production begins.

Proportional Spacing

A method of spacing whereby each character is spaced to accommodate the varying widths of letters or figures, thus increasing readability. Books and magazines are set proportionally spaced, and most fonts in desktop publishing are proportional. With proportionally spaced fonts, each character is given a horizontal space proportional to its size. For example, a proportionally spaced "m" is wider than an "i."

Pt.

Abbreviation for point.

Pull Quote

An excerpt from the body of a story used to emphasize an idea, draw readers' attention, or generate interest.

QuarkXPress

A popular page-layout application.

Queue

A set of files input to the printer, printed in the order received unless otherwise instructed.

QuickDraw

Graphic routines in the Macintosh used for outputting text and images to printers not compatible with PostScript.

RAM

Random Access Memory, the "working" memory of a computer that holds files in process. Files in RAM are lost when the computer is turned off, whereas files stored on the hard drive or floppy disks remain available.

Raster

A bitmapped representation of graphic data.

Raster Graphics

A class of graphics created and organized in a rectangular array of bitmaps. Often created by paint software, fax machines, or scanners for display and printing.

Raster Image Processor (RIP)

That part of a PostScript printer or imagesetting device that converts the page information from the PostScript Page Description Language into the bitmap pattern that is applied to the film or paper output.

Rasterize

The process of converting digital information into pixels at the resolution of the output device. For example, the process used by an imagesetter to translate PostScript files before they are imaged to film or paper. See also RIP.

Reflective Art

Artwork that is opaque, as opposed to transparent, that can be scanned for input to a computer.

Registration

Aligning plates on a multicolor printing press so that the images will superimpose properly to produce the required composite output.

Registration Color

A default color selection that can be applied to design elements so that they will print on every separation from a PostScript printer. "Registration" is often used to print identification text that will appear outside the page area on a set of separations.

Registration Marks

Figures (often crossed lines and a circle) placed outside the trim page boundaries on all color separation overlays to provide a common element for proper alignment.

Resample

Alter the resolution of an image. Downsampling averages the pixels in an area and replaces the entire area with the average pixel color at the specified resolution. Subsampling chooses a single pixel and replaces the entire area with that pixel at the specified resolution; it is not recommended for high-resolution printing.

Resolution

The density of graphic information expressed in dots per inch (dpi) or pixels per inch (ppi).

Retouching

Making selective manual or electronic corrections to images.

Reverse Out

To reproduce an object as white, or paper, within a solid background, such as white letters in a black rectangle.

RGB

Acronym for red, green, blue, the colors of projected light from a computer monitor that, when combined, simulate a subset of the visual spectrum. When a color image is scanned, RGB data is collected by the scanner and then converted to CMYK data at some later step in the process. Also refers to the color model of most digital artwork. See also CMYK.

Rich Black

A process color consisting of sold black with one or more layers of cyan, magenta, or yellow.

Right Indent Tab

An option to position the text at the right indent position following the insertion of the Right Indent Tab command.

Right Reading

A positive or negative image that is readable from top to bottom and from left to right.

Right Alignment

Straight right edge of text with a ragged, or uneven, left edge.

Right-angle Fold

A folding method in which any successive fold of a signature is at right angles to the previous fold.

RIP

See Raster Image Processor

ROM

Read Only Memory, a semiconductor chip in the computer that retains startup information for use the next time the computer is turned on.

Rosette

The pattern created when color halftone screens are printed at traditional screen angles.

Rotation

Turning an object at some angle to its original axis.

RTF

Rich Text Format, a text format that retains formatting information lost in pure ASCII text.

Rubylith

A two-layer acetate film having a red or amber emulsion on a clear base used in non-computer stripping and separation operations.

Rules

Straight lines, often stretching horizothally across the top of a page to separate text from running heads.

Running Head – (Header)

Text at the top of the page that provides information abot the publication. Chapter names and book titles are often included in the running head.

Saddle-stitching

A binding method in which each signature is folded and stapled at the spine.

Sans Serif

Sans Serif fonts are fonts that do not have the tiny lines that appear at the top of and bottom of letters.

Saturation

The intensity or purity of a particular color; a color with no saturation is gray.

Scaling

The means within a program to reduce or enlarge the amount of space an image will occupy by multiplying the data by a scale factor. Scaling can be proportional, or in one dimension only.

Scanner

A device that electronically digitizes images point by point through circuits that can correct color, manipulate tones, and enhance detail. Color scanners will usually produce a minimum of 24 bits for each pixel, with 8 bits each for red, green, and blue.

Scheme color

One of the colors defined in a color scheme. If you fill an object with a scheme color, the object's color changes whenever you choose another color scheme for that publication.

Screen

To create a halftone of a continuous tone image (See Halftone).

Screen Angle

The angle at which the rulings of a halftone screen are set when making screened images for halftone process-color printing. The equivalent effect can be obtained electronically through selection of the desired angle from a menu.

Screen Frequency

The number of lines per inch in a halftone screen, which may vary from 85 to 300.

Screen Printing

A technique for printing on practically any surface using a fine mesh (originally of silk) on which the image has been placed photographically. Preparation of art for screen printing requires consideration of the resolution of the screen printing process.

Screen Shot

A printed output or saved file that represents data from a computer monitor.

Screen Tint

A halftone screen pattern of all the same dot size that creates an even tone at some percentage of solid color.

Search Engine

A program that uses keywords supplied by Web users to search databases of Web sites and other resources the the World Wide Web for information on a specific topic. Search engines create indexes of Web sites, which are then searchable databases. See World Wide Web.

Section

A range of pages having a different numbering sequence from other pages in the document. For example, the frontmatter, projects, glossary, and index all have their own numbering systems.

Selection

The act of placing the cursor on an object and clicking the mouse button to make the object active.

Self-Cover

A cover for a document in which the cover is of the same paper stock as the rest of the piece.

Separation

See Color separation.

Serif

A line or curve projecting from the end of a letterform. Typefaces designed with such projections are called serif faces.

Service Bureau

A business that specializes in producing film for printing on a high-resolution imagesetter. An organization that provides services, such as scanning and prepress checks, that prepare your publication to be printed on a commercial printing press. Service bureaus do not, however, print your publication. To find out if you need to use a service bureau, talk to your printing professional.

SGML

Standard Generalized Markup Language, a set of semantics and syntax that describes the structure of a document (the nature, content, or function of the data) as opposed to visual appearance. HTML is a subset of SGML (see HTML).

Shade

A color mixed with black: a 10-percent shade is one part of the original color and nine parts black. See tint.

Sharpness

The subjective impression of the density difference between two tones at their boundary, interpreted as fineness of detail.

Shortcut

1. A quick method for accessing a menu item or command, usually through a series of keystrokes. 2. The icon that can be created in Windows95/98 to open an application without having to penetrate layers of various folders. The equivalent in the Macintosh is the "alias."

Silhouette

To remove part of the background of a photograph or illustration, leaving only the desired portion.

Skew

A transformation command that slants an object at an angle to the side from its initial fixed base.

Small caps

A type style in which lowercase letters are replaced by uppercase letters set in a smaller point size.

Smart Quotes

The curly quotation marks used by typographers, as opposed to the straight marks on the typewriter. Use of smart quotes is usually a setup option in a word processing program or page layout application

Snap-to (guides or rulers)

An optional feature in page layout programs that drives objects to line up with guides or margins if they are within a pixel range that can be set. This eliminates the need for very precise, manual placement of an object with the mouse.

Soft or Discretionary Hyphen

A hyphen coded for display and printing only when formatting of the text puts the hyphenated word at the end of a line.

Soft Return

A return command that ends a line but does not apply a paragraph mark that would end the continuity of the style for that paragraph.

Spectrophotometer

An instrument for measuring the relative intensity of radiation reflected or transmitted by a sample over the spectrum.

Specular Highlight

The lightest highlight area that does not carry any detail, such as reflections from glass or polished metal. Normally, these areas are reproduced as unprinted white paper.

Spine

The binding edge at the back of a book that contains title information and joins the front and back covers.

Spot Color

Any pre-mixed ink that is not one of or a combination of the four process color inks, often specified by a Pantone swatch number.

Spot-color Printing

The printing method in which one or two colors (or tints of colors) are produced using premixed inks, typically chosen from standard color-matching guides. Unlike process colors that reproduce color photographs and art, spot colors are typically used to emphasize headings, borders, and graphics, to match colors in graphics, such as logos, and to specify special inks, such as metallic or varnish.

Spread

1. Two abutting pages. Readers Spread: the two (or more) pages a reader will view when the document is open. Printers Spread: the two pages that abut on press in a multi-page document. 2. A trapping process that makes the lighter color larger.

Stacking Order

The order of the elements on a PostScript page, wherein the topmost item may obscure the items beneath it if they overlap.

Standard Viewing Conditions

A prescribed set of conditions under which the viewing of originals and reproductions are to take place, defining both the geometry of the illumination and the spectral power distribution of the light source.

Step-and-repeat

A layout in which two or more copies of the same piece are placed on a single plate. This is useful for printing several copies of a small layout, such as a business card, on a single sheet. Also called a multiple-up layout.

Stet

Used in proof correction work to cancel a previous correction. From the Latin; "let it stand."

Stochastic Screening

A method of creating halftones in which the size of the dots remains constant but their density is varied; also known as frequency-modulated (or FM) screening.

Stripping

The act of manually assembling individual film negatives into flats for printing. Also referred to as film assembly.

Stroke, Stroking

Manipulating the width or color of a line.

Stuffit

A file compression utility.

Style

A set of formatting instructions for font, paragraphing, tabs, and other properties of text.

Style Sheet

A file containing all of the tags and instructions for formatting all parts of a document; style sheets create consistency between similar documents.

Subhead

A second-level heading used to organize body text by topic.

Subscript

Small-size characters set below the normal letters or figures, usually to convey technical information.

Subset

When exporting documents as EPS or PDF files, the ability to include only the portion of a font that actually appears in the document. This is particularly useful when decorative drop caps are used, or when a specific symbol is used from a pi font.

Substitution

Using an existing font to simulate one that is not available to the printer.

Subtractive Color

Color which is observed when light strikes pigments or dyes, which absorb certain wavelengths of light; the light that is reflected back is perceived as a color. See CMYK and Process Color.

Superscript

Small characters set above the normal letters or figures, such as numbers referring to footnotes.

SWOP

Specifications for Web Offset Publications

System Folder

The location of the operating system files on a Macintosh.

Tabloid

Paper 11 inches wide x 17 inches long.

Tagged Image File Format (TIFF)

A common format for used for scanned or computer-generated bitmapped images.

Tags

The various formats in a style sheet that indicate paragraph settings, margins and columns, page layouts, hyphenation and justification, widow and orphan control and other parameters.

Template

A document file containing layout and styles by which a series of documents can maintain the same look and feel. A model publication that you can use as the basis for creating a new publication. A template contains some of the basic layout and formatting, and perhaps even some text and graphics that can be re-used in future publications.

Text

The characters and words that form the main body of a publication.

Text Attribute

A characteristic applied directly to a letter or letters in text, such as bold, italic, or underline.

Text Converters

Files that convert word-processing and spreadsheet documents created in other programs into files that you can import into Publisher.

Text Wrap

See Wrap.

Texture

1. A property of the surface of the substrate, such as the smoothness of paper. 2. Graphically, variation in

tonal values to form image detail. 3. A class of fills in a graphics application that give various appearances, such as bricks, grass, etc.

Thin Space

A fixed space, equal to half an en space or the width of a period in most fonts.

Thumbnails

1. The preliminary sketches of a design. 2. Small images used to indicate the content of a computer file.

TIFF (.tif)

An acronym for Tagged Image File Format. A popular graphics format. See Tagged Image File Format.

Tile

1. A type of repeating fill pattern. 2. Reproduce a number of pages of a document on one sheet. 3. Printing a large document overlapping on several smaller sheets of paper.

Tint

1. A halftone area that contains dots of uniform size; that is, no modeling or texture. 2. The mixture of a color with white: a 10-percent tint is one pat of the original color and nine parts black. See shade.

Tip In

The separate insertion of a single page into a book either during or after binding by pasting one edge.

Toggle

A command that switches between either of two states at each application. Switching between Hide and Show is a toggle.

Tracking

Adjusting the spacing of letters in a line of text to achieve proper justification or general appearance. You may want to squeeze letters closer together to fit into a frame, or spread them apart for a special effect.

Transfer Curve

A curve depicting the adjustment to be made to a particular printing plate when an image is printed.

Transform

Application of rotation, shear, scaling or other effects to an object.

Transparency

A full color photographically produced image on transparent film.

Transparent Ink

An ink that allows light to be transmitted through it.

Trapping

The process of creating an overlap between abutting inks to compensate for imprecise registration in the printing process. Extending the lighter colors of one object into the darker colors of an adjoining object. This color overlaps just enough to fill areas where gaps could appear due to misregistration.

Trim

After printing, mechanically cutting the publication to the correct final dimensions. The trim size is normally indicated by marks on the printing plate outside the page area.

Trim Page Size

Area of the finished page after the job is printed, folded, bound, and cut.

TrueType

An outline font format used in both Macintosh and Windows systems that can be used both on the screen and on a printer.

Type 1 Fonts

PostScript fonts based on Bézier curves encrypted for compactness that are compatible with Adobe Type Manager.

Type Family

A set of typefaces created from the same basic design but in different weights, such as bold, light, italic, book, and heavy.

Typesetting

The arrangement of individual characters of text into words, sentences, and paragraphs.

Typo

An abbreviation for typographical error. A keystroke error in the typeset copy.

UCR (undercolor removal)

A technique for reducing the amount of magenta, cyan, and yellow inks in neutral or shadow areas and replacing them with black.

Undertone

Color of ink printed in a thin film.

Unsharp Masking

A digital technique (based on a traditional photographic technique) performed after scanning that locates the edge between sections of differing lightness and alters the values of the adjoining pixels to exaggerate the difference across the edge, thereby increasing edge contrast.

Uppercase

The capital letters of a typeface as opposed to the lowercase, or small, letters. When type was hand composited, the capital letters resided in the upper part of the type case.

Utility

Software that performs ancillary tasks such as counting words, defragmenting a hard drive, or restoring a deleted file.

Varnish Plate

The plate on a printing press that applies varnish after the other colors have been applied.

Varnishing

A finishing process whereby a transparent varnish is applied over the printed sheet to produce a glossy or protective coating, either on the entire sheet or on selected areas.

Vector Graphics

Graphics defined using coordinate points, and mathematically drawn lines and curves, which may be freely scaled and rotated without image degradation in the final output. Fonts (such as PostScript and TrueType), and illustrations from drawing applications are common examples of vector objects. Two commonly used vector drawing programs are Illustrator and FreeHand. A class of graphics that overcomes the resolution limitation of bitmapped graphics.

Velox

Strictly, a Kodak chloride printing paper, but used to describe a high-quality black & white print of a halftone or line drawing.

Vertical Justification

The ability to automatically adjust the interline spacing (leading) to make columns and pages end at the same point on a page.

Vignette

An illustration in which the background gradually fades into the paper; that is, without a definite edge or border.

Visible Spectrum

The wavelengths of light between about 380 nm (violet) and 700 nm (red) that are visible to the human eye.

Watermark

An impression incorporated in paper during manufacturing showing the name of the paper and/or the company logo. A "watermark" can be applied digitally to printed output as a very light screened image.

Web Press

An offset printing press that prints from a roll of paper rather than single sheets.

Web Site

One or a collection of Web pages stored on a computer on the World Wide Web.

White Light

Light containing all wavelengths of the visible spectrum. Also known as 5000°k lighting.

White Space

Areas on the page which contain no images or type. Proper use of white space is critical to a well-balanced design.

Widow

A short line ending a paragraph, which appears at the top of the page. See orphan.

Wizard

A utility attached to an application or operating system that aids you in setting up a piece of hardware, software, or document. A Publisher tool that helps you create a publication or change an object in a publication.

World Wide Web

(commonly shortened to WWW, or simply Web) The popular multimedia branch of the Internet that presents not just text, but also graphics, sound, and video. On the Web, exploring (sometimes called surfing) can all be done with point-and-click simplicity, and users can easily jump from item to item, page to page, or site to site using hyperlinks. See Internet.

WYSIWYG

An acronym for "What You See Is What You Get," (pronounced "wizzywig") meaning that what you see on your computer screen bears a strong resemblance to what the job will look like when it is printed.

X-height

The height of the letter "x" in a given typeface, which represents the basic size of the bodies of all of the lowercase letters (excluding ascenders and descenders).

Xerography

A photocopying/printing process in which the image is formed using the electrostatic charge principle. The toner replaces ink and can be dry or liquid. Once formed, the image is sealed by heat. Most page printers currently use this method of printing.

Zero Point

The mathematical "origin" of the coordinates of the two-dimensional page. The zero point may be moved to any location on the page, and the ruler dimensions change accordingly.

Zip

1. To compress a file on a Windows-based system using a popular compression utility (PKZIP). 2. A removable disk made by Iomega (a Zip disk) or the device that reads and writes such disks (a Zip drive).

Zooming

The process of electronically enlarging or reducing an image on a monitor to facilitate detailed design or editing and navigation.

Student CD-ROM
Adobe® Illustrator® 9
INTRODUCTION TO DIGITAL ILLUSTRATION
AGAINST THE CLOCK

System Requirements

Windows:

- Intel Pentium II or higher processor

- Windows 98/NT 4.0, or Windows 2000 or higher

- 64 MB RAM or higher

- 105 MB free hard drive space for installation

- Monitor with resolution of 800 x 600 pixels

- Adobe PostScript Level 2 printer

- CD-ROM dri

Macintosh:

- PowerPC 604 processor or higher

- System 8.5 or higher

- 64 MB RAM using virtual memory or 96 MB with virtual memory off

- 105 MB free hard drive space for installation

- Monitor with resolution of 800 x 600 pixels

- Adobe PostScript Level 2

To use the additional resources available on this CD-ROM, you will need to have the appropriate applications installed on your system and enough free space available if you copy the files to your hard drive. This product does not come with the application software required to use the data files on this CD-ROM.